The European Monetary Union

The European Union is at a crossroads. This book analyzes the historical roots of the EU's monetary and financial institutions in order to better understand its struggle to maintain an economic and monetary union, as well as the ongoing problems facing the euro. The institutions of the EU are based on the operation of free markets, a common monetary policy, and the European Central Bank. These founding policies have created many of the imbalances at the root of the ongoing European recession. Reemerging threats of populism and localism are poised to further disintegrate the European construction and may spark fierce opposition between countries. Nicola Acocella engages with these risks, suggesting detailed actions for reform within the EU and its institutions that may steer it away from further conflict, allowing it to better serve its member states and citizens.

NICOLA ACOCELLA is professor emeritus of Economic Policy at the Sapienza University of Rome. He is the author of *Rediscovering Economic Policy as a Discipline* (2018) and coauthor of *Macroeconomic Paradigms and Economic Policy* (2016), among other books.

The European Monetary Union

Europe at the Crossroads

NICOLA ACOCELLA
Sapienza University of Rome

CAMBRIDGE
UNIVERSITY PRESS

CAMBRIDGE
UNIVERSITY PRESS

University Printing House, Cambridge CB2 8BS, United Kingdom

One Liberty Plaza, 20th Floor, New York, NY 10006, USA

477 Williamstown Road, Port Melbourne, VIC 3207, Australia

314–321, 3rd Floor, Plot 3, Splendor Forum, Jasola District Centre,
New Delhi – 110025, India

79 Anson Road, #06–04/06, Singapore 079906

Cambridge University Press is part of the University of Cambridge.

It furthers the University's mission by disseminating knowledge in the pursuit of
education, learning, and research at the highest international levels of excellence.

www.cambridge.org
Information on this title: www.cambridge.org/9781108840873
DOI: 10.1017/9781108892858

First published 2020

A catalogue record for this publication is available from the British Library.

Library of Congress Cataloging-in-Publication Data
Names: Acocella, Nicola, 1939– author.
Title: The European Monetary Union : Europe at the crossroads / Nicola Acocella,
Sapienza University of Rome.
Description: New York, NY : Cambridge University Press, 2020. | Includes index.
Identifiers: LCCN 2020007278 (print) | LCCN 2020007279 (ebook) | ISBN
9781108840873 (hardback) | ISBN 9781108744102 (paperback) | ISBN
9781108892858 (ebook)
Subjects: LCSH: Economic and Monetary Union. | Monetary unions – European
Union countries. | European Union.
Classification: LCC HC241.2 .A6317 2020 (print) | LCC HC241.2 (ebook) |
DDC 337.1/42–dc23
LC record available at https://lccn.loc.gov/2020007278
LC ebook record available at https://lccn.loc.gov/2020007279

ISBN 978-1-108-84087-3 Hardback
ISBN 978-1-108-74410-2 Paperback

Dedicated to Andrew Hughes Hallett, an author of many books and a coauthor of mine in some of them, who recently died.

Contents

Figures

Tables

Preface

In this book we argue that the institutional setup for any instance of international coordination must be carefully designed in order to ensure effective and consistent working of markets and public institutions. This is a difficult task, as differences in terms of visions and interests are likely to be more pronounced between countries than at local levels. In fact, the policy orientation of different countries may diverge, also as a result of differences in past history and the weights of interest groups, whereas at least the common past history tends to reduce differences in policy orientations and the institutional choice within a country.

The book follows this line of argument. In Part I (Chapters 1, 2, and 3) we describe the historical and institutional background for the analysis of the imbalances — the object of Part II — that emerged over time, which are central to our inquiry. After having traced the path of European institutions built since the 1950s, we sketch those of the European Monetary Union (EMU) and the roots of the institutions in terms of the theories and the interests shaping them. This makes it possible to understand in Part II (Chapters 4–7) the imbalances that arose in the Union, descending from preexisting asymmetries as well as its institutions and the policies that were implemented. These imbalances led to the specific European features that compounded the financial crisis and its bad management in the Union. The final part of the book (Part III, which includes Chapters 8–11) first deals with the theoretical advances of the recent decades and then indicates our proposals for institutional and policy changes that descend from them.

In contrast to a common tradition and culture, based on largely similar philosophical and religious foundations, Europe has a history of fierce opposition and wars among national states that culminated in World War II. An important impulse to some kind of

European cooperation came exactly from the attempt to counter this tradition of conflicts, even if the past was still weighing.

This largely explains the long process through which European institutions have reached their current state as well as their "incompleteness," from the point of view of a more "mature" one, of the kind of a federalist structure. Incompleteness derives from a strong measure of persistent national and, thus, independent decision-making that interacts and overlaps with the common institutions and often dominates them.

The history of European institutions shows that there was an evolution in their coverage in terms of both content and features, especially with respect to the balance between public and private institutions. The realm of the initial cooperation, through the European Coal and Steel Community (1951), was limited, but this Community was characterized by active inter-country coordination and cooperation, with limits to free market. This orientation evolved into one almost of an opposite kind, the European Economic Community (usually called the Common Market) (1957), christening the predominant role of markets. The change seemed to be turned upside down again with the Werner Plan, which designed a wide spectrum of common policies, but was never implemented. Finally, the free-market orientation in all fields, with the exception of monetary policy and some constraints on national fiscal policies, returned with the Maastricht Treaty (1992). The European history, institutions, and policies until the establishment of the EMU are traced in Chapter 1.

The Maastricht Treaty originated the European Union (EU) and the European Economic and Monetary Union (commonly called the European Monetary Union). The former now gathers twenty-eight countries, pending implementation of the United Kingdom's decision to withdraw. The latter had only eleven members when it started in 1999 and has now enlarged to nineteen. The institutional architecture of the EU is investigated in Chapter 2, which also underlines its possible faults. The EMU's design is founded on a few common institutions, a single currency, and the free operation of markets, as well as some harmonization of rules. All the other policy instruments are to be managed by the member states, with constraints on some policies, especially fiscal policy. Thus, most national borders are maintained. In the mind of the founding fathers of the Union, these common institutions were necessary and sufficient conditions for getting rid of frictions and the uneven distribution of resources and opportunities across the countries, thus resulting in a uniform process of growth of the whole Union.

The monetarist and new classical macroeconomics theories, popular at the time when the institutions of the EMU were devised, played an important role for the choice of the institutional design. However, the existing theories were only partly implemented (e.g., the requirements of the optimal currency theory were not satisfied) and later revisions of the accepted theories – asking for a different orientation of the initial institutions and current policies – have been ignored. Other factors, of the nature of vested interests, added to existing theories and can explain together with them both the institutional design and the policies implemented by the Union (Chapter 3).

This sequence of institutions developing in Europe brought progress in economic integration and possibly also some political success, such as banning of armed conflicts. However, with respect to the former, the increase in growth and employment of the first decades was followed by some kind of relative stagnation, starting in the 1970s and the 1980s (the so-called Eurosclerosis). The lasting imbalances in the domestic and external accounts of each country that emerged when the Union began operating laid the ground for a crisis. This had certainly originated elsewhere but developed in forms and with an intensity that appear as built-in in the way European institutions were devised as well as in the different growth strategies pursued by the various countries (Chapter 4).

Then, the Great Recession came in 2008 and lasted – with a double dip – up to 2013–14 in Europe. This was the deepest depression suffered by advanced countries since the 1930s. Its consequences on indicators of macroeconomic and microeconomic efficiency and equity are investigated in Chapter 5.

The policies implemented and the differences with the United States are described in Chapter 6, adding to the negative consequences of the institutional differences.

Chapter 7, differently from the previous chapter, focuses on the consequences of the EMU institutional setup. It shows that the signals and information about the imbalances that can arise do not flow clearly and effectively across states, contrary to what happens within them, and are often noisy or carry wrong messages to markets and governments. Thus, they do not offer sufficient incentives for change in the right direction.

Chapter 8 starts from the observation that the theoretical foundations are largely outdated and have shown a number of faults. These can be summarized in the fact that there are frictions at work – which mainly derive from existing national borders – and adjustment issues that are not tackled, at least in a reasonably long period, by the single currency, free markets, and constraints on national policies.

The chapter suggests the broad lines along which the EMU could be reformed and indicates different growth and short-term strategies for the institutions as well as macroeconomic and microeconomic policies. It must certainly be realized that the economic performance in Europe has been nourished not only by the inadequacies in the Monetary Union institutions but also by the way European policymakers, at all levels, operated, first in facilitating the development of the Great Recession in Europe and then in compounding its solution. In fact, the policies implemented to face the recession can make it clear why it prolonged beyond the period over which it hit the United States. Thus, the possible benefit of avoiding military confrontation between European countries must be balanced against the rising populism and resentment of some European countries against the others as a consequence of the clear insufficiency of European institutions and policymakers in dealing with the crisis. Institutions (and policies) can have lasting negative political consequences on the future of the Union. The need then arises for a deep reform of the EMU.

Chapters 9 and 10 outline, respectively, necessary changes to the existing macroeconomic and microeconomic institutions and policies. The reforms should radically change the balance of powers between the Union and the country level as well as reliance on the different policy tools.

Chapter 11 closes the book. It deals with two polar cases in the Union institutions. The first one discusses radical changes in the structure of the EMU, including the possibility of its breakup. The second deals with the prospect of political and institutional changes that reinforce the existing structure, in particular with reference to solutions for overcoming its democratic deficit.

The focus of the book is on institutions, on how they orient and constrain policies as well as on how they determine the economic performance, namely microeconomic and macroeconomic imbalances. As to policies, most attention is devoted to macroeconomic tools, but microeconomic policies also are considered as a necessary complement of macroeconomic instruments. The need for this is clear when one thinks of the complementarity between wage policy and other labor market policies or between microeconomic and macroeconomic regulation, or of industrial and regional policies as instruments for addressing the microeconomic imbalances that are behind the macroeconomic ones, or, finally, of the implications for antitrust legislation of differences in the tax treatment of companies as between different countries.

The book should be easy to follow by any reader having a basic knowledge of economics.

Acknowledgments

In preparing the book, I benefited from previous research on the topic and related issues. Some of this was done together with other authors, whom I now thank again for their collaboration.

I was also assisted by the advice and criticism of many friends and colleagues. I must thank in particular Philip Arestis, Filippo Cesarano, Francesco Farina, Grazia Ietto Gillies, Massimo Giuliodori, Luciano Milone, Michele Morciano, Roberto Tamborini, and, mostly, Francesco Saraceno.

My final thanks go to Augusto Frascatani, for his kind technical assistance in (re)drawing the figures.

Abbreviations

AMIF	Asylum, Migration and Integration Fund
APP	Expanded Asset Purchase Programme
ARRA	American Recovery and Reinvestment Act
BCBS	Basel Committee on Banking Supervision
BIS	Bank for International Settlements
CAC	Collection Action Clause
CAP	Common Agricultural Policy
CEEC	Central and Eastern European countries
CF	Cohesion Fund
DMC	Domestic Material Consumption
DSTI	Debt service-to-income ratio
EBA	European Banking Authority
ECB	European Central Bank
ECU	European Currency Unit
EDA	European Debt Agency
EDIS	European Deposit Insurance Scheme
EEC	European Economic Community
EFB	European Fiscal Board
EFSF	European Financial Stability Facility
EFSI	European Fund for Strategic Investments
EIF	European Integration Fund
EMF	European Monetary Fund
EMFF	European Maritime and Fisheries Fund
EMS	European Monetary System
EMU	European Economic and Monetary Union
ERDF	European Regional Development Fund
ERM	European Exchange Rate Mechanism
ESBs	European Safe Bonds

ESCB	European System of Central Banks
ESF	European Social Fund
ESFS	European System of Financial Supervision
ESM	European Stability Mechanism
ESRB	European Systemic Risk Board
ETS	Emissions Trading System
EU	European Union
EZ	Eurozone
FEAD	Fund for European Aid to the Most Deprived
FG	Forward Guidance
GSE	Government-sponsored enterprise
ICN	International Competition Network
IMF	International Monetary Fund
LSAP	Large-scale asset purchases
LTRO	Long-term refinancing operations
LTV	Loan-to-value
MBS	Mortgage-backed securities
MFF	Multiannual Financial Framework
MIP	Macroeconomic Imbalance Procedure
NAIRU	Nonaccelerating inflation rate of unemployment
NAWRU	Nonaccelerating wage rate of unemployment
NCBs	National Central Banks
NPL	Nonperforming loans
NTBs	Nontariff barriers
OCA	Optimal currency area
OECD	Organisation for Economic Co-operation and Development
OEEC	Organisation for European Economic Cooperation
OMT	Outright Monetary Transactions
QE	Quantitative easing
REs	Rational expectations
RES-E	Renewable energy sources
SBBS	Sovereign bond-backed securities
SEM	Single European Market

SGP	Stability and Growth Pact
SMP	Securities Markets Programme
SRF	Single Resolution Fund
SRM	Single Resolution Mechanism
SSM	Single Supervisory Mechanism
TARGET2	Trans-European Automated Real-time Gross Settlement Express Transfer-2
TARP	Troubled Asset Relief Program
TINA	There is no alternative
TLTROs	Targeted longer-term refinancing operations
WTO	World Trade Organization
ZLB	Zero lower bound

PART I The Historical and Institutional Background

I   The Preparation of the European Economic and Monetary Union

I.I   THE STEPS OF EUROPEAN INTEGRATION AND THE UNDERLYING PROBLEMS

This chapter deals with the steps of the European construction and its structure. It also hints at the issues arising from an incomplete union.

The foundations of European integration can be traced to issues raised immediately after World War II (WWII) (Baldwin, Wyplosz, 2006). The central question was political: "How can Europe avoid another war?" It can then be easily understood that the current step of the integration, i.e., the European Economic and Monetary Union (EMU),[1] is the result of a nonlinear process, much "less an economic project than a political one" (Minkinnen, Patomäki, 2012: 9). In particular, in the minds of a large part of the European élites it was a step toward European political unification. The euro was considered as a symbol of European unity.[2]

After the war, different proposals were suggested. The one which ultimately prevailed was pursuit of some kind of integration, but its nature was far from being clear until the late 1940s.

At the beginning of the Cold War, the United States too tried to promote integration between European countries to counter the emerging power of the Soviet Union. Economic, military, and political

---

Some paragraphs of this introduction are drawn from Acocella et al. (2016), with adaptations.

[1]   In the following, we will also use the terms Euro-area (EA) or Eurozone (EZ) to refer to the countries belonging to the EMU.

[2]   This implied risks, however. In fact, this project came to the detriment of an alternative possible symbol characterizing European countries, i.e., the welfare state. However, these risks should be balanced against a possible benefit of the EMU project, which could at least partly relieve Europe from the pressures of international markets.

interests suggested adoption of a US aid program for European countries (the Marshall Plan – officially, the European Recovery Program), which made aid conditional on effective cooperation between European governments and the gradual liberalization of trade and payments in order to avoid the rivalries of the 1930s. The Organisation for European Economic Cooperation (OEEC) was established in the Western European countries in order to both organize reconstruction and give way to structural reforms.

However, the US attempt to favor integration received a cold response from a Europe still deeply divided as a consequence of the war. Genuine European economic cooperation only began with the federalist project traced in the Schuman Declaration of 1950, which led to the constitution of the European Coal and Steel Community (ECSC) in 1951.

It strengthened and expanded further with the Treaty of Rome of 1957, which established the European Economic Community (EEC, usually called the European Common Market) and the European Atomic Energy Community (Euratom) between Belgium, France, Germany, Italy, Luxembourg, and the Netherlands (the Six).

Thus, political integration started from the economic sphere and remained focused around it for a long time. The pragmatic need to introduce European-wide policy coordination gradually and the limited scope of the initial approach to economic integration were prompted by the difficulty of proceeding with cooperation in other fields or full political integration. Evidence of this is shown by the failure of proposals to create a European Defense Community, suggested by the French Prime Minister René Pleven, in 1952, and a European Political Community, inspired by the Italian Prime Minister Alcide De Gasperi, in 1954. The main explanation for this failure lies in the opposition of the French Parliament to plans implying loss of national sovereignty. The favor met by the common market and Euratom can be explained in terms of the almost general acceptance in its member countries of the prospect of the further economic gains that could accrue to countries whose economies still needed further growth to solve their problems.[3]

In the beginning, the common market was not much more than a customs union, devoted to lowering internal duties and setting a single external tariff for countries and a few specific common policies, notably in agriculture, transport, and antitrust legislation. There was still not only a push at avoiding conflicts and implementing cooperation but also reluctance to give up national sovereignty due to the need to more easily control the orientation of policies.

The European policies were inspired, at least initially, by two opposite views that clearly appear if we compare the attitudes taken toward industry, on the one hand, and agriculture, on the other. Free-market competition and internal trade were promoted in the industrial sector (through the customs union), whereas a complex protectionist system was created within Europe and between it and the United States in the agricultural one to defend agricultural incomes against internal and external, especially US, competition (Common Agriculture Policy). The common denominator of the two views – and a partial explanation of the final choice – was that both required limited supernational coordination to be implemented. This position, expressing a pragmatic approach to integration, also needed two institutions complementary to free circulation of goods: a common transport policy and antitrust legislation.

Thus, the dominant attitude was in favor of free markets, with the exception of agriculture. This can easily be explained on the grounds of the interests of the rising industry, looking for the possibility to exploit scale and scope economies. Political considerations advised protecting the interests of small peasants, of special relevance for support in some countries.

---

[3] France, in particular, favored the project of a common atomic institution, to provide a source of energy that could substitute for the exhausting coalmines and be more reliable than oil provision, whereas the Benelux countries and Germany preferred a common market.

On a theoretical ground, the pro-market orientation can be justified at least partially by the fact that the concept of both microeconomic and macroeconomic market failures had not penetrated the political sphere and, to a large extent, also the academic circles.[4] Looking at real economic life, policymakers could see no apparent market failure. The years in which the common market was born were in fact years of rapid growth sustained by the postwar recovery – which was fueled by catching up technologies and emerging entrepreneurship energies – and with a positive trend for the other main macroeconomic goals for nearly all European countries. In fact, inflation was low and unemployment tended to fade, also in its disguised form. The balance of payments was not a problem, as low wages and new technologies promoted exports toward countries external to the Market. When the US aid was terminated, it was partly substituted by their direct investment.

This integration also involved acceptance of some international governance in Europe. In fact, European countries were part of the Bretton Woods system. However, even before its collapse, there was a discussion about being relieved of the constraints imposed by the US leadership. France was seeking European monetary unification in order to lessen Europe's dependency on the US policy.

Discussion reached a higher level with a plan for creating an independent monetary union associated with integrated macroeconomic policies, notably fiscal policy. The ambitious Werner Plan of 1970 (Werner, 1970) devised a prospect of currency unification, a common fiscal policy and coordination of regional and structural policies, as being ancillary to economic integration. Reducing and then eliminating fluctuations in the exchange rate were based on the idea that trade significantly benefits from fixed exchange rates (now a more controversial issue; see the review by Baldwin, Wyplosz, 2006, and, more recently, the "post EMU mea culpa" by Glick, Rose, 2016).[5]

---

[4]   This is the case at least of Germany, Italy, and other Continental countries.
[5]   Glick and Rose offer a rather positive assessment of the effects of the monetary union on trade.

Interestingly, at that time coordination of fiscal, regional, and some other structural policies, together with a single currency (but not a common central bank, at least in the first instance), was devised. The plan was deemed necessary for coping with the divergences that had been emerging in the performance of the different European countries. In addition, it followed a period of turbulence in foreign exchange markets, rising deficits in the balance of payments of the United States, and their decision in 1968 to limit gold convertibility of the dollar to central banks. The plan – presented in 1970 – was commissioned by the heads of state or government of the common market countries, thus with the agreement of France and Germany. It was rejected by the European Council, which only endorsed the prospect of the common currency, largely due to internal political disagreements, mainly by France (partly reflecting the US opposition).

The Marjolin Report (European Communities, 1975), in criticizing the Werner Report, suggested new designs for common institutions. However, it recognized the need for a relevant budget managed by a central fiscal authority, a social security system ensuring a certain degree of redistribution, and a common Unemployment Benefit Fund, as in federal states.

The idea of some common action in the field of fiscal policy surfaced again in 1977, with the MacDougall Report,[6] which recommended a progressive increase in the budget of the European Communities, starting from the level of 5–7 percent (or 7.5–10 percent, if defense were included) of gross domestic product (GDP) also in order to implement redistribution between their members. In time, the level of the federal budget could reach that of the United States or the Federal Republic of Germany, to about 20–25 percent. This recommendation was never implemented.

European cooperation in the monetary field, instead, continued with the creation of the "snake" (1972) and the European Monetary System (EMS) (1979) to stabilize intra-EU exchange rates. After the

---

[6] See Commission of the European Communities (1977).

dollar devaluations, beginning in 1971 and especially after 1973, the system of fixed exchange rates had been abandoned, in practical terms, first, and in statutory terms, later (after the Jamaica accords of 1976). The underlying justification for the need for stabilization was that fixed exchange rates would favor (or force) convergence of wages and prices. In addition, after the dollar devaluation, this was favored by the US "abuse" of its dominant role in the International Monetary Fund to create excess money and its apparent inability to ensure international monetary stability and later (around the turn of the 1980s) by the transatlantic tensions (Ludlow, 1982; Story, 1988; Story, De Cecco, 1993, cited by Sadeh, Verdun, 2009; Henning, 1998).

In the early 1980s, a pause in the process of European integration followed. This lasted until 1984, when the Treaty for European Union establishing the European Political Cooperation was agreed upon. This foresaw the Single European Market (SEM) – agreed on in 1986, after the 1985 White Paper on completing the Internal Market – to be implemented by the end of 1992 through the free movement of the factors of production and further market integration as an outcome of elimination of any residual nontariff barriers (NTBs). This included open access to public procurement and to all markets by firms being licensed to do business in one member state, common professional recognition, a minimum of common labor market standards (the "Social Chapter"), open access to all markets by firms being licensed to do business in one member state, common commercial laws, and so on. It also set out new objectives for European action in the areas of the environment, technological research, economic and social cohesion, and health and safety in the workplace. Numerous long-term objectives were confirmed, such as continuing progress toward economic and monetary union and institutional changes, including a shift from unanimous to qualified majority voting in the Council of Ministers. The Treaty mentioned the necessity to exploit "the experience acquired in cooperation within the framework of the European Monetary System (EMS) and in developing the ECU"[7] (article 102a, p. 311) but did not raise the issue of monetary unification.

The proposal of a single currency was revived in the late 1980s. The French President Mitterrand's push toward monetary unification seems to have played an important role in this. Later, German reunification convinced the leaders of other countries, notably France and Italy, of the necessity to accelerate the steps for some kind of European integration as a way to keep the new Germany tied to the rest of Europe.[8] The Werner Plan was set aside, and the decision was taken to go ahead with fastening the preexisting institutions, notably the fixed exchange rate mechanism.

According to Gros and Thygesen (1992), there was also the idea that the emergence of imbalances in the current account of some countries derived not only from divergent fiscal policies but also from different wage and price dynamics. This progressively made the target of fixed exchange rates and monetary integration to prevail over the others devised by the Werner Plan,[9] as a way to correct for the different wage and price dynamics.

Thus, the Maastricht accords, amending again the Treaty of Rome, were agreed upon in December 1991 and were followed by the Maastricht Treaty, signed on February 7, 1992. They heralded the formal birth of the EU and established the future creation of the EMU. As said, at the time of its formal start, January 1, 1999, it had eleven members only (out of the fifteen countries composing the EU), which soon after (2001) were joined by Greece.

---

[7] The ECU was the prototype of a common money (more in Section 1.2).

[8] This is also the idea supported by Thygesen (2016: 13), who criticizes instead the position that there are main problems with the argument according to which "there was a bargain in which Germany acquiesced in moving towards monetary union and in giving up the DM in return for support from European partners for German reunification."

[9] This plan resulted from a fragile compromise between the different positions expressed, on the one hand, by France and Belgium, which were in favor of monetary integration as a first step toward an economic union, and, on the other, by Germany, insisting on economic convergence as the precondition for monetary union.

Simultaneously to the progress of economic integration, there was also a "spatial" evolution of both the EU and the EMU, making its management more complex since the enlargements increased both the number of decision-making centers and the imbalances. Membership of both the EU and the EMU progressively grew, amounting, respectively, to twenty-eight and nineteen countries in 2019.[10] Various further institutional changes have been implemented since the advent of the euro, notably those of the Lisbon Treaty, which also contains a clause providing for a member to leave the EU (not the EMU).[11]

In a way similar to the Bretton Woods system, which had the IMF as a coordinating institution and could work only through the US hegemony, monetary institutions emerged in Europe – or, at least, were conceived – as coordinating, albeit imperfect, devices to ensure existence and unicity of the equilibrium. The EMS had the European Commission (actually the monetary policy committee) as a social planner in its initial phases, but later that role fell de facto to the Bundesbank as central bank to the EMS regime.

The rest of this chapter deals with the monetary aspects of European integration. It is structured as follows. Section 1.2 discusses the initial structure of the EMS up to the crisis of 1992–3. Section 1.3 describes this crisis. Section 1.4 discusses the reasons for this crisis underlined by the "impossible trinity," offering an economic justification of the currency union, which was foreseen in the Maastricht Treaty. It also discusses the Maastricht criteria, how they originated and were implemented. Section 1.5 sketches the main line of argument in the next chapters.

---

[10]   As of November 2019, the EMU's members are Austria, Belgium, Cyprus, Estonia, Finland, France, Germany, Greece, Ireland, Italy, Latvia, Lithuania, Luxembourg, Malta, the Netherlands, Portugal, Slovakia, Slovenia, and Spain. The EU members also include Bulgaria, Croatia, the Czech Republic, Denmark, Hungary, Poland, Romania, Sweden, and the United Kingdom. In 2016, this latter country decided to withdraw from the Union, which should be implemented in due course.

[11]   Withdrawal from the EU is allowed under Article 50 of its Treaty: "Any Member State may decide to withdraw from the Union in accordance with its own constitutional requirements." No similar prospect is envisaged for withdrawal from the EMU only, but the issue is discussed whether the latter is possible, with no exit from the EU (Chapter 11).

I.2 THE EUROPEAN MONETARY SYSTEM

Following the Werner Plan and the monetary turmoil caused by the declaration of dollar inconvertibility in August 1971, in April 1972 a number of European countries reacted to the ensuing widening of the exchange rate fluctuation bands at the world level by narrowing the bands between their currencies (the *snake*). In 1979, they decided to strengthen and extend this agreement, which had proved extremely difficult to implement within the emerging international system of floating rates, by establishing a fully fledged EMS of fixed – but adjustable – exchange rates. To some extent, the initially numerous adjustments (realignments) were reduced, especially after 1983, when their high frequency declined. However, in 1992–3 – after German reunification and as a consequence of it (see next section) – speculative attacks caused five realignments and a very substantial widening of the permitted bands of fluctuation (from ±2.25 percent, the band initially allowed, to ±15 percent), while some currencies (notably the pound sterling and the Italian lira) exited the system altogether. The advantage of wider bands was, first, that they allowed countries greater freedom of maneuver to resolve their financial, budget, or trade imbalances. Moreover (and more important at the time), they imposed large risks on those who would speculate against a currency. In fact, wider bands removed the one-way bet aspect of the EMS and produced a more stable system. Until the euro appeared in 1999, there were no more adjustments in the exchange rates of the countries that had remained within the EMS.

In addition to their shared desire to create an area of monetary stability, and therefore economic and political stability within the EEC, the countries had independent motives that nonetheless converged on a system of fixed exchange rates. On the one hand, low-inflation countries (i.e., those in the German mark area) wanted to use the system to prevent competitive devaluations (or depreciations) by high-inflation countries. On the other, higher-inflation countries sought to introduce an external element of extra discipline on the behavior of unions and firms[12] and to increase the credibility of their anti-inflation policies.[13]

The final structure of the system and the way it was implemented were the result of a compromise between the various interests and largely reflected political considerations.

In the EMS two essential elements were

(a) the European Exchange Rate Mechanism (ERM), which was intended to reduce fluctuations in the exchange rates between EU currencies. Not all the members of the then EEC participated in the ERM; and

(b) a mechanism for providing credit to countries with balance-of-payments difficulties. All EEC members participated in this.

According to the ERM, a "grid" of bilateral parities was first established: that is, a central rate was set for each pair of currencies. As said, central rates could be changed, but participating countries were supposed to keep them stable. The system initially called for a limited fluctuation band and reproduced the fixed (but adjustable) exchange rate mechanism of the IMF without the latter's reference to gold and the apparent leadership of a country. Over time, however, conditions evolved to confer leadership to Germany.

When an exchange rate between two currencies hit the upper or lower limit, both countries involved had to intervene in foreign exchange markets to comply with the limit. In practice, the mechanism to ensure that exchange rates remained fixed operated asymmetrically. Interventions were more urgent and costlier for countries with a balance-of-payments deficit than for those with a surplus. In fact, the former might use up their reserves and find it difficult to borrow to stay within the existing bands, while the latter faced only the possibility of an unwanted increase in the

---

[12] The game was in fact more complex. Firms, and often the central banks, also had the objective of preventing the government and parliament from running up budget deficits.

[13] These higher-order "objectives" will be discussed later. In any case, a number of comments highlighting the hegemonic position acquired by Germany are in James (2012, especially chapters 6 and 9).

domestic money supply, which they could in any case offset with sterilization.

A basis for a more symmetric fluctuation mechanism had also been devised, following the issues debated at the original Bretton Woods Conference and Keynes's proposals. This was the European Currency Unit (ECU), which was created as a "basket currency" containing a weighted average of the currencies of the EEC members that could indicate the countries whose currency deviated and had then to adjust.[14] It would have ensured greater symmetry than a system based on a parity grid in signaling tensions across the board rather than on a bilateral basis, and the currencies responsible for them. Then, the country that should bear the burden of adjustment could be decided accordingly. This would have been a more balanced instrument for initiating coordination of the economic policies of the EMS countries. However, in practice it did not work for a variety of reasons.[15] Thus, only Germany, the main surplus country, was in a position to decide its monetary policy and to some extent to exert monetary discipline on the behavior of private and public agents in other countries. In other words, the EMS had become a unilateral near currency union, not a multilateral union as intended.

The question can be debated of how successful this discipline was in influencing union, firm, and government action in higher-inflation countries, adding *credibility* to their anti-inflationary policies – and, conversely, to what extent it imposed an excessive sacrifice in terms of high interest rates and a worsening of public debt. This issue still needs to be addressed in a dispassionate fashion,

[14] Bilateral exchange rates could not signal that. When a currency was at its lower limit, and another currency was at its upper limit, no one can say which country had determined this situation – e.g., through a restrictive policy – unless the situation of other currencies is taken into account. This can only be known by considering the quotation of each currency in terms of the basket of all currencies, i.e., the ECU.

[15] The most important reason was the absence of a firm obligation to intervene with monetary and fiscal adjustment policies (by both deficit and surplus countries), should a currency quotation show a divergence with respect to its central value in terms of the ECU. The difference between the ECU value corresponding to the central rates of the various currencies and the ECU value in terms of the market value of these currencies was an indicator of their divergence. It revealed the currency responsible for the deviation. However, no practical consequence derived in terms of policy obligations for the country.

especially in the light of the devaluations that occurred in 1992–3 and of the subsequent events until the present time.

As said, the policy of fostering an appreciation in the real exchange rate, i.e., adopting a "hard exchange rate" policy instead of a "devalue and then inflate" policy, was aimed at imposing discipline on the behavior of public and private agents in higher-inflation countries.[16] In addition, the overvaluation of the exchange rate could give an innovative stimulus to industry, by pressing it to innovation.[17] Policymakers expected that achieving this goal, together with restraint in wage increases and fiscal deficits, would reduce inefficiencies and inflation, thus leading to a reduction in foreign account imbalances and stabilization of the real exchange rate over time. The real appreciation of weak currencies, however, lasted for a long time, with apparently scarce effects, which was unexpected. The persistence of this appreciation may be due to the long lags in the effects of the hard exchange rate policy, which is likely to be more effective and rapid in financial markets (if credible) than in the labor markets, the more so after the liberalization of capital movements implemented in the 1980s. Considering the fact that nominal interest rate differentials with Germany remained large in countries with large current account deficits, it seems difficult to imagine that, even before the realignments of 1992–3, the financial markets believed in the commitment to fixed nominal exchange rates or the possibility of maintaining them.

1.3 THE EMS CRISIS OF 1992–1993

The 1992 speculative attacks against the EMS can be illustrated as the result of three factors: (1) its bad design and poor implementation; (2) bad luck; (3) a weak and distorted leadership.

---

[16]   Many economists and politicians saw this institutional architecture as imposing a strong network of ties on the conduct of the agents, both public and private, in the countries with higher inefficiencies. It was thought that these ties would – almost naturally – compel them to change their conduct and enact the needed reforms (Giavazzi, Pagano, 1988). This conviction is critically discussed in Tavlas (1993b). Its application to the EMU is dealt with in Chapter 7.

[17]   On the effects of the appreciation of the exchange rate on the distribution of productivity across firms, see Tomlin, Fung (2015).

Full capital mobility, which was a part of the Single Act, established a system where free capital mobility, fixed exchange rates, and independent monetary policies had to coexist. However, coexistence was impossible.

To intuitively grasp the implications of this arrangement, we refer to the "Tinbergen rule," which prescribes that the number of instruments should at least equal that of targets (Acocella, 2018). Each government should aim to achieve: (1) a fixed exchange rate, (2) monetary autonomy for stabilizing GDP fluctuations, and (3) free capital movement to stimulate growth or, otherwise, to avoid over-saving. As the three goals are interconnected, if the government did not impose capital controls, it had only two independent instruments (monetary and fiscal policy) to pursue them. This was then an "impossible trinity," and we will further discuss it in the next section.

Persistent differences in the structural features of the member countries in terms of inflation trends can explain the EMS crisis of 1992–3. To some extent, the founding fathers of the EMU did not take sufficient account of these differences and relied too much on the virtues of a single currency and free (unregulated) markets to overcome them. Given these differences and free capital mobility, some countries (in particular those suffering from a decline in their current account) were subject to speculative attacks.

Up to 1992–3, the attacks were limited and the countries under attack, when they did not devalue their currency, usually reacted by adopting severe domestic deflationary measures, while the surplus countries, like Germany, tended not to implement expansionary policies, as said before.[18] This did not ensure symmetry, thus running against the initial conception of the system.

The bad luck, paradoxically, was related to the German unification, which represented a big shock that called for very tight monetary

---

[18] In 1992–3, the attacks were too strong and scarcely sustainable, due to capital movement liberalization. (The asymmetric reaction to speculative attacks illustrates another feature of the system, i.e., the generally deflationary bias in the EMS economies, which has recurred also in the EMU experience.)

policy in Germany and misaligned the German goals from those of the other EU countries. In fact, the shock did not trigger the crisis directly, but contributed to worsening financial market expectations about the sustainability of the EMS. The underlying roots were instead in the wrong design of the EMS and persistent imbalances between countries. Policies following unification only were aggravated by those imbalances. The negative response of the Danish referendum on the Maastricht Treaty in June 1992 christened the negative expectations. After an attempt to face the attacks, in September 1992 the Bundesbank finally gave up unlimited support of existing exchange rates, thus undermining EMS credibility. Then, the de facto German informal leadership somehow failed in promoting the European stability implied by this role, in order to support the domestic situation.[19]

The crisis in 1992–3 can be illustrated by a simple figure (based on an IS/LM model), where prices are assumed to be fixed for simplicity. The initial situation (E_1 and U_1) was characterized by equal interest rates in Germany and the United Kingdom as requested by free capital mobility, which calls for equalization of international (nominal) interest rates up to expected changes in exchange rates.

After unification, the German government tried to bring infrastructures in former East Germany to standards similar to those existing in the West. Fiscal expansion led to a large shift to the right of the IS curve (reunification shock). The Bundesbank then hiked real interest rates by a monetary restriction to keep the GDP on planned target and inflation under control. This shifted to the left the LM curve (not shown in the picture for simplicity), thus moving the German economy to point E_2.

---

[19] Eichengreen, Wyplosz (1993) model the attitude of Germany as a leader after reunification and the effects of this on the crisis of the EMS of 1992–3. Hefeker (1994) traces back the multiple roots of the Bundesbank's position essentially to three reasons: first, a kind of revanche toward the German government for not accepting the conversion rate between the Deutsche Mark and the Ost Mark it had suggested, which caused its loss of reputation; second, opposition to the increase in public spending deriving from reunification; finally, a signal to the German government for not accepting the route taken with the Maastricht Treaty, which would reduce its power, in an attempt to block the EMU.

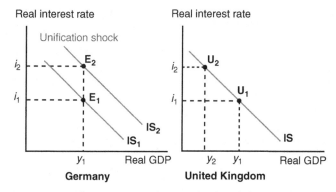

FIGURE 1.1 The German unification shock and the 1992 EMS crisis

The German policy called for monetary restriction in the United Kingdom too. As the result of free capital mobility, the initial real interest rate differential should be maintained in order to keep the exchange rate fixed. The British government faced the dilemma to accommodate German policy by raising its interest rate too, thus keeping the exchange rate fixed and paying the cost of a recession (to U_2) or to keep the money supply unchanged, thus exiting the EMS (U_1). Speculators bet on the exit (i.e., devaluation), selling pounds in the forward market, and the increase in pounds supply put more pressure on the devaluation, making it more costly to defend the parity; in the end the United Kingdom (and Italy) left the EMS.

The actual operation of the EMS led to increased speculative attacks even after Italy and the United Kingdom had withdrawn from it. In August 1993, the band was widened to ±15 percent for all countries in order to counter attacks on the French franc.

1.4 GERMAN UNIFICATION, THE IMPOSSIBLE TRINITY, AND THE MAASTRICHT TREATY

1.4.1 *The Economic Justification of the EMU: The Impossible Trinity*

The actual design of the EMU was contained in the Delors Report. This is the common name of the Report (dated April 1989) of a committee established by the European Community (Committee for the Study of Economic and Monetary Union, 1989). In addition to a common currency, it required "binding rules" on the "size and the financing of national budgetary deficits," while rejecting increases in the size of the European budget as well as any other centralized European institution for the pursuit of economic policy, such as wage or industrial policy. Implementation of this Report was decided by the Maastricht Treaty. The reasons underlying its conception and/ or acceptance can be analyzed in terms of strictly political, or of a political economy type, or strictly economic considerations. We refer to each in turn.

Strictly political arguments can explain the Accords. The German unification made some kind of stronger tie between European countries necessary, which could also be seen as a continuation of the older argument of the necessity to keep Europe united in order to avoid political or even military confrontation.

Undoubtedly, German unification had increased the power of this country. Thus, the desire became stronger "to strengthen the binds of the newly united Germany to the western nations" (Sadeh, Verdun, 2009: 280), even if the prospect for monetary unification had been devised before the destruction of the "Wall" by the Werner Plan and the Delors Report. In turn, "Germany agreed to EMU in return for international legitimacy for its unification and to prepare the then European Community to its eventual enlargement to the east" (Sadeh, Verdun, 2009: 280). Therefore, the Maastricht meeting of 1991 that decided the establishment of the monetary union formally accepted the whole content of the Delors Report, deciding applicability of the subsidiarity principle to all policies, with the exception of monetary policy. This represented the European political response to German unification. In particular, the Accords were a political bargain by the two most important members, France and Germany, as each tried to secure its vital objectives (Baun, 1995–1996).

As to underlying political economy factors, American authors in particular tended to view the Treaty as a European response to globalization, aiming at strengthening cooperation and instituting some kind of governance (Keohane, Hoffmann, 1994). Neo-functionalists, instead, see the Accords simply as an inevitable outgrowth of previous common policies, in particular the Single Market (Tranholm-Mikkelsen, 1991).

Also strictly economic considerations are various: (1) One sees the EMU as a "natural" evolution of previous institutions; this can recall one of the previous political economy considerations, but is based on a more strictly economic argument. It has to do with the impossible trilemma, or "trinity," which states the impossibility of simultaneously pursuing the following three objectives: a fixed exchange rate, free capital movements, and independent monetary policies.[20] We deal with this justification in the remaining part of this section, as it is strictly related to the topics discussed before. (2) Another justification can be found in the benefits *accruing to all countries adopting a single currency* as an effect of forming a currency area, independently of whether conditions for an optimum currency area were satisfied or not before. We will discuss them in Chapter 3, from the point of view of the theory of optimum currency areas, and will debate the foundations of this theory in Chapter 8, from the point of view of recent contributions. (3) An additional argument in terms of the benefits that accrue to countries with less efficient economies from joining a currency union derives from the argument of the external tie. Again, we will defer discussing this, to Chapter 7.

The reasoning underlying the impossible trinity is based on the *uncovered interest rate parity* condition, which states equalization of international (nominal) interest rates up to expected changes in exchange rates as the outcome of free capital movements. The following three situations could arise, which show the reasons for the impossibility in detail:

[20] The trilemma can be derived from the Mundell (1963)-Fleming (1962) model. It was applied to the EMS by Padoa Schioppa (1982), who spoke of an impossible quartet (the fourth element being free trade), and was popularized by Krugman (1987, 1999).

1. If there are to be independent monetary policies in the various countries together with free capital movements, there would be a tendency to changing exchange rates, as capital would move from countries with lower to those with higher interest rates, in case exchange rates remain fixed.
2. If there are to be credibly fixed exchange rates and free capital movements, there should be no independent monetary policies, as these would cause capital flows pressing on fixed exchange rates.
3. If we aim at having independent monetary policies and fixed exchange rates, we cannot have free capital movements. If these are free, they would push for higher returns, making it impossible to keep the rates fixed.

As the three objectives mentioned above cannot be pursued at the same time, an international institution will have to opt for one of three policy options, respectively, with reference to the conditions just indicated: (1) independent monetary policies, free capital flows, and flexible exchange rates; (2) fixed exchange rates, free capital movements, no independent monetary policies; (3) fixed exchange rates, independent monetary policy, no free capital flows.

In devising new institutions for the Eurozone (EZ), the Maastricht Treaty reacted to the memory of the failure of the EMS and its underlying factors and chose the second option. The other two options were seen as either dangerous with respect to the final aims of European integration or politically unacceptable, in that they involved a departure from free-market principles and/or from monetary discipline and price stability. Free markets were thought to be helpful in furthering integration and economic progress.

1.4.2 The Maastricht Criteria

For some time, discussion and disagreement had continued inside the Committee of Governors of the EMS countries (and, more generally, the policymakers of the countries interested in the Maastricht Treaty) as to supporting symmetric or asymmetric responsibilities of "strong" and "weak" countries. In fact, on both sides of the spectrum no yardstick could be defined a priori as to the extent to which each had to put a remedy to the situation, without a central point "around which symmetry or asymmetry should develop. ... The issue was solved only once it was recognized that there was one criterion (price stability) that identified 'the right' monetary policy and that all countries had to behave consistently with this principle" (James, 2012: 380).

However, this was not sufficient to identify the exact measure of price stability to serve as a pivot. The view of a monetary policy ensuring a "strong" currency finally prevailed and monetary unification, under the guidance of an independent and conservative central bank, was held capable of ensuring the alignment of the conduct of agents in higher-inflation countries to that of Germany, which was considered to be the most "virtuous" country together with a few other Northern European countries.[21] Thus, fixed exchange rates, monetary discipline, and price stability materialized also because an external constraint was desired not only by the "virtuous" countries, but also by the élites in higher-inflation countries asking for discipline to be imposed on private and public agents (more on this in Chapter 7).

According to the Maastricht Treaty, unification should involve only those members of the EU that met certain specified convergence standards, i.e., price stability, close convergence of long-term interest rates to those of the countries with the lowest inflation, a demonstrated ability to live with exchange rate stability, and a commitment to maintain their government budget deficit to GDP ratio within the limit of 3 percent as well as a tendency of the debt to GDP ratio to fall toward 60 percent. We deal further with them below.

Three stages were foreseen by the Maastricht Accords before the start of the EMU. Stage One, up to December 1993, required removing

---

[21] The criterion of price stability, however, could help only up to a point, as the experience of the EMU showed. In fact, it has been observed in the EMU as a whole, but imbalances have continued, mostly likely with the contribution of both surplus and deficit countries (Chapter 4).

exchange controls, setting the economic convergence criteria just mentioned. Stage Two would end in December 1998, after having established the European Monetary Institute as the forerunner of the European Central Bank (ECB), with the main task of strengthening monetary cooperation between the member states and their national banks. In December 1995, the name of the new currency (the euro) as well as the duration of the transition periods were chosen. In 1998, the Stability and Growth Pact (SGP) was adopted and the following year a new mechanism (the Exchange Rate Mechanism, ERM II) replaced the previous ERM that should be applied to the countries that would enter the EU in the future (more in Section 2.5). In May 1998, the European Council also selected the eleven countries that would participate in the third stage initially, from January 1, 1999, as they had fulfilled the requirements for admission. On June 1, 1998, the ECB was created and, on December 31, 1998, the conversion rates between the eleven participating national currencies and the euro were established. From the start of 1999, Stage Three was on, the euro became the common currency, and a single monetary policy was introduced under the authority of the ECB. A three-year transition period was required before the introduction of actual euro notes and coins, and the euro was used only for electronic payment. The national currencies ceased to circulate at the end of February 2002.

The euro convergence criteria (also known as the Maastricht criteria) are the criteria that all EU member states are required to comply with to adopt the euro as their currency. They held not only for the countries that would initially enter the EMU, but are required also for any further accession. In order to check their fulfillment by the EU members aspiring to euro adoption, the ECB publishes a Convergence Report at least every two years before accession.

The five convergence criteria required from EU member states were (and are):

1. The harmonized CPI must not exceed by more than 1.5 p.p. its reference value, given by the unweighted arithmetic average of the CPI in the three EU member states with the lowest CPI.
2. The ratio of the annual general government deficit relative to the GDP at market prices must not exceed 3 percent.
3. The ratio of gross government debt to GDP at market prices must not exceed 60 percent at the end of the preceding fiscal year. Or, if the debt-to-GDP ratio exceeds the 60 percent limit, the ratio shall at least be found to have sufficiently diminished and must be approaching the reference value at a satisfactory pace.
4. (i) The countries should not have devalued the central rate of their euro-pegged currency during the previous two years; (ii) for the same period the currency stability shall be deemed to have been stable without "severe tensions"; (iii) the countries should have participated in the EMS for two consecutive years.
5. Long-term interest rates (taken with reference to ten-year government bonds in the past year) shall be no more than 2.0 percentage points higher than the unweighted arithmetic average of the similar ten-year government bond yields in the three EU member states with the lowest CPI.

The situation assessed in May 1998 in order to decide on admission of the first members of the EMU was as shown in Table 1.1.

The eleven countries admitted to become members of the EMU were thus: Belgium, Germany, Spain, France, Ireland, Italy, Luxembourg, the Netherlands, Austria, Portugal, and Finland. The countries that were admitted to the EMU later were Greece (2001), Slovenia (2007), Cyprus and Malta (2008), Slovakia (2009), Estonia (2011), Latvia (2014), and Lithuania (2015).[22]

---

[22] As to partial fulfillment of criteria by Ireland, the European Monetary Institute held that "over the reference period from February 1997 to January 1998 the average rate of HICP inflation in Ireland was 1.2%, i.e., well below the reference value of 2.7%. . . . Seen over the past two years, HICP inflation in Ireland has been low and has fallen to a level which is generally considered to be consistent with price stability" (European Monetary Institute, 1998: 178).

Table 1.1 *Convergence criteria to EMU assessed in 1998 (Source: European Central Bank)*

| | Inflation | Government budgetary position | | | | | | Exchange rates | Long-term interest rates[4] |
| | HICP[1] | Existence of an excessive deficit[2] | Deficit (% of GDP)[1] | Debt (% of GDP) | | Change from previous year | | ERM participation | |
	January 1998	January 1998	1997	1997	1997	1996	1995	March 1998	January 1998
Reference value	2.7[5]		3	60					7.8[6]
B	1.4	Yes[7]	2.1	122.2	-4.7	-4.3	-2.2	Yes	5.7
DK	1.9	No	-0.7	65.1	-5.5	-2.7	-4.9	Yes	6.2
D	1.4	Yes[7]	2.7	61.3	0.8	2.4	7.8	Yes	5.6
EL	5.2	Yes	4.0	108.7	-2.9	1.5	0.7	Yes[8]	9.8[9]
E	1.8	Yes[7]	2.6	68.8	-1.3	4.6	2.9	Yes	6.3
F	1.2	Yes[7]	3.0	58.0	2.4	2.9	4.2	Yes	5.5
IRL	1.2	No	-0.9	66.3	-6.4	-9.6	-6.8	Yes	6.2
I	1.8	Yes[7]	2.7	121.6	-2.4	-0.2	-0.7	Yes[10]	5.7
L	1.4	No	-1.7	6.7	0.1	0.7	0.2	Yes	5.6
NL	1.8	No	1.4	72.1	-5.0	-1.9	1.2	Yes	5.5
A	1.1	Yes[7]	2.5	66.1	-3.4	0.3	3.8	Yes	5.6

P	1.8	Yes[7]	2.5	62.0	-3.0	-0.9	2.1	Yes	6.2
FIN	1.3	No	0.9	55.8	-1.8	-0.4	-1.5	Yes[11]	5.9
S	1.9	Yes[7]	0.8	76.6	-0.1	-0.9	-1.4	No	6.5
UK	1.8	Yes[7]	1.9	53.4	-1.3	0.8	3.5	No	7.0
EU	1.6		2.4	72.1	-0.9	2.0	3.0		6.1

[1] Percentage change in arithmetic average of the latest twelve monthly harmonized indices of consumer prices (HICP) relative to the arithmetic average of the twelve HICP of the previous period.

[2] Council decisions of 26.9.1994, 10.7.1995, 27.6.1996, and 30.6.1997.

[3] A negative sign for the government deficit indicates a surplus.

[4] Average maturity ten years, average of the last twelve months.

[5] Definition adopted in this report: simple arithmetic average of the inflation rates of the three best-performing member states in terms of price stability plus 1.5 percentage points.

[6] Definition adopted in this report: simple arithmetic average of the twelve-month average of interest rates of the three best-performing member states in terms of price stability plus two percentage points.

[7] The Commission is recommending abrogation.

[8] Since March 1998.

[9] Average of available data during the past twelve months.

[10] Since November 1996.

[11] Since October 1996.

1.5   THE LINE OF ARGUMENTS IN THE NEXT CHAPTERS

At this point, it may be useful to trace the line of the argument that we will follow in the next chapters of the book. The solution found for avoiding the impossible trinity emerging with the EMS led to adoption of a common currency (which is equivalent to adopting irrevocably fixed exchange rates) together with a unique independent and conservative (i.e., giving an overriding weight to keeping a low inflation rate) European Central Bank, having no possibility to act as a lender of last resort to governments as its main coordinating institution (Chapter 2). The limits of the Monetary Union derive exactly from this choice, as its institutions also miss common regulatory and fiscal policies. They must be traced to acceptance of mainstream theories of the time when the Union was designed, associated to vested interests by countries and sections of the population in each country, which can explain the forces behind the choice of the institutional design of the EZ (Chapter 3). The limits of the fundamental disequilibria and imbalances accumulated over the years (Chapter 4) emerged clearly with the onset of the financial crisis (Chapters 5 and 6). Absence of proper signals indicating the imbalances implied scarcity of proper incentives for change and the elimination of asymmetries (Chapter 7). Hence, suggestions for reforming the institutional design are in order (Chapters 8 to 11).

2 The Institutions of the European Economic and Monetary Union

2.1 INTRODUCTION

In 1992, the Maastricht Treaty established the creation of the EMU and envisaged common polices for education, vocational training, culture, and health.

Behind the institutional setup of the EMU there are some original "biases" that we will explain in Chapter 3. To understand their nature and reach, it is preferable to describe the institutional design itself, which we do below.

The eight main institutions of the EU are the following:

- The European Parliament, which approves the budget, appoints the president of the European Commission, and votes its approval of the Commission and monitors its activity;
- The European Council, made up of the heads of state or government of the member states and the president of the European Commission;
- The European Commission, composed of independent members designated by the president in common accord with national governments, having powers of initiative, execution, management, and oversight;
- The Council of the EU, made up of the ministers of the member states responsible for the specific areas addressed on the agenda of a given meeting;
- The Court of Justice;
- The Court of Auditors;
- The European Investment Bank;
- A number of other institutions, such as the European External Action Service, the European Economic and Social Committee, the European Committee of the Regions, the European Ombudsman, the European Data Protection Supervisor and Interinstitutional bodies;

- The European Central Bank (ECB), which strictly speaking is not a Community institution as it has independent legal personality. However, its president is appointed by a qualified majority vote of the European Council, usually those who have adopted the euro, for an eight-year nonrenewable term.

The EMU public institutions and policies are mainly based on the single currency and a common monetary policy. Additional – rather loose – common rules were laid down since the beginning of the Union or have been added recently, especially under the effects of the financial crisis, as in the case of the banking union. Then the correct working of the economy is mainly based on the common currency and the operation of markets, which should ensure attainment of the policy goals.

In the following sections of this chapter, we deal first with macroeconomic policies, i.e., monetary, fiscal, wage, and exchange rate policy as well (Sections 2.2–2.5) and then with microeconomic policies, starting from competition policy to regional policy (Sections 2.6–2.12). We merge discussion of macroeconomic and microeconomic regulation of credit, in dealing with both in Section 2.11, as they appear to be strictly intertwined. In Section 2.13, we underline the institutional faults of the Union. In Chapters 8 to 10, we will discuss the missing institutions and instruments for a correct and beneficial working of the European economy also in the light of the theory of the optimal currency area (OCA); we will also suggest amendments to the existing ones.

2.2 MACROECONOMIC POLICIES: MONETARY POLICY

Monetary operations for the EZ are decided by the ECB's Governing Council and carried out by the National Central Banks (NCBs) of the area under ECB instruction.[1] The European System of Central Banks (ESCB) also includes, in addition to those of the EMU, the NCBs of all

---

[1]   The term "Euro-system" refers to the ECB and the NCBs of the Eurozone.

the other EU member states, which autonomously decide their monetary policy.

Various types of open market operations are the main instrument of the ECB. After some initial hesitation, the ECB also adopted a compulsory reserve system.

The duties assigned to the ECB reflect a restrictive interpretation of the tasks of a central bank. In fact, the ECB is forbidden by its statute to perform a *lender-of-last-resort* function with respect to the EU or national governments (apparently in order to avoid moral hazard), nor, until recently, did it have a regulatory or supervisory role in the financial system. Those tasks were carried out exclusively by the NCBs or other national institutions under domestic legislation in the member states. However, the regulation and oversight of the systemically most important banks or financial institutions has recently been passed over to the financial stability wing of the ECB. It is this institution that must decide on any resolution or lender-of-last-resort actions for the private sector, to be carried out by a combination of the European Stability Mechanism (ESM)[2] and national financial regulators. We deal specifically with financial regulation in Section 2.11.

In performing its functions, especially in defining and implementing monetary policy, the primary objective of the ECB is to maintain price stability. The Governing Council defined price stability as an annual average medium-term rise of below (later corrected to "below, but close to") 2 percent in the harmonized index of consumer prices in the EZ countries. *Without prejudice to that objective*, the ECB shall support the general economic policies in the Community, acting in accordance with the principle of an open market economy with free competition, favoring an efficient allocation of resources.

---

[2] This is a mechanism established in 2012 in order to provide financial support to member states hit by the crisis. The ESM lends to countries setting up an economic recovery program, conditionally on implementation of tough reforms. The mechanism raises the money it needs in financial markets by selling bills and bonds to investors.

In setting duties for the ECB, a very specific political decision was made to assign a preeminent role to the objective of price stability with respect to other macroeconomic objectives. The model for this arrangement was the Bundesbank, rather than the US Federal Reserve, which is charged with seeking full employment as well as price and financial stability. However, differently from the Bundesbank, which operated discretionally, but was protected by a reputation of conservatism, the ECB has decided to solemnly commit to an explicit inflation target to acquire credibility.

This and a strict practical implementation, at least until recently, of the conservative "mission" imposed on the new bank added to the mixed effects for this mission of the other differences in the institutional design of the ECB with the Bundesbank noted by Fratianni (1994). One refers to representation of national interests by the members of the ECB Council. The lower number of members in the ECB Board would represent the interests of the Union as a whole and should thus operate in the opposite direction. In addition, voting for interest rate decisions should follow a rotation system in this Council. This system could, however, increase volatility in the attitude of the ECB toward inflation. The other difference has to do with the relatively greater clarity for the ECB about targets with respect to instruments.

The ECB *political* (or *target*) *independence* – in addition to *operational independence* – is in the first instance safeguarded by the constraint on its ultimate inflation target. The only possible outside influence on the ECB could come from the provision of the Maastricht Treaty that gives the Council of Ministers responsibility for establishing the exchange rate of the euro. We will deal with that in Section 2.6. The ECB may acquire government securities only in the secondary market (i.e., as part of its open market operations). Until recently, basically only very short-term temporary open market transactions were conducted to influence short-term market interest rates. In addition, overnight refinancing and deposits facilities for commercial banks were envisaged to provide or absorb overnight liquidity, to

signal general monetary policy intentions, and to set a limit to fluctuations in overnight interest rates.[3] Recently, the financial crisis
showed that market arbitration – which is usually supposed to transmit impulses from this very limited segment of the financial market
to other, longer-term, ones – did not work properly. Thus, a series of
longer-term refinancing operations (unconventional policies) were
introduced. These policies go under the name of "quantitative easing"
(QE) and aim at easing the transmission mechanism from short- to
long-term interest rates by direct purchase of long-term assets by the
ECB. Also other unconventional policies, like forward guidance (FG)
over the future course of the monetary stance, have been introduced
(Chapter 5).

However, the ECB has not agreed to intervene directly in the
primary debt markets for distressed sovereigns in the financial crisis
begun in 2007, in order to reduce firms' borrowing costs or keep
domestic financial markets operating. Nor has the ECB embraced
the idea that fiscal deficits and debt are often the result of one or
more of following facts: (a) "sudden stops" of capital inflows or their
reversal; (b) debt overhang and high deleveraging needs after a period of
high private-sector indebtness; (c) liquidity shortages which make the
expected value of a unit of common currency different in different
places; (d) a lack of competiveness and high borrowing costs (if market
interest rates differ due to different risk *premia*) that turn the current
account into a deficit, which is difficult or expensive to finance long
term.

An issue of separating the private financial sphere from public
finance has also arisen in relation to financial regulation (more in
Section 2.3).

Overall, the tasks originally assigned to the ECB, its mission, its
status seem to reflect both the vision and interests of Germany and the

---

[3] These provisions set a ceiling and a floor for the short-term market rate to fluctuate and
create a "corridor" for overnight interest rates around the intervention rate. The width
of the corridor can be changed, as the ECB did in 2008, when it lessened it in order to
reduce market volatility.

analytical orientations prevailing at the time in favor of a "conservative" central bank, i.e., monetary action guided by a clear preference for price stability over other targets (Rogoff, 1985), independent of fiscal policy and not supporting "irresponsible" governments. However, this has not led to an overall better performance by EMU countries with respect either to other comparable EU, but non-EMU, countries or to the United States (Chapters 4 and 5). While monetary conservatism will be dealt with again in Section 2.5 in relation to the issue of coordination between monetary and decentralized fiscal policy, we will defer mention of the recent advances in the issue of the optimal long-run inflation target to Chapter 9.

2.3   FISCAL POLICY AND CONSOLIDATION

Fiscal policy in the EU remains largely the responsibility of national governments.[4] A partial exception is offered by the so-called Juncker Plan launched in November 2014 by the newly elected president of the European Commission, Jean-Claude Juncker (officially, the "European Fund for Strategic Investments," EFSI), which started in 2015. This envisages a €22.5 million loan agreement, supported by the EFSI or Juncker Plan, part of which – for €11.5 million – has been released in mid-2019, while the other €6 and €5 million tranches will be released in the following years subject to the achievement of some conditions by the companies that will be financed. These should stimulate, through multiplying effects on private investment, a predicted €315 billion Investment Plan over the next three years. The Juncker Plan aims to reinvigorate the sluggish European economy and create jobs, by reviving investment in strategic projects around Europe to ensure that money reaches the real economy. The Plan provides funding for economically viable projects, including those with a high risk profile, in sectors of key importance, including digital, transport and energy, education, R&D, innovation, renewable energy, and resource efficiency, and support for small and medium

---

[4]   On this see, more extensively, Acocella (2018).

enterprises. Even if of a limited size and of an exaggerated optimism,[5] the Plan is the main exception to the passive attitudes toward the crisis dominating European countries and institutions, which represent a coordination failure of the deflationary spirals having their origin in a collective movement of fear and risk aversion that creates negative externalities (De Grauwe, 2009).

Another partial exception to national authority over fiscal policy derives from the institution of fiscal boards. In 2015, a European Fiscal Board (EFB) was introduced, having the task to cooperate with the national fiscal councils[6] as well as to provide the Commission with an assessment of the appropriateness in the EU of the SGP and more generally the fiscal stance at a national level as well as to produce an independent view of the fiscal policy in the whole Union.

Apart from this, there is no other active fiscal policy provision at the EMU level, in particular to face asymmetric shocks, which was indicated as a main defect of the project of monetary unification. By contrast, rules have been established to limit the action of a country facing such shocks. In fact, fiscal policy at the country level operates within the constraints imposed by the SGP – both in the EZ and in other members of the EU – and the more recent Treaty on Stability, Coordination and Growth (TSCG), commonly referred to as the "fiscal compact," equally effective in the whole EU, except Croatia, the Czeck Republic, and the United Kingdom.[7] The original rules of the SGP stated that member states were supposed to have budgets in surplus or balance over the medium term, i.e., over the business cycle. The maximum permissible normal budget deficit as a percentage of GDP in a year was the same as that envisaged in the Maastricht Treaty for admission to the monetary union (3 percent),

---

[5] Perotti (2017) shows that the multiplier assumed by the Plan is highly unrealistic and that the amounts to be invested by the EU are too limited.

[6] On these, see International Monetary Fund (2013b) and Acocella et al. (2016).

[7] This is an intergovernmental treaty, which was signed in March 2012 and entered into force on January 1, 2013, by all the twenty-seven members of the time, except the Czeck Republic and the United Kingdom. Croatia entered the Union only starting 2013.

with a debt constraint on public debt of 60 percent of GDP.[8] The fiscal compact prohibits *structural* deficits higher than 0.5 percent of GDP, as measured over the business cycle, and prescribes reductions of the debt/GDP ratio each year by at least 1/20th of the excess over 60 percent. In addition, the compact prescribes adoption of consistent constitutional rules by each member state. The concept of debt considered by the SGP and the fiscal compact is one of "gross" – not "net" – debt, as it includes only public "liabilities" and does not consider the addition that a part of public expenditure, i.e., investment, can generate to public "assets." Net debt would instead derive from the difference between assets and liabilities.

Justifications for introducing similar constraints on national fiscal policies are manifold. A first argument lies in the disappearance of two watchdogs against fiscal policy failures, i.e., domestic central banks and international foreign exchange markets. Other arguments include avoiding moral hazard, free-riding, and negative spillovers on the following: international interest rates, the risk of repayment by other countries of excessive debt accumulations (Casella, 1989; Lindbeck, Niepelt, 2006; McKinnon, 1996;[9] Eichengreen, Von Hagen, 1995), and the risk for financial stability and the growth rate itself of the EZ deriving from the high debt of some countries. The foundation of these arguments lies possibly in the idea inherited from the Delors Report that "the constraints imposed by market forces might either be too slow and weak or too sudden and disruptive" (Committee for the Study of Economic and Monetary Union, 1989: 24) or that countries should be given an incentive to correct fiscal behavior for gaining admission to the EMU, or offer a proof of ability

[8] The Pact was agreed upon in a very short time. Information about negotiations is in Buti and Franco (2005). According to Arestis and Sawyer (2004: 10), "the source of the 3 percent and 60 percent figures was never clear, though some suggested that the 3 percent figure came from a combination of the average budget deficit of Germany and the average public capital expenditure."

[9] According to this author, the default risk would increase alongside the higher debt that would arise, due to the impossibility of monetary financing of government expenditures. This was contradicted by the perceptions of financial markets until the financial crisis erupted.

similar to the Quest in Greek mythology (Frankel, 1993). Another argument, underlying debt ceilings to be respected according to the fiscal compact, is that these can improve growth, not only because they ensure financial stability, but also for their claimed expansionary effects. Consolidation is thus considered to be virtuous with reference to both the short and the long run.

On the opposite side, i.e., as for the shortcomings of the SGP and the fiscal compact, one must say, first, that the watchdog represented by NCBs was only apparent or, better to say, acted as such only in "normal" periods, as the possibility always existed for governments to behave as sovereigns and to command their central banks to play the role of lender of last resort in exceptional times. This would lay down a barrier against speculation and self-fulfilling crises. Another shortcoming of the fiscal constraints – keeping deficits at a level lower than 3 percent (or even at a lower one, in order to fulfill the fiscal compact, in case of a debt higher than the 60 percent ratio of the GDP) – derives from their limitations of the operation of automatic stabilizers, especially in countries with a strong welfare state (see, e.g., Eichengreen 1998b; De Grauwe, Ji, 2015b) such as those of the Western part of the EU. Similar findings come from an agent-based model: the SGP makes the economy more volatile, raises unemployment, and is likely to produce deeper crises and have depressing effects also in the long run (Dosi et al., 2014). In contrast with these positions, according to Buti and Sapir (1998), the limit of 3 percent is sufficient to make automatic stabilizers work. We will deal further with this in Chapter 9.

Reforms of the SGP have been mostly rejected. A milder version nevertheless emerged in 2005, sponsored by France and Germany, which had breached the Pact and wanted to avoid sanctions. The reform allowed for a longer span of time to reduce the deficit below 3 percent or to reach the medium-term objective, depending also on the debt situation, together with some exemptions from the application of sanctions. However, the fiscal compact was later added, prohibiting, as said, *structural* deficits higher than 0.5 percent of GDP, as an effect of the sovereign debt crisis that badly hit the "peripheral" (higher-inflation) countries[10] and threatened financial stability, if not default, across the Euro-area.

2.4 WAGE AND INCOMES POLICY

No common wage guidelines were envisaged before the EU institution or have been provided later at the EU level and systems of wage formation widely differ across countries. In some of them, there is centralized wage bargaining (e.g., in Finland); in others, a decentralized system prevails at the firm level (e.g., Sweden), while elsewhere bargaining takes place at a sectoral level (e.g., traditionally in Germany). Also articulated, i.e., mixed, systems occur – as in Italy, with sectoral- and firm-level agreements, and in Germany, where bargaining can take place also at a regional level and a growing number of companies resort to collective bargaining at a firm level. Some studies (e.g., Andréasson, 2014) find a positive linkage between decentralization at the firm level and firm productivity.[11]

As to the source of agreements, sometimes bargaining derives from free decisions of the relevant subjects, at least worker and firm unions, but often also public organizations. In other cases, legislation dictates guidelines of industrial relations. Also, from the point of view of the rates of growth of wages, there are wide differences, as in some cases they are below the productivity trend, whereas in others the opposite is true. National minimum wage regulations are in some cases envisaged. Usually, statutory national minimum wages are set, but sometimes minimum rates are negotiated by sectoral agreements.

The effect of wages in terms of growth is difficult to detect. It passes through their impact on demand, technology, and productivity as well as employment. In some cases, the effects are ambiguous and possibly depend on other features of the economic system, e.g., whether the economy is wage- or profit-led (Storm, Naastepad, 2012).

---

[10]   We also call these countries GIIPS, by their initials, i.e., Greece, Ireland, Italy, Portugal, and Spain. The other EMU countries are part of the "core."

[11]   Really, productivity can be considered as exogenous only as a first approximation.

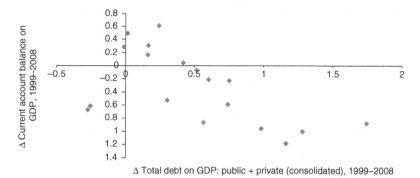

FIGURE 2.1 Export-led versus credit-led growth models in the EZ, 1999–2008 (Source: Acocella, Pasimeni, 2018).

The increase in wages before the crisis was rather diversified across countries. Particularly striking was their drop in Germany, which is the real outlier. The problem of some peripheral countries, instead, was more on the side of productivity growth, whose low profile worried Italy and, to a less extent, Spain. Overall, wage moderation improved competitiveness and net exports and, possibly, might also have had a positive effect on investment, due to increased profitability. However, it acted negatively on the side of consumption. This can explain the dichotomy between the growth models experienced by different countries (export-led vs. demand- or credit-led growth) before the Great Recession (Stockhammer, 2011; Stockhammer, Onaran, 2012), as indicated by Figure 2.1. Apart from a few exceptions, the countries that experienced higher increases in total (public and private) debt had higher reduction in their current account balances.

After the crisis, there has been a drop in the (real) wage share of peripheral countries, with the exception of Italy, and of the real wage per hour at least in Greece.

We must say that some authors (Albonico et al., 2018a) negate this dichotomy and challenge the view of an expansionary credit cycle driving demand in Italy and Spain, while emphasizing the role of technological factors rather than loose domestic (private and/or public) demand conditions. However, in our opinion there are over-whelming factors in favor of the dichotomy, and in the following analysis we offer various factors supporting it.

2.5 THE EXCHANGE RATE POLICY

At the start of 1999, the various NCBs contributed part of their reserves, totaling €39.5 billion, to the ECB. Some 15 percent of the reserves consist of gold, while the remainder is in convertible curren-cies. The management of the reserves still controlled by the NCBs must not interfere with the ECB's conduct of monetary and exchange rate policy.

Having eliminated (or more precisely, irrevocably fixed) the exchange rates among the currencies of the countries participating in European monetary union, the EZ's exchange rate policy is aimed at regulating the exchange rate of the euro with the currencies outside the area, including those of other EU members and non-EU countries. Determining the desired exchange rate of the euro against other cur-rencies is a task of the European Council, but the ECB must be con-sulted on this and has operational responsibility in the area. A conflict can then arise between the Council's intentions and the ECB's main "mission": in fact, the Bank could be required to intervene to cause a depreciation of the euro and, therefore, to create monetary base in an amount and in a situation that might conflict with its price stability objective. An expansionary monetary policy that caused the euro to depreciate does not necessarily imply a threat to internal price stability in case of unemployed factors of production, if one accepts Keynesian analysis, but the ECB governing bodies do not necessarily agree on this.

According to Arestis and Sawyer (2004: 17),

> It is very important for the EMU to formulate an official exchange rate policy and abide by it. At the moment the slightest indication by any of the EMU officials on the exchange rate results in "brutal" (according to the ECB chairman) gyrations in the euro exchange rate with inevitable and undesirable uncertainties creeping in, which

hurt an already fragile economy, with unacceptably high rates of unemployment.

The need for stabilizing the exchange rate of the euro is raised if one wants to increase the international role of the currency. The president of the European Commission Juncker in his State of the Union Address of September 2018 highlighted the strategic importance of the euro and the need to allow it to play its full role on the international scene. This position was repeated in a Communication of the Commission of December 2018, where he noted also that "the volume of euro-denominated foreign debt issuance reached a peak at 40 % before the crisis (in 2007) and now stands just above 20 %, similar to its share in 1999" (European Commission, 2018).

A case of harmonic policy has occurred recently, as the need to revive the economy and escape from the deflation trap has induced the ECB to expand its assets through QE. This has caused for some time a depreciation of the euro. The ECB has thus assumed a role that should have pertained to the European Council, but this has been accepted as an instrument for expanding the economy, a badly needed goal, pending the financial and economic crisis.

As said, at the start of Stage 3 of monetary union, the EMS was replaced by a new exchange rate mechanism (ERM), informally the ERM II, or EMS II, which is a kind of "waiting room" for joining the EMU of the EU. The currencies taking part to it should usually obey the fluctuation bands of ±15 percent, with the exception of the Danish krone. This is allowed to have an oscillation band of ±2.25 percent, as it was part of the new mechanism since January 1, 1999, even if it has never adopted the euro.[12]

2.6 MICROECONOMIC POLICIES AND THE BUDGET

Active microeconomic policies are not peculiar to the EMU or to other EU countries. In this and the following sections, we will refer to the

[12] More generally, the exception is for those countries that were member of the EU before the birth of the EMU.

existing policies for the EU as a whole, not to those at the country level, even if some of the former are designed as complementary to national ones.

An important role has been played by the EU in the field of regulation, not only with the initial cancellation of nontariff barriers (NTBs). A number of such barriers have been removed and regulatory standards and rules have been leveled out, under the impulse of the EU Commission, states, and interest groups (Thatcher, 2006). Quality and safety of consumers and workers, environment protection, better access to markets, and interoperability have been the main goals of harmonization. However, important fields are still to be covered, as we will say shortly.

A large part of microeconomic policies that are different from those just mentioned, as well as antitrust action, are implemented through the EU budget. The EU funds most of its social and agricultural policies as well as some other microeconomic policies through its own budget. The total amount of this is, however, tiny, now 1 percent of the European GDP on average, after the negotiations for the Multiannual Financial Framework (MFF) referred to 2014–20, when expenditures were reduced by .12 p.p. with reference to the previous period (European Commission, 2013).

In May 2018, the EU Commission presented the MFF for the next seven years (2021–27), but the Parliament adopted two resolutions whereby it raises some objections to its content, making it difficult for the MFF to be passed before the end of 2019. The level of the budget has been raised to 1.11 percent of the EU 27 gross national income (GNI), in order to meet new requirements, such as defense, border security, migration, and development aid, an (complementary) unemployment insurance scheme, and investment, while subsidies to agriculture and tertiary education should be reduced or suppressed and charged to countries (but the EU Parliament insisted that they should remain constant in real terms).

More than one-third of the total current budget (37 percent) goes to "sustainable growth and natural resources" expenses (mostly, agricultural funds). Another one-third of the budget is absorbed by "economic, social and territorial cohesion" (49 percent for regional policy, almost one-fifth for the Cohesion Fund, and 16 percent for competitiveness). Finally, 12 percent of the total budget is for "competitiveness for growth and employment" (research and innovation, infrastructures).

The EU budget must be balanced. Of its total finance, 98 percent comes from: the EU's own resources (customs duties on imports from outside the EU and sugar levies); member states' transfers of a standard percentage of their GNI to the EU; most importantly, a uniform rate of 0.3 percent levied on the harmonized value-added tax (VAT) base of each member state. Methods for the assessment of the amount of net contributions by each member to the EU budget differ, but their common message corresponds to a net contribution by richer countries and a net payment to lower-income countries, notably the "new" member states.

The budget finances the policies indicated through structural funds. They are as follows:

1. The *European Regional Development Fund* (ERDF), which is intended to reduce regional inequalities through investment in infrastructure, R&D, educational and healthcare facilities and trans-European networks. The ERDF focuses on several key priority areas ("thematic concentration"): innovation and research; the digital agenda; support for small and medium-sized enterprises; the low-carbon economy. The ERDF resources allocated to these priorities will depend on the category of region. In more developed regions, at least 80 percent of funds must focus on at least two of these priorities. In transition regions (less-developed regions), this focus is for 60 percent (50 percent) of the funds;

2. The *European Social Fund* (ESF), which seeks to increase employment by financing training and adjustment programs for workers affected by industrial transformations. This is Europe's main tool for promoting employment and social inclusion, as it helps people get a job (or a better job) and integrates disadvantaged people into society, thus ensuring fairer life

opportunities.[13] Every year, the Fund finances a wide range of organizations – public bodies, private companies and civil society – which give some fifteen million people practical help to find a job, or stay in their job, or to improve their skills to find work in future. This assuages the consequences of economic crisis, especially the rise in unemployment and poverty levels, and, in the longer term, tends to create a more inclusive society. In the period 2014–20, it will provide some €80 billion (in current prices) for improving education, training, and the quality of public services

3. The *Cohesion Fund* (CF), which is aimed at member states whose GNI per inhabitant is less than 90 percent of the EU average. It aims to reduce economic and social disparities – thus making for convergence of the different economies – to promote competitive and sustainable development and to increase trans-boundary cooperation. For the 2014–20 period, the Fund benefits mainly more recent member countries, notably former "transition" countries.[14] Its role has been reduced over time since its creation by Jacques Delors' initiative. In the current period, it allocates a total of €63.4 billion to activities directed to the following:

- - trans-European transport networks, notably projects of European interest as identified by the EU. The Cohesion Fund will support infrastructural projects under the Connecting Europe Facility;
- - environment, in support of projects related to energy or transport (energy efficiency, use of renewable energy, developing rail transport, supporting intermodality, strengthening public transport, etc.).

These three funds absorb about one-third of the total EU budget. The EU also foresees redistribution and sectoral policies through other programs, such as the following:

4. The *Common Agricultural Policy* (CAP), introduced in 1962, which implements a system of agricultural subsidies and other programs that have undergone several changes since then. It is based on two pillars:

---

[13] On the many aspects of social inclusion in Europe, see Atkinson et al (2017).

[14] The receiving countries are: Bulgaria, Croatia, Cyprus, the Czech Republic, Estonia, Greece, Hungary, Latvia, Lithuania, Malta, Poland, Portugal, Romania, Slovakia, and Slovenia. The financial assistance of the Cohesion Fund can be suspended by a Council decision (taken by a qualified majority) if a member state shows excessive public deficit and if it has not resolved the situation or has not taken the appropriate action to do so.

(a) the European Agricultural Guidance and Guarantee Fund, which contributes to the cofinancing of direct payments to farmers according to national aid schemes for agriculture and actions involving agricultural structures as well as promoting the environmentally compatible development of rural areas in a variety of ways, including the diversification of agricultural activities;

(b) the European Agricultural Fund for Rural Development, which aims at promoting economic efficiency and innovation through governmental micromanagement, either on a sectoral basis (farming) or on a territorial basis (rural areas), in particular for promoting the provision of public goods, especially in the environmental realm.

The new agreement on CAP reform reached in 2013 maintains the two pillars, but increases the links between them, thus offering a more integrated approach to policy support. It introduces a new architecture of direct payments: an enhanced safety net and strengthened rural development for a more competitive and sustainable EU agriculture. The CAP budget has shrunk relatively from 71 percent in 1984 to around 37 percent of the total EU budget in 2018. The amounts for the CAP agreed under the new EU MFF for 2014–20 are frozen, in nominal terms, at the level of 2013 for both pillars of the CAP for 2014–20. In real terms, CAP funding decreases compared to the previous period.

5. The *European Maritime and Fisheries Fund* (EMFF), which has replaced other previously operating funds starting Autumn 2015 and is intended to support restructuring in the fishing sector, including processing of final products and aquaculture.

These funds have become a way to control efficiency of public expenditure in the member states, even if sometimes bureaucratic checks by the European Commission may appear excessive.

Other funds have added to them that have been created in the last decade or so, mainly concerning immigration policy. These, however, are not part of the EU budget, as participating countries contribute to them directly. They include the following: (i) the *European Integration Fund* (EIF) for non-EU immigrants, covering the period

2007–13, which aims at ensuring the successful integration of migrants into their host societies by granting them comparable rights, responsibilities, and opportunities; (ii) the *Asylum, Migration and Integration Fund* (AMIF), set up for the period 2014–20, with a total of €3.137 billion, to promote the efficient management of migration flows and the implementation, strengthening, and development of a common Union approach to asylum, legal immigration, strategies for return of immigrants to their countries of origin, solidarity to countries of arrival from other EU States. Special incentives are provided by the AMIF to support the Union Resettlement Programme, for the transfer of beneficiaries of international protection from an EU state with high migratory pressure to another; (iii) the *European Return Fund* for the period 2008–13, with a total of €676 million, in order to improve return management as well as to encourage the development of cooperation between EU countries and with countries of return; (iv) the *Fund for European Aid to the Most Deprived* (FEAD), created in 2014, to provide nonfinancial assistance to the most deprived. However, these funds are insufficient for coping with the size and the nature of the immigration flows. With reference to the latter, suffice it to say that most immigrants remain unemployed, not only in the short, but also in the medium term, even in the most advanced European countries, as in Germany. More recently, in January 2017, under the German presidency of the EU, a Marshall Plan for Africa has been devised in order to halt irregular immigration flows, introducing to this end the strategy of aid with a true partnership tending to develop Africa's energies through a "bottom-up" approach, in the words of a German document (Federal Ministry for Economic Cooperation and Development, 2017). The Plan was then agreed upon in an EU-African Union summit in November 2017.

2.7 COMPETITION LEGISLATION

We will deal with the community-level legislation, first, and then with the national rules in the EU countries and the existing international coordination with non-EU countries.

2.7.1 Community-Level Rules

The competition legislation was devised in the Common Market Treaty. However, some European countries had no competition legislation whatsoever until recently. This was the case of France, which introduced legislation in 1986, and Italy, which enacted such laws only in 1990. In some cases of both older (United Kingdom) and newer competition law (France), industrial policy concerns tempered the goals of competition policy, leaving scope for concentrations or even fostering the creation of national champions, which were often public enterprises.

Such industrial policy considerations did not bypass the Eastern European Countries (EEC). Especially in the 1960s and 1970s, it was often claimed that the practical implementation of competition law had weakened the ability of Europe's economy to fend off the competition of foreign rivals.

European competition law is broadly based on US legislation and is founded in articles 101, 102, and 108 of the Treaty on the Functioning of the EU as well as in the EU Regulation 139/2004.

Article 101 prohibits as incompatible with the common market all agreements (such as agreements to fix prices, share markets, and limit production) and concerted practices that may prevent, restrict, or distort competition within the common market. This unless they contribute to an improvement in the production or distribution of goods by promoting technical or economic progress, or allow consumers a fair share of the resulting benefits (e.g., through the establishment of common standards).

The Commission may initiate proceedings following a complaint or if it notes signs of collusive behavior in a given sector and may suspend the agreement and impose penalties on the firms involved, or it can informally request that the accord be dissolved or amended in such a way that it does not harm competition.

Article 102 prohibits any abuse of a dominant position in the relevant market for the product(s) involved (the "relevant market" or "marché en commun") as incompatible with the common market insofar as it may affect trade between member states. The reason why a dominant position is subject to sanctions only in the event of actual abuse of that position can be expressed as follows: a dominant position achieved through either internal or external growth may involve gains in productive efficiency and, at the same time, an increase in market power and hence a possible deterioration in allocative efficiency. Economies of scale do not always materialize, although they have often been assumed. Concentrations must be notified beforehand to the Commission, which may refuse to allow the operation to go ahead.

Article 108 of the Treaty establishes that "any aid granted by a Member State or through State resources in any form whatsoever which distorts or threatens to distort competition by favoring certain undertakings or the production of certain goods shall, in so far as it affects trade between Member States, be incompatible with the common market." Such aid comprises that granted for exports and investment.

By contrast, the following categories of aid are not considered to distort competition and hence are compatible with the common market:

(a) Regional aid, namely that to promote the economic development of areas where the standard of living is abnormally low or where there is serious underemployment (such areas are those with a per capita GDP of less than 75 percent of the community average or an unemployment rate above the community norm)
(b) Horizontal aid, such as aid for R&D, the environment, energy conservation, SMEs, and promotion of non-EU exports
(c) Sectoral aid, regulated by the Commission (such as, in the past, in steel, shipbuilding, synthetic fibers, and automobiles) or other categories of aid specified with a decision of the Council, which decides with a qualified majority on proposals from the Commission.

Even if the EU competition law draws inspiration from the United States, it has taken account of some European specificities, deriving from the different extension of state interventions in the two cases. In addition, especially in the past decades, the enforcement of

EU legislation has been tougher, which has originated various situations of conflict with foreign countries, the more so the larger the foreign projection of firms.

2.7.2 Legislation in EU Member States and International Coordination

The laws of individual member states normally complement EU legislation, fully incorporating its underlying principles. This is especially true in the case of Germany and Italy, less so for France and the United Kingdom, whose basic position is that competition is essentially neutral, generating positive or negative effects according to the circumstances. The main difference between EU rules and French law regards the control of concentrations, with France placing considerable emphasis on what it perceives as a need to strengthen its national productive system. The United Kingdom also gives weight to forms of efficiency other than allocative efficiency. The differences between the criteria adopted in these countries and those at the EU level have, then, multiple foundations. These range from the preeminent role assigned to nonallocative efficiency (and the partial acceptance of the Schumpeterian argument regarding the advantages of monopoly) to only partly economic considerations (the need for "national champions" to ensure the independence of the economy from the domination of foreign capital).

In case of a conflict, obviously EU rules prevail over national legislation. However, EU legislation and national legislation have some relatively distinct and nonconflicting areas of application, leaving room for laws based on partially different criteria. In fact, European rules prohibit only restrictive agreements and abuses of dominant positions that affect trade between member states, which excludes almost all such practices in the services sector and many agreements in agriculture and industry. Moreover, the existence of a minimum threshold for economic concentrations to be considered at the European level introduces a separation between the two spheres even sharper than the rules governing collusive agreements and dominant positions.

The national or regional scope of most competition legislation hinders its effectiveness when dealing with firms whose operations cross national borders. International economic relations and international trade suffer as a result (Tizzano, 2000). Competition legislation, as with any economic policy measure taken at the national (or regional) level, may differ from, or conflict with, similar measures taken in other countries. This is all the more likely the greater the level of globalization and the determination of a government to regulate anticompetitive behavior not only within its national frontiers but also abroad. This is the case of the United States, which seeks to control the action of its firms abroad that has an impact on competition at home. However, even simple differences between national laws or the orientation of competition authorities in different countries can cause problems. Take, for example, a cross-border merger (i.e., a merger involving firms that operate in various countries). Such an operation could be assessed differently by the competition authorities of the countries involved.

In recent years, we have seen the emergence of agreed or bilateral competition action between the United States and the EU or the United States and Canada. On a multilateral plane, at the Doha intergovernmental conference in November 2001, the World Trade Organization (WTO) decided to initiate multilateral negotiations to achieve cooperation among national competition authorities. In October 2001, the International Competition Network (ICN) was established to bring together all countries with competition regimes, of which 132 are currently participating. The network seeks to foster a collaborative environment for solving the substantive problems of combating anticompetitive behavior.

A final point to discuss is the relation between competition law and macroeconomic policy, in particular as to taxation. Different taxation in the various countries can lead to ineffectiveness of, or even infringements to, antitrust legislation. This is the case in general for different ordinary tax bases and tax rates and in particular of tax rulings, which offer a case of unfair competition, due to an illegal state aid. In 2014, the European Commission requested Luxembourg to provide complete information on its tax rulings practices. At Luxembourg's refusal, it opened infringement procedures. Similar procedures have been conducted against Belgium and the Netherlands, finding in all three cases that tax rulings violated the state aid rules.

2.8 SOCIAL AND COHESION POLICIES

In this section, we consider social policies, which have a multiple role, mainly redistributive, but also growth-promoting and environment-protecting. In fact, in this case provisions are implemented in a way that, in reducing the social and economic imbalances between the various regions of the Union (or inside each of them), they can also strengthen the productive structure and foster innovation.

The role of European social policy as envisaged in the funds created in the EU budget and additional special funds is only a minor one, given their limitation, with respect to the role for this policy played by each country's welfare state. In fact, the Treaty of Rome leaves this policy mainly under the responsibility of member states, which have established a variegated and uneven, but rather comprehensive, set of provisions in different fields. These range from subsidies to unemployed and poor people and pensions to health, education, and housing. Social policy thus involves multilevel decisions.

Nevertheless, in the last two to three decades some progress toward common rules has occurred, at least in some areas, such as working conditions and equal treatment at work of different categories of workers. Some authors claim that a still-fragmented but specific EU welfare dimension has been created and advocate a common approach to social policy, even if decisions and implementation remain at the national level. In November 2017, an EU Summit on Social Rights decided to relaunch the Union's activity for asserting and implementing social rights, through the following: mainstreaming social priorities (e.g., by an Investment Plan for Europe); modernizing coordination of social security systems (in particular, of legislation on health and safety at work); introducing fair and enforceable rules for labor mobility (by better coordination of social security systems and the institution of a European Labour Authority); investing in youth and skills (e.g., through Erasmus Programs); relaunching social dialogue (in particular, through a Quadripartite Agreement).

Because of its fragmentation, social policy in the EU suffers from a constitutional asymmetry with respect to policies promoting market efficiency. This is due, on the one hand, to the relevance attributed to unification of markets and the common monetary policy in order to attain higher efficiency and, on the other, to the separation of national social policies, with built-in differences between the various countries due to their different visions, stages of development, etc. (Atkinson, 2002; Scharpf, 2002). The asymmetry was rather limited until the Union enlarged to new members, with the exception of Britain, as the other members shared the features of the European Social Model.[15] It further enlarged as an effect of the Great Recession, which hit the ability of some countries to offer social provisions.

A tension between the European Social Model and macroeconomic policy was built in the Union institutional architecture, due to the role that the theory of integration based on the idea of a catching up of backward countries and regions with respect to more advanced ones had possibly played in the Union foundation.[16] This role is reflected in the limited strength of social and regional policies, their

[15]   These features can be described in different ways. According to Frangakis et al. (2010: 1), the basic "elements of the European Social Model include a relatively strong sense of social solidarity instead of competitive individualism, and a positive role for the state, which should bear responsibility for the welfare of individuals."

[16]   The idea that integration would be a smooth process and would lead to growth of all countries and regions was certainly central in the minds of the EU constituents. However, if the operation of catching up is accepted, pure economic analysis would rule out regional funds.

management left to countries together with other policies, whereas macroeconomic management was geared at the EU level, through monetary policy, the SGP, and, later, the fiscal compact. Failure of catching up and the financial crisis led to a higher level of debt and the fiscal compact put severe limits on the possibility to ensure maintenance in the future of the current level of the European Social Model, at least in the most indebted countries.

The critique of the "divorce" of social and economic policy and the quest for integration of social inclusion policy are long-dated. The route taken by the evolution of the EU policy in the past decade has been disappointing with respect to the hopeful prospect devised by some authors. Disappointment is even deeper if one considers the progress of globalization, with its threat to jobs and national social welfare policies, and the pressure of immigration due to political or economic causes.

Cohesion policy has passed through a long and painful process. Divergences as to the principles for sharing the burden of the cohesion policy have been marked, in particular by mid-2000s, on the occasion of the enlargement of the Union, when the list of beneficiaries radically changed. The very principle of solidarity – and not the simple allocation of funding among members – was then questioned (Bachtler et al., 2016). More recently, the program for the years 2014–20 seems to insist more on a perspective of regional growth aiming at emphasizing competitiveness as a prerequisite for regional convergence, instead of pursuing the traditional goal of promoting balanced socioeconomic development (Avdikos, Chardas, 2016).

It must be noted that recent cohesion policy has served also to create support for further integration and broaden consensus to widen and to deepen EU competencies (Brunazzo, 2016) as well as to facilitate intergovernmental bargaining on various topics. However, the foundations of cohesion policy have been the object of theoretical and empirical controversy, due to the evolution in the underlying economic paradigm and the discussion on the effectiveness of the EU action (Begg, 2016).

2.9   REGIONAL POLICY

Regional policy can be of two kinds: One kind refers to occasional divergences between regions or countries of a comparable living standard that are due to some kind of asymmetric shock. This kind of regional policy should be implemented – at a union or country level – through fiscal policy, as in a currency union each country gives up its own monetary policy.

Disparities in income and living conditions between regions (and countries), as well as structural backwardness and the relative uncompetitiveness of some regions, are instead the object of the second kind of regional policy, through specific microeconomic policies. These are one of the most important issues facing the Union, involving its very cohesion (Begg et al., 1995). This kind of regional policy can have many economic foundations, in addition to strict considerations of solidarity, equity, and cohesion. First, there are structural deficiencies of some regions, due to market rigidities, the type of productions, etc. Of specific relevance is also the aim of improving macroeconomic performance and policy, by lowering differences in inflation and unemployment rates. In addition, the spatial impact of integration must be considered (Jovanović, 2015). In fact, no convergence in per capita real income emerged between 1970 and 2010 in either the EU or EMU countries. Borsi, Metiu (2015) identify "convergence clubs," suggesting a clear long-run separation between old and new members, with no catching up of the latter, even if they show a higher growth performance. A separation between Northern and Southern countries also emerges. The need for structural policies then arises. The financial crisis has indeed increased divergences both across and within countries. Disparities between regions inside countries tend to rise for some time after integration – when more advanced industries and regions are favored and expand to the detriment of more backward ones, as technological innovation spreads and transport costs diminish – thus following a kind of inverse U-shaped pattern. But catching up of backward regions is not guaranteed and must be supported (Camagni, Capello, 2011).

The determinants of regional disparities are multiple. They are not only of an economic, but also of a social, historical, and institutional type. As to the former, market mechanisms tending to reduce income disparities do not work properly. Labor mobility is in fact low, except from the new Central and Eastern European Countries (CEEC) members to more developed EU countries, and has problems of its own we will deal with below. Moreover, in some of the cases where there is mobility, this can become one of the factors of further deepening of the differences, as more backward regions are often impoverished of their more talented labor force. Sometimes growth and development propagate from one region to another, but it often happens that other factors operate causing a circular cumulative causation that leads to polarization and regional differences (Myrdal, 1957).

In the case of the EMU, according to the European Economic Advisory Group (EEAG, 2015: 76), it was the elimination of exchange rate uncertainty that produced capital movements depressing wages in the core, i.e., in countries with a lower inflation trend, and raising them in the periphery, thus reducing "disparities both in terms of labour productivity and unemployment ... across countries, while disparities across regions within countries did not change much."[17]

We will show that: (i) the direction of causality from capital movements to wage depression in the core can (should) be reversed; (ii) the reduction of unemployment in the periphery was only

---

[17] Here and in the rest of the book, we refer to this simple dichotomy between core and peripheral countries, where the former are the countries with a lower inflation and surplus current account profile (Germany, Belgium, the Netherlands, Finland, Austria, and possibly France), whereas the latter show opposite trends of these variables (mainly Spain, Greece, Portugal, Italy, and Ireland). We thus leave out of our analysis East European countries, mainly because all of them accessed the Eurozone after 2007.

temporary, as it did not last beyond the financial crisis; (iii) the increase in productivity in the periphery occurred only in some countries.

As a matter of fact, as we saw above, a large part of the EU budget is devoted to regional policy, especially in favor of CEEC. However, funds are limited by the low level of the budget. In historical terms, on the occasion of Maastricht agreements, Spain and other three low-income countries insisted on an increase of regional funds, but the promise they received was later denied. EU funds are assigned to projects presented by interested countries for regions having a per capita income lower than, or equal to, 75 percent of the EU average. The principles governing the EU regional policy are as follows: concentration of assistance on priorities, coordination of various policies and funds, partnership with member states and other subjects, subsidiarity, multiannual and multiproject programming, and additionality with respect to other expenditures by public or private bodies (Armstrong, Taylor, 2000).

In a recent econometric analysis, Bachtrögler et al. (2019) show some features of the distribution of the EU regional funds. In less- (higher-) developed regions, they are devoted mainly to transportation infrastructure (fostering labor market and social inclusion), whereas in all regions a large share of the amount is taken by environment, innovation, and R&D. Small firms are in general favored, except for less-developed and urban regions.

As to the effectiveness of the EU regional policy, Becker et al. (2018) find that the picture is really mixed, as, in particular: on the one hand, EU funds have a positive income multiplier effect, but this is not very long lived and is lower during the crisis and their employment effects are usually scarce (higher during the crisis); on the other hand, in poor regions with scarce human capital and abundant corruption effects are lower.

2.10 INDUSTRIAL, AGRICULTURAL, AND TRADE POLICIES

The EU (and, before it, the EEC) has undertaken numerous industrial policy actions over the years.[18] Of special interest are the sectoral initiatives taken in the 1970s and 1980s, notably in the steel industry, for which a system of national quotas was developed. Little remains of this sectoral intervention, except in agriculture, as said.

This approach initially encompassed information technology (IT), telecommunications, new materials, and various energy projects. More recently, many new programs have been devised, such as the Research and Innovation Plan, in order to fulfill the Europe 2020 goals. This is also called "Europe 2020" or "Horizon 2020," a ten-year strategy proposed by the European Commission in 2010 to realize greater coordination of national and European policies in order to pursue "smart, sustainable, inclusive growth." In particular, it aims at "improving the conditions for innovation, research and development ... (and) ... increasing combined public and private investment in R&D to 3% of GDP" by 2020. It has nearly €80 billion of funding available over seven years (2014–20) – in addition to the private investment that this money will attract (European Commission, 2014c). An important, even if declining, role among industrial policies has been played by agricultural policies, as can be derived from their relevance among the structural funds.

Apart from these fields, the EU's industrial policies have been chiefly passive in nature, taking a liberal approach to the market. Toward the end of the 1980s and continuing along the line of the industrial policies devised in the Treaty of the Common Market (with antitrust legislation), the focus of industrial policy shifted toward boosting "horizontal" actions, such as R&D spending as a proportion of GDP, favoring the elimination of obstacles to the

---

[18]　For a historical review of the EU industrial policy, see Mosconi (2015). For a discussion of different perspectives and suggestions for industrial policy, see Pitelis, Kelmendi (2011).

Single Market and fostering cooperation between the member states in the area of technological innovation. Early initiatives sought to encourage basic research, but were subsequently broadened to applied research projects jointly proposed by firms, research centers, and universities from different EU countries. Although in principle targeted at a wide variety of sectors (in that it was expected that the programs would generate dynamic external economies in a range of areas), European research policy has in fact been selective, picking projects in sectors where it was felt appropriate to concentrate funding as circumstances dictated.

The most important instrument of these policies has been the elimination of NTBs within the Union, with measures aimed at creating the Single Market. A "new approach" to technical standards was also initiated in the 1980s, envisaging harmonization of health and safety requirements and implementation of the principle of mutual recognition in the Union of national standards in conformity with essential safety requirements – and thus of free circulation of products legally manufactured in one member state. The EU has liberalized many sectors, such as public-interest services, which were previously dominated by public monopolies (railways, energy, water, and postal services), and financial services (banking, insurance, and investment).

Economic integration can be hampered or distorted by differences in tax systems, as far as indirect, income, and capital taxes are concerned. The EEC has long since adopted a unified system of taxation on consumption, based on the VAT. Its base and rates are harmonized to a large extent, starting from the 1977 Sixth Directive, and there are now limited interstate distortions, as the tax is levied under the destination principle (exports free of taxes, imports taxed) (however, see Genser, 2003, for a discussion on the best VAT regime for the Single Market).

The field in which the need for tax coordination is higher is that of capital taxation, as tax competition can result in inefficient and unfair outcomes. Any attempt to harmonize the tax treatment of investment income has failed so far. By contrast, the Commission has repeatedly recommended removing all tax barriers to the free flow of financial movements. Whether, in view of the theory of the second best, this would make the financial system more stable and efficient is an open question.

Differences in corporate tax bases and rates create obstacles to cross-border investment in the EU and affect its location. To deal with at least the most blatant divergences in capital taxation at the end of 1997, the Ecofin Council approved the "Code of Conduct on business taxation" (European Commission, 1997). This is a non-binding agreement aimed at avoiding tax competition in the form of tax preferences to highly mobile investment activities, including foreign direct investment, and nontransparent administrative practices. The Code is, however, silent on competition in the form of uniformly low corporate income tax rates (Zodrow, 2003). Following the approval of the Code, the focus shifted to enhancing coordination among the member states, combined with a good dose of tax competition, for example in the area of business taxation.

To remove obstacles to cross-border investment, while favoring the creation of European business structures, the Bolkestein Report (2001) focused on tax base uniformity rather than tax rate harmonization. It proposed to establish a system of common base taxation (uniform rules for computing taxable profits for firms with cross-border operations) and a home state taxation (taxation of foreign operations in the member state where headquarters are located, based on the principle of multilateral recognition).

Efforts to induce governments in tax havens to at least cooperate in cases of suspected tax evasion continue under the aegis of both the EU and the Organisation for Economic Cooperation and Development, OECD, born in 1961, which now brings together thirty-six of the world's most advanced economies. However, in addition to absence of tax harmonization, as said some EU countries have adopted procedures of "tax rulings," granting a tax treatment even more favorable than the usual one to transnational countries that intend to invest in the country in question.[19] On this practice, the EU Commission has opened a procedure for unfair competition and unlawful state aid. In January 2016, the EU Commission envisaged an "Anti Tax Avoidance Package" to fight tax avoidance practices. More recently, in 2017 the European Parliament made plans to clamp down on aggressive tax competition. It has also set up two special committees on tax rulings. At the same time, the EU Council of Ministers implemented a directive introducing a common framework for the automatic exchange of information about tax rulings and preventive agreements on transfer prices. An inquiry committee has also been set up by the European Parliament to look into the "Panama papers," a dossier listing about 214,000 offshore corporations and their shareholders, including some that are located in European countries, flying to "tax holidays" to reduce their tax burden.

In other fields, despite a number of official efforts, there are still many differences favoring segmented markets. A couple of examples can be clarifying. First, if you want to connect your computer to a plug in an EU country different from yours, often you still need an adaptor. Second, rules on certification and protection of branded products are still very different, allowing those countries that have most delocated their production to continue to sell goods produced abroad as made in their countries.

2.11 FINANCIAL REGULATION, MICRO-PRUDENTIAL AND CREDIT POLICY

A substantial deregulation of the financial sector and a wrong way of arranging the remaining supervisory system of controls played a key

---

[19] On the side of transnational corporations, this is a way to reduce their tax burden, which enables them to implement the procedure of transfer pricing for lowering their fiscal burden. Even if in practice their main operating places remain elsewhere, by transferring their parent company to a country where tax rates are lower, in particular as a consequence of a tax ruling agreement, parent companies can, e.g., impute unexisting costs, such as for R&D or for counseling to the subsidiaries in countries with higher tax rates, or in order to lower the profits of these subsidiaries (on transfer pricing see, e.g., Tørsløv et al., 2018). On the side of the countries granting lower taxes, this represents a beggar-thy-neighbor practice, even if with little increase in production and employment.

role for the development of the crisis in the EZ, as in the United States. The financial sector was significantly affected by the creation of the Single Market, and this had a decisive influence on international trade in services, even more than trade in goods. In addition to foreign exchange controls, NTBs were (and to some extent still are) represented primarily by the various regulatory systems adopted by member states. These regulations, which were justified because of the need to safeguard the stability of their financial systems, certainly imposed different restrictions and rules from country to country, thereby segmenting the individual national markets. However, with some exceptions, they have not been substituted by proper regulation at the EU level until recently, when the banking union and macroprudential regulation have been introduced (Section 9.2).

The EEC first and the EU later sought to reduce existing barriers between the various financial markets with a series of interventions, notably: complete liberalization of capital movements, as envisaged in the Delors Report of 1989; harmonization of certain key parts of financial legislation, involving adoption of the universal bank model and establishment of minimum capital requirements and ratios of own funds to assets (leverage coefficiency and, in the long run, solvency ratios); mutual automatic recognition of financial institutions (bank or investment companies) authorized to operate in an EU member state by all the other countries (single banking license); home country supervision over all the activities of a bank, including its foreign branches, with low or no European-level regulatory or supervisory power, until 2014. Only since then, partial regulation and supervision by the ECB came into play at the European level for the largest banks, backed by a relatively small bail-out fund (the ESM); introduction of a specific payment infrastructure, called TARGET ("Trans-European Automated Real-time Gross Settlement Express Transfer System"); its version TARGET2 was inaugurated in 2008. Country balances are recorded, cleared, and settled by the ECB credits or debits. They are settled daily for countries outside the EZ, but can build up as credits or liabilities with respect to the ECB system. Each NCB acts as a counterpart of cross-border payments. At the end of the day, it has either a net inflow or a net outflow of payments done, and the accumulated net positions since the start of TARGET can be calculated.

2.12 ENVIRONMENTAL POLICY

The EU began devoting attention to environmental policy around 1970, not because environment was perceived as an important policy issue per se, but as a way to complete the common market, mainly as different standards adopted by its members could be an obstacle to the free movements of goods. Its objectives and instruments have evolved over time, however, also following the evolution in the interest for this topic per se and development of new broader concepts, such as that of sustainable development, to which the Union committed in 2002. In the period 1987–92, environmental policy underwent a process of legal and institutional consolidation as an official field of activity within the Single European Act, with indication of aims (even beyond those relating to trade policy) and procedures for its implementation (qualified majority decisions in the Council of Ministers). After 1992, there was a revision and integration of environmental targets into other policy areas, but environmental policy lost its previous driving force (Knill, Lieffering, 2013).

In 2005, under the pressure of many interests an Emissions Trading System (ETS) regulating pollution was implemented (Gawel et al., 2014), setting caps for emissions and instituting a trade system of permits to pollute. The ETS is a "cap and trade" system tending to combat climate change. It is the key EU tool for reducing greenhouse gas emissions cost-effectively, limiting emissions from heavy energy-using installations operating in the EU countries and covering around 45 percent of the EU's greenhouse gas emissions. A cap – tending to be lowered over time in order to reduce total emissions – is set on the total amount of certain greenhouse gases that can be emitted. Companies receive emission allowances within their cap that, in case their emission is lower than the cap, they can (partly) sell to other firms that cannot respect their cap. The limit on the total number of allowances available – properly determined according to an assessment of current emissions – ensures that they have a value. The ETS sectors include power and heat generation, combustion plants, oil refineries, coke ovens, iron and steel plants, and factories making ante operam (a.o.) cement, glass, lime, bricks, and ceramics.

This is now the world's largest system of this kind. The procedures are an important aspect of this policy, as a system of multilevel governance has been introduced (Newig, Koontz, 2014). However, implementation is still to be improved. In fact, the emission caps have been set at too a high level, with the consequence that a rather low carbon price has resulted, implying a low value of the externalities created by emissions and a low stimulus to carbon-use saving and its replacement by renewable energies.

After 2005, the outbreak of the crisis offered an alibi for not pressing on environmental policy, in order not to hinder growth and jobs. Also the enlargement of the Union to CEEC since 2004 implied some resistance in implementation coming from new members, in particular the Visegrad countries (Baldock, 2016).

An improvement can derive from the 2011 Low-Carbon Economy Roadmap for 2050, aiming at an 80–95 percent reduction of greenhouse gas by that date. In 2014, an intermediate target was set to cut emissions by at least 40 percent by 2030. As a complementary goal to the use of carbon caps, each member state should develop by 2020 renewable energies amounting to a total target of 20 percent of the whole sources of energy.

Now the main objectives of the environmental policy are as follows: preserving, protecting, and improving the quality of the environment; protecting human health; prudent and rational utilization of natural resources; promoting measures at international level to deal with regional or worldwide environmental problems; and in particular combating climate change.

Major areas of environmental policy concern are water, air quality, waste management, ensuring protection of biodiversity and natural habitats, and compatibility with environment protection of aid
programs and all sectoral policies, to be subject to an environmental
impact assessment. Some areas, such as soil protection, are still
a matter of competence of states.

In addition to the tradable pollution permits of the ETS, the
instruments of environment policy are legislative measures, financial
support, environmental taxes (but only a few countries have imposed
these, primarily Denmark, Finland, Germany, the Netherlands, and
Sweden), and voluntary agreements to achieve environmental objectives, such as Ecolabel and Ecoaudit.

The EU has undertaken an ambitious type of policy coordination, namely the attempt to design environmental policy as closely
associated to the development of its other policies, but implementation has proven to be hard, due to its fragmented institutional and
political structure, with the risk of remaining on paper. Indeed, the
very evaluation of the practical implementation of previous policy has
proved to be hard. A program for environmental research and innovation has also been designed that is financially supported by Horizon
2020.

The EU is engaged in international environmental negotiations
and has subscribed to all major Multilateral Environmental
Agreements on environmental issues. In 2016, EU ministers agreed
to subscribe to the Paris universally binding climate change agreement that will limit global warming to "well below 2°C."

2.13   FINANCIAL ASSISTANCE TO THE COUNTRIES

The European Financial Stability Facility (EFSF) was the first EZ
bailout fund. It was created by the Euro-area member states in
June 2010 as a temporary crisis resolution mechanism. The EFSF has
provided financial assistance to Ireland, Portugal, and Greece through
the issuance of bonds and other debt instruments on capital markets.
Also, specific funds outside the EU budget finance the ESM, which was

introduced in 2012 by an intergovernmental treaty, as a successor to the EFSF. The ESM has capital of €80 billion contributed by the member states, but can raise €620 billion through bonds which pay very low interest rates, given the reliability of the mechanism. The ESM acts as a lender of last resort to the euro sovereigns in need of financial assistance, if it is necessary to safeguard the financial stability of the EZ as a whole and of ESM members. Assistance is conditional on submission of proper tough adjustment programs. The countries that have received such assistance are Spain, Cyprus, and Greece. The interest rates applied to countries can be low, given the low interest paid to bonds holders (in 2019, they are even lower than 1 percent), thus leading to some kind of support for the budgets of the debtors.

2.14 THE LOGIC AND THE FAULTS OF THE INSTITUTIONAL DESIGN. A PERSPECTIVE VIEW OF INTEGRATION POLICIES

The logic underlying the EMU institutions has been properly underlined by Andreozzi, Tamborini (2017: 1–2), who say:

> Indeed, one of the pillars of the Treaties ruling the EMU is the doctrine of exclusive national responsibility in all economic matters, except monetary policy. In this view, in a context where monetary policy is committed to maintaining price stability, each member country retains full sovereignty, only being required to comply with the fiscal rules established by the Treaties, and with the policy recommendations put forward by the European Commission ... the performance of each country ... is mostly seen as the result of its own responsibility. In the end, there is no such a thing as "the EMU," which is just the statistical average of what the single countries are doing. ... Consequently, the blame for failures, and the need for reforms, is mostly placed at the level of single countries, whereas the general institutional setup is kept out of discussion.

It is this logic – contrasting with the rising needs that derive from the interrelations between the different countries and the imperatives arising from the crisis – that has made it necessary to introduce a complex and tangled regulatory framework.

As a general rule, EU decisions are taken by means of the "Community" method, an ingenious device suggested by Jean Monnet to enable "the federalist founding fathers of European integration to sidestep the politically intractable barrier of national sovereignty" (Laffan, Mazey, 2006: 32). Each of the EU institutions has rather definite tasks and uses a decision method. The institutional design of the founding Treaties was a compromise between two different approaches, intergovernmentalism and federalism, each of which presents some advantages and shortcomings. Intergovernmentalism implies unanimity and ensures a veto power to each participating country. It derives from consensus about certain policies only between some countries and is exactly a way to accommodate diversity. Federalism, instead, delegates decision powers to supranational institutions. It is reflected in the existence and the decision method of the European Commission – requiring a qualified majority voting – and the Court of Justice, whereas the Council of Ministers reflects more directly the wills of national governments, generally acting unanimously. However, the Lisbon Treaty of 2007, amending the Treaty of Rome and the Maastricht Treaty, has introduced important changes toward supranationality, shifting the voting procedure in the Council of Ministers for at least forty-five policy areas – e.g., budgetary, appointment, and quasi-constitutional procedures – from unanimity to qualified majority. This procedure does not apply to some important areas, such as direct taxation or transnational aspects of family law, which still require unanimity. The various decision procedures represent a balance of the changing needs to ensure national interests as well as deepening of integration, as a result both of the new emerging problems and the progress in integration.

In addition to the faults in specific institutions – such as the targets assigned to the ECB – indicated in the previous sections, we must address those that derive from the whole institutional architecture and failure to guarantee coordination in different areas. As an example of these, think of the free movements of factors and goods without complementary rules and action that refer to common public finance and debt. As Stiglitz (2017) points out, free movement of labor, capital, and goods without a harmonized system of taxes and expenditures, as well as a common debt, distorts allocation and leads to inefficient allocation of production, creating agglomeration and concentration, external effects, both positive and negative. In addition, the Single Market principle for financial institutions and capital can lead to a race to the bottom in financial regulation. Absence of common regulation and of funds for bailing out banks leads to capital flights from countries with lower-bailing-out capacity. Other faults will be indicated in the following chapters, in particular in Part II.

An important fault refers to the lack of democratic representation in the main EU institutions, not only the ECB, but also the European Commission whose powers have been enhanced by the recent "two-pack" discipline that introduced in 2011 additional coordination and surveillance of budgetary processes for EZ countries.

In order to show other institutional faults, it can be useful to introduce a distinction between the various policies. We borrow it from Knill, Lehmkuhl (1999), who distinguish between: "positive integration," prescribing a concrete and active institutional model to which the member countries must comply; "negative integration" directed at changing the opportunity structures of these countries simply by introducing rules to be obeyed by public and private agents; and "framing integration," aimed at changing beliefs and expectations.

From what we have said so far, there have been few policies of positive integration, the single currency and the ECB and a few and limited macroeconomic and microeconomic policies (banking union, social, and regional policies). Most European policies were initially of the types prescribing negative policies (such as the completion of the Single Market, fiscal policies, through limits to public deficits, antitrust legislation). As we will see in Chapter 7, the change in the incentive structures of private and public agents (i.e., framing integration) was especially relevant and effective in the process to admission, possibly much less afterward, when perverse incentives probably acted in peripheral countries.

As a whole, we can say that scarcity of positive integration and resilience of powers retained at a country level can be due to a conscious, but dangerous, strategy based on the expectation that "incomplete and partial integration could always be overcome with further integration, in a 'chain-reaction' towards an 'ever-closer union'. The euro, with its institutional incompleteness and shortcomings, is a child of this strategy" (Spolaore, 2015: 444). The political factors determining incompleteness of the European integration should be interrogated further, since the crisis has generated deep reservations on the side of public opinion (on this, see also Pisani-Ferry, 2016).

A decisive move toward an institutional setup featured by more "positive" and "framing" integration would derive from the EU Commission plan launched in December 2017 to be implemented by 2025, aiming at completing the EMU by enhancing its unity, efficiency, and democratic accountability. This plan continues along the road indicated by the Five Presidents' Report of June 2015 (Juncker et al., 2015) and the Reflection Papers on the Deepening of the Economic and Monetary Union and the Future of EU Finances of Spring 2017. A European Monetary Fund (EMF) should be established, to substitute the ESM, in assisting member states in financial distress, providing the backstop to the Single Resolution Fund (SRF) and acting as a lender of last resort to facilitate the resolution of distressed banks. The substance of the fiscal compact should be integrated into the legal framework of the Union, thus adding to its democratic legitimacy, but its requirements would be weakened or changed, since in some cases they are against the EU Treaties. The EU budget should also support the needs of structural reforms of member states and their convergence in the process of joining the euro as well as for stabilizing countries hit by large asymmetric shocks. Moreover, the need arises to shift from a system of rules and guidelines to a system of further sovereignty sharing. Finally, a European Minister of Economy and

Finance, serving as vice president of the Commission, chairing the Eurogroup and answerable to the EU Parliament, would be appointed.

Some of the indicated reforms can be agreed on, while some others are not fully satisfactory, as we will see later, and can indeed stress some defects of the current setting (Chapters 8 to 10).

3 Theoretical Foundations and Practical Interests behind European Institutions

Behind the institutional setup of the EMU, there are some original "biases" that derive from two roots. One has to do with the theoretical orientation that had developed before the Maastricht Treaty since the end of the 1960s. The essence of the credo it inspired was based on the virtues of free markets and policy rules, contrasting with the ineffectiveness and inefficiency of discretionary government action. The German doctrine of ordoliberalism (*Ordnungspolitik*) added to it. The credo was channeled to the European public and the governments through experts and political élites, in particular the monetary and financial élites and central bankers, who tended to limit the discussion about EMU to monetary and financial affairs, promoting consensus over the merits of macroeconomic discipline, price stability, and central bank independence from politicians (Sadeh, Verdun, 2009). The treaties setting its institutions, in fact, embed the principles of the neoliberal doctrine. Fitoussi and Saraceno (2006, 2013) depict EU institutions as the fruit of a true Berlin-Washington Consensus, reproducing – in some cases, anticipating – the Washington Consensus. Such principles have been shown later to be theoretically flawed, as we will see in Chapter 8. In fact, in prescribing structural and deflationary policies, they do not consider, e.g., the link between current output and potential output, thus condemning the EZ to lasting low growth. Suffice it to say here that the predominant theoretical influence was that of monetarism and the rational expectations (REs) theory.

The other bias of the EMU design derives from the sectional and country interests that promoted its implementation or benefitted from it, also when the various elements of the theoretical setting were criticized or became obsolete.

Obviously, the two biases are linked one to another. Nevertheless, one can clearly trace, on the one hand, the predominant vision that led to adoption of an institutional setup based on rules, rigor, and markets, rather than flexibility and adaptability and, on the other, the interests at play for both the institutional setup and policy actions, especially after the emergence of the financial crisis.[1]

In the next three sections, we deal at length with the predominant influence of the theories developed in the two decades after the end of the 1960s. The biases deriving from the different interests involved at the time of the Maastricht Treaty and the bargaining powers of the various countries are dealt with in Section 3.4.

3.1 THE VIRTUES OF MARKETS IN A CURRENCY UNION

3.1.1 Why Markets?

A growing consensus emerged among economists from the end of the 1960s on the failure of Keynesian policies as well as on the virtues of neoliberal policies and "sound" money for reducing inflation and unemployment, while raising growth rates (e.g., Marcussen, 1997). The institutional design of the EMU fully reflected this exaggerated confidence in the operation of markets within a single currency and negative preconceptions about the action of government.

As said in the previous chapter, until recently markets and the single currency played the dominant role. Other rules aimed at constraining the action of both the only common public institution and the countries' governments. The former consisted in the choice of a model of an independent and conservative central bank. The latter

---

[1]   To cite an example of the connection between the expectations of different countries and ideas, Brunnermeier et al. (2016b) deal at length with what they label as the "German" (or Nordic) and the French (or Southern) view, tracing them, respectively, to Kant and Machiavelli or, with reference to the recent history of economic ideas (and, possibly, economic interests), to the clash between rules versus discretion. The German view led also to avoidance of bail-outs, while the Southern view favored liquidity provision as a way out of some difficulties. This is clearly tied to the interests, on the one hand, of prevailing German groups (i.e., savers) and, on the other, of Southern countries, where bureaucracies and people depending on government spending prevailed.

were expressed by the SGP. Thus, rules, together with markets, seem to be central to the EMU construction. They derived from the conviction of the possibility of markets to solve problems, on the one hand, and the need for constraining the action of public agents at the country level by conservative fiscal policies, while ensuring a unique and conservative monetary policy to act as a further constraint on countries, on the other.[2]

By looking at the report "One market, one money" (and the background studies prepared for it), which evaluated the benefits and costs (indeed, the former more than the latter, in the perspective of the report) to be derived from the EMU, one can realize how profoundly this assessment and the track suggested for monetary unification were influenced by the then dominant theories (European Commission, 1990, 1991). Buti (2003) explicitly recognizes the importance of the debate in the 1970s and 1980s and of the theories then prevailing on the EMU construction, in addition to the decisive influence of the national central banks, in particular the Bundesbank. The theoretical foundations of EMU institutions can thus be traced back to a number of analytical contributions introduced, mostly since the second half of the 1960s up to mid-1980s, even if not to the theory of the OCA, as we will see in the next subsection.

However, tracing the theoretical roots of EMU institutions can be done only in an approximate way, as they have to do with an array of rules that were agreed upon in a rather long period, partially as a result of compromises and bargaining. Thus, there may be several possible rationales for this institutional setup, and more than one theoretical approach can often be linked to the real institutional architecture that has developed. The basic idea of the European construction was that benefits could be derived from implementation of

[2]   This position seems to have forgotten the motto of Tage Erlander, the prime minister of Sweden from 1946 to 1969 and possibly the greatest reformer of the last century, who is reported as saying, "The market is a useful servant, but an intolerable master" (Grunfeld, 2017), thus echoing what Francis Bacon had said with reference to money. Possibly, a unitary monetary policy ruled by stringent rules might have "served" and not been "intolerable."

free markets, not only of goods but also of capital, in order to ensure efficiency. The many static and dynamic failures plaguing these markets were disregarded. The process of liberalization of markets – in particular of the market for capital – was rapidly accomplished, being completed by the end of the 1990s. Simply adding a single money to a unitary market could solve most problems deriving from the (possibly) diverging conduct of private agents in each submarket, keeping also undisciplined public agents in line. However, given the power of command of the latter, together with scarce effectiveness of their instruments as well as the potential dangers that could result from their use, adding constraints on their conduct was necessary.

Eichengreen (1992) summarizes the rebalancing institutions or channels that should work in a currency union to ensure efficient allocation of resources and avoid the costs deriving from asymmetric shocks as follows: (1) domestic wage and price adjustments; (2) interregional migration; (3) interregional flows of private and public capital, ensuring operation of risk-sharing, a requirement for rebalancing softer than (1) and (2); and (4) interregional fiscal transfers.

However, each channel has its limits, which are either political or economic. As to the first channel, from a practical point of view, it operates (and operated in our case) only to some extent. Since labor markets tend to remain sticky, working of this channel becomes a policy target rather than a condition. With reference to flexibility in the product markets, competition and intervention by EMU authorities to restore it may be needed. Competition policy is a cornerstone of the EU design since the very beginning of the common market, as we know from Chapter 2. The initial inspiration is liberal, but this policy should have pursued more than one target at a time (Monti, 2002), which charged it with too much weight. Its implementation has drawn at times from the conception of the Freiburg School and in other cases from that of the Chicago School, as there is scarcely a single coherent goal of EU competition. Certainly, pursuit of allocative efficiency is one such goal, at times the prevailing one. This would require price flexibility, which, however, is not ensured and would be harmful from other points of view (in some cases, for macroeconomic stability). Channel (2) did not operate between countries, because of economic, cultural, and linguistic barriers, and conveys mixed blessing. In fact, it can cause deprivation of the countries hit by shocks of their best human capital, if outflows of migrants are not temporary. In addition, according to some sources it can raise problems of equity deriving from access of immigrants to welfare state provisions paid by presumably higher-skilled native workers. As to capital movements and international risk-sharing (channel 3), the experience at a world level accumulated in the 1990s (and the ensuing evolution of the literature), as well as the financial crisis begun in 2007 showed that this rebalancing channel was subject to theoretical objections and practical failures. We will deal with the latter in Chapter 4 and will refer to the former below, in Sections 8.3–8.6. Channel (4) does not refer to markets properly, but was not implemented for political reasons (opposition of some countries to devolving the fiscal lever to common institutions) and the operation of markets was deemed to be a good substitute for it. Thus, the conditions for rebalancing did not operate or found obstacles to their operation.

3.1.2 Justifications of the Union. The EMU as an Optimal Currency Area?

The EMU can be justified on various grounds. We will first and mostly refer to its economic foundations, which have been searched for in the theory of optimal currency unions. Later we will briefly expose other justifications.

Ingram (1959) is one of the forerunners of this theory. However, the most famous and apparently general analysis of a currency area or union is in Mundell (1961), who originally stated the conditions for its smooth functioning and viability. Most of the basic assumptions of this theory – and their later removal – are indicated by Cesarano (2013), who raises the issue of the OCA puzzle, along the lines of previous authors. Mundell intended to criticize the case for flexible exchange rates made by Friedman and Meade, but found that, with fixed exchange rates, internal balance can be obtained only when borders are redrawn in a way that within them labor mobility or price and wage flexibility are ensured. From this point of view, as many observed at the time, the EZ did not possess the necessary prerequisites of an OCA (e.g., Krugman, 1993). A drastic position against the project of a single currency was expressed by Eichengreen (1993: 1322), according to whom the project of monetary unification was a "leap in the dark." Portes (1993: 2) had the idea that "permanently fixed exchange rates" is an oxymoron. Tavlas (1993a), partly summarizing previous contributions, maintained the ex ante "criteria approach" and defined a number of prerequisites which – if satisfied – would have reduced the risk of asymmetric shocks. These include, in addition to factor mobility and price and wage flexibility, similarity of inflation rates, degree of openness and size of the economy, commodity diversification, goods market integration, fiscal integration, and political will.

By contrast, De Grauwe and Vanhaverbeke (1991) held a more optimistic assessment of the existence of the preconditions for an OCA. In fact, they found that the growth rates of output and employment tended to diverge less at the national level than at the level of regions of the same countries and asymmetric shocks were higher at the regional level. Thus, the presumption of the literature on the OCA held relatively well. An increase in labor mobility could be enough to substitute for the limited exchange rate variations that were necessary in the past and appear to be realistic in the currency union. Otherwise, only one of the two models, the Northern and the Southern one (the former involving higher labor mobility and being more balanced), would prevail in the Union, which would be harmful for some countries.

Complements to, and divergences from, Mundell (1961) were introduced later by other authors and Mundell himself (Mundell, 1973a). The former contributions emphasize factors such as the need for demand policies (for redirecting production) and product diversification – as a way of attenuating occurrence of asymmetric shocks. In his 1973 contribution, Mundell was more optimistic about the possibility of success of the European currency union and in the course of time became an advocate of the EMU. In order to differentiate this position from his previous one, the term "Mundell II" has been used in a debate originated by McKinnon (2002). The many reasons – also political – in favor of the EMU are argued for in Mundell (1973b), who underlines the equilibrating factor offered by international risk-sharing, as an effect of interpenetration of capital between countries. This factor might have played some role up to 2008, as the core countries accumulated credits toward peripheral institutions. However, it turned into an opposite role, after the eruption of the crisis, when other different factors began to operate, which led to a capital flow reversal and a sudden increase in interest rate spreads between the core and the periphery.[3]

Later on, much of the economic discussion shifted to the endogenous effects of currency unions on optimum currency criteria. Frankel and Rose (1997, 2002) inaugurated the so-called endogenous theory of optimal currency areas. Even if some countries do not respect the conditions for an OCA *before* adopting a common currency, they can fulfill them *in progress*, by the very effects of the single currency, as this can triple trade among them (because foreign goods will be cheaper), and, as a consequence, lower the differences in inflation rates.[4] This would enhance business cycle correlation, thus reducing risks of asymmetric shocks. However, Eichengreen (1992) and Krugman (1993) had suggested the possibility that integration could lead to agglomeration effects. Increasing trade specialization would in turn lead to a negative correlation of output between countries.

---

[3]   A GVAR analysis shows that in core countries this was caused by international risk aversion, whereas in the periphery it depended on the high value of public debt and low competitiveness (Croci Angelini et al., 2016).

[4]   The additional argument of the external tie as a way of constraining inefficient countries to lower their inflation rate and to improve their trade position will be developed in Chapter 7. The possibility was disregarded of the occurrence of significant financial shocks that could threaten the sustainability of the Union, by hitting it in midstream, i.e., while there is still heterogeneity among its member countries (Masciandaro, Romelli, 2018).

Empirical findings support the specialization paradigm against the endogeneity hypothesis, as they show that larger intra-EMU trade flows did not result in greater synchronization across the EZ, thus suggesting the need for a higher degree of policy coordination between the EZ members. In fact, Goodhart (1998) had stressed the point of separation of monetary policy from fiscal and other policies, the former being entrusted to the EMU level, while the latter would remain in the hand of the participating nation states, thus not ensuring the necessary coordination. The EMU was a "unique" event that could raise some problems, as markets might not react in a favorable way. A general review of the reasons in favor of and against the EMU as an OCA is in Krugman and Obstfeld (2003).

Some authors (e.g., De Grauwe, Ji, 2016; Marelli, Signorelli, 2017, also for references) think that one can jump over the issue of similarity or divergence in the structural composition of production of the various countries and consider their convergence. This may refer to their per capita GDP or to GDP growth rates or to the coefficient of correlation of these rates or other measures of convergence as indicators of the likelihood of asymmetric shocks hitting the EZ.

These remarks do not consider other effects arising in the process of integration that can enhance imbalances or make them unsustainable and favor asymmetric shocks. We will deal with them in Sections 4.3 and 4.4 as well as in Chapter 8. Moreover, the critiques referred to above are more a refinement of the optimality criteria than a recognition of the need to consider other essential elements of a monetary union, ensuring internal adjustment. Among these, of specific relevance are those related to the "border effect," which indicates the existence of forces capable of ensuring rebalancing at a country level, due to existence of common institutions and rules as well as availability of more information and a range of various instruments for dealing with regional imbalances. This effect implies incompleteness of a monetary union and its exposure to the effects of asymmetric shocks when policies other than the monetary one are left to participating countries, as in the EMU. This entraps reequilibrating forces at the national level and does not extend them at the EMU level (on this, see more in Chapter 8). In order to introduce the missing requirements for a common currency area, the need arises for interventions at the EU and/or the country level. Sometimes, actions by member countries that can satisfy some of the conditions stated for the optimality of the currency area (such as flexibility in wages and prices[5]) may be required by the EMU. However, these and policy requirements by the EMU in other fields, as those currently requested, may be insufficient.

Apart from these interventions, the countries participating in the Union lacked the conditions for forming an OCA. Indeed, these conditions can be absent also in the case of regions within single countries adopting a common currency, which often do not form an OCA, without calling into question the stability of the currency. Stability is in fact ensured in this case by the existence of the border effect. Critiques of the OCA theory say that it may be useful only in the case of small states (which fix their exchange rates), or microstates (giving up their currencies altogether), which all have limited power. These considerations stress the relevance of noneconomic justifications for the countries that formed the EMU. These have been suggested by some authors, according to whom this is mostly a political project, not based on considerations of efficiency (e.g., Willett, 2000).

Apart from the issue of whether or not the countries forming the EMU satisfied the conditions for an OCA, some authors say that the real justification for adopting a currency union was the need to ensure against the possibility of monetary policy time inconsistency (e.g., Marimon, 2018). We do not discuss the current situation and then whether the Union is still to be viewed as an anchor against it. Our problem is whether the initial decision to build a monetary union

---

[5]   Cesarano (2013) stresses the relevance of the "border effect."

The indication of the actions to be implemented by member countries corresponds to a situation where the original Mundell argument has been reversed and member states must implement institutional reforms in order to become an OCA. "The Europe 2020 strategy and the Euro Plus Pact invoke exactly this logic of monetary integration as a reform lever" (Schelkle, 2013: 40).

despite inexistence of the conditions for an OCA could be influenced by the need to avoid time inconsistency in the member states, if these were uncommitted to a common monetary policy. This kind of situation of the Union certainly could not be accepted by Germany, in particular by the Bundesbank, especially after the 1992 withdrawal from the EMS of Italy and the United Kingdom, who reneged on their commitment to adoption of fixed exchange rates. However, withdrawal happened only after the Maastricht accords and therefore could not influence them.

Replacement of the various currencies of the member states with a single currency has major implications, generating both benefits and costs for the group of countries as a whole and individually. Direct and indirect benefits accrue from lower transaction costs (fewer currency exchanges or calculations, less risk insurance due to the common currency), reduced uncertainty (due to absence of potential exchange rate fluctuations), and increased competition (for greater transparency and comparability of prices).[6] Benefits are all the greater the closer the initial integration among the countries that adopt the single currency. These benefits in turn raise integration further through increased trade and cross-border investment. Monetary union also has costs. In particular, these arise in the presence of permanent asymmetric demand shocks as between the different countries, differences in labor market institutions, and other structural asymmetries.

3.2   GOVERNMENT IS THE BEAST: FINDING THE APPROPRIATE SETTING FOR THE CENTRAL BANK

In the vision of the EMU architects, problems do not come from markets, which should indeed be freed of any obstacle (at least of most regulations and obstacles deriving from government

---

[6]   Mundell (1973a) offers a very detailed account of the benefits deriving from common monies: international risk-sharing, saving of reserves, economies of scale for transaction costs, reduced intermediation costs, greater information, and the innovative character of the new money, which is superior to the old currencies in terms of size and stability.

action[7]), a position that received public support and consensus without much scrutiny (McNamara, 1998, 2006).

Problems come from discretionary action of public agents, as in each period these tend to pursue targets that are unattainable in the presence of private agents having either backward- or forward-looking expectations. If expectations are backward, some targets can be met only in the short run. With forward-looking expectations, governments are immediately fooled by the private sector and a suboptimal outcome results also in the short run: discretionary monetary and fiscal policies are ineffective with respect to real variables and the first best desired by public agents can never be obtained. However, complying with some kinds of rules can at least ensure a second-best outcome.

3.2.1 The Role of Monetary Policy

In more technical terms, with backward-looking expectations monetary policy aiming at higher employment and income is ineffective in the long run, when there is no trade-off between unemployment and inflation (the long-run Phillips curve is vertical) (Phelps, 1967; Friedman, 1968). Any monetary expansion trying to reduce the "market" rate of unemployment below the "natural" one is doomed to failure and can only cause inflation.[8] Monetary policy should pursue a target of monetary stability, rather than trying to influence real variables. This can justify assigning to the ECB a predominant monetary target (price stability), rather than a dual or multiple mandate with objectives having no ranking, as in the case of the Federal Reserve. To be sure, *price stability* would not be the proper objective, as the Friedman (1969) rule should be obeyed, ensuring (at least in a completely flexible price context) a zero nominal interest rate and a *deflation* rate equal to the real interest rate on safe assets. However, the decision taken by the ECB to choose an

---

[7]   What G. Carli called "lacci" and "lacciuoli" (Carli, 2003).
[8]   In any case, discretionary monetary policy can even aggravate cyclical oscillations because of a long and variable effect time lag. Then, stable rules must be adhered to in monetary action, also in the short run (Friedman, 1960, 1962).

inflation target less than, but close to, 2 percent – then a positive one – is only apparently or partially contrary to the Friedman rule, as in reality prices are not completely flexible and hedonic prices may be of some importance (more in Section 8.4).

The issue of ECB independence seems more remote from Friedman's thought. In his opinion, attributing the central bank an independent status is a second-best option, for political as well as for economic considerations. As far as the latter are concerned, rules are preferable to independence, as the main objectives of monetary policy are to avoid money itself being a factor of major disturbances in the system and to offer a stable background for the economy.

We must thus refer to theoretical inspirations for the ECB design and target other than those drawn from Friedman's thought, even if Friedman's (1962) argument contains the seeds of further thought justifying an independent and conservative central bank. This anticipation of further developments can be linked to one of his arguments: in fact, in the case of an independent central banker, he is a critic of the uncertain degree and the personality of those in charge with monetary control, who may or may not give an assurance of steady and firm conduct. This argument is a prelude to the assertion of the virtues of commitment and of a conservative central banker, which are linked to the passage from backward- to forward-looking expectations.

3.2.2 *Rational Expectations, the Neutrality Proposition, and the Need for a Conservative Central Bank*

Introduction of REs led, first, to a statement of the ineffectiveness of monetary policy that was even more forceful than that claimed by Friedman (Sargent, Wallace, 1975). Similarly, with forward-looking expectations, fiscal policy was considered to be ineffective as an instrument for managing income levels (Barro, 1974), a result we will consider into detail shortly. A proposition of policy neutrality or policy "invariance" of the system was thus stated with regard to the two most important macroeconomic policy instruments. From a more general point of view, Lucas (1976) showed that if the private sector has REs, it can fool any attempt by either the central bank or the government to pursue a given target for any real variable through the use of any instrument.

In the same vein, any promise by governments that is time inconsistent is deemed not to be credible by private agents having forward-looking expectations (Kydland, Prescott, 1977). This result can be avoided by self-restraint of the policymaker, whose temptation to cheat is balanced by a fear that he might lose his *reputation* and no longer be able to act effectively, in case of repeated interactions with the private sector. However, in a world with uncertainty, signals are more difficult to interpret and then the best practical solution to the problem of time inconsistency is that the policymaker credibly *commits* to some rule (Barro, Gordon, 1983).

A consensus thus emerged in the 1970s and 1980s from these contributions as well as the monetarists' with reference to the need to eliminate the tendency to create inflation – the inflation bias – that may be present in the constituency and the government (including the central bank) (McNamara, 1998). A "conservative revolution" in favor of economic policy tending to but one goal, abating inflation, also conquered the European left (Marcussen, 1997).

In order to eliminate this bias, many possible rules were suggested, such as those tying money growth to some macroeconomic indicator. An alternative is for the constituency or government to delegate monetary policy to a conservative central banker, i.e., to a banker assigning employment a lower *weight* than the society or the government. Rogoff (1985) shows that this banker would be able to attain a lower level of inflation without reducing employment. Appointing a conservative central banker originates a conflict with the government that can be avoided by introducing rules that govern the independent monetary authority, i.e., by establishing a *target* conservative central bank (Svensson, 1997). This represents the best way for obtaining a commitment not to pursue inflationary, but ineffective, policies. We are thus (almost) back to Friedman, with two (not insignificant) details added. One is that rules are a way to cope with a more general problem faced by governments, that of their credibility. The other is that, once price stability is not in question – since a rule has been introduced prescribing its pursuit, setting a cap on the inflation rate – stabilization policies are possible. This is exactly the description of the status of the ECB, which has to guarantee a certain inflation rate in the medium run as its preeminent target, but can also pursue other objectives, provided that these do not compromise the attainment of its predominant one.

As a final remark in this section, we can recall Goodhart's notation according to which there is a significant overlap between the solution devised for monetary policy – more generally, the EMU institutional design – and "advocating a reduced role for the State in economic affairs" (Goodhart, 1998: 425).

3.3 AGAINST DISCRETIONARY AND COORDINATED FISCAL ACTION

The rules for fiscal policy set by the EMU have numerous specific theoretical roots, apart from the need for commitment to avoid time inconsistency, an argument that, as said, can be applied not only to monetary policy, but also to any other public action and, thus, also to fiscal policy. These roots range from political economy contributions to those about the ineffectiveness of fiscal policy due to the low values of multipliers and the negative effects on the price level of fiscal action coordination between countries.

Political economy contributions – which we deal with in Section 3.3.1 – can first offer an analytical justification for the assumption underlying Barro and Gordon's (1983) model, according to which the government's desired unemployment rate is lower than the natural one. In this way, one goes to the roots of time inconsistency. Moreover, this literature can explain the tendency of discretionary fiscal action toward accumulation of public deficit and debt, which offers an additional specific justification for constraints imposed on it. Ineffectiveness of this action due to ultrarationality (Barro, 1974) and the low values of multipliers deriving from time inconsistency and

REs go in the same direction (Subsection 3.3.2). Finally, the possible negative influence of fiscal action coordinated between countries and the capacity of monetary counteraction, the object of Subsection 3.3.3, justifies absence of fiscal coordination and application of the principle of subsidiarity to this matter.

3.3.1 The Political Process as a Collection of Self-Interested Decisions and the Need for Rules

Both macroeconomic and microeconomic policies involve issues pertaining to the goals to be pursued. All of them have redistributive consequences for groups of countries and individual countries or even different groups of people in each country. These consequences can explain the populist or egoistic tendencies of politicians who aim at maintaining or gaining power or exploiting it to their personal interests or in favor of other people and the need to limit such tendencies. This visual angle is useful for both understanding some theoretical bases of the EMU monetary policy (in addition to those already indicated) and explaining introduction of fiscal policy rules in the institutional setup.

These aspects of fiscal policymaking have first been explained by the school of public choice, starting from the idea of the political process as represented by a collection of self-interested decisions (Buchanan, Tullock, 1962). This applies not only to voters and politicians, but also to bureaucrats. As noted, as far as politicians are concerned, by referring to this idea one could first have an analytical justification for the assumption underlying Barro and Gordon's model. In fact, a number of reasons can lead politicians to attempt to reach an employment target higher than the natural one, possibly by running budget deficits, accumulating public debt, etc: the attempt of politicians to maximize the length of their office (Downs, 1957) or to win elections (Nordhaus, 1975), their partisan inclinations (Hibbs, 1977; Wittman, 1977), or their representation of interest groups.

The kind of electoral system chosen – e.g., proportional representation – or electoral uncertainty can exacerbate the tendency to enlarge expenditure and deficits. Politicians' attempts can be successful because principal–agent problems arise, as an effect of "rational ignorance" (Downs, 1957) or asymmetric information (also Dixit, 1996). Similar problems affect not only macroeconomic policies but also the provision of public goods and other policies and are particularly important if the principal is composed of a large group of individuals (Olson, 1965).

Thus, concepts of political economy can add specific justifications for constraints imposed by the Union on discretionary fiscal action: e.g., the possibility to limit people's propension to profligacy, since the governments can justify restrictions as due to European rules; the need to avoid pernicious strategic coordination of national fiscal policies against monetary policy (Fatàs, Mihov 2003a, 2003b; von Hagen, Eichengreen, 1996).

The need then arises to devise rules, especially constitutional ones, to be decided by following a unanimity procedure. Quasirational individuals could agree to limit the temptation to draw short-run benefits and agree on such subjects as balanced budget rules, limits to governmental growth, and transfers (e.g., Brennan, Buchanan, 1980). One could thus explain both the reason why the SGP was required to be constitutionally grounded (Inman, 1996) and the recent introduction of the fiscal compact, according to which constitutional rules constraining discretionary fiscal policy should be passed or, at least, the fiscal compact – which, as said, is now, an intergovernmental agreement – should be included in the European law.

In addition, this literature gives support to transferring some decisions to institutions not plagued by time inconsistency and opportunistic behavior to make a credible commitment. This can be done by delegating some decisions to agents with different time preferences or with incentive structures different from those of politicians as in the case of independent central banks (e.g., De Haan, Sturm, 1992) and other independent authorities (Majone, 1996). Moreover, political economy arguments have been at the basis of the analysis not only of the EMU, but also of all the other European institutions. Political economy considerations can also be useful with respect to the way interest groups influence the action of EU policymakers, which can derive from two sources:

(i) The more traditional supply-side source, highlighting the cases where groups mobilize to protect the interests of either business groups or sections of the civil society through a logic either of arguing or of political exchange; as to the way interest groups operate, an important distinction is between insiders and outsiders: the former, mainly business groups, tend to influence policymakers directly; the latter, mainly – but not only – civil society groups, operate prevailingly on the public opinion (on this, see more recently Dür, Mateo, 2016);

(ii) A demand-side source, as interest groups' action can be requested by various external sources, in particular the government itself: e.g., these groups can be asked to subsidize parties and other institutions and give "suggestions" about the agenda and composition of policy bodies.

Other studies referring to the EU case offer support for both sources. The double type of activity of interest groups justifies the approach taken by Richardson (2006b), who suggests looking at the EU's governance as resulting from the impulse of multiple stakeholders.[9]

3.3.2 Ineffectiveness of Fiscal Policy: Low Value of Multipliers

Turning to other theoretical orientations, both the neoclassical and the New Keynesian (NK) approach[10] usually incorporate some sort of Barro–Ricardo (consumption smoothing) effect and thus assert a low value of multipliers and tend to suggest ineffectiveness of expansionary fiscal policy. Even in these models, separable utility, deep habit consumption, rule-of-thumb consumers, liquidity-constrained

---

[9]   Apart from the classic contribution by Olson (1965), for a recent overview of interests groups in the United States and Europe, see Dür, Mateo (2014), Dür et al. (2015).

[10]   The NK approach emerged first at the beginning of the 1990s, but it was not until the 2000s that it was refined in such a way as to allow for some positive real effect of fiscal policy. Then, it had scarce or no practical influence on EMU institutions, differently from other, more traditional, neoclassical theories.

consumers, spending reversals could restore positive and significant Keynesian-like effects of public spending increases on output (Hebous, 2010). However, in the absence of such mechanisms some kind of Barro–Ricardo effect would not only imply ineffectiveness of Keynesian policies, but also suggest the need for fiscal consolidation. In addition, in case of a crisis, fiscal contraction would be in order, under the form of either a reduction in expenditure or a rise in taxes. These suggestions would be strengthened when considering also the negative long-term effect of debt on growth.

Indeed, some empirical researches found a positive effect of government expenditure cuts both in a short- and a long-run perspective. This was the conclusion of the doctrine of "expansionary austerity" asserted by Giavazzi and Pagano (1990), who explained the positive effects on consumption of the cuts of the 1980s in the Danish and Irish public expenditure as deriving from households' expectations of permanent cuts in the level of government budget. Along similar lines followed Alesina and Perotti (1995, 1997); Giavazzi and Pagano (1996); and, more recently, Alesina and Ardagna (1998), Amendola et al. (2017), and others. The negative effect of the debt on growth had been stated first by Modigliani (1961) and others long before Reinhart and Rogoff (2010).

This *"fin de siècle"* credo of low or negative values of multipliers and of negative effects on growth deriving from the accumulation of debt was certainly not in favor of traditional Keynesian fiscal action against imbalances and can be thought of as influencing the draft of the EMU institutional setup. In addition, it also inspired the idea of an expansionary fiscal consolidation that was at the basis of exit policies from the crisis (Sections 8.3–8.5).[11]

In this perspective, it is not strange that the SGP and (more recently) the fiscal compact have been agreed on and active fiscal

---

[11] A much milder version of the "expansionary austerity" argument is that based on the beneficial effects in the long term of the austerity, as this lays down the possibility to produce the much-needed changes in the long-lasting relative price imbalances that caused the crisis after 2009 (EEAG, 2014: ch.3). Then, the benefits of any fiscal expansion are limited and some austerity measures are inevitable.

policy has been restricted. However, these limitations on discretionary fiscal policy cannot be fully understood without considering open economies explicitly, in the context of other European institutions, which we do in the following subsection.

3.3.3 Inefficiency and Negative Spillovers of Fiscal Policy Coordination

Theoretical models of open economies are of specific interest to us. In this context, the impact of budget policies on the real exchange rate plays an important role in determining the size of the multiplier effect, as this could be increased by the ensuing real exchange rate depreciation, a possibility investigated by a number of authors. Other effects must be taken into account in an open economy, such as the existence of incomplete international financial markets and the possibility of a home bias in consumption: both increase the expansionary impact of public expenditure. Finally, in an open economy context there are also negative or positive spillover effects. The former refer to the increase in the interest rate of the whole area. The latter operate via trade and have a special interest. Fiscal expansion stimulates domestic activity, which leads to more foreign imports and, hence, higher foreign output. It is then natural to argue in favor of fiscal coordination in order to increase the multiplier effects.

Some of the positive effects on the size of multipliers are scarcely relevant in the context of a monetary union. In fact, changes in the real exchange rate are possible only to the extent to which the price levels change. Prices in the country with an expansionary fiscal policy tend to increase and the opposite may happen abroad.[12] As a conclusion on this point, the relative increase of home country prices tends to reduce the multiplier effect. Then, the possible effect of a country's expansion on the euro real exchange rate is likely to be doubtful and empirically negligible (Wyplosz, 2006). Financial markets are still incomplete, but incompleteness in the EMU is reduced

---

[12]   The conjectural character of this statement about falling prices abroad is tied to their downward inflexibility.

with respect to the wider global economy. The home bias is limited in the EU as far as the effect of national protectionist policies is concerned, as both trade and NTBs have been drastically lifted. In fact, the income multiplier is reduced by the high value of the propensity to import (about 25 percent on average) from other EU countries. This high propensity, instead, while having a negative impact on expansionary fiscal action in one country only, would support a coordinated fiscal action. As to negative spillovers, the rise in the interest rates of the whole area due to expansion *in one country* is practically nil, at least in the first approximation.

The conclusion in favor of fiscal policy coordination would miss interactions between fiscal and monetary policies, which have an impact on the nature and the value of spillovers and fiscal multipliers. In a monetary union, any expansionary fiscal action by one country has an impact on the union's price level and thus calls for a deflationary intervention by the ECB. Beetsma and Bovenberg (1998), and some more recent papers,[13] while using different modeling approaches, all find negative effects on income from fully coordinated fiscal expansion, due to the deflationary reaction of the central bank.

According to Beetsma and Bovenberg, there are justifications not only for a conservative central bank, due to the need to avoid time inconsistency, but also for avoiding coordination of national fiscal policies. In fact, monetary unification enhances the strategic position of the monetary authority and introduces a disciplinary effect on governments. Fiscal coordination would eliminate this disciplinary effect and worsen the strategic position of the central bank. It is true that coordination always improves welfare in the absence of strategic behavior and asymmetric information, but this conclusion is not always guaranteed if the underlying assumptions are removed, as must be done in our case. The need for introducing subsidiarity in fiscal policymaking is thus asserted.

---

[13]   See also, more recently, Beetsma and Giuliodori (2010). This paper and the one cited in the text do not use micro-founded models, whereas other papers use an NK model.

Apart from the issues of the spillover effects of fiscal policy in a monetary union and of fiscal policy coordination, the only problem left is whether the existence of a committed central bank alone and unconstrained (and noncoordinated) national fiscal authorities can avoid the negative effects on price stability of free-riding by these authorities. In fact, Chari and Kehoe (2008) show that time inconsistency can cause a free-riding attitude of trade unions or governments if other institutions are absent that may be needed to complement the type of central bank that has been chosen for ensuring price stability. The free-riding problem can be reduced by introducing some kind of constraint on the action of operators different from monetary authorities. Others claim that a pact of the kind of the SGP can reduce the negative spillovers arising from political distortions that can be exacerbated in a monetary union.[14] A monetary policy rule for price stability with no limit to fiscal policy could be insufficient for ensuring price stability, according to the "unpleasant monetarist arithmetic" of Sargent and Wallace (1981), due to REs. Given this kind of expectation, bond financing of public expenditure could cause immediate inflation, even if tight money is ensured. Along similar lines, Woodford (1996) applies the fiscal theory of the price level to the case of the EMU and absence of fiscal self-discipline of governments. Finally, Casella (1989) suggests that a country's fiscal deficit – per se and therefore apart from the reaction of the common central bank – has negative spillovers on the interest rates and the bonds' prices of the area and should be limited.

Then, in the years preceding the constitution of the EMU, the economic rationales are laid in favor of limits to national fiscal policy and against its coordination within the Union. To summarize, these are as follows: (1) political economy considerations; (2) ineffectiveness of fiscal action, with possibly negative – or, at best, very low – multipliers and negative effects of accumulated public debt on growth; (3) under REs, unconstrained fiscal action could impair attainment of

---

[14]   This issue is reviewed at length in Beetsma and Giuliodori (2010: section 7).

price stability; (4) in any case, fiscal coordination, while increasing the value of multipliers (under the best assumption), would worsen the strategic position of the central bank and lead to its reaction and thus to higher interest rates; (5) negative spillovers on the real interest rates in other member countries would derive from fiscal deficits in one country.

The SGP was only the legal transposition of these statements, reflecting the idea that the true problems of the EMU setup were not only that of setting an independent and conservative central bank but also of ensuring that no harm could derive from fiscal policy.[15]

3.4 THE ROLE OF INTERESTS

There are three reasons at least why the role of theories in the EMU construction and the revision of its institutions should not be emphasized.

The first reason for downgrading the role of theories derives from the fact that the theoretical setup existing at the end of the 1980s also included a theory – that of the OCA – that was disregarded by the European institutional setup. Prescriptions of this theory were neglected, which justifies why authoritative commentators on the recent performance of the EMU have spoken of a kind of "vindication" of the OCA theory (Krugman, 2013). Then, adoption of the specific institutions of EMU – free markets and a single currency centered on an independent and conservative central bank, to the exclusion of other common institutions – appears somewhat strange and contradictory, if we look at the EMU as a heritage of the economic theories of the time only.

The second reason is that it is well known that policy actions only partly depend on (changes in) economic theory. There are a number of other factors explaining why theoretical innovations may not translate into adopted policies: among them, the role of inertial factors (see, e.g., Galbraith, 1987). In addition, the evolution

[15]   Buti (2003: 5) quotes Mervyn King as saying that the real obsession of central bankers is not inflation but fiscal policy (King, 1995).

of real phenomena can have an impact on policy action. Similarly to the rejection in the 1970s of the Bretton Woods agreements and their substitution with a system of flexible exchange rates, once free movements of capital were allowed,[16] adoption of a currency area can be seen as the product of the "impossible trinity," deriving from the increase in capital mobility (McNamara, 1998).

The third reason has to do with the role of vested interests and some autonomy in the dynamics of political orientations, which can explain policy actions, even if it is quite a difficult task to separate their part from that of theoretical orientations and say anything about the specific role of interests with respect to ideas. Keeping them separate from theoretical arguments can only be done as a first approximation, as interests and ideas are not mutually exclusive and often interact simultaneously or sequentially (Börzel, Risse, 2000). Considerations of political economy on the possible influence of vested interests and the different bargaining power of the various countries, especially those having a strong currency, as well as reflections of a not strictly economic nature, would be in order. These are largely outside the realm of the present book and we deal here with some of them briefly. Later we consider vested interests other than those of countries.

In general terms, it was the interests of some countries (or of some institutions inside them) that influenced the EMU decisions. Bailer et al. (2015) represent the interaction and clash of ideology and structural features and interests in the EU Council of ministers. By examining the position taken over the years in the Council by each country, they conclude that rich countries do not usually oppose suggested policies in favor of integration, as they are more interested in facilitating it. By contrast, minor countries tend to show their opposition under the influence of some domestic lobby, by abstaining

---

[16] The success of Bretton Woods agreements highly depended on low capital movements, while their failure derived from the practical rejection of the capital controls that had been devised in the agreements and the IMF interventions in favor of countries hit by capital account imbalances.

or voting against proposals arriving at the Council. In our opinion, while this is indicative of opposing interests, there may be a bias, as rich countries have the power to facilitate the path to have their proposals discussed in it.

We refer now specifically to the interests of Germany. According to some authors (Sadeh, Verdun, 2009), Germany did not act as a leader except during crises before the EMU. Monetary authorities neither sought to "lead" nor is there evidence that they purposely tried to influence other monetary authorities, except perhaps for crisis episodes. In fact, the Bundesbank objected to the EMS from the outset, and obtained the "Emminger letter" of November 1978, defined as "infamous" by Bibow (2013: 15), which allowed it to renege on its commitments if it deemed price stability in Germany to be in danger. In securing their commitment to the EMS other monetary authorities simply followed (or paid close attention to) German monetary policies. The Bundesbank was from the outset similarly cautious about EMU, if not critical of it. It was not alone in this stance; a considerable part of the German public, both laymen and experts, were skeptical of EMU when it was being created (e.g., Barkin, 1996; Dornbusch, 1996). In December 1991, after the negotiations of the Maastricht Treaty had been completed, *Bild Zeitung* ran a front-page headline explaining that the end of the Deutschmark was near, which caused great distress among the population.

Independently of whether German decision-makers had or did not have a desire to dominate monetary policy in Europe, Germany never possessed the formal power to actually coerce EU member states into accepting its rules, or to punish those who break the rules. The only (formal) sanction available to Germany at the outset was not to agree to the establishment of EMU or to stay outside. According to some authors, German influence did not translate into monetary dominance, as it was not a hegemonic leader in the traditional sense, during either the EMS period or in the EZ design.[17] According to other

[17]   The empirical estimation contained in Bajo-Rubio, Montávez-Garcés (2002) tends to support a weak version of the Germany dominance hypothesis, as this country,

authors, Germany tended to affirm its authority or even dominance over regional agreements like the EMS – as a consequence of its bargaining power over the rules of monetary cooperation due to its strong currency and, thus, absence of a reserve constraint – and, later, in the Union. During the EMS, the Bundesbank had imposed its monetary discipline, which caused two effects: a positive one, as it ensured disinflation in Europe, and a negative one tied to the double-digit unemployment rate experienced by other European countries and the low growth rate of the whole area (Wyplosz, 1997).

In addition, one should also consider that in time this role of Germany strengthened, in parallel with the stronger bargaining power acquired after reunification. Let us refer, first, to the antecedents of the Delors Report and the Single Act, which are well represented by Gros and Thygesen (1992): a French and an Italian memorandum had criticized the bias of the EMS against "deficit" countries as well as absence in this system of mechanisms designed to achieve structural change and growth and requested a rapid pursuit of the monetary union. The German answer was of a monetarist kind, in asking for the establishment of a central bank having price stability as its pre-eminent target, since these could act as catalysts for achieving the necessary convergence of economic policies in the member states. The German reply, anticipating real developments in the European institutional architecture, was thus closely linked to the theoretical innovations since the end of the 1960s as well as to the traditional stance of the Bundesbank as independent from political bodies since its creation and pursuing the priority target of low inflation.[18]

The effectiveness of the German position was heavily influenced by some practical circumstances that had matured in the

---

although not being strictly the dominant player, played a certain leadership or special role. It would be necessary to update estimations, in particular because the role of Germany seems to have increased after the early 2000s.

[18] Bini Smaghi (2015) refers on his blog of the German PM Adenauer trying to influence the Bundesbank not to raise interest rates at a time when this could have threatened employment and growth. This led to the opposite decision by the Bank to implement a rise higher than that previously planned.

previous two decades. Notable was the rising weight and bargaining power of Germany among European countries, due to its rapid growth and – after 1989 – unification with Eastern Lander. This country was thus able to pursue its low interest in implementing appropriate policies to close long-run divergences in the economic performance between countries, while relying on markets and institutions that tended primarily to price stability and adjustment by peripheral countries. German dominance in the EMS – or, at least, its leadership expressed by its ability to implement an independent monetary policy, as well as to influence the conduct of the other countries that followed it – is well documented.[19] However, there were different positions between the different German institutions. In fact, Oatley (1998) underlines the conflict of the government with the Bundesbank in the implementation of the EMS. For this reason, one must be careful in attributing positions of specific German institutions to the country as a whole.

With reference to the dominant political objective that was certainly common to many German institutions, Iversen et al. (2016) hold that the preference for a deflationary environment featuring the EMU was the outcome not of a rejection of Keynesianism, but of a rational choice of the supporters of an export-oriented growth (more explicitly the neo-mercantilist attitude of Germany, well rooted in its past action) trying to reduce the competitive position of other countries such as Italy[20] and their bargaining power in the EZ. The truth may be that this position added to the widely diffuse anti-Keynesian doctrines and both converged in favoring the deflationary inclination expressed by German institutions. And this country made use of its hegemonic position to be granted privileges when asking for exemptions for the violation of the SGP rules in the early 2000s.

---

[19] Smeets (1990), De Grauwe (1991) and, more recently, Bajo-Rubio, Montávez-Garcés (2002).

[20] Even if running a higher inflation rate, these countries could compete with Germany through periodic devaluations of their currencies. Adoption of a common currency would cancel this opportunity, while imparting a deflationary inclination to the Union.

Really, the hegemonic position of Germany remained hidden, as this country preferred to remain backstage and became manifest only after the eruption of the crisis, which impinged on its interests.[21]

In the most indulgent interpretation of the German "vision" underlying the EMU construction, a common currency could integrate European economies and make them further converge in due time: monetary unification could ensure the structural changes necessary for creating a stable macroeconomic context (in particular, uniform wage and price dynamics), while ensuring a looser monetary regime and allowing for German reflation.[22] Other, less favorable, interpretations are, however, possible. One of them could simply be that Germany intended to establish an institutional architecture stronger and tougher than that of the EMS. This would have permitted it to pursue the goals of a mercantilist monetarism and to further the interests of its savers and the banking industry. Alternatively, at least it did at some point actually exploit the agreed institutional set up to pursue such a strategy. As to institutions, in order to preserve its veto power for key future decisions, in facing new problems of common interests, Germany tended to prefer intergovernmental agreements to higher supranational powers for the EMU. In any case, its export-led model of growth made it unaffected – or little affected – by the deflationary bias of the EMU. At the same time, the specular image of its export surplus, i.e., its position as a creditor country, empowered it to decide solutions for the crisis more suited to its interests.

Germany must certainly be credited for being able to create at home a system powerful enough not to suffer from the deflationary bias of the EMU institutions, due to the real devaluation it operated

---

[21]   On the opportunities and risks deriving from this position, see Bolaffi and Ciocca (2017).

[22]   We have used the adjective "further" in referring to convergence, not to run counter to the proposition according to which Germany pretended of having some kind of economic convergence before unification, which was certainly the Bundesbank position (Wyplosz, 1997). However, inexistence of common policies other than the single currency implies that this was deemed to be able to ensure durable convergence of the various economies.

since the 1990s, in particular in the early 2000s, and for its ability to build a successful system to compete in Europe (and to some extent outside the area) through the quality of its products (Storm, Naastepad, 2015). However, these very credits constitute acts of distrust toward the construction of a true common institution. Germany might have some justifications for that in the inactivity of peripheral economies, but not before 2003–4.

Apart from Germany, the attitudes of other countries were influenced, at least to some extent, by the assessment and the positions taken by important interest groups. In the United Kingdom, the financial sector was successful in being against participating to the EMU, as a way to keep its supremacy unaffected, whereas in Italy both the financial and the industrial sector were interested in the long-term benefits, even if the latter feared that in the medium term it would lose the benefits of periodically devaluing the exchange rate.

Peripheral countries (most of the GIIPS) still think that they may draw some profit from the external constraint of fixed exchange rates and from other EMU institutions. They might like to reform some of these institutions, but are not powerful enough to counter German opposition. This helps explain why they have accepted a number of institutional changes, among which are the incredibly asymmetric provisions of the Macroeconomic Imbalance Procedure (MIP) on current accounts, and the fiscal compact. The MIP was devised in 2011 and requires member countries not only to comply with the prescriptions of the SGP, but also to adjust their current account imbalances, prescribing that current account deficits cannot be higher than 4 percent of GDP on a three-year average, whereas the boundary for surpluses is 6 percent. It is then clear that it has been tailored to German and Dutch interests and that these prevail, as in practice even this privileged 6 percent limit has been disregarded by Germany for many years. As for fiscal policy, the SGP requires budgets in surplus or balanced over the medium term. This allows countries such as Germany to run a surplus for a long time, which makes elimination of imbalances asymmetric and deflationary. The fiscal compact has an additional deflationary impact on each country, thus making it more difficult to raise the revenues needed to comply with the Pact and implying, in turn, a deflationary impact on the rest of the EZ.

A further consequence of this deflationary bias is that fragmentation between the different European countries is thus rising, even if it appears to have been repressed until now.

In emphasizing the role of Germany and the interests of other surplus countries to create an asymmetric MIP and to require fiscal discipline, one should not forget the many shortcomings in the conduct of peripheral countries. These tolerated inefficiencies in the public and private sectors, which have not been overcome either before the crisis or – in many cases – later, as well as the interests of the financial and construction sectors in fostering a financial-led growth with soaring asset prices. Obviously, policymakers in these countries did play an important role, in tolerating inefficiencies and the specific interests of those sectors, to the detriment of the interests of the whole system. This is clear if one reflects on the role of self-interested politicians in being elected on the basis of a program of soft budget constraint.

Politicians in these countries could have looked for a gain in reputation, in order to have greater bargaining power and be admitted as members of the European club. This would have led them to accept the "social" norm of hard budget constraint, even with the prospect of a lower level of income, as an effect of the constraint (Fitoussi, 2007). As a consequence, Featherstone (2014) is right when he says that the *vincolo esterno* (external constraint) and EMU only encouraged a reform direction, but did not determine "the choice of content" and implementation of the reforms. However, in our opinion he misses the point when adding that the external constraint was a means to try to internalize the norms and values of EU policies, at least in most peripheral countries. This might have been, or really was, the case before admission to EMU, when élites encouraged reforms in public administration and the private sector, as they – and the general public – expected gains from participation in the currency union. However, this does not appear to have been the case after admission, least in some of the peripheral countries cited by Featherstone, also because the *vincolo esterno* appears to have been not much of a constraint. As to core countries, one can also have doubts about the realism of Featherstone's idea that they were closer to the demands of EMU, if this is to be intended as adherence to its norms and values. Otherwise, it would be difficult to reconcile this statement with pursuit by some of these countries of an export-led strategy by means of true beggar-thy-neighbor policies and their violation of agreed norms (the SGP).

3.5 THE INFLUENCE OF EMU INSTITUTIONS IN A LONG-TERM PERSPECTIVE AND SECULAR STAGNATION

In this perspective, two aspects of the influence of EMU institutions must be analyzed. They refer, first, to the past and, second, to the future.

Having a look at the figures for the past performance of the EMU can be useful. The lack of appropriate institutions for facing asymmetric shocks in the EMU seems to have generated what to some extent can be called a negative symmetric shock for the whole area. Apart from the appropriateness of the other institutions dealing with shocks, also choice of an independent and conservative central bank has proved to be scarcely founded. In fact, it has produced outcomes for EMU countries that are generally worse than those of the EU – but non-EMU – members at a comparable stage of development (Denmark, Sweden, and the United Kingdom). This statement holds in terms not only of unemployment rates and rates of GDP growth, but also of inflation, both in the run-up to establishment of the currency union and in the new century up to the Great Recession. As to inflation

Table 3.1 *A comparison of growth, unemployment, and inflation rates in the EMU and some EU, but non-EMU, countries, 1991–2016 (Source: Eurostat database)*

Period	1991–98	1999–2007	2008–16	1999–2016
Percent GDP growth rates at constant prices				
EZ 12	1.8	2.3	0.4	1.4
DK, SW, UK*	3.2	2.7	1.0	2.1
Unemployment rate changes in the period (p.p.)				
EZ 12	1.8	−2.0	2.5	0.6
DK, SW, UK*	2.1	−0.7	0.7	1.0
Inflation rate (CPI, %)				
EZ 12	3.0	2.1	1.3	1.7
DK, SW, UK*	2.1	1.6	1.8	1.9
• *Weighted average of the three countries*				

rates, since 1999 to 2016 the EMU countries succeeded in reversing the gap with non-EMU countries that they had experienced before 1999: the former were more inflationary in the 1990s, while being less inflationary after 1999. However, paradoxically – given the conservative nature of the ECB – this was only due to the "deflationary" effects of the Great Recession, as monetary policy did not succeed in keeping the inflation rate "below, but close, to 2%" (Table 3.1).

Having a look at the EMU performance vis-à-vis other regions, we note that the rates of growth of the latter – not only other developed countries and some emerging countries like China, but also the United States – have been higher or much higher (Figure 3.1). Similarly, the unemployment rates have been lower outside the EZ (Figure 3.2), thus figuring a prospect of stagnation in

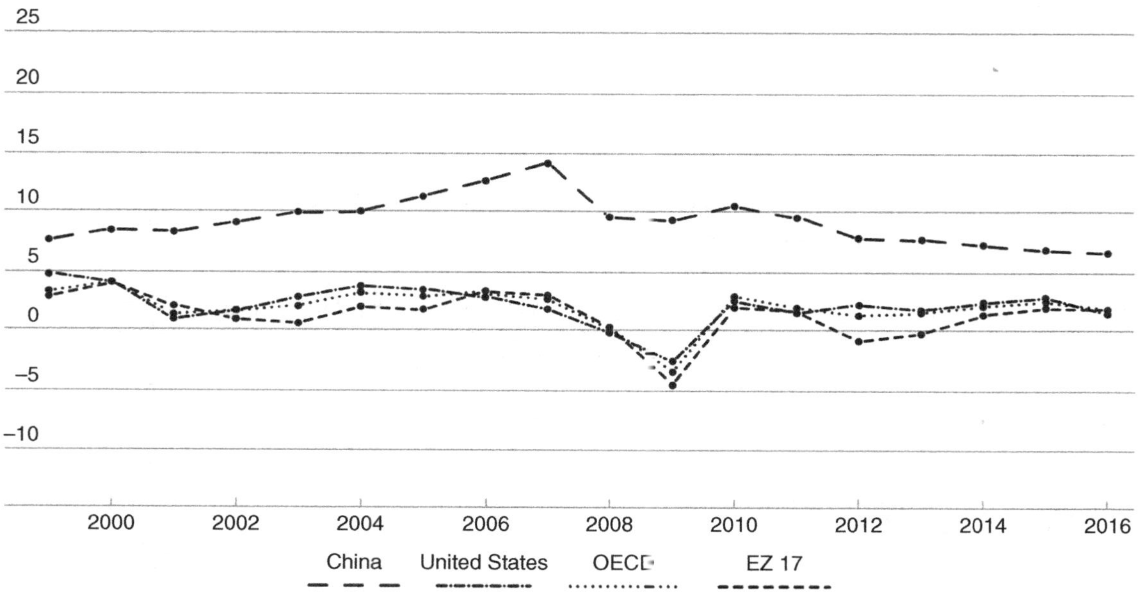

FIGURE 3.1 GDP growth rates in the EZ, the United Sta es, and China, 1999–2016 (Source: OECD)

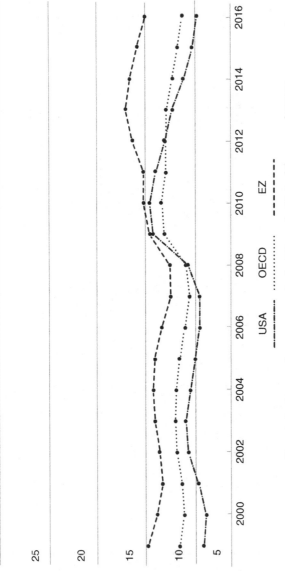

FIGURE 3.2 Harmonized unemployment rates in the EZ 19, the United States, and OECD, 1999–2016

the latter. Austerity has been a characteristic not only of the EMU, but – even if to a less extent – of the whole of Europe. Japan is another country with the same problem of relative stagnation. However, the sources of low growth in the EZ and Japan are different, as we clarify in Figures 3.1 and 3.2.

PART II Institutions and Policies in Action

4 Asymmetries, Macroeconomic and Microeconomic Imbalances

Expectations for the possible accomplishments of the European Monetary Union were high (e.g., Commission of the European Communities, 1990, 1991). Only a few critiques, which grew later, were raised against the project of a monetary union, claiming that this was deprived of some essential preconditions for its proper functioning and aimed almost exclusively at achieving monetary stability while not being complemented by other institutional pillars tending to cope with imbalances and stimulate growth in an uneven environment.

Let us look at the issue from a number of points of view. Seen from the perspective of each participating country, loss of one instrument (monetary policy) in favor of a centralized authority might not imply a parallel loss in the ability to control the economy, as entering the monetary union would also imply a parallel drop in one target, that of the balance of payments equilibrium (more in this same section). One might think that loss of the instrument of monetary policy also implied loss of another target, i.e., low inflation. However, the EU monetary authority would ensure reaching this target only for the EZ as a whole. Ensuring low inflation for any given country would not be guaranteed by the ECB, and inflation differentials are precisely one of the factors behind the imbalances within the Union, which we will deal with later in the chapter.

Some authors expected that the countries entering a Union with a unitary monetary policy would be biased in favor of excessive debt accumulation. In fact, in a country not taking part in a currency union, a credibility effect would rise from the inability of the central bank to commit to an anti-inflationary policy. This would lead fiscal authorities of that country to reduce accumulation of public debt. Monetary unification makes the credibility of the common central bank less effective, even if this is conservative, because the fiscal authority of each country has a reduced incentive to contribute to the credibility of the bank (a true public good), thereby boosting debt accumulation. This justified imposition by the EU of ceilings on fiscal budget and debt. As a conclusion, a country's ability to self-govern was compromised and this contributed to the formation of asymmetries and imbalances with other countries. The true issue is that the EU did not care for them, thinking that the issue of asymmetries had largely been solved in the phase before the admission and, in addition, that other factors would then operate to definitely clear them.

From the point of view of the Union as an integrating area, there were asymmetries between the different countries. These were due to behavioral and structural factors – also of an inertial kind – in peripheral countries (but also in the core to some extent). Asymmetries showed themselves mainly in the public accounts of some of them as well as in other features of the economies of all peripheral countries, such as higher inflation rates. These derived mostly from diffuse inefficiencies, but also, to some extent, from the Balassa-Samuelson effect. These asymmetries had been reduced, but not eliminated, in the transition to the EMU and also afterward. Some inefficiencies have been documented for peripheral countries. To offer only two examples, in Italy they derived from both the ownership pattern of its productive structure (e.g., with the high distortions deriving from the relevance in this country of family- and government-controlled firms) and misallocation of capital and labor within the production sectors. Misallocation was diffuse not only in backward sectors and small and medium firms, but also in advanced sectors and big firms and was due in particular to underinvestment in R&D, the difficulty of filling positions that required a high level of specific skills, and the distorting support of unemployment benefits. Gopinath et al. (2015) document a significant increase in productivity losses from capital misallocation after 1999 in Spain. Facing the inefficiencies and high costs of peripheral countries, Germany cut its wages both before and after the establishment of the EMU.

If these structural differences between peripheral and core countries persisted, together with the high (low) level of domestic demand deriving from high (low) public spending, the current account of the balance of payments of the former (the latter) would tend to be negative (positive). However, this did not worry the majority of scholars for two reasons. First, because any imbalance in the current account would be cleared by free movements of capital. Blanchard, Giavazzi (2002: 186) conclude that "although benign neglect may not be optimal, it appears to be a reasonable course of action." A country could enter the currency union at no cost. In fact, as said, it would lose one instrument (exchange rate), but would also be relieved of one target (or constraint), that of current account (or, more generally, of the balance of payments) equilibrium. On the other hand, it could reap benefits by relying on well-functioning markets. Another argument in favor of participation in a currency union is that of the benefits from the external constraint, already dealt with in the previous chapter (also Chapter 7).

In any case, over time, the common currency as well as integration of markets and limits to public deficits and debts would induce policymakers and other agents to change their conduct. They would introduce needed reforms, with the result of eliminating public accounts imbalances, reducing public debt, increasing competitiveness, and reducing risk prospects (see, e.g., Commission of the European Communities, 1990, 1991; Fernandez-Villaverde et al., 2013). This would occur not only in higher-inflation countries, but also in other countries such as France, which suffered from other kinds of imbalances.

This change in the conduct of public and private agents in higher-inflation countries was at least an implicit assumption behind the institutional design of the EMU. In more detail, a beneficial impulse for rebalancing would derive from the following:

- The impossibility for governments to maintain unemployment any longer below its natural rate by expansionary demand policies; this would be the effect of the SGP and a conservative central bank, which would force governments to change their conduct; reduced public imbalances would contribute to lower demand and curb excess inflation, with positive effects on current account imbalances;
- The impossibility of private decision-makers to rely on competitive exchange rate devaluations in order to regain the competitiveness lost due to inefficiencies, rent-seeking, and wrong conduct. In fact, workers, unions, and firms in higher-inflation countries could no longer earn "monopoly" rents. They would thus change their conduct in order to bring inflation in those countries back in line with that of more stable countries, with beneficial effects on current account imbalances;
- The wider context and opportunities for comparisons and choice (especially for asset returns, once these were cleared of the currency risk component) would induce public and private agents to adopt a more cautionary conduct, implying even in nontradable sectors beneficial changes in the conduct of agents as an effect of higher pressure from consumers and the government or of higher competition induced by increased foreign direct investment (e.g., Commission of the European Communities, 1990, 1991).

The existence of a "misfit" – to make use of a concept developed by Börzel and Risse (2000) – between European and some countries' institutions and conduct was recognized, but it was thought that this would be a condition necessary for change, and that some additional factors could facilitate it.

In summary, existing differences in the structure and conduct of agents of the different economies did not worry economists and policymakers too much. They would clear away as the integration proceeded. Failures in this outcome and the possibility that external shocks could interact with residual structural differences and imbalances, producing asymmetric effects, were downplayed or not taken into account. Some authors even dared to drastically claim that this event "would be eliminated under a monetary union with perfect capital mobility and currency substitution" (Weber, 1991: 204), even if, according to a few others, this was more problematic.

In the next section, analyses of the foundations of the EMU as a currency area are discussed. In Section 4.3, the main features of developments in the Union up to the financial crisis are outlined, whereas the imbalances accumulated in the area and later exploded as a consequence of this crisis are dealt with in Section 4.4, together with their links and the interdependence with structural differences (including preexisting asymmetries). However, in this chapter we mainly refer to theoretical issues, whereas in the next chapter we deal with this interdependence with a view to the recent performance of EMU countries.

4.2 MECHANISMS OF ADJUSTMENT TO SHOCKS IN A CURRENCY AREA

Differences between the mechanisms of adjustment to shocks of single currency areas and those of a monetary union being also a political entity had already been noted by Friedman (1953) and Kaldor (1971). More recently, see, e.g., also Fratianni (1994) and Cesarano (1997, 2013).

As shown in Figure 4.1, the impact of these shocks can be viewed in terms of aggregate supply and demand curves. To illustrate: in Italy, a country that is assumed to be hit by a negative demand shock, the aggregate demand curve will shift to the left; while that, say, in Germany, which is hit by a positive demand shock, will move right. This prompts a reduction in output in Italy and an increase in Germany.

Both countries will face adjustment problems, since Italy will experience a recession with an increase in unemployment while the German economy will expand, with possible inflationary pressures. These problems could be managed with automatic adjustment mechanisms, first by labor mobility. However, this is problematic in Europe, even if at a regional level (i.e., within countries) it is not that different from the one in the United States. The differences with the

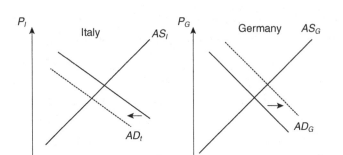

FIGURE 4.1 The impact of asymmetric shocks (Source: Acocella, 2005)

US labor market, characterized by high mobility, due also to quite homogenous culture, are notable. In fact, cultural and language barriers are likely to persist in Europe. However, the geographical mobility of workers as an immediate response to shocks in the EU has significantly increased over time in the last two–three decades, especially for higher-educated people, in both the South European and the Baltic states.

An alternative mechanism, effective in the short term, is wage flexibility, with a reduction in wages in Italy and an increase in Germany induced by autonomous reactions of self-interested agents or wage policies at a country level. This would shift the aggregate supply curve to the right in Italy and to the left in Germany. The original level of output in the two countries can be restored, but with prices lower than their preshock level in Italy, and higher in Germany. This is shown in Figure 4.2, where proper shifts of the supply curves can cope with the previous shocks to demand. There may be limits to the operation of this mechanism, if the wage bargaining institutions are strong, or if wage and nonwage costs (for minimum wage laws, payroll taxes, social contributions, hiring/firing costs) are inflexible and social support/unemployment benefits generous and do not enhance incentive to work. Moreover, limits derive

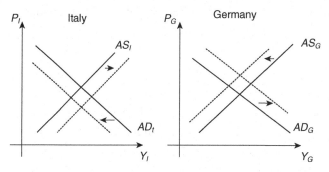

FIGURE 4.2 Asymmetric shocks with wage flexibility (Source: Acocella, 2005)

from absence of proper signals of the shock and of its effects, possibly due to other shocks that apparently compensate them (Chapter 7).[1]

An effect similar to that of wage flexibility could be produced by the industrial policies implemented in order to change productivity trends and other factors influencing the dynamics of competitiveness between the two countries. Lack of perceived signals, the limitations imposed on member countries by union institutions, and deficiencies in country policymaking can make this solution unfeasible.

As an alternative, Germany could seek to curb aggregate demand. Doing so, however, might solve its inflation problem, but not Italy's unemployment, and the demand level for the area as a whole would be lower.

Were the two countries not part of a currency union, both problems could be solved by revaluing the German currency (the mark) against the Italian currency (the lira), which would increase demand for Italian products, reduce that for German goods, and return the aggregate demand curves to their original position in both countries. However, this option – which was available in the EMS – is no longer available in the monetary union.

An alternative solution to the problem of adjusting to asymmetric demand shocks would be for higher taxes to be raised in

---

[1]   However, one must consider that there would be costs to implementing supply-side policies, when there is an aggregate demand shortage.

Germany to finance public spending in Italy. However, the EZ is only a monetary union, with no centralization of fiscal policy at the European level or transfers between countries. Fiscal policy remains entirely in the hands of the individual member states and fiscal schemes providing an insurance system against shocks, while not having distributional consequences as between countries, are difficult to devise (Eichengreen, 2014). In addition, other limits to deficit spending are imposed by the SGP. Regional policies in favor of countries hit by shocks could also be useful, but – as seen – the amount of money devoted to them in the EU is meagre. Even in the absence of a fiscal union or of an adequate regional policy, perfect functioning of financial markets and no previous accumulation of public debt could put Italian policymakers or private agents in the position to borrow the funds from Germany necessary to allow deficit spending to offset the shock. This has happened to some degree in the EZ. However, the conditions required to allow this to happen to a sufficient extent, and without risk or penalizing interest rates, were not met in the EZ. What happened after the start of the recent financial crisis was just the opposite: the capital invested by some countries (e.g., Germany) in the countries hit by the crisis flew back to the countries of origin and interest rates soared to very high levels in the periphery.

Differences in labor market institutions between countries can also cause problems in a monetary union hit by common supply shocks. For example, take a supply shock, such as that generated by the oil crisis, affecting all countries in the Union. If labor and product market institutions differ from country to country, the reaction of wages and prices to the shock will also differ, causing the aggregate supply curve to move differently as well, thereby producing situations similar to those seen with asymmetric demand shocks. These are cases of structural asymmetries. Once again, the scope for adjustment is reduced since exchange rate variations are not possible in a monetary union.

Additional difficulties can be caused by differences in growth rates or in governments' preferences for inflation and unemployment, which can give rise to imbalances in goods movements of the sort discussed earlier.

The balance between the benefits and costs of a monetary union therefore depends on a number of circumstances, such as the extent of real and monetary integration, the degree of differentiation between the structural factors, and the size and type of any shocks that might hit the various countries. A monetary union raises tricky problems in a variety of areas, such as the labor and financial market and the wage, industrial, and fiscal policy, that need to be addressed in order to prevent the emergence of imbalances. If this is not done, as in the EMU, a monetary union can become a trap and cause current account and financial imbalances, and may set the member economies up for a full-blown financial crisis (Chapter 5).

In contrast with this kind of prospect, the expectations of favorable outcomes seemed to be confirmed before the crisis burst. Until 2007 EMU, countries showed a rather good performance in terms of some microeconomic and macroeconomic indicators. However, the EMU, while sharing some tracts of the new policy stance and priorities against inflation that had emerged all over the world since the end of the 1970s, did not outperform other economies in microeconomic and macroeconomic terms. In addition, differences between the member countries persisted or aggravated and some critical imbalances began to emerge as an effect of the absence of proper institutional mechanisms and policies, even if at the most masked by the bubbles arising in peripheral countries.

We will deal here with the effects of EMU from its establishment to 2007, while deferring the analysis of the sources and the impact of the crisis (Chapters 5 and 6) and of the role of improper signaling of the looming imbalances (Chapter 7).

We refer to the situation in the EZ in terms of the various indicators of efficiency and distribution. We do this separately. However, in considering the former we will also examine the spatial dimension of efficiency, as in some cases the performance in terms of efficiency for the Union as a whole would be somewhat meaningless without its breakdown for the various countries. This, in any case, will give a first idea of issues of equity between the different European countries.

4.3 REALIZATIONS: THE SITUATION AT THE ONSET OF THE CRISIS

4.3.1 *Static and Dynamic Indicators of Efficiency*

Indicators of Pareto inefficiency are difficult to devise, but it is common knowledge that there was (and still is) a wide gap in terms of organizational efficiency of both private and public institutions between the different member countries – and sometimes, within each country between different institutions and regions.

As for the choice of indicators of the various types of efficiency, the European Commission has only recently prepared a European Resource Efficiency Platform whose objective is – at least – to double productivity of resources by 2030, "in order to boost competitiveness and maintain a high quality of life." In this perspective, the Platform provides guidance to the Commission, member states and private agents to direct them toward a more resource-efficient economy (European Commission, 2014a). In order to pursue this target, the Commission began to investigate some aspects of allocative efficiency, notably that of the efficient use of resources, and has provided some rough specific indicators for this, such as the "Resource Productivity" (GDP/DMC, expressed in euro/tonne[2]) as the leading indicator. It has also devised a road map to more deeply monitor the issue (European Commission, 2011a).

As to microeconomic dynamic efficiency, an indicator can be found in the growth of total factor productivity. According to this indicator, the EU as a whole was lagging behind the United States and Japan. In addition, differences between the EU countries are remarkable, as indicated in Figure 4.3.

---

[2]   DMC stands for Domestic Material Consumption.

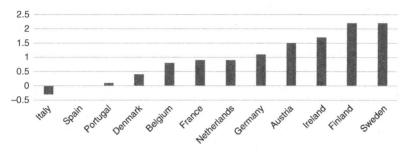

FIGURE 4.3 Annual total factor productivity growth (%) in the EU, selected countries, 2001–2007 (Source: OECD)

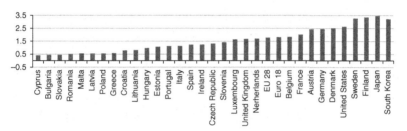

FIGURE 4.4 R&D intensity (%) in Japan, the United States, and South Korea, 2007 (Source: Eurostat)

In terms of factors contributing to total factor productivity, R&D expenditures are relevant. In 2007, the EU 28 (EMU 17) had an R&D/GDP ratio equal to 1.84 percent (1.88 percent), only slightly increased since 1999, when it amounted to 1.77 percent (1.76 percent). This compared to a ratio of 2.62 percent for the United States (also slightly up from 2.5 percent), 3.21 percent for South Korea (jumping up from 2.17 percent), and 3.47 percent for Japan (also up from 2.98 percent).[3] Only a few EMU countries like Austria, Germany, and, even more, Scandinavian countries had an R&D intensity comparable to (or higher than) that of the United States, Japan, and South Korea (Figure 4.4).

---

3   Consider, however, that the definition of R&D expenditures is different among the different countries.

Before discussing other achievements up to the crisis, it is worth remembering that the tradition of the EU construction assigns a high weight to the role of markets versus active policies and institutions. Theories stated in the two decades since the end of the 1960s favored the free-market attitude of the EMU, together with adoption of an independent and conservative central bank. They supported a shift in economic policy attitudes whose most popular examples were Thatcher's, Volcker's, and Reagan's. Thus, there was a clear change in policymakers' preferences and the Great Inflation changed into the Great Moderation all over the developed world (and elsewhere) (Figure 4.5). In contrast with the reduction of overall inflation rates due to the Great Moderation, unemployment rates in the same countries decisively increased after 1970 until the early 2000s.

Unemployment rates in the OECD countries as a whole increased from about 3 percent in 1970 to 8.1 percent in 2013. Similarly, they rose from 5.0 percent to 7.5 percent in the United States, from about 1.2 percent to 4.5 percent in Japan, and, finally, 0.6 percent to 5.4 percent in Germany.

Unemployment rates, employment rates, and other variables can be taken as indicators of macroeconomic (static) efficiency. Let us begin with the first such indicator. Considering pre-crisis data, the average unemployment rate for the EU 15 (EMU 12) had dropped from 8.6 percent (9.5 percent) in 1999 to 7.1 percent (7.5 percent) in 2007. Data for individual countries in 2007 were scattered around these averages (Figure 4.6).

In fact, the variance (standard deviation) – calculated with reference to EU (EMU) countries – was as low as 4.11 (2.03). This picture, derived in terms of unemployment, is confirmed by the evolution of another Europe 2020 target, i.e., employment rates, whose average value had increased since 1999 to 2007 from 66.0 to 69.8 percent for the EU 28 and even more, from 64.6 to 69.8 percent, for EMU 18. Over the same period, the United States experienced a reduction from 76.9 percent to 75.3 percent, whereas Japan increased its employment rate from 74.1 percent to 75.3 percent (Figure 4.7).

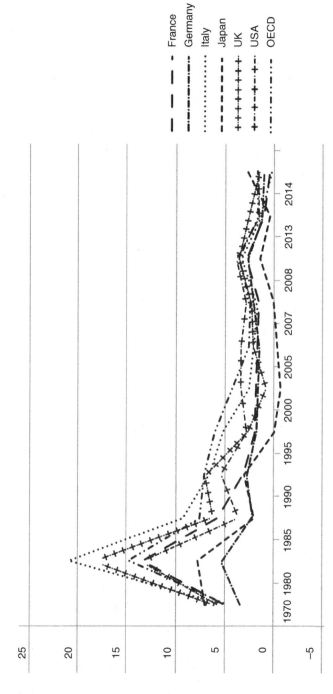

FIGURE 4.5 Inflation rates (%), various developed countries, 1970–2014 (Source: OECD)

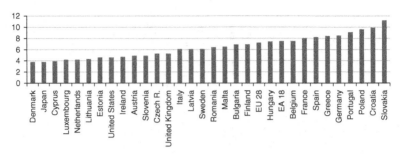

FIGURE 4.6 Unemployment rates (%) in the EU and the United States, total, 2007 (Source: Eurostat)

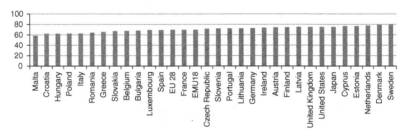

FIGURE 4.7 Employment rates (%) in the EU and the United States, age 20–64, 2007 (Source: Eurostat)

Moving to macroeconomic dynamic indicators of efficiency, in the first nine years since monetary unification the EU GDP increased at a rate of 2.5 percent per annum. The EMU's growth performance was more modest, but certainly appreciable, at an annual pace of 2.3 percent. This compares with better US performance (2.5 percent) and worse of Japan (1.3 percent).

4.3.2 Equity Indicators

The (increase in the) dispersion of indicators of efficiency across member countries already implies a (growing) inequality between the member countries, or at least a failure to improve the integration process and reduce the income differential of the members. Other, more explicit, indicators of equity can also give an idea of (the evolution of) equity

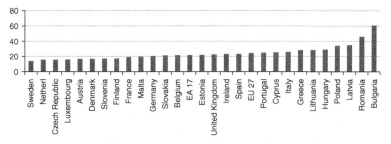

FIGURE 4.8 People at risk of poverty and social exclusion in various countries (%), EU 27, 2007 (Source: Eurostat)

within each country. One such indicator is the risk of poverty and social exclusion, a Europe 2020 goal. In 2007, 24.4 percent (21.7 percent) of the population in the EU (EMU 17), totaling about 120 (71) million people, were at risk of poverty and social exclusion (Figure 4.8).

4.3.3 Other Imbalances: Public Finances, Current and Capital Accounts

Reliance on the virtues of markets and monetary unification has also proved to be partly misleading for other imbalances. Those in public finances went through different patterns before the crisis within the EMU. In peripheral countries, public debt slightly reduced in the years both before admission and after (mainly because of a lower interest rate due to the fall in the risk premium, even if the larger financing facility induced governments to increase borrowing), with the main exception of Portugal and Greece (Figure 4.9). Paradoxically, public finance imbalances rose also in some core countries, France, and Germany, even before the crisis.

For current account imbalances as a percentage of GDP, the picture is rather different. Figure 4.10 shows that Germany had a rising current account surplus over the whole period for which (three-year average) data have been calculated.[4] At the beginning it

[4]   As the legend may not be easy to detect in the figure, we can simply say that the various bars indicate values of the current account/GDP starting from 2002 until 2013.

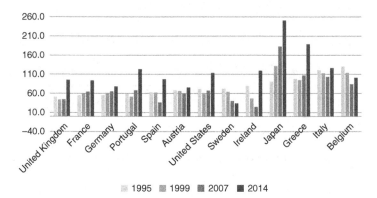

FIGURE 4.9 General government debt/GDP (%), selected countries, 1995, 1999, 2007, 2014 (Source: Eurostat)

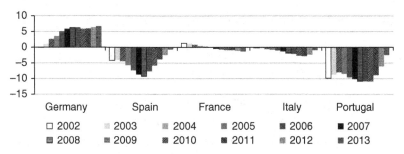

FIGURE 4.10 Current account/GDP (%), selected EMU countries, 2002–2013 (three-year moving average) (Source: OECD)

was small, and then it rose to levels of more than 6 percent with respect to GDP. Other countries, such as the Netherlands, behaved in a similar way. On the other side, France had first a small positive account and then a deficit, behaving like peripheral countries.[5] These show negative and rising accounts (as a percentage of GDP) up to the crisis (Eurostat database). Consequently, Greece, Ireland, Portugal, and Spain accumulated net external liabilities close to 100 percent of

---

5   As Matthijs and Blyth (2015: 254) say, France looks like "a core member state with periphery characteristics."

GDP. The relevance of external factors having to do with the shocks deriving from third countries at a world level (mainly, competition from China and other developing countries) or to facts, institutions, and policies transcendent to the EMU (such as the rise of global value chains) cannot also be denied. However, these are external factors to add to those we have underlined before, in referring to the internal EMU dynamics.

Germany's current account imbalance is to be analyzed in more detail. This country pursued an export-oriented strategy even before 1999 and then with labor market reforms (Hartz reforms) in 2003–4 and managed to tighten fiscal policy, while acting also on the other factors that affect efficiency and prices. Peripheral countries did not catch the implications of this and were lulled by their apparent prosperity due to expansionary budget balances (in some countries) and capital inflows from the other EMU countries that were experiencing a fall in relative inflation (notably, Germany).

The many channels through which German wage cuts negatively influenced other countries are listed by Bofinger (2015). These were as follows:

- A very weak real domestic demand in Germany, which strongly decelerated due to the wage moderation. In fact, the annual rate of wage increases from 2000 to 2005 declined to 0.1 percent (as contrasted with the 1.7 percent rate in the period 1995 to 2000). The comparable rates for the rest of the EZ were 2.0 percent (3.2 percent) in the two periods (Figure 4.11).

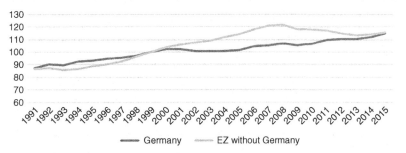

FIGURE 4.11 Domestic demand (at 2010 prices), 1991–2015 (Source: Bofinger, 2015)

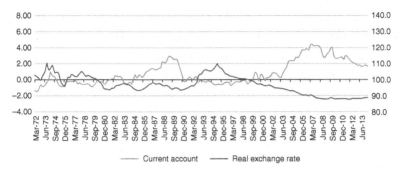

FIGURE 4.12 Germany: real exchange rate and current account balance vis-à-vis EZ, March 1972–June 2013 (Source: Bofinger, 2015)

- An improvement in German price competitiveness and its exports over time, which is shown in Figure 4.12.

The drop in domestic demand and the improvement in competitiveness caused an improvement of the current account in the years 2000 to 2007 (e.g., Kollmann et al., 2015), different from previous years, when Germany's imports from, and exports to, the rest of the EZ did grow in parallel.

- German inflation was for many years below the ECB's target rate and also below the average inflation of the rest of the EZ.

The ECB pursued for some time a relatively mild expansionary policy, which had the advantage of moderating an otherwise deflationary bias in the EZ, but did not help prevent the speculative bubbles that loomed in peripheral countries.[6]

In fact, net capital flows need a closer look. Schmitz and von Hagen (2011) shift the emphasis away from current account to net capital flows, finding an increase in their elasticity with respect to per capita incomes within the Euro-area (EA), as opposed to practical invariance in the case of other countries. This is evidence of increasing financial integration in the area and possibly of some financial

---

[6] However, as we know from Chapter 2, monetary policy is not the proper tool to deal either with the formation of imbalances or with asset bubbles.

diversion, which could simply have derived from adoption of a single currency, with diverging inflation – and thus real interest rates. As a matter of fact, Schmitz and von Hagen's result disappears in a model also including other variables (Nieminen, 2014). Anyway, capital flows appear to have been an important – and novel – determinant of external imbalances within the EMU, to be related to its specific institutions. In addition, capital inflows had a detrimental impact on a number of other EMU countries' macroeconomic and microeconomic variables, such as the GDP, sectoral composition of production, and average productivity growth (Benigno et al., 2015).

In summary, imbalances were to a large extent the effect of a specific strategy of some countries – aiming at lowering public deficit, curbing wages, and increasing exports – coupled with short-sightedness of peripheral countries, in an institutional environment, that of the EMU, lacking a common growth strategy and where the main common institutions were markets and the single currency. This only added to the other factors of imbalance.

Existing EMU institutions have proved not to be able to issue the right signals and incentives for prompting both private and public agents to remove the existing asymmetries originating the imbalances in the current and capital account, public finance, taxation, welfare, and reward systems (Acocella, 2016). Asymmetries and imbalances have thus lasted, nourishing the roots of the crisis as it developed in Europe.

4.4 IMBALANCES WITHIN EUROPE: THEIR TIES

The situation in Europe after adoption of the euro was marked by the preexisting imbalances that had not been eliminated – but only reduced – in the process preceding admission to the third stage of the monetary union.

Contrary to the previous opinions, the structural and behavioral changes that were expected as a consequence of implementing the Union's institutional design and should eliminate the residual differences between the various countries did not take place or were only partial, at least in some countries, i.e., in peripheral countries. Neither the action of agents of change nor formal and informal institutions (i.e., those leading to consensus-building and cost-sharing) acted, at least in a way to avoid the formation or permanence of large imbalances.[7] Thus, the monetary union has even further increased macroeconomic divergences. Our analysis will try to explain the role played by the EZ monetary institutions and policies.

The imbalances, which in some cases became stronger in the early 2000s, were both macroeconomic and microeconomic. The former had to do with public finance and the current account. The latter had to do with inefficiencies in the private and public sectors, especially of higher-inflation countries, and with the microeconomic policies of lower-inflation countries. The latter imbalances were important determinants of the former, but the two interacted in a way to make imbalances stronger. A review of the reasons why the optimistic forecasts about the viability of the EMU went wrong is offered by Pisani-Ferry (2013, 2014).

4.4.1 The Macroeconomics of Imbalances and Mistakes in Constraining a Part of Them Alone

National accounts establish some fundamental identities that must be considered for understanding the relevant issues and implementing appropriate solutions.[8] For any open economy, the following identity holds:

$$S - I = (G - T) + CA \tag{4.1}$$

where S is private saving, I is fixed investments, G – T is budget deficit (public spending less revenues), and CA = X – M + NI is the current account balance (exports minus imports plus net investment income).

This identity links the private financing imbalance to the external and the government's fiscal imbalances. It shows how external imbalances, even in the absence of fiscal irresponsibility, can lead to

---

[7] Here we are using concepts indicated in Börzel and Risse (2000).

[8] This section partially draws on Alessandrini et al. (2014) and Acocella et al. (2016).

accumulating public debt, capital outflows, and a financial sector liquidity crisis in which private debt[9] must be replaced by public debt. Fiscal irresponsibility, as in the case of Greece, simply adds to this underlying imbalance.

In fact, excess of investment over private savings $(S - I < 0)$ can be associated with either a government budget surplus $(G - T < 0)$ or a current account deficit $(CA < 0)$ or both. Thus, attention has to be given to all imbalances, and the factors that each one depends upon, because if one goes further out of balance, then the others will go further out of balance too. One imbalance can easily turn into another imbalance and the causality can, and does, flow either way. Then, there are three potential imbalances to control in a static context, and policymakers need three independent policies to control them. Financial regulation can address private financing imbalances; fiscal controls can ensure public account balances; structural measures (and, when possible, monetary or currency policy) could ensure competitiveness and current account balances.

All three policies must be carefully coordinated together, since each policy, while being mainly directed to one target, also has an influence on the others. In presence of macroeconomic imbalances as basic as these, in fact, it is no longer feasible or sensible to pretend that they do not interact or materially affect each other – as much of the literature has tended to do in the past. Change in each one of them has the capacity to undo the balances to which the policy has not been assigned and thereby destroy the impact of other policies on the balances assigned to them. One of the lessons of the recent financial crisis is that the only way out is to use coordinated (jointly determined) packages of policies rather than to design separate fiscal, monetary, and regulation policies for each given situation. The picture is complicated in a monetary union, since deep economic

---

[9] When using the term "private debt," we want now to refer to the debt of both financial and nonfinancial private institutions. When dealing with the trends in private debt after 2007, we will instead refer to the private nonfinancial institutions, but we will be specific on that.

and financial integration makes changes swifter and imbalances more difficult to control at country-level only. Some kind of common coordination is called into action, especially in the financial sector, but financial regulation of capital flows and other policies can be problematic.

In the light of this discussion, we can try to trace the main imbalances that arose in the EMU after its start. A summary view on the European sovereign debt crisis emphasizes that countries in the South of the EZ were fiscally irresponsible and failed to implement pro-competitive supply-side policies. This is the most common view of existing imbalances.[10] However, it can be challenged by referring to the fiscal conduct of some peripheral countries and by analyzing the other macroeconomic imbalances, which reveal different aspects and responsibilities. In fact, the crisis reflected a deep divide between the external (but also fiscal) surpluses of the North and the external deficits of the South, associated to public budget deficits in some countries of the latter only.

The general picture up to 2007[11] can be depicted as follows, by grouping most EMU countries under three types (the abbreviations of their names are after the indication of the type of imbalances):

1. $S - I > 0, G - T \leq 0, CA > 0$ D, NL, A

In this group of countries, a private credit problem was originated by their low inflation rates, which – given the equal nominal interest rates – gave an incentive to lend abroad to other EMU countries. The counterparts to this were current account surpluses, arising out of tight fiscal policies – which in Germany really began only after 2003–2004 – and the lower-inflation profile, which added to competiveness in all these countries. In some cases, as in Germany, we can

---

[10]   De Grauwe and Ji (2014a) are an exception, as they make the case that the sovereign crisis after 2009 cannot be attributed to a previous government's profligacy for all peripheral countries.

[11]   After this date, the picture has changed a lot. There are now countries – such as Italy with a high public debt, but a low private one.

speak of a true *export-led strategy* favored by both private (unions and firms) and public institutions.

2. $S - I < 0, G - T > 0, CA < 0$ GR, P, (IT)

The second group includes countries with fiscal profligacy and high inflation rates, which, on the one hand, led to current account deficits and, on the other, stimulated (or derived from) excess investment over savings, associated to asset bubbles. This exemplifies a case of (public) *debt-led* growth.

3. $S - I < 0, G - T = 0, CA < 0$ S, IR, (IT)

In the third group, there was no fiscal profligacy, even if the high inflation rates led to capital account surpluses (and thus deficits in terms of current account) and excess investment over savings, associated with asset bubbles. This is again a case of (private) *debt-led growth.*

This picture shows that there were two drivers of growth in the EMU, export and debt (either private or public). It also shows that not all the governments of peripheral countries accumulated or increased public imbalances, which is true for those of group 2, not for group 3. This negates the view of the European sovereign debt crisis as due to governments in the peripheral countries that were fiscally irresponsible and failed to implement pro-competitive supply-side policies. Such a view is absolutely partial. Our analysis reveals that the crisis reflected a deep divide between the external current account surpluses of the lower-inflation countries and external deficits of the others as large as the divide between the fiscally profligate economies and the fiscally thrifty economies. In fact, from a certain point of view one could reverse the argument.

The main common driving factor can be indicated in the foreign account imbalances, to which fiscal profligacy added in some countries.[12] By contrast, thriftiness of other countries added in the

---

[12] Feld et al. (2016a) dissent from the common view that indicates foreign account imbalances as the main culprit of the EZ crisis. In their opinion, the crisis was due to a lack of economic and fiscal policy discipline and absence of credible mechanism for crisis response regarding bank and sovereign debt problems.

opposite sense.[13] Also wage behavior can largely explain that. In fact, Stockhammer et al. (2009) find that wage moderation (1 percent reduction in the wage share of GDP) leads to a decrease in demand (0.2 percent of GDP). Thus, German wage moderation can have had the effect of lowering domestic demand, while propelling export growth (Stockhammer, Onaran, 2012). Consider what we said before about the almost null wage increases in Germany after 1999 and before 2007 – an effect also of decentralization of wage bargaining (Stockhammer, 2008) and exploitation of lower-paid (sometimes immigrant) workers.

The picture can be seen also from the symmetric point of view of capital account balances. Accumulation of debt by the Greek "sinners" does have a *pendant* in terms of French and German "saints." Opposing a sin of those that borrowed is the sin of lenders, who irresponsibly lent their money to unlikely solvent banks.[14] Also from this point of view, one can say that "it takes two to tango." De Grauwe (2015b) says: "For every reckless debtor there must be a reckless creditor."

Then, the responsibilities for the capital account imbalances should have been shared between the creditors, for extending too much credit, and the debtors, for being responsible for taking too much debt. By contrast, the idea underlying policy intervention for settling the exposures of peripheral countries toward core countries was that of the "Eigenverantwortung" (personal responsibility) of debtors in borrowing too much. However, with reference to whether the European crisis is the result of excessive borrowing or excessive lending, we can note that the correspondence of liberty and responsibility is a fundamental principle of a market economy laid down by Friedrich A. Hayek (1960).

---

[13] This clarifies why Lagarde (2010) spoke of the need for two people to dance a tango. In other words, imbalances of current accounts should be seen as being symmetric: some countries carry on a current account deficit; at the same time, others carry on a surplus and imbalances of both are due to "wrong" or "irresponsible" policies.

[14] The expressions "sinners" and "saints" are used by Matthijs and McNamara (2015).

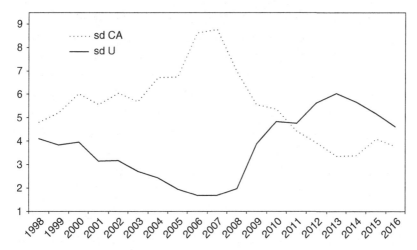

FIGURE 4.13 Divergences (standard deviations) in current account and unemployment rates in the EMU, 1998–2016 (Source: Acocella, Pasimeni, 2018)

The initial increase (decrease) in current (capital) account, mirrored by a reduced (increased) divergence in unemployment rates, continued up to the eruption of the financial crisis, when the divergence in current (capital) account flows began to shrink (rise) while differences in unemployment tended to move in the opposite direction (Figure 4.13).

One can look at capital flows directed from low- to high-inflation countries from different perspectives. In principle, they could have been a de facto substitute of the fiscal union and other institutions (Chapter 7), allowing interregional risk sharing of asymmetric shocks (Mundell, 1973a) – i.e., acting as a "private insurance channel" (Chapter 8). But this role would mainly refer to *gross* (and balanced) capital flows, as regards the pooling of risks through portfolio diversification. In fact, assets issued in a country that is hit by a negative shock are held by owners in different countries, some of which are not hit by the shock, whereas residents of the countries hit by the shock hold assets issued also by the countries exempt from the shock. These have in principle a stabilizing role, as they can support international risk sharing and enhance capital market efficiency. Gross capital flows have certainly increased as an effect of the common currency and absence of exchange rate risks. However, there are cases when they can increase macroeconomic and financial risk, if they generate relevant *net* capital flows, subject to a sudden reversal (in this sense, see also, Zemanek, 2010; Lane, 2013).

In fact, the most relevant aspect of capital movements within the Union was the huge increase in net capital flows and the accumulation of one-sided net capital positions of some countries vis-à-vis others. As said, this derived from the equal nominal interest rate – the outcome of a single monetary policy and disappearance of currency risks in the perception of investors as christened by wrong "official" rating by private agencies – to which corresponded different inflation rates, and thus different real interest rates, in the various countries. This raised (lowered) investment and domestic demand and stimulated capital outflows (inflows) in higher- (lower-) inflation countries.

The functioning of such a mechanism is illustrated by the two specular dynamics of private indebtedness in deficit countries and banks' exposure in surplus countries. Credit booms and asset price bubbles in the former provided banks in the latter with strong incentives to increase their lending. Hale and Obstfeld (2016) find evidence that, after the introduction of the euro, banks in surplus countries increased their borrowing from outside the EMU in order to raise their lending to the deficit countries within the EMU. Financial integration played a very relevant role, as is shown also by Cesaroni and De Santis (2015), who find that it contributed to explain current account deficits in peripheral countries, particularly in the post-EMU period. This behavior increased the fragility of the whole banking sector (Pasimeni, 2016).

Before commenting on the situation further, one could ask whether there was some kind of priority between the two aspects of foreign imbalances, current and capital account. These should be symmetric, but the question can be useful to put in order to understand if there is a prevailing direction of causality that might have shaped further development of imbalances.

A position that does not privilege one or the other direction seems to be expressed by Hobza and Zeugner (2014: 16). According to them,

> a priori, it is not possible to establish a direct link between bilateral financial flows and the total external financial balance (and thus the current account balance). Under efficient financial markets, any savings-investment gap in a deficit country can be financed under the same conditions irrespective of the source of financing [either from EMU or from external countries]. However, the presence of a financial "euro bias" due to the absence of exchange rate risks could make the total balances of its members depend more on credit supply and demand within the EZ than outside. ... In addition – or as an alternative explanation – the emergence of external imbalances in the EZ could depend on the impact of excessive real appreciations in peripheral countries on their trade performance.

Capital account imbalances could have been due to (overly) optimistic expectations about convergence in the peripheral countries, which could start an asset price bubble. This is entirely possible; as such, expectations were diffuse in peripheral countries.

One of the common factors stimulating both current and capital account imbalances is inflation divergence between the EMU countries (Figure 4.14). This seems to be a valid explanation, even if its explanatory power may decline over time, and several studies had proved that, particularly in the EZ, changes in relative price competitiveness were not the significant determinant of current account imbalances (Gaulier, Vicard, 2012; Gabrisch, Staehr, 2015).

In addition, significant divergences in inflation trends could have been more a consequence than a cause of current account imbalances. These would have been triggered by capital flows, reacting to rather small inflation (and real interest rate) differentials. In

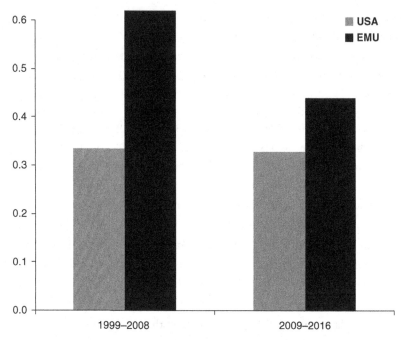

FIGURE 4.14 Standard deviations of annual average inflation rates in the United States and the EMU, 1999–2008 and 2009–2016 (Source: Acocella, Pasimeni, 2018)

favor of the plausibility of this explanation of current account differentials, there could be the following argument. Its explanatory factor is in the end the same as that of the explanation pointing at current account imbalances as being more important than capital account imbalances. However, the well-known faster (and possibly stronger) reactions to imbalances of capital with respect to goods could give priority to the explanation favoring priority of capital account imbalances. The role of trust in a rapid convergence of economies would not be denied as, in the absence of such expectations, there could not have been real interest rate differentials. In empirical terms, econometric evidence strongly indicates that the credit boom derived from capital movements from the core to the periphery acted first, causing net capital inflows and current account deficits in Europe's periphery

(Lane, McQuade, 2013[15]), while differences in the real unit labor costs started to increase only later (Gabrisch, Staehr, 2015; Storm, Naastepad, 2016).[16] In turn, capital movements, or at least exchanges of bonds within the Union, were favored by elimination of country risks and harmonization of financial regulation across the EMU (e.g., Hale, Obstfeld, 2016).

The increase in net capital flows acted as an internal system of transfers, operating through the private sector *via* financial markets, rather than through a common fiscal capacity, but the effects were quite similar. The transfers allowed a reduction of unemployment in peripheral countries and contributed there to higher inflation and asset bubbles, thus avoiding a deflationary environment. This had a kind of multiplier effect on itself, as behind inflation there were not only – or mainly – inefficiencies, but also the asset bubbles created by capital inflows. (To both, fiscal profligacy in some countries is to be added.)

In fact, this changed the functioning of the EMU into the opposite of an insurance mechanism and originated, according to Krugman (2013: 444), what he calls a kind of large shock, asymmetric and endogenous, even if a relatively gradual one, a shock "that was, in a bitter irony, caused by the creation of the euro itself." We could add that the asset bubble created in peripheral countries, by pushing their inflation rate and, to some extent, real economic activity further up, lulled the governments of these countries by the idea of a period of increasing prosperity (Acocella, 2016). As said, some of them did not even reduce their debt.

However, the extent to which we can speak of an asymmetric shock is limited by the circumstance that the countries that adopted an export strategy also benefitted from growth in peripheral countries. In fact, on the one hand, the first group of countries continued to

---

[15]   They conclude as follows: "Our analysis confirms that the current account balance is a misleading indicator in understanding the relation between international capital flows and domestic credit growth, in view of the striking differences in the co-variation of domestic credit growth with net debt flows and net equity flows" (p. 20).

[16]   The idea that capital flows are responsible for current account balances (and not vice versa) goes back to Böhm-Bawerk (1924).

maintain a high growth rate, even if the distance between the two groups of countries narrowed, and, on the other, this asymmetric shock was only a prelude to the symmetric one, which emerged later.

In fact, after 2007, the situation changed radically. The EMU proved to be financially fragile, because of the imbalances that had been created, with only partial control of them. This financial fragility was derived from the absence of proper control at the right, i.e., the Union, level of other imbalances and had many implications. First, in a situation of crisis, it imposed in the EZ a kind of "creditor rule," similar to the power of big banks in the United States, deemed to be too big to fail (partly tempered when Lehman Brothers had gone bankrupt). For this and other reasons, rescheduling of the Greek debt was preferred to default and write-offs.[17]

According to Pasimeni (2016), during the crisis, as much as one-half of the EA's fiscal and financing problems were associated with external imbalances and the consequent liquidity stops and capital reversals. The size and the speed of capital movements back to their countries of origin were emphasized by the composition of capital flows, mainly of a debt, rather than of equity, nature:[18] divestment was thus easier, as it did not imply possible capital losses. Spreads not only increased, but also became more volatile. This caused a huge welfare cost, higher than the gain deriving from the reduction in trade costs following adoption of a common currency (Lama, Rabanal, 2012).

One of the lessons is thus that there had been policy failures that could (or should) not be rectified by fiscal consolidations alone.

---

[17] By studying sovereign debt relief in a long-term perspective, Reinhart and Trebesch (2016) draw the conclusion that the situation of debtor countries improves significantly after post-default debt relief operations, only if these involve debt write-offs. However, this solution may be inferior, considering that sovereign debt restructurings *prior* to a payment default can avoid this and imply lower output losses (Asonuma, Trebesch, 2016).

[18] In fact, one of the determinants of capital flows in the EMU, elimination of the exchange rate risk, is a relatively minor factor in the valuation of equity-type flows, so that the euro effect was necessarily smaller for them than for the debt category (Lane, 2013).

Policies to enhance competitiveness, a strict financial regulation for intra-EA capital flows, and activist monetary policies would have been just as important or more. Another lesson has to do with the unbalanced view about imbalances. According to De Grauwe (2015b), "[W]hat is surprising is that the European Commission accepted to become the agent of the creditor nations in the EZ – pushing austerity as the instrument to safeguard the interests of these nations."

As a result of the prevailing line, at the beginning there was an asymmetric adjustment, hitting debtor countries, which bore "the full brunt of the adjustment," by reducing wages and prices relative to the creditor countries (an "internal devaluation") as well as internal demand, without the existence of compensating internal revaluations and demand stimulus by Northern countries. Reduction in output and employment in the Southern countries thus followed. An institutional rule preventing excess saving by creditor countries would have prevented imbalances as well as the extension and depth of the crisis in the EA.

4.4.2 The Underlying Microeconomic Imbalances and Their Link with Macroeconomic Imbalances

The common factor sustaining both current and capital account imbalances was higher inflation in peripheral countries and lower (below target) inflation in Germany and other core countries. The determinants of the inflation differentials are to be further discussed. Problems may be caused by the following: (1) higher unit labor cost increases in peripheral countries; (2) the Balassa-Samuelson effect; (3) inefficiencies, in particular in the service sector, both public and private, of those countries.

We can say that inflation differentials were the effect of different wage costs more than productivity, even if the latter operated to some extent. Labor costs in Germany were in fact lower than those of its main competitor and the EMU average. By contrast, the productivity trend was somewhat, but not particularly, higher. Only with respect to Italy and, to some extent, Greece, this performance of Germany in terms of productivity contributed to the difference in unit labor costs. The other GIIPS countries, not to mention the formerly planned EMU economies and the EU nonmember countries of the monetary union, showed a growth of productivity substantially higher than in Germany. Thus, changes in relative productivity trends cannot be the primary determinant of the inflation differentials between the GIIPS countries and Germany. Export-led strategies in Germany were based at first on wage cuts and also on the strengthening of the existing industrial structure. Wage cuts lowered domestic demand and increased inflation differentials of Germany with other EU countries, thus raising both a current account surplus and an excess of savings over investment.[19]

As to the Balassa-Samuelson effect, its relevance for peripheral countries has been the object of different claims. Recent findings accord with an amended version of Balassa-Samuelson interpretation, incorporating sectoral productivity shocks and a labor market wedge, in contrast with previous studies. For peripheral economies, an important addition to the Balassa-Samuelson effect could derive from the direct effects of bubbles on inflation and their indirect effects arising from the diversion of investment from sectors more productive than those affected by bubbles (Subsection 4.3.3).

This leads to the importance of differences in productivity dynamics due to true inefficiencies in the tertiary sector. In particular, these featured the public and the private service sector of some countries, deriving from patronage, protection from competition, etc. A recent investigation for the period 1980–2007 (Di Meglio, Visintin, 2014), based on parametric analysis of the tertiary (private and public) sector at an aggregate level, finds three different clusters in a sample of countries: that of high performers (Central-Nordic European countries, namely Belgium, Denmark, the Netherlands, Sweden, and Finland); average performers (Germany, Austria, Italy, and Spain); and Anglo-Saxon nations (Australia, the United States, and the United

---

[19] This also makes it clear that the export-led growth model in the core and the debt led growth model in the periphery are closely interdependent (e.g., Hein, 2012).

Kingdom); and, finally, low performers, mainly Eastern European countries (Hungary, the Czech Republic, and Slovenia) and Japan. The position of Germany and Japan seems to be at odds with the tradition of these countries. However, part of the explanation for the nonexcellent performance of Germany can be found in the fact that these are aggregate data for the whole tertiary sector and do not have a regional breakdown that could have shown the result to depend, at least to some extent, on the backward position of the Eastern Lander.

These results might also suggest that other factors, i.e., nonprice factors of competitiveness or demand fluctuations due to financial bubbles, are more important than relative price competitiveness in explaining the current account imbalances in the EA. They also confirm what had been pointed out in the recent literature on current accounts in the EA: the hypothesis that intra-EMU trade imbalances were caused not so much by changes in relative cost competitiveness, but rather by demand shocks (Storm, Naastepad, 2015).

As to the relative unimportance of price competitiveness, Sanchez and Varoudakis (2013) draw the conclusions that in the EZ deficit countries, unit labor costs played a "negligible" role in explaining growing external imbalances. Our reaction is that this can be only partly accepted. Labor costs might have played a rather minor role in determining the growing external imbalances within the EZ. However, reductions in wage costs in Germany might have supported in this country, on the one hand, an increase in savings over investment[20] and, on the other, a change in the structural composition of aggregate demand, with a growing importance of exports outside the EMU and a lower relevance of investment and public expenditure. The demand shock determined by financial bubbles could have been

---

[20] Kollmann et al. (2015) explain the export surplus of Germany as a reflection of a succession of shocks, starting from a positive shock to the German saving rate and to the foreign demand for German goods. The rise in the saving rate was due to households' concerns about rapid population aging and pension reforms in the first years of the new century. These, on the one hand, lowered state-funded pensions and, on the other, created tax incentives for private retirement saving. In addition, German labor market reforms and other positive aggregate supply shocks – such as innovation and other improvements in its industrial structure – contributed to the export surplus.

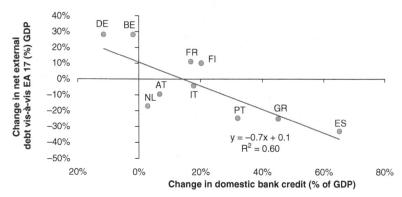

FIGURE 4.15 Precrisis correlation between change in domestic credit and change in the net external debt position vis-à-vis other EZ countries, 2003–2008 (Source: Merler, 2015)

the key driver of external imbalances within the EZ, but efforts to improve relative competitiveness in some surplus countries (e.g., in Germany, by wage restraint after 1999, when wage gains no longer kept pace with productivity, as they had done during the 1990s) also contributed.

The strong correlation between net debt inflows and domestic credit growth during the precrisis period found by Lane and McQuade (2013) and Merler (2015) is depicted in Figure 4.15. Credit growth was reinforced by direct credits to agents from consumers and firms that bypassed the credit system. This increased financial vulnerability (Gourinchas, Obstfeld, 2012; Schularick, Taylor, 2012), by causing bubbles and misallocation of capital. When the first signs of the incoming crisis arrived, capital stock adjustments with respect to accumulated credits were of a high order of magnitude and gave way to panic and overpricing of country risks.

4.4.3 Could Imbalances Have Been Avoided?

Imbalances within Europe cannot be discussed without noticing that they are part of the imbalances arising at a world level, which are one of the major features of the precrisis global environment

(Lane, Milesi-Ferretti, 2012). At the world level too, an export-led growth model and a debt-led growth model can be detected: some South-Eastern Asian countries experienced the former together with Germany, whereas the United States shared the latter with South European countries.

However, the sources of the two imbalances, their speed, and their relevance appear different between European countries and the others, even if some commonalities exist. To exemplify, even if deregulation is the common factor for the growth of the financial sector, the shock to real interest rate differentials within the members of the currency union was more relevant and acted faster in causing capital movements. In fact, for this area the friction role of the exchange rate and the risk of its possible change did not operate, which is not the case of other countries that experience current account imbalances, but are not part of a union. With respect to states that are part of a federal union, we have clearly indicated the differences that can ensure rebalance, whereas divergences between states being members of a pure currency union are difficult to eradicate. As a consequence, in a currency union imbalances leave the deficit countries vulnerable to a sudden capital stop or reversal of capital flows.

Thus, currency zones, rather than solving the problem of international (or regional) payments imbalances make it even harder to solve, in the absence of other common institutions (Johnston, Regan, 2016). Increased competition may reduce inflation, but does not guarantee growth convergence. Therefore, a common currency does not eliminate the need for internal adjustments. The point is that the situation described earlier is fragile and any financial stress can disrupt the precarious equilibrium, putting pressure on high-inflation countries that have attracted international capital flows to balance their trade deficits.

Once the imbalances manifested themselves, EMU policymakers adopted a position of benign neglect and did not remove their roots. This was done in some higher-inflation EMU countries, which implemented not far-reaching policies but only short-run labor market reforms to restrain appreciation in their real exchange rate. Some other countries thought they should try to resolve their problems on their own, as in the case of Germany, but the strategy it implemented, as early as in the 1990s, to cope with the stagnation that inevitably followed the reconstruction of this country after unification and the ensuing monetary contraction aggravated other countries' problems. This of course meant beggar-thy-neighbor policies with respect to the rest of the EZ.[21]

Indeed, there are several reasons that can explain the failure of the policies undertaken by peripheral countries. First, reforms were often not effective or properly implemented in some of them. In addition, as the divergence has two sides, catching up with Germany was difficult, since the dynamics of unit labor costs and nonwage costs in this country were trimmed well below the EMU average.

Finally and most importantly, to be effective, such reforms should have been designed as complements to proper (i.e., not so restrictive) monetary institutions and labor market and industrial policies (such as coordination and common guidelines on wage bargaining; policies to foster innovation and industrial restructuring). These were either out of reach of each country (as for monetary policy) or not featured in the EMU design and peripheral countries did not enact the policies they still controlled. The potential crisis became reality also due to the absence of any common financial supervisor, regulator, or rescue body. This absence made it possible for the bubble to grow and burst following a financial crisis largely imported from the United States: saving financial intermediaries required intervention of national governments and an increase in public deficits, thus threatening the entire European financial system. The booms or, at least, growth-sustaining bubbles in higher-inflation countries, together with the imperfection of the "system of signals" at the European

---

[21] This interpretation of the German policymaking as a sort of neo-mercantilism, shared also by Flassbeck and Lapavitsas (2015), is disputed by Kollmann et al. (2015), according to whom the positive effects of wage restriction appeared only after 2005. This is largely true, but the implementation of a noncooperative policy that could endanger other countries started certainly at the latest in 1999.

level that would trigger action from local policymakers, can at least partially explain why policymakers did not implement long-term policies for addressing imbalances in these countries.

This is reflected in the pricing of sovereign bonds. According to Beirne and Fratscher (2013), in the precrisis period sovereign risk for European economies might not have fully represented economic fundamentals. A note of caution might derive from the findings of Bernoth and Erdogan (2012) and Bernoth et al. (2012), who stress the relevance of public deficit and debt. However, these tended to fall in peripheral countries, more than in some countries of the core, such as France and Germany. Overall, this can suggest that optimistic assessment of an ongoing trend toward integration and convergence between the member countries pervaded financial markets.

In the next chapter, we study how the crisis materialized and evolved in the EMU, after the contagion of the financial crisis from the Anglo-Saxon countries. The intervention of national governments and the increase in public deficits and debts were required to save financial intermediaries. This raised concern also about solvency of sovereign subjects and led to contractionary fiscal policy and a general recession throughout the EA.

5 The Great Recession
How It Developed in Europe

5.1 INTRODUCTION

The determinants and the evolution of the US financial crisis are well known.[1] In Europe, the financial crisis appeared initially under forms similar to those characterizing the United States, but soon assumed a very different form. This was due first to the different type of financial system in Europe, with no central control, supervision, and bailout facilities for the whole EZ, even if the central control in the United States over the financial system had been dismantled by deregulation.[2]

An additional role was played by the specific financial imbalances that appeared in the EMU as a consequence of the formation of a currency area. As said, the accumulation of private debt in some countries (not only the GIIPS, i.e., Greece, Ireland, Italy, Portugal, and Spain) was built into the way the EZ institutions were (and are) shaped, which caused macroeconomic imbalances. Preexisting imbalances became more intense when Germany decided to cope with the difficulties of a mature economy and unification with its Eastern Lander by

---

[1] We can summarize its main components: high levels of debt and real-estate bubbles, promoted also by the US housing policy; a mix of excessive borrowing and risk-taking by households; widespread bankruptcies of nondepository financial institutions; breakdowns in corporate governance; systemic violations of accountability and ethics; financial deregulation and policymakers and regulators ill prepared for the crisis (Yellen, 2009). An overview of different aspects of the US crisis and its transmission to Europe is in Melvin and Taylor (2009). An empirical analysis of the factors determining the crisis is in Feldkirchery (2012).

[2] Absence of central control is the only commonality between the two areas. However, in the EZ it was structural, i.e., due to the nature of its institutions, whereas it was the effect of the deregulation implemented in the United States in 1999, by the Gramm Leach-Bliley Act, which finally repealed the Glass-Steagall Act.

adopting an export-led growth model supported by real devaluation and a careful redesign of its productive role and specialization, especially with respect to Eastern European countries. Finally, the monetary union lacked support from other active common policies, in particular fiscal policies. After around 2005, most peripheral countries began having a rising current account deficit also with respect to countries outside the EZ (China, CEEC, and oil exporters) because of the increasing trade penetration of these, stimulated by trade liberalization and euro appreciation. Then, European financial integration allowed for persistent net lending from core countries to peripheral countries, which compensated for the current account of the latter toward not only the former but also countries external to the EA.

The imbalances reflected first in interbank loans across boundaries: banks in peripheral countries had borrowed from their homologues in core countries. When the Anglo-Saxon financial crisis threw panic over the EMU financial system, the capital flow reversal already hinted at began to materialize, hitting the financial sector of peripheral countries. At a later stage, unlike the United States, it evolved into a sovereign crisis, due to the specificity of shocks, the state intervention to save ailing banks, and the peculiar institutions of the EMU. More recently, the crisis has again changed its nature, as sovereign debt has been absorbed by banks, thus causing a problem for them and, in turn, again for the public finances that had to face bank failures.

The following section describes a few data about the nature of the crisis. In Section 5.3, we deal with one of the determinants of the crisis, i.e., deregulation of the financial sector. Section 5.4 studies the dynamics of the crisis in its two components, the private and the public debt. Section 5.5 investigates the growth components. Section 5.6 analyzes the effects of the crisis in terms of efficiency and equity. Section 5.7 indicates some of the consequences of the Great Recession, in terms of secular stagnation.

5.2 A FEW FACTS AND FIGURES

The financial turmoil initiated in 2007 in the United States and turned into a deep crisis in terms of the main macroeconomic indicators. It soon hit Europe too and evolved into a long recession. In 2009, the GDP went down by 3.1 percent in the United States and by 4.4 percent in the EA. Initially, the shock hitting Europe was symmetric, as it involved practically all the EMU countries, not only peripheral ones. The shock became asymmetrical when misreporting of public finances in Greece was announced, in October 2009, and the year after, as a consequence of the solution given to the Greek debt.[3]

This solution, on the one hand, relieved French, German, and Italian banks from their credits to Greece (for around, respectively, €60, €30, and €10 billion) and the public finance problems that would arise in these countries from coping with the crisis following insolvency. The bank exposures were shifted to the Union and the IMF. According to Janssen (2010: 1), Greek sovereign debt was "transferred from the balance sheets of banks to the balance sheet of European governments, the real purpose of the entire operation . . . (being) to save European banks by relieving them from holding debt titles upon which a potential default could be looming."

On the other hand, in Greece repeated programs of budget restriction (including relevant wage cuts to public employees) were implemented, together with liberalizations, privatizations, and other structural adjustments. This country received credits for €110 billion in three years from the newly built European Financial Stabilisation Mechanism (EFSM),[4] first, and, since 2012, from the ESM, which substituted it.

---

[3] The newly elected government announced that the deficit/GDP ratio for 2009 was almost 15 percent, against the value of 6 percent announced by the previous government. Indeed, there were growing fiscal and current account deficits in Greece since its entry into the EMU, in 2001.

[4] This mechanism drew funds from financial markets that are guaranteed by the EU budget.

On top of the private debt problem – and largely as an outcome of public policy measures enacted to cope with it – a public debt issue arose in peripheral countries. Sovereign debts in these countries were hit by speculation and a "flight to quality" of financial institutions. Spreads between the interest rate paid on them and that of the German Bund – which had lowered to almost zero after the EMU inception – soared to unsustainable levels.

Markets misperceived risks: they were dominated by overly optimistic predictions up to 2007, underestimating risks, and rather suddenly moved to a too pessimistic orientation, after the first signs of the crisis emerged. There was indeed an oscillation of the pendulum from a "flight to risk" attitude, up to the crisis, to a "flight to safety" obsession, afterward. In particular, especially in the first months of the Greek crisis, the spread between the interest rate paid by this country and that on the German Bund soared to incredibly high levels, leading interest rates on them almost up to 35 percent for ten-year government bonds in April 2012[5] (Figure 5.1). The solution given to the crisis overburdened the Greek economy, which fell into a depressive loop.[6]

Also, governments in other countries restrained public expenditures and raised taxes, in an attempt to raise market confidence and in order to comply with European rules. In due course, practically the whole EMU economy precipitated again into recession. This was a consequence of the policy response dictated to the EA, a type of policy that appears as self-defeating, also due to disregard of the value of the multipliers. Core countries too suffered from this policy. In fact,

---

[5]   Spreads reflected the market predictions over risk for sovereign debt, which, in turn, became highly sensitive – even overly sensitive and unrelated to deteriorating fundamentals – to credit rating changes for both Greece and other peripheral countries, at least for some time. A radical change in market sentiments that caused a sharp decline in the spreads followed implementation of Outright Monetary Transaction (OMT) operations (Section 6.3).

[6]   Janssen (2010: 1) was a good prophet in forecasting that "three years from now, Greece will be facing an even higher debt burden." Jones (2003) had made a similar prediction much earlier, pointing at the current account deficits that were being accumulated by Greece and Portugal.

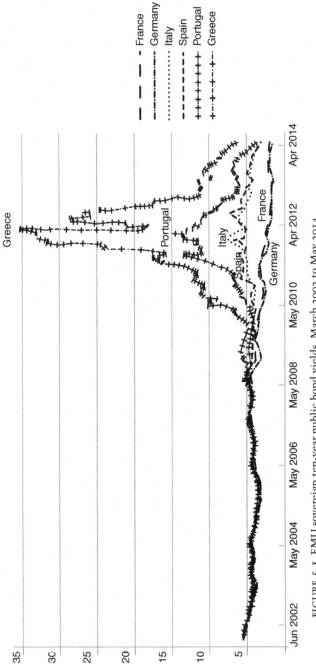

FIGURE 5.1 EMU sovereign ten-year public bond yields, March 2002 to May 2014
(Source: Sensoy et al., 2015)

Table 5.1 *A comparison of growth, unemployment, and inflation rates in the EMU and the United States, 2007–2016*

	2007–16		2010–16	
Variable/date	EMU	US	EMU	US
Growth (%, annual)	0.4	1.3	0.9	2.2
Unemployment rate (p.p. change)	2.0	0.2	–0.5	–4.9
Inflation rate (CPI, %)	1.4	1.6	1.2	1.6

Note: Unemployment rate change refers to the EU 16, rather than to the EZ
(*Source:* OECD, database)

Germany and other countries faced recession again, as net exports to other EMU countries dropped. Meanwhile, the United States, had largely recovered.

As can be seen in Table 5.1, in the six (nine) years after 2010 (2007), EMU GDP grew at an annual rate of 0.9 (0.4) percent, to compare with 2.2 (1.3) percent for the United States. The American unemployment rate in 2016 was –4.6 (+1.6) p.p. higher than in 2010 (2007), whereas the EMU one rose by –0.5 (2.0) p.p. in the same period. The inflation performance was worse in the United States (1.6 percent) than in the EMU (1.4 and 1.2 percent) for the whole period, but this is largely due to the deflation that hit the EZ up to 2014. This different performance of unemployment and inflation, especially in the last period, denotes a higher inflationary bias for the United States, partly deriving from the relative interdependence between the Fed and the government.

5.3   THE CRISIS: THE EMU'S FINANCIAL AND FISCAL FRAGILITY

5.3.1   *Financial Deregulation*

A substantial deregulation of the financial sector and a wrong way of arranging the remaining supervisory system of controls played a key role in the development of the crisis in the EZ, as they had done for the

United States. The financial sector was significantly affected by the creation of the Single Market, and this had a decisive influence on international trade in services in the European Community first and the EU later, even more than trade in goods. In addition to foreign exchange controls, NTBs were (and, to a lesser extent, still are) represented primarily by the various regulatory systems adopted by member states. These regulations in the field of financial services, which were justified because of the need to safeguard the stability of financial systems, certainly imposed different restrictions and rules from country to country, thereby segmenting the individual national markets. However, they were not substituted by proper regulation at the EU level.

The Community and the EU sought to reduce existing barriers between the various financial markets with a series of interventions, notably: (1) complete liberalization of capital movements, as envisaged in the Delors Report of 1989; (2) harmonization of certain key parts of financial legislation, involving adoption of the universal bank model and establishment of minimum capital requirements and ratios of own funds to assets (*solvency ratios*); (3) automatic mutual recognition of financial institutions (bank or investment companies) authorized to operate in an EU member state by the other countries (*single banking license*); (4) home country supervision over all the activities of a bank, including its foreign branches, with low or no European-level regulatory or supervisory power, until 2014. Only since then, partial regulation and supervision by the ECB came into play at the European level for the largest banks, backed by the ESM; (5) introduction of a specific payment infrastructure, called TARGET ("Trans-European Automated Real-time Gross Settlement Express Transfer System"), version TARGET2 of which was inaugurated in 2008. We deal with this in the next subsection.

5.3.2   The Working of TARGET2 and the Ensuing Issues

TARGET2 imbalances have piled up until now (Figure 5.2). There are two fundamentally different causes for that. The first has to do with the abnormal capital flows during the worst years of the financial

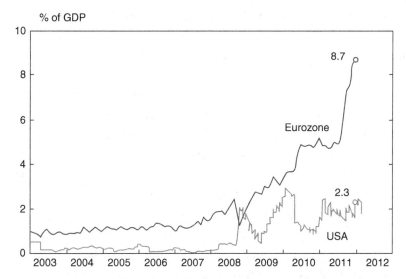

FIGURE 5.2 Gross TARGET claims and gross Interdistrict Settlement Account claims relative to the corresponding GDP, 2003–2012 (Source: Sinn, 2012a)

crisis. The second has arisen as a consequence of the asset purchase program performed by the ECB.

Let us first deal with the former kind of imbalances. If banks in peripheral countries face capital repatriation and withdrawal of credits from banks or other creditors based in core countries, thus facing a liquidity crisis, they turn to their central bank for credit. The contrary happens with the banking system in core countries, which faces excess liquidity that is absorbed by their central banks. This system allowed the balance of payments deficits of peripheral countries emerging from current and/or capital accounts deficits to be somewhat financed by the banking system of core countries (De Grauwe, Ji, 2012).[7] This avoided a precipitous crisis when – starting from 2009–10 – capital inflows in these countries no longer compensated current account deficits, as capital flew back to its countries of origin

[7] They say: "Somewhat like a car company that lends consumers the money to buy their cars, the German banking system was lending the money to other Eurozone countries to allow them to buy surplus German products – a highly risky affair."

(Cesaratto, 2013). The liquidity obtained from central bank by banks in peripheral countries was largely used to fund payments to banks in core countries, thus building up the TARGET surpluses of these countries.

A similar arrangement works for the regional banks of the Federal Reserve System, through the Interdistrict Settlement Account. However, Sinn (2012a) notes that there are relevant differences in size between the two systems, as shown in Figure 5.2, which underlines the jump in the EZ imbalances in the hottest period of the crisis and compares them with the much less pronounced rise in the Interdistrict Settlement Account claims in the United States.

The TARGET imbalances in this contingency were a symptom of differential liquidity and funding conditions across the EZ banking system. The EZ used the TARGET mechanism to deal with the major shift in the direction of capital flows. This was an important achievement. However, the TARGET system is intended to deal with liquidity needs and is, therefore, expected to be in balance except over short periods. As such, its possible costs and benefits would be distributed casually. Lasting imbalances in the same direction can cause strains to the system. Imbalances should not be interpreted as a measure of the risk exposure of the central banks of creditor countries. This does not mean that, under certain conditions, TARGET2 imbalances cannot be suggestive of the difficulty that banking systems in some EZ peripheral countries have in funding themselves in the markets without public support.

Given the size of imbalances, the return to balance has been long and has required adjustments to reduce current account deficits.

Some authors have calculated the current losses and profits deriving for each country from the system, neglecting the costs of a possible EZ collapse or a member country exit. Profits derive from the real interest rate currently earned by creditor countries. Losses derive in perspective from the real exchange rate appreciation needed for reestablishing equilibrium trade balance in the long run. In drawing this balance, a high net cost for Germany has been calculated along the lines followed by Jin and Choi (2012) for China. This implies an implicit distributional mechanism worth about €30 billion (Erler, Hohberger, 2014). This method of assessing costs and benefits of the payment system is, however, open to critique. First, the huge imbalances in net payments shown in Figure 5.2 really arose mostly after 2009 as a consequence of the repatriation of credits extended by the banks of core countries to peripheral ones. The method followed by Erler and Hohberger does not take account of the huge benefit drawn by German savers and banks from that. The liquidity provided by the ECB, which is reflected in the TARGET system, made it possible for German banks to bring their money back home when the financial crisis erupted in peripheral countries. Absence of the ECB's intervention could have led to defaults in the banking sector with possibly huge losses for German savers (Dullien, Schieritz, 2012). Moreover, the TARGET2 system ensures a smooth functioning of the payments system, which would not be the case if Sinn and Wollmershäuser's (2011) proposal to restrict its functioning was implemented. This would lead to the end of the euro and Germany would incur severe difficulties. The German taxpayer would pay a much higher cost, as the new German currency substituting the euro would likely appreciate (Whelan, 2012). In fact, Germany's export-oriented economy would suffer and its commercial banks would find that their assets in former EMU countries no longer covered their liabilities, due to the German currency's nominal appreciation toward foreign currencies.[8] To avoid the dangers associated with the prospect of a euro breakup, the TARGET2 system is imperative. And a limitation of TARGET2 imbalances could imply that the basic functioning of the EMU might be impaired (Buiter et al., 2011b).

As to the second and more recent kind of increase in TARGET2 imbalances, their reemergence during the period of the asset market

[8]   There are ways for Germany and other creditor countries to avoid losses in case of a break up (De Grauwe, Ji, 2012), and protective clauses such as Collective Action Clauses can largely do that (Section 9.3). Sinn (2012b) argues that in case of a euro breakup Germany would suffer a loss, since TARGET balances are real wealth that would be lost.

programs "does not signal increases in financial market stress or fragmentation, nor does it signal unsustainable balance of payments developments" (Eisenschmidt et al., 2017: 4). It is instead tied to the decentralized implementation of the intervention in the asset market and the concentration of international financial activities in particular centers. Liquidity is provided by the ECB to each national central bank according to its share in the ECB's capital. Then each national central bank can buy assets that can be held in other countries. The individual payments settled in TARGET2 at the end of each business day, deriving from all cross-border payments sent from accounts at one central bank to accounts at all other participating central banks, are summed algebraically and indicate the net position inflow or outflow of each central bank with respect to all the other participating central banks. The total sum of these positions is zero, but there may be a persistent net inflow or outflow position of each central bank over time, rising after 2011. This has caused a situation of imbalances, with Germany, Luxembourg, the Netherlands and Finland as the main creditors and Spain, Italy, France, and Greece as the main debtor countries. In this case, TARGET2 balances are not tied to imbalances of the balance of payment and are supply driven, whereas the previous kind of balances strictly depended on such imbalances and was demand driven. Thus, they should fade along with a reduction of the ECB intervention in the asset markets.

5.4   THE DYNAMICS OF THE CRISIS IN THE EMU

5.4.1   *Introduction*

The EZ crisis is usually characterized by the dynamics of public debt in specific countries, in particular the peripheral ones.[9] This characterization should be corrected or completed for a number of reasons.

First, to some extent the imbalances we dealt with in the previous chapter predate the creation of the EZ, even if they increased since then

---

[9]   For example, this is the characterization offered by Corsetti et al. (2013, 2014). While this characterization is a theoretically plausible one, from a historical point of view the prevailing causation runs from a private to a public debt crisis.

in some countries – due to both the design faults in the EZ's institutional framework and inaction by national and European policymakers. Second, private debt imbalances were more important than public debt (especially in the period of the US financial crisis) and, to a large extent, preexistence of the former caused the latter to arise (a "morphing" problem, as we explain later in the chapter). The ensuing public debt crisis, in turn, generated a new private debt crisis, in what Brunnermeier et al. (2011) have described as a "diabolic loop." Third, the basic determinants of the European private debt crisis were often different from those that had first started the financial crisis in the United States, as they derived from balance of payments imbalances between countries, in a situation of incomplete economic union. Lastly, the financial crisis in the United States was only the firelighter that ignited the specific financial crisis of Europe. In order to understand the roots, the dynamics, and the effects of the crisis, the complex ties between not only private and public debt but also growth and its features should be discussed.

The next subsection explains how a private debt crisis arose in Europe, also as an effect of the features taken by growth in the various countries. Subsection 5.4.3 shows how the public debt crisis emerged to a large extent as a consequence of the private debt crisis, and how EMU policies helped the public debt crisis to precipitate into a depression.[10]

5.4.2 The Trend in the Direction of Capital Movements before 2007 and Its Reversal

As said, the European financial crisis was ignited by the American crisis, but sprouted and developed in forms very different from those characterizing the United States. Obviously enough, many European financial institutions – especially in Ireland and the United Kingdom, but also in other countries – had invested in Certificates of Deposits and were thus exposed to the same risks as the American banks.

---

[10]   We follow the line of reasoning in Acocella (2015a).

Indeed, their financial exposure was about one-third of the total outstanding US Asset Backed Securities, far higher than Japan's and China's, and they suffered an even higher share of total losses (around 50 percent), between the last quarter of 2007 and the last quarter of 2008 (Gourinchas et al., 2012).

As said, free capital movements and a common monetary policy that was expansionary until 2006 actually fueled a process of financial transfers between core countries and the GIIPS. In the latter, debt exposure toward the former soared to very high levels. German banks had lent to Ireland for around 250 percent of the latter's GDP, to Greece for almost 50 percent, and to Portugal and Spain for more than 60 percent, while France credits accounted for around 120 percent of the Irish GDP, 80 percent of the Greek and about one-third of the Portuguese and Spanish. Because of speculative operations in the real estate and stock markets (e.g., Lane, McQuade, 2013), peripheral countries were heading toward overheating of their economies before the crisis as an effect of speculative bubbles. Van Oyen and Elmer (2016) identify the bubbles with reference to the European technology stock market, which showed behavior similar to the American NASDAQ bubble in the dot-com hype. Jones (2015) offers an explanation of the persistence of asset bubbles unrelated to behavioral errors, limits to learning, and arbitrage.[11] He points instead to the incentives of asset managers in the investment industry and the principal–agent relationship, together with the growing presence of institutional investors. This has an influence

---

[11]   Keynes's (1936) "Old Maid" and "beauty contest" as well as Shiller's (2015) "irrational exuberance" are usually the fruit of irrational behavior. A game of Snap, of Old Maid, and of Musical Chairs is a pastime in which he is the victor who says Snap neither too soon nor too late, who passed the Old Maid to his neighbor before the game is over, who secures a chair for himself when the music stops. In a beauty contest, participants are asked to choose the six most attractive faces from many photographs and are eligible for a prize for those who picked the most popular faces, not those who indicated the most beautiful ones (according to some criterion of beauty). A number of examples of such episodes will be cited in this book. The most recent addition to them – and a possible cause of crisis – might be the case of "bitcoins."

on remedies, which should go beyond countercyclical monetary and macroprudential policy (Chapters 9 and 10).

Expectations of high real growth deriving from asset bubbles and the increase in consumption convinced people of the sustainability of debt (EEAG, 2011) and made the signals coming out of imbalances noisy, not only for ordinary citizens but also for banks and policymakers. Analytical contributions by economists with a reputation contributed to induce people not to care for current account imbalances.

Again, absence of EMU financial regulation made it possible for the bubble to grow. Its burst required intervention of national governments to save financial intermediaries and implied an increase in public deficits, thus threatening the whole European financial system, as we will see in the next subsection. As for current account imbalances, once they appeared, they could not be dealt with properly under the existing EA's institutional arrangements (in particular Harashima, 2011). Sticking to these rules, i.e., with no innovation introduced in the institutional architecture of EMU, each country should undertake policies to resolve the imbalances on its own, even if the deflationary effects could snowball. In fact, different countries tried to cope in different ways. Most GIIPS countries (the exception being Greece) acted in some way. Some took a contractionary budget stance; others did not, preferring, as said, to maintain higher employment in the short run, and instead enacted questionable labor market reforms to remedy the deterioration in the real exchange rate. Labor market flexibility thus increased substantially in a number of EMU countries (e.g., Damiani et al., 2011). Contrary to the opinion of some authors (Zemanek et al., 2010, and references therein), this did not significantly reduce inflation differentials, first of all because Germany had further trimmed wage increases since 2003–4 and, in addition, the reforms were not really effective in some countries when the crisis erupted. Finally and most importantly, reforms could not have been effective in the absence of proper monetary institutions and policies and ran contrary to alternative ways of ensuring price stability such as wage bargaining coordination (e.g., Hein, Trueger, 2005) and adoption of common wage guidelines. Introduction of labor market reforms created an army of temporary workers that compounded the recession (typical is the instance of Spain).

Capital flows to the periphery suddenly ceased (an example of "sudden stop" of lending; see Calvo, 1998) from the end of 2007. In addition, as said, their direction reversed after the appearance of the first signals of the financial crisis and this flowback gained momentum in the following few years. This implied deleveraging of financial institutions and firms in the GIIPS countries (Pisani-Ferry et al., 2013). Most of the burden fell on public debt.

5.4.3   Public Debt

Thus, public debt after the crisis is strictly linked to private debt. Before it, instead, unlike private-sector debt, public debt in the area as a whole fell from 71 percent of GDP in 1999 to 66 percent in 2007 (Eurostat, 2011). It had been reduced in all EZ countries, except Germany, Greece, and Portugal. As to peripheral countries, their past histories are quite varied, but debt had lowered in Ireland, Italy, and Spain. It had risen only in Portugal (but to a level only a little higher than Germany's) and Greece. So there is not much basis for the analysis of EEAG (2011), according to which these countries were marked by excessive public spending and borrowing. In practice, the only such country was Greece. And, as said, there was no sign of significant public debt tensions before the crisis. In addition, the EEAG report is mistaken in attributing the crisis to moral hazard, i.e., a lax attitude on the part of the GIIPS governments owing to the expectation of being bailed out by other European countries (more in Chapter 7). Apart from the analysis of the real culprit, which we will be developing in the next pages, the relevant difference between the core (notably, Germany) and the peripheral countries was that the former had shaped their economy in a way that better resisted the crisis. In particular, the public accounts of the core were not overburdened as a consequence of countering the shock. As a matter of

Table 5.2 *Government budget balance/GDP (%) in various EU countries, 1999–2017 (Source: Eurostat)*

GEO/TIME	1999	2007	2014	2015	2016	2017
EU (curr. compos.)	:	−0.9	−2.9	−2.3	−1.6	−1.0
EA 19	−1.5	−0.7	−2.5	−2.0	−1.5	−0.9
Germany	−1.7	0.2	0.5	0.8	1.0	1.3
Ireland	2.4	0.3	−3.6	−1.9	−0.5	−0.3
Greece	−5.8	−6.7	−3.6	−5.7	0.6	0.8
Spain	−1.3	1.9	−6.0	−5.3	−4.5	−3.1
France	−1.6	−2.6	−3.9	−3.6	−3.4	−2.6
Italy	−1.8	−1.5	−3.0	−2.6	−2.5	−2.3
Portugal	−3.0	−3.0	−7.2	−4.4	−2.0	−3.0
UK	0.7	−2.6	−5.4	−4.3	−3.0	−1.9

Table 5.3 *General government debt/GDP (%) in various EU countries, 1999–2017 (Source: Eurostat)*

GEO/TIME	1999	2007	2015	2016	2017
EU (curr. compos.)	:	57.5	84.5	83.3	81.6
EA 19	70.7	65.0	89.9	89.0	86.7
Germany	60.0	63.7	71.0	68.2	64.1
Ireland	46.6	23.9	76.9	72.8	68.0
Greece	98.9	103.1	176.8	180.8	178.6
Spain	60.9	35.6	99.4	99.0	98.3
France	60.5	64.5	95.6	96.6	97.0
Italy	109.7	99.8	131.5	132.0	131.8
Portugal	51.0	68.4	128.8	129.9	125.7
UK	39.9	41.9	88.2	88.2	87.7

fact, the situation of sovereign debt after the crisis was heavier than before, especially for peripheral countries, even if core countries' positions also worsened (Tables 5.2 and 5.3).

The theoretical literature on sovereign defaults has focused on adverse shocks to debtors' economies, tending to suggest that defaults are of an idiosyncratic nature. Even so, sovereign debt crises are also of a systemic nature, clustered around panics in the financial center, such as the sovereign debt crisis under examination in the aftermath of the US Subprime Crisis in 2008. Crises in the financial centers are rare disasters and, thus, their effects on the periphery can only be captured by looking at long spells of time. In examining sovereign defaults from 1820 to the Great Depression, with a focus on Latin America, Kaminsky and Vega-García (2016) find that 63 percent of the crises are of a systemic nature, arising in a financial center.[12] Crises of an idiosyncratic nature, due to country-specific shocks to the debtor's economy, are different. Both the international collapse of liquidity and the growth slowdown in the financial centers in the core are instead typical of systemic crises, with global shocks triggering longer default spells and larger losses for investors.

The main causes of the sovereign crisis can be found in the sequence of the following factors: (1) a sharp rise in the sensitivity of financial markets to fundamentals, a "wake-up" call contagion among peripheral countries, which was absent before the crisis, when markets did not fully reflect the fundamentals (Beirne, Fratzscher, 2013; Giordano et al., 2013); (2) as a consequence of this, a reversal of capital movements back to their countries of origin; (3) a large expansion of budget deficit and debt in peripheral countries due to the rescue of ailing banks; (4) "herd" behavior,[13] transmitting pricing up of sovereign risk between the markets of GIIPS countries (Beirne, Fratzscher, 2013); (5) transmission of the contagion through the different fiscal positions of peripheral countries; (6) persistence of contagion, with asymmetries across countries (Giordano et al., 2013; Hondroyiannis, 2014).

In the process, the size of the deficit and the debt/GDP ratios depended on the EMU governments' responses to the private debt

---

[12] Idiosyncratic shocks are seldom the main cause of financial crises. These often originate in the periphery as a consequence of panics in the financial center (Kaminsky, Vega-García, 2016).

[13] Herd behavior is related to Keynes's (1936) "beauty contest." Before the creation of the EMU, the first models of such behavior in the economic field were suggested by Banerjee (1990) and Scharfstein and Stein (1990).

crisis, specifically on two factors: the public intervention to save ailing banks; and the deflationary fiscal policies initiated in 2010 by all the EMU countries. The former was not limited to some peripheral countries, even if it assumed different forms. In fact, "total commitments (from capital injections to liability guarantees) ranged from roughly 20 percent to over 300 percent of GDP across EZ countries" (Shambaugh, 2012: 190). As to the latter, apart from the negative effects on GDP of the deleveraging of banks and firms after the sovereign crisis (as an effect of the financial accelerator[14]), an additional negative impact derived from the kind of public reaction. In fact, each government, acting separately, sought to ward off its insolvency; this tended to curb the numerator of the deficit/GDP ratio, but eventually reduced the denominator too. Absence of a common fiscal policy and requirements by the EMU of "sound" fiscal policy from each government, in particular of peripheral countries, implied a fallacy of composition and the paradox of thrift.

To be more specific on the dynamics of the crisis, tensions within the EMU, after a limited rise soon after the crisis emerged in the United States, exploded almost by chance, as said, in Greece, followed by Ireland, as a direct consequence of the need for government intervention to save banks. Expectations of insolvency then arose, causing a wide increase of differentials in public bond yields, which had slightly risen beginning September 2008, after Lehman Brothers' bankruptcy.

Sensoy et al. (2015) show the precise date when the high-average dynamic conditional correlation between EMU sovereign bond yields that had emerged in the previous ten years began to falter, reaching its minimum in spring 2012. Reichlin (2014) and Bologna and Caccavaio (2014) note a progressive dismantling of financial integration and concentration of bank loans in fiscally sound economies as an effect

---

[14] The negative effect in Italy of the Greek sovereign crisis – which was deployed through the lending banking channel and its impact on investment, particularly of small and medium firms – is highlighted in Bottero et al. (2015). A similar effect might apply also to other EU countries, which showed a structure, in terms of both profitability and capital structure, comparable with other Western countries.

of the crisis. Bank exposures to foreign depositors and lenders dropped in the most vulnerable countries (by about 40 percent in the EZ), returning to their precrisis level. This led to a significant increase in the cost of credit in all peripheral countries (Neri, 2013). Neri's counterfactual analysis shows that the increase might have been of the order of magnitude of 60 to 130 basis points on average (according to the type of loans) at the end of 2011, with respect to the case when interest rate spreads remained constant at their levels, in April 2010.

The negative effects in the EZ of the crisis originated in the banking and financial sector, transmitted soon to sovereign financial assets, reflected back in the financial sector of peripheral countries, causing a rise in interest rates, reduction in credit demand, and, finally, causing a reduction in GDP and a rise in unemployment. Real effects, in turn, transmitted to other member countries through trade and confidence factors. According to Neri and Ropele (2015) – who use an econometric model to assess the impact of the negative asymmetric shock deriving from the declaration of the Greek government in 2009 – this shock transmitted first to the EZ countries with weak fiscal and macroeconomic conditions. In progress, it transmitted to core countries via the trade and confidence channels. As a result, credit market conditions deteriorated, economic activity was lowered, while the unemployment rate increased.[15]

Some analysts (e.g., EEAG, 2011) hold that the shocks would have been avoided simply by enacting a stiffer SGP and a credible no-bailout clause. However, this would not have worked with Greece, which could still have violated it, misreporting the true state of its public finances. In the case of Ireland, this would simply have made it harder to rescue banks. Moreover, the measures proposed would have had an extra deflationary effect, causing additional difficulties for

---

[15] A recent empirical analysis tests the validity of the link between economic sentiment (in particular, consumer confidence) and economic activity. It finds that "consumer confidence has the closest co-movement with economic and financial variables, and most of the correlations are contemporaneous or forward-looking, consistent with the view that economic sentiment is indeed a driver of activity" (Nowzohour, Stracca, 2017: 4).

other countries. In fact, the burden of the bank rescue was aggravated by the bad design of the EFSF. By charging high interest rates, it sent a signal of significant default risk to markets (De Grauwe, 2011a). Finally, making the SGP more rigid would have aggravated its deflationary effects.

As a way of provisional conclusion, institutions were central to the impact of the financial crisis as it developed in the EMU. We will deal further with this in the next section.

5.5 THE COMPONENTS OF GROWTH BEFORE AND AFTER THE CRISIS

The difference between the dynamics of growth and employment inside and outside the EZ has already been outlined in Chapter 4. Similarly, we already dealt with the determinants of growth up to 2007, indicating the different drivers of growth in the various countries that had led to a bifurcation or duality between them.

These components of growth and their fragility did not emerge to some observers of the EMU achievements after ten years. In contrast with the position of some of the skeptics[16] at the time when the EMU was devised, they gave no weight to existing imbalances and the reasons why the situation could look acceptable only to careless observers, being the result of a kind of drug and, thus, precarious (Barrell et al., 2008). Christodoulakis (2009) and most contributors to Maćkowiak et al. (2009), while recognizing a few remaining challenges, gave a very positive assessment of the achievements of the EMU. The Commission even dared to clearly state that "Ten years into its existence, the euro is a resounding success" (European Commission, 2008: 3). Wyplosz (2006: 208) stated that academic research, while being rather critical at the launch of this unique experience, has later generally recognized that, in the end, "the launch

---

16 Two very skeptical positions must be recalled as notable. Taking some of the words of Dornbusch (1996), "the combination of overly tight monetary policy and determined budget-cutting suggests a tough time ahead for Europe." Friedman (1996) was even more impressive, in warning about the "suicidal nature" of participating in the Union.

of the euro has been a major success." However, he noted that it was early to tell whether the EMU could suffer from asymmetric shocks, since it had not been submitted to the test (p. 222). Nickell (2007: 252) even dared to forecast the possibility of Greece and Italy running into difficulties. Both were thus cautious enough. By contrast, most other analysts and the markets did not catch the signals that were already apparent at the time and should have been recognized. Tabellini and Wyplosz (2006) underline that the different performances of the various countries can be ascribed to the different extent to which they undertook supply-side reforms, whereas other aspects of the EU action, such as absence of centralization or the Open Method of Coordination, were irrelevant.

More recently, some analysts (only a few, really) have raised doubts about the soundness of the European construction. In particular, François et al. (2014) find that not macroeconomic variables, but other factors, affected support for the EU before accession. After 2004, citizens attributed responsibility to the EU and not to their country for the state of the economy in terms of unemployment and inflation, thus reallocating responsibility to the new ruler. The waves of Euroskepticism and Europhoria, both among and within EU member states, are instead the object of Olsson (2009). This author suggests that support for the EU can derive (to a variable extent) from minority nationalists, or regions with strong identity that seek to bypass their central states in order to achieve their policy goals at the EU level.

Looking at the factors of growth after 2007, overall, in the EMU investment has been lacking and public expenditure has been the main support to domestic demand. This, in turn, has been the main driver of growth. However, in Germany exports have remained an important component of it, which explains why this country suffered less from the crisis. In fact, until recently, even if large output gaps have remained in peripheral countries, which implied reduction in their demand for German goods, other countries outside the EZ have absorbed them.

In the EU countries external to the EZ, the major component of growth has been internal demand (mainly consumption), but no specific role has been played by the public sector. The external sector did impress an impulse only in some countries, even if the exchange rate lever could have been used to this end by all of them.[17] This shows that another course of action on the route out of the crisis would have been possible by using the exchange rate lever, with no constraints put on the components of domestic demand and no inflationary impulse. The same route could have been followed by peripheral countries, certainly not as a way to solve their structural problems, but only to face the crisis.

The case of the United States is still different, as private consumption supported by the strength of the financial market has been the main driver of expansion there, both before and after the crisis. Exports have been stimulated by the weakness of the dollar after the crisis up to 2013–14. Before the crisis, the export share of GDP had practically remained constant. Thus, the only novel aspect of the US strategy with respect to that pursued before the crisis is the role of the foreign sector, which has complemented the role of finance-led growth.

By contrast, growth has been very low in Japan in the last decade. "Abenomics" has tried to revive it since 2013 by using a variety of instruments, ranging from "quantitative and qualitative easing" to traditional budget policies and the so-called Revitalisation Strategy, based on a number of microeconomic reforms. The results appear encouraging in the last four to five years, mainly in terms of the unemployment rate, with the very comforting value of 2.4–2.5 percent in 2018, a bit lower than the record values of the 1980s, before the start of the Japanese stagnation (Japan Statistics Bureau, n.d.).

---

[17] It was actually used in a significant way by the United Kingdom, Sweden, the Czech Republic, and Poland, between the end of 2007 and 2009.

5.6   EFFICIENCY AND EQUITY IN THE EMU BEFORE AND AFTER THE CRISIS

We use the same indicators of efficiency and distribution as those examined with reference to the situation before the crisis, with the same proviso concerning the information on equity that can be derived also from the breakdown of indicators of efficiency in spatial terms.

5.6.1   *Microeconomic Indicators of Static and Dynamic Efficiency*

Let us first consider *dynamic efficiency* in microeconomic terms. In the period 2008–15 it apparently increased on average in the EU, which is to be considered as a direct consequence of the crisis and is scarcely indicative of long-run trends, apart from possible effects on stagnation (as discussed later). We often use data referred not to the latest year for which they are available, but mainly to 2014 (or 2015, if it is the case) to show the highest incidence of the crisis.

In terms of factors contributing to total productivity, the crisis had an apparently positive impact on the relative position of the EU. In fact, the R&D intensity for the EU (EMU) increased to 2.06 percent (2.15 percent) in 2017, up by 1.2 (1.1) p.p. since 2008, reducing differences with the United States (2.79 percent), but not with Japan and South Korea, whose research intensity soared to 3.2 percent and 4.56 percent, respectively, in the same year. Apart from the apparently positive result, the target contained in Europe 2020 (an R&D intensity equal to 3 percent) still appears to be very distant. The country distribution of these values for the EU is indicated in Figure 5.3, which shows the lagged position not only of the periphery and CEEC, but also of the United Kingdom.

The apparent improvement is partly illusory. In fact, it has been shown that the absolute amount of R&D expenditure has remained constant (Veugelers, 2014) for the EU as a whole, which is anyway a positive aspect of the situation: the crisis had no negative impact on

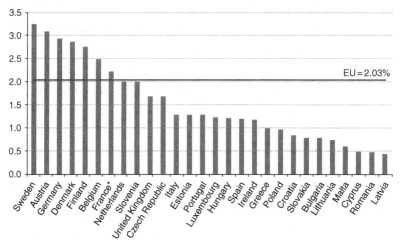

* 2015 data instead of 2016

FIGURE 5.3 R&D intensity (%) in the EU and various countries, 2016 (Source: Eurostat)

overall R&D outlays, even if it made private and public agents cut their expenditure in some cases. But, while the absolute values for innovation-leading countries have even slightly increased, there have really been disastrous effects of the crisis on followers and laggards, in particular on countries experiencing fiscal consolidation problems (Veugelers, 2014), as a part of a more general cut in investment there. Thus, practically the improvement in total EU research intensity is entirely explained by the drop in GDP, as happened in the United States in the worst years of the crisis there. If this is the general picture of research in Europe, there are wide differences among different member states. Some of them (Finland and Sweden) now have R&D/GDP ratios even higher than Japan's (but not South Korea's); others (not only Cyprus and Malta, but most CEEC, with the exception of the Czech Republic and Slovenia) have a much lower one. As an effect of the crisis, the standard deviation for the EU as a whole has risen from 0.82 to 0.89 since 2007 (Eurostat, 2017).

Considering the current state of research intensity, both the average 3 percent goal for research intensity and the country-specific targets set by Europe 2020[18] appear as still rather far away, also taking account of the very slow progress toward them. A fast recovery of the European economy could help governments, the EU, and private agents to refocus on this essential ingredient of growth. However, if R&D expenditures do not rise enough, whereas recovery is fast, the impact in terms of GDP could prevail, i.e., the denominator of the research intensity could increase more rapidly than its numerator, thus frustrating achievement of this Europe 2020 target.

Other targets set by Europe 2020 – which can be considered relevant for dynamic efficiency, in its double meaning of innovative efficiency and adaptive efficiency, thus reflecting progress toward a knowledge-based and innovative economy – refer to education and seem to show a more positive trend. Reducing below 10 percent the rate of early school leavers of young people aged 18–24 may prove to be in progress, as it dropped to 10.7 in 2016, not far from the Europe 2020 target of 10.0 percent, even if there was a ratio of up to 6 between the best and the worst performers (Figure 5.4). At the same time, the share of 30–34-year-olds completing third-level education is approaching its 40 percent target (in 2016: 39.1 percent for the EU, 37.4 percent for the EMU 18), which is closely related to the education rate of younger people. However, one can again doubt that these achievements are an effect of the crisis[19] rather than the prosecution of an undeniable trend, as the European Commission itself recognizes (European Commission,

[18] European Commission (2010). Setting this and other targets for the whole EU started from the recognition of the urgency of strong cooperation, which is certainly a goal of interest, even if it lacks implementation of proper instruments. Also of interest is indication of goals at a national level, which should enhance countries' responsibility to better the quality of national institutions and their ability and willingness to learn from best practices abroad and implement them. We must, however, warn that the indicators should be assessed carefully, also because they do not show why attainments can diverge from the targets. Some apparently favorable or unfavorable situations might derive not only from the countries' policies, but also from the EU (or EMU) institutions and policies as well as their consequences on each country.

[19] The Southern European countries seem to perform better in reducing school leaving in recent years (for Portugal, the rate even drops from 36.5 to 14 percent, and for Greece and Italy it is lower than the target, even if this is common to other countries too), but this might be tied to the higher difficulty of finding a job.

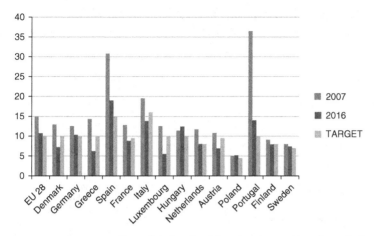

FIGURE 5.4 Rate of early school leavers of young people aged 18–24 (%) by sex in EU and various countries, 2007, 2016 (Source: Eurostat)

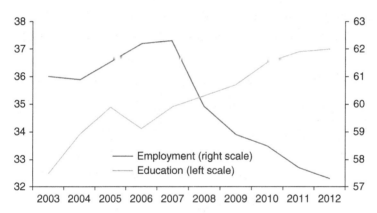

FIGURE 5.5 Employment rate and share of people participating in education (%), ages 15–24 years, EU 28, 2003–2012 (Source: Eurostat)

2014b: 14). In fact, they might be biased and tend to fade away with a recovery of growth and employment, which could increase prospects for job enrollment, as an alternative to education, as perceived by many young people. This has happened in the past as Figures 5.5 and 5.6 show.

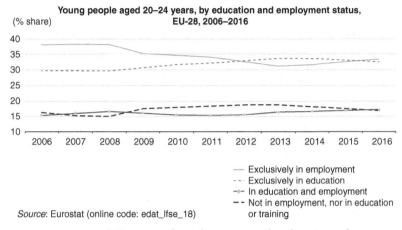

FIGURE 5.6 Young people aged 20–24 years, by education and employment status, EU 28 (2006–2016, % share) (Source: Eurostat)

As to the environmental goals, which are also set in the project of Europe 2020, the trend in the evolution toward the various specific targets is positive or very positive for most indicators (greenhouse gas emissions also in non-ETS sectors, primary and final energy consumption), less satisfying for the share of renewable energy. On all of them, there could have been a beneficial effect of the crisis (possible only apparent, as nondurable). This is evident in greenhouse gas emissions in non-ETS sectors, for which mainly GIIPS countries have reached their targets or have even gone much beyond them in 2015.

5.6.2 Macroeconomic Indicators of Static and Dynamic Efficiency

After the crisis, the picture of unemployment rates (Figure 5.7), employment rates, and other variables dramatically changed with respect to the previous situation. In 2018, the average unemployment rate had lowered by around 3 p.p. (4.6 percent in the EU and 5.2 percent in the EZ), but had slightly risen to almost 7.3 percent and 7.6 percent respectively, in 2013. In addition, much of the previous ranking has been reversed. Most CEEC and Germany were at the bottom, whereas

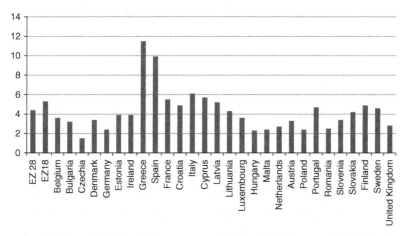

FIGURE 5.7 Unemployment rates (%) in the EU, Japan, and the United States, 2016 (Source: Eurostat)

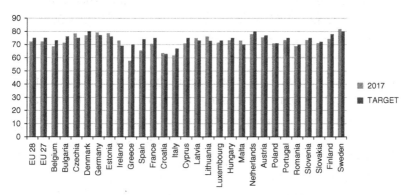

FIGURE 5.8 Employment rates (%) in the EU, Japan, the United States, and other countries, ages 20–64 years, 2016 (Source: Eurostat)

some GIIPS countries were at the top (Greece, Spain, and Italy). The variance (standard deviation) of unemployment increased to 95.01 (7.4) for the EU and to 96.01 (9.8) for the EMU.

Employment rates (Figure 5.8) rose in 2016 to 71.1 percent in the EU from 70.3 in 2008, whereas they dropped to 69.9 percent from 70.2 in 2008. After 2007, the dispersion, as measured by the variance (standard deviation), increased sharply for the EMU, to 126.56 (11.25), but less than for the EU, where it climbed to 156.25 (12.5).

Moving to macroeconomic dynamic indicators of efficiency, after 2007 the EU – and even more the EMU – suffered negative growth, with an annual reduction of GDP of 0.13 percent and 0.8 percent, respectively.[20] According to some assessments, it could take twenty-five years for Europeans to regain their precrisis standard of living. OECD projections of growth to 2060 for European countries made in 2012 (OECD, 2012) – according to which the crisis would have no long-term effects on trend growth – are likely to prove too optimistic, not only because of the further fall in growth due to the prolongation of the crisis, but also as an effect of the requirements for fiscal consolidation and the delays in the implementation of much needed supply-side reforms (Crafts, 2013).[21] Crafts's calculations lead to a projected growth rate between 2012 and 2030 "closer to 1% per annum, as opposed to the pre-crisis rate of 2.3%" (Crafts, 2013: 45).[22] In fact, apart from the negative effects of the crisis on investment – and then on innovation – there are those on unemployment, especially on youth and long-term unemployment, which have a lasting impact on human capital (Acocella, 2018). Germany, Austria, Denmark, and the Netherlands are the EU countries that have been hit less in terms of youth unemployment, thanks to their dual training system, by which young people and young adults experience apprenticeship, while completing their theoretical training at school.

The different performance of the various member countries is indicated in Figure 5.9.

There are no synthetic reliable indicators for sustainable growth, but the environmental goals mentioned before can serve this purpose as

[20] The negative performance of the non-EMU members during the crisis is mainly due to the United Kingdom in 2008 and 2009.

[21] However, we must put emphasis on the need to implement these reforms especially out of the crisis, not to aggravate contraction deriving from demand.

[22] More recent projections by OECD, from 2010 to 2030, prospect a total growth of about 35 percent for the EZ, as opposed to more than 58 percent for the United States (http://stats.oecd.org/viewhtml.aspx?datasetcode=EO95_LTB&lang=en).

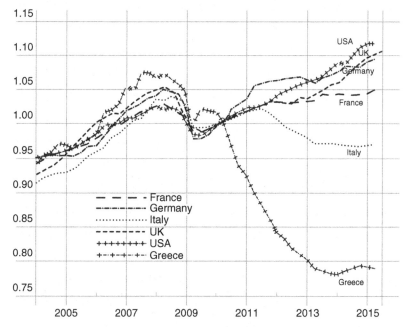

FIGURE 5.9 GDP growth rates in EU countries and the United States, 2005–2015 (Source: Coley et al., 2013)

one important determinant of sustainability, even if the link between these indicators and long-term growth should be a matter of further inquiry and include other variables – such as the nature of technological progress, income distribution, and institutions – as well.

5.6.3 Equity Indicators

Equity was hit badly by the crisis, as shown by Figures 5.10 and 5.11. Between 2007 and 2016, the average rate of poverty and social exclusion[23] rose by 1.4 p.p. to 23.1 percent in the EMU, while

---

[23] This indicator is more comprehensive than the poverty rate. In fact, it is multidimensional, going beyond the static indications deriving from poverty, since it refers not only to monetary poverty, but also to other components: these are material deprivation, which affects future prospects for the poor, and a situation of living in households with low work intensity, which is at the root of poverty. On this concept, see, e.g., Atkinson et al. (2002a, 2002b), World Bank (2007), Atkinson (2009a). For comparisons over time, see Lelkes and Gasior (2012).

FIGURE 5.10 People at risk of poverty and social exclusion in various EU countries (%), 2014, 2015 (Source: Eurostat)

■ 2015 — 2014

[1] 2015: estimate
[2] 2015: not available

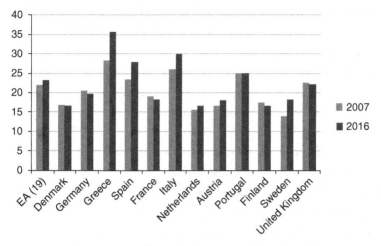

FIGURE 5.11 People at risk of poverty and social exclusion in various EZ countries (%), 2007, 2016 (Source: Eurostat)

decreasing in the EU, from 24.5 to 23.4 percent (not shown by the figures). The increase in poverty in the EMU, especially in terms of percentage rates but also in absolute amounts, appears to have been rather limited, but this conclusion would be largely misleading. The figures, in fact, undervalue impoverishment and social exclusion, since the crisis significantly lowered the average and median per capita income, especially in some countries.[24] Moreover, the EU variance sharply reduced in the period, from 100.11 to 48.33, while the value for the EMU of this indicator soared, from 14.95 to 29.12.

In addition, we must consider that containment in the increase of the poor derives from the existence of the welfare state. To show the importance of its role we must refer to one component of the risk of poverty and social exclusion, i.e., poverty rates, as this measures the monetary aspect of poverty only. This component is calculated considering net disposable income, which is significantly affected by

[24] Apart from the GIIPS and some CEEC countries, some of the leading countries of the EU, such as France and Germany, also have significantly been affected by the crisis (Insee, 2014, Bundeszentrale für politische Bildung und dem Wissenschaftszentrum Berlin für Sozialforschung, 2013). In Germany, the situation of the Eastern Lander has particularly worsened after the crisis.

taxes and social transfers. Data about this component in different EU countries before and after all social transfers (including social pensions)[25] show how significant are transfers as a part of disposable income. If we consider their contribution not only at the deepest point of the crisis, but also more recently, they amounted to almost 9 percent of the median income for the EU in 2015, lowering the share of people at risk of poverty from 26.0 percent to 17.3 percent (Figure 5.12). The contribution was much higher for some countries (not only Scandinavian countries, but also the United Kingdom and other countries) than for new-accession countries.[26] The share of the poor before social transfers was similar in Finland (at 26.8 percent) and in Romania (29.3 percent). While Finland experienced the second largest decrease in the EU of the rate of poverty after social transfers (14.4 p.p.), in Romania the share of the monetary poor only fell slightly (3.9 p.p.) as a result of such transfers.

Over time, the rates of people at-risk-of-poverty before and after social transfers have moved in different directions. The former was relatively stable in the EU between 2010 and 2015,[27] while the latter increased slightly over the same period. This could mean that either the amounts of social transfers paid have fallen or such transfers have become less effective over time. Anyway, as transfers are countercyclical, we can deduce that the member states performed a high-

---

[25] One could say that data about poverty rates before and after social transfers (including social pensions) are not a suitable indicator, as social pensions largely represent an intergenerational transfer between the same people, rather than a transfer among different people of the same generation. But data show that the substance of our argument holds (and really it is possibly emphasized) if they are excluded.

[26] The impact of (total) social transfers reduces the average number of material deprivations by 2.2 percent in Germany and Greece and by 1.9 and 1.8 percent in Poland and the United Kingdom, and even more if we consider only worse-off recipients. The reduction in at-risk-of-poverty rates is usually even higher (Notten, Guio, 2016). In 2016, the Greek at-risk-of-poverty rate before all social transfers (i.e., excluding both social benefits and pensions from the total disposable household income) was 52.9 percent. It dropped to 21.2 percent after consideration of social transfers. Thus, the inclusion of total social transfers contributed to a total decrease of 27.7 p.p. in the at-risk-of-poverty rate.

[27] One must remember that, given the definition of the rate of poverty in terms of the median income, a reduction in the former does not necessarily imply a reduction in the number of the poor.

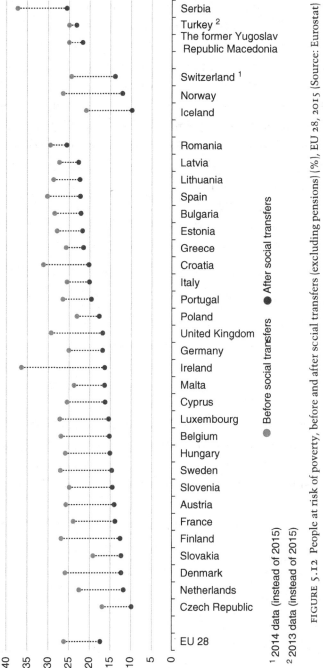

FIGURE 5.12 People at risk of poverty, before and after social transfers (excluding pensions) (%), EU 28, 2015 (Source: Eurostat)

profile task in compensating for the negative effects of the crisis on monetary poverty. However, performance of this role entailed higher public deficits and debts all around the EU, implying the risk of making the burden of the welfare state unsustainable, unless this is cut, as has been done in some countries.

Poverty is relevant, but also inequality should be taken into consideration. In some way, similarly to poverty, inequality can refer to a number of "spaces" such as consumption, income, wealth, utility, and capability. The most common spaces are income and wealth.[28] As to income inequality within specific countries, the findings of various studies – referring to different periods, countries, and indicators – differ. From the end of the Civil War in the United States to the start of World War II, inequality increased as an effect of rising monopolization, while for European countries in terms of the Gini coefficient it diminished mainly as an effect of "the wars of the twentieth century that, to some extent, wiped the past and transformed the structure of inequality" (Piketty, 2013: 118).

More recently, the trend in income inequality has changed. With reference to the last three decades, inequality – again in terms of the Gini index – has risen more in transition countries (mainly the Baltic countries), the United Kingdom, and some Nordic countries. It has increased less in other countries, such as Italy, and has remained largely unchanged in Austria, Denmark, France, and Germany, in particular after the eruption of the Great Recession (Salverda et al., 2014). Using a measure of personal inequality different from the Gini index, this picture is confirmed and some aspects of the changes are enlightened. In the United Kingdom the top 1 percent income share

[28]   Utility and, even more, capability are instead less common and more difficult to assess. For each space, there can be different dimensions. As to income, dimensions of equality can be factor distribution, personal, or geographic distribution. Similar dimensions can be the object of analysis of other indicators. Wealth inequality can refer to total wealth, net of debt, or to specific wealth items, houses and land, or financial wealth. For each space and dimension, different indices can be calculated. As an example, personal distribution of income can be assessed by using synthetic indicators such as the Gini or the Theil indexes or more detailed ones, referring to deciles, quartiles, or other percentages of income earners.

has risen less than in the United States and has stayed almost constant in major Continental European countries (Alvaredo et al., 2013; Piketty, 2013).

Strictly tied to personal inequality of income is personal inequality of wealth, which varies highly between countries, being higher in the United Kingdom, France, and the Scandinavian countries, while Spain, Ireland, and Italy have lower inequality levels (Maestri et al., 2014).

Personal inequality of both income and wealth is linked to worsening factor inequality and, to a large extent, also depends on it (e.g., Dabla-Norris et al., 2015; Stockhammer, 2015). However, in our case, rather strangely, improvements in personal income equality before 2007 were accompanied by falling labor income shares, whereas more recently deterioration in personal inequality pairs with more or less stationary labor shares. This is in contrast with what usually happens, as declining labor shares and improved macroeconomic performance do not translate into improvements in the distribution of personal income (Atkinson, 2009b). And data also show that a higher capital share is accompanied by higher inequality in personal distribution (Piketty, 2013). This implies that other factors must have been more relevant. One such factor is sources of income other than from labor for some workers at least that can be related to the accumulation of relevant financial assets during the period up to 2007. The subsequent financial crisis can then easily account for deteriorating personal equality even with rather unchanged labor income. More recently, it has also been shown that policies other than those specifically devised for equality have been able to influence it. In fact, Lenza and Slacalek (2018) find that QE also caused a reduction in inequality, by lowering the number of families being unemployed and thus compressing the income distribution.

As a conclusion to this analysis, we can say that the crisis had a relevant negative impact on both efficiency and equity. Thus, the reasons underlying the crisis appear worthy of being analyzed. We do this in the next chapter.

5.6.4 The Effects of the Crisis in a Short- and Long-term Perspective, with Specific Relevance to Distribution

The effects of the crisis on distribution were variegated. In the United Kingdom, they were negative, similarly to what happened also in other Anglo-Saxon countries (Figure 5.13). By contrast, in Continental European countries they were almost absent, due mainly to the more intense action of the welfare state in them (Figure 5.14), as already said before.

These findings are substantially confirmed by more recent analysis of income distribution in developed countries (Bourguignon, 2018). This same source also offers evaluations of the share of the higher percentile in the same countries, but it stops at 2012 and coincides with Alvaredo et al.'s findings in some cases, whereas in others they differ. Counterfactual simulations show that the expansionary monetary policy of the ECB contributed to counteracting the negative effects of the sovereign debt crisis mitigating the negative effects of the sovereign debt crisis on both the banking sector and the

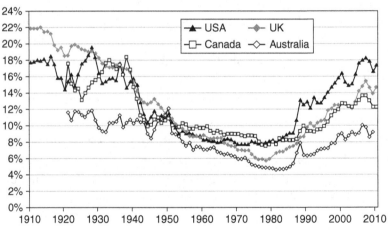

The share of top percentile total income rose since 1970 in all Anglo-Saxon countries, but with different magnitudes. Sources and series: see piketty.pse.ens.fr/capital21c.

FIGURE 5.13 Share of income of the richest 1 percent of the population in Anglo-Saxon countries, 1910–2010 (Source: Alvaredo et al., 2013)

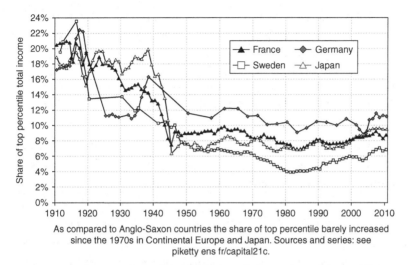

As compared to Anglo-Saxon countries the share of top percentile barely increased since the 1970s in Continental Europe and Japan. Sources and series: see piketty ens fr/capital21c.

FIGURE 5.14 Share of income of the richest 1 percent of the population in selected countries of Continental Europe and Japan, 1910–2010 (Source: Alvaredo et al., 2013)

real economy, not only in individual countries but also in the EZ as a whole.

The economic crisis produced not only a bank and sovereign debt crisis, but also a slowing down, certainly differentiated across the Union, of economic growth in most of Europe. This is first due to the implication, as is the case for all crises, in terms of hysteresis and potential growth and, in addition, to the burden of sovereign debt of some countries, which had to implement consolidation plans to reduce it. These implications have and will in the future negatively impact not only on these countries' rate of growth but also on the rate of growth of the most "virtuous" countries via trade linkages.

The long-term effects of the Great Recession are not limited to the economic realm directly. They extend to the field of political implications, which, in turn, could have economic implications on future prospects. Among these political effects, most important seems to be the impulse to a movement, which certainly had other roots and had begun to manifest itself before the recession, i.e., populism and localism at a national level, as opposed to international governance.

5.7   PROSPECTS OF STAGNATION IN THE EA: THE IMPACT OF THE GREAT RECESSION, RISING INEQUALITY, GLOBALIZATION, AND INSTITUTIONS

The crisis, inequalities, globalization, and institutions are relevant also as they affect the determinants of secular stagnation. Let us discuss each point in turn.

The Great Recession has raised the issue of the prospect of stagnation in various ways: first by increasing the burden of the debt accumulated during the crisis; second, through its hysteresis effects, discouraging future investment. As to the latter channel, falling GDP has negatively influenced potential output (Ball, 2014a; Eggertsson, Mehrotra, 2014; Hall, 2014; Krugman, 2014; Fatás, Summers, 2016a).[29] The median loss in potential output in 2014 among the nineteen OECD countries experiencing a bank crisis over the period 2007–11 has been estimated to be 5 ½ percent, which is to be contrasted with an estimated loss across all OECD countries of about 3 ½ percent in the same year (Ollivaud, Turner, 2015). In fact, the recovery has not represented a return to the former potential. The future trend is threatened mainly by reduced capital investment and, to a lower extent, by a decline in the hours of work (Summers, 2014: 66).

Eichengreen (2015) suggests four possible causes of stagnation, which he defines as a falling downward tendency of real interest rates: an excess of savings over investment; a rise in savings rates due to the higher propensity to save of emerging markets; a decline in attractive investment opportunities or in the relative price of investment goods; a decline in the rate of population growth.[30] This implies that both the demand- and the supply-side perspectives are relevant and explain

---

[29]   As this negative effect of the recession on potential output begins to materialize, while the recession is fading out (thus raising the current growth rate), the gap between the two tends also to disappear. This fact could be an explanation alternative to Gordon's (2014) argument according to which the reduction in the gap shows that the hysteresis effect is of scarce relevance.

[30]   On this, see also Thwaites (2015).

why Krugman and Gordon, who represent these two points of view, largely agree (Gordon, 2014; Krugman, 2014).[31]

Ollivaud and Turner argue that the most adverse effects derive from a lower productivity trend. This is to a large extent influenced by investment, which dropped during the Great Recession. Many countries have limited their public deficits, in particular in order to comply with institutional limits, just by curbing public investment (and, within it, the items that are more sensible for productivity growth, such as educational expenditures), due to the relatively larger flexibility in their management with respect to almost fixed current expenditures. In this perspective, Fatás and Summers (2016b) underline the permanent negative effects deriving from fiscal consolidation. The role of the various determinants of the trend in productivity is difficult to ascertain, but some authors are critical about the possibility of continuing to have high rates of productivity growth in the future.[32]

Also demographics can have an impact on secular stagnation, which, according to some authors, can be even more important than that of technology. Aging and increased life expectancy are a feature of demographic trends in many countries, especially in Europe (notably, Italy and Germany), the United States, Japan, and China.[33]

---

[31]   On the supply-side perspective, see also Gordon (2012).

[32]   Data are difficult to collect, as indicators such as R&D expenditures and patent registrations can be biased and misguiding, and some other measures of productivity growth may be illusory, concerning largely tertiary sectors, where productivity is difficult to ascertain, due to absence of material content of production (Cowen, 2011). According to Gordon (2014), productivity growth in the next decades is predicted to be as high as it was in the five previous decades, even if, to some extent, the effects of technological progress may appear less relevant in some countries, namely the innovation leaders, due to the geographical distribution of its implementation in a globalized world. In fact, innovations devised in one country – such as those derived from information technology – can be implemented in other countries, due to decentralization of production. In addition, technological progress appears to be more relevant for investment than for consumption goods, for which the weight of services tends to grow.

[33]   The a priori impact of demographic trends on aggregate demand and real interest rates is complex. On the one hand, increased savings can derive from the section of the population having a higher propensity to it, due to the increase in longevity. On the

In addition to the Great Recession, the tendency to stagnation is due to globalization, which has transmitted the financial crisis and stagnation from the regions initially more affected to other regions, showing the shortcomings of current international institutions. These look incapable of acting in a way to reap the benefits of globalization, while protecting from its evils. Among the latter, notable is the international transmission of shocks and crisis.

The rising poverty and inequality has reinforced these negative effects.[34] The impact of poverty and inequality on long-term growth has been the object of inquiry of a number of modern theoretical and empirical studies that reach different conclusions.

Some theoretical analyses show positive effects linked to the top part of the income distribution, as this can boost savings available for investment and allow at least some individuals to acquire a good education and accumulate the minimum needed to start businesses (Barro, 2000). Some other analyses indicate negative effects, depending on the share of the bottom part of income distribution, since it: (i) deprives the poor of the ability to stay healthy and accumulate human capital (Perotti, 1996; Aghion et al., 1999; Galor, Moav, 2004); (ii) generates political and economic instability that reduces investment (Alesina, Perotti, 1996); and (iii) impedes the social consensus required to adjust to shocks and sustain growth (Rodrik, 1999).[35] The relationship between inequality and growth may be nonlinear: "increases in inequality from low levels provide

other, the larger share of older people – having a lower propensity, consistently with the life-cycle theory (Modigliani, Brumberg, 1954) – will act in the opposite direction. The net effect on real interest rates is, thus, uncertain (Favero, Galasso, 2015), the more so – we can add – as account should be taken of possible changes in the retirement age, some of which have already been implemented. A final effect of demographic trends is to be noted: reduction in the working cohorts of the population lowers its direct contribution to growth, unless the retirement age is prolonged. Intuition thus suggests that aging population can reduce growth. However, in practice this might not be so, as the positive effect of higher automation – in response to the demographic trend – can counteract this effect (Acemoglu, Restrepo, 2017).

[34] On the other hand, it was one aspect of globalization, i.e., capital account liberalization, that increased inequality (Furceri, Loungani, 2015; see also Ostry et al., 2018).

[35] See also Ravallion (2016).

growth-enhancing incentives, while increases past some point encourage rent-seeking and lower growth." The net effect is indeterminate, depending on the relative strength of each and the overall inequality (Ostry et al., 2014: 8).

Empirical analyses can then be useful, even if they cannot be considered as diriment, since they only indicate some possible regularities across countries subject to the influence of history and the whole set of institutions and the economic and social conditions of each country. Nevertheless, results of such analyses are striking in indicating the negative impact on growth of different features of inequality (Cingano, 2014).

In the debate about the causes of secular stagnation institutional aspects and political mistakes are also to be considered. Secular stagnation has been surfacing in some regions like Europe and Japan in the last couple of decades. In Japan, wrong policies as well as the effects of aging population have prevailed. In Europe, it has mainly been an effect of the deflationary design of institutions and to some extent of wrong policies (De Grauwe, 2015b). Crafts (2014) emphasizes that the risks of stagnation are greater for Europe than for the US hypochondria, due to a number of factors, among which are institutional factors such as the burden of fiscal consolidation and the ECB's focus on low inflation.

Other barriers to growth can be low education, increasing government debt, energy shortage, and environmental problems.[36] In particular, as to education, Gordon (2014) complains about the rising number of dropouts in the United States, but fortunately this is not the case for Europe, where the rate of early leavers has been decreasing since 2002. As to the other factors, instead, Europe is certainly in a worse position than the United States, which could negatively influence its long-run growth. Dew-Becker and Gordon (2008) study some factors in the labor market, such as unions, affecting the role of

---

[36]   From the point of view of a specific country such as the United States, also the interaction of globalization and ICT can be a problem, as it has caused or facilitated outsourcing.

the slowdown of European productivity growth and find signs of a positive effect on per capita output of employment protection legislation and unemployment benefits, with roughly no effects of product market regulation and the tax wedge.

Finally, globalization, while in many ways contributing to growth, can raise risks, negatively affecting it. In fact, external imbalances – associated with financial liberalization and the fragility of the international financial system – represent one of the fundamental causes of the global financial crisis and, then, of the prospects of stagnation.

6 Policies and Institutions Put to the Test of the Great Recession

6.1 POLICIES IN THE UNITED STATES AND THE EMU

The content of the policies implemented in the two areas was rather different. More importantly, the evolution of the crisis and the outcomes of policies differ remarkably. In Europe, the original determinants of the crisis derived from private financial sources, as in the United States. However, they evolved into a sovereign debt crisis, which was not the case in the United States. We attribute this largely to the different institutions in the two areas, in addition to the policies enacted, which were anyway to a large extent constrained by these institutions. Policymakers were either incapable of taking the opportunity to reform them or interested in keeping them and making them serve national or other interests. Monetary policies have prevailed in both the United States and EMU, but in Washington they have been complemented by federal fiscal policies in the initial, decisive, phase of the crisis. By contrast, no similar expansionary policy was implemented in Europe, where fiscal policies were managed at the state level and were generally deflationary. In the following section, we illustrate policies in Washington, while those implemented in the EZ are dealt with in Section 6.3. Section 6.4 tries to trace back the differences to the different institutional design, illustrating more specifically the influence on policies of the EMU institutions. The final section sketches new emerging tendencies.

6.2 POLICIES IN WASHINGTON

Expansionary monetary policy was soon enacted in the United States. It first tended to support ailing financial institutions, through ordinary operations (open market operations with broker-dealers) changing the aggregate quantity of reserve balances that banks held at the Federal Reserve. This was done by lending directly to commercial banks and other depository institutions at the "discount window" (with its maximum maturity lengthened to ninety days) and by creating a range of emergency liquidity facilities to meet the funding needs of key non-bank market participants at interest rates close to zero. The main issue, however, was that of relieving various financial institutions from the risks and losses of securities markets, which had taken a dominant role. A joint action of the Fed with the Treasury in November 2008 was intended to restart these markets, by establishing the Term Asset-Backed Securities Loan Facility (TALF), with the Fed supplying the liquid funding and the Treasury assuming the credit risk. In 2009, the new Obama administration proposed a new investment fund financed by private and public resources to relieve banks of their "toxic assets." The plan was passed, but was criticized by Krugman (2009) and Stiglitz (2009).

A delicate issue was that of the final impact of monetary action on the real economy, which mainly depends on the level of the long-term interest rate. Arbitrage is usually supposed to operate the transmission mechanism from short-term to long-term rates. However, it tends to work in an imperfect way, depending on expectations of future rates as well as on the preference for very short-term assets, which is very high in times of financial panic. In order to influence long-term rates, the Federal Reserve implemented two types of unconventional monetary actions: forward guidance (FG) and quantitative easing (QE). The former had been introduced first by the Fed itself in August 2003 and was implemented again in December 2008, under a rather loose form, as an "open-ended" promise by the central bank about the continuation of its expansionary stance for "an extended period" (Kohn, 2010). In order to issue a kind of guaranty of the expansionary nature of its attitude for a certain time, in August 2011, after analogous moves by the Bank of Canada and the Swedish Riksbank in April 2009, the Fed strengthened the type of promise conveyed by FG, by turning it to a "time-contingent" form.

Finally, in December 2012 it shifted to an even more informative attitude by adopting a "conditional" type of FG, i.e., by tying its expansionary stance to the achievement of the threshold values of its target values of unemployment rate (6.5 percent) and inflation rate (2.0 percent) (Acocella, Hughes Hallett, 2018).[1]

In order to have a direct impact on longer-term rates, the Fed inaugurated various rounds of QE, all having the purpose of buying longer-term securities, whereas its usual operations are short-term ones. The effects of these measures were lower long-term yields and higher asset prices that have induced positive wealth effects. The first round of QE – usually referred to as quantitative easing 1 (QE1) – addressed to buying large-scale asset purchases (LSAP) of government-sponsored-enterprise (GSE) debt, agency debt, mortgage-backed securities (MBS), and Treasury securities – began toward the end of 2008. The second round of QE (QE2) started in the second half of 2010 and concentrated on purchases of US Treasury securities. In September 2011, the Federal Reserve rediscovered "Operation Twist," a commitment to extend the maturity of the securities held, experienced first in 1961. In September 2012, a third and final round of QE, QE3 – lasting up to October 2014 – was inaugurated, focusing on the purchase of MBS, acting directly on markets' expectations, through explicit announcements and communication about future trends in policy.

In May 2013, the announcement by President Bernanke of the possibility of a future exit action from the expansionary stance negatively hit domestic and international financial markets, which jumped the gun on the recovery. He had to correct the announcement to signify that the current stance would not be abandoned until the Fed's targets (in terms of either unemployment and growth or inflation) would not be hit.

Unconventional operations have been very effective in lowering sovereign yields, raising equity markets and GDP growth rates (e.g., Cecioni et al., 2011; Meinusch, Tillmann, 2014; but see Chen et al.,

---

[1] "Open-ended" and "time-contingent" (or "date-based") FG are of a "Delphic" form, whereas the "conditional" (or "threshold") type has an "Odyssean" content.

2012, who find rather low effects on GDP) not only in the United States, but also in other countries, as an effect of portfolio reallocation and repricing of the risk in global financial markets (Fratzscher et al., 2013; Georgiadis, 2015). Unconventional measures have also helped to lower bank funding volatility and to increase loan supply (Carpenter et al., 2013). However, relying too much on them for too long can cause a liquidity glut and speculative capital movements both in the country where they are implemented and in other countries (e.g., Cho, Rhee, 2013; Bhattarai et al., 2018).

Fiscal policy too has always been expansionary in the United States. Discretionary measures were taken, beginning with G. W. Bush's October 2008 Troubled Asset Relief Program (TARP) (implying a $700 billion purchase of nonperforming financial assets from the balance sheet of private banks, infusion of funds into GM, Citigroup, and AIG). They continued with President Obama's American Recovery and Reinvestment Act (ARRA) in 2009, which led to additional expenditures and tax cuts for an amount of $787 billion. It is true that part of this huge discretionary impulse could simply be explained by a structural feature of that country, i.e., paucity of automatic stabilizers (Dolls et al., 2012), and that its net effect on GDP growth and employment has been rather small for a number of reasons. However, social security benefits and personal income taxes can play an important role in stabilizing asymmetric shocks, especially so if a discretionary program of extended benefits is implemented (Nikolov, Pasimeni, 2019). In any case, it testifies to the will of the American administration to counter the recession, even at the cost of public debt accumulation.

6.3 POLICIES IN FRANKFURT AND AROUND

Practically all the EZ countries, Germany included, responded to the crisis with a moderately expansionary fiscal stance, up to 2010. Some authors (e.g., Marelli, Signorelli, 2017), echoing an American song, speak of a "too little, too late" attitude in the EU reaction to the crisis. This is true to some extent, but the real problem is that the expression should refer mainly to EU policymakers' attitude toward structural imbalances, in particular before the crisis.

As to the following decisions, we should instead speak of a "too much, too early, too tough (and, above all, wrong) attitude." In fact, after the emergence of a public debt issue in some EMU countries the initial policy was followed by a contractionary orientation of fiscal policy. Strengthening the SGP was then decided, through the fiscal compact in 2012. This has failed to pursue its claimed target, i.e., a fall in the deficit/GDP and debt/GDP ratios, in order to get rid of speculation. In fact, a first recessionary wave was followed by another one. The double-dip recession lowered the denominator of those ratios and conjured up the spectre of a future crisis of confidence. In the seven years to 2014 – the year when it reached its maximum level – the debt/GDP ratio has soared, as seen in the previous chapter, not only in peripheral countries, but also in Germany, even if the peak (82.4 percent) was reached in 2010 in this country. The negative effects on real economic activity were largely underestimated. Wyplosz (2012) commented: "Adopting contractionary fiscal policies in the teeth of a double-dip recession never made sense."

The burden of expansionary action fell on monetary policy. As a whole, its response was expansionary until April 2011 through the usual open market operations, even if: (i) it started late; (ii) in May 2010, the ECB claimed that its intervention tended simply to smooth the policy transmission mechanism; (iii) at some point later, the ECB conducted a premature exit strategy for some months, as we say below. The ECB also used twelve-month and thirty-six-month longer-term refinancing operations (LTRO) (a form of nonstandard measures) since 2009. These operations have continued in 2011 and 2012. In addition, the ECB instituted a Securities Markets Programme (SMP) running since May 2010, by which it purchased bonds issued by the countries under speculative attack to the tune of several hundred billion euros. In this sense, European monetary policy shared some features with the Federal Reserve's policy of QE.[2] The SMP was

---

[2]   Apart from comparisons with the United States, an empirical analysis of the effects of LTRO has shown that these have different effects according to whether standard

conceived as a program intending to buy a limited amount of bonds for a limited time, which increased the panic pervading investors at the height of the sovereign debt crisis. This was complemented, again in May 2010, by the first governmental bailout fund, the EFSF, which, however, charged high interest rates and sent a signal of significant default risk to markets (De Grauwe, 2011a) like that of the SMP.

There have been many differences with the US monetary policy. First, in Europe, the expansionary policy began too late, as the ECB kept its more important rate, that on the main refinancing operations, at 4 percent until July 2008, even raising it by twenty-five basis points until October that year (Albonico et al., 2018b), and, as said, later on, in 2011 it raised again this policy rate. One further difference with the US's unconventional monetary policy, where the Fed purchased assets outright, is that European banks used funds obtained through the LTRO not only to face liquidity problems, but also to buy more public debt, which strengthened the link between private and sovereign debt and thus the risks.

An additional difference is that after April 2011, despite the feebleness of the economic recovery in that year, the ECB prematurely initiated an exit strategy and insisted on this course for some months. At last, in November 2011 this stance was abandoned and substituted again by an expansionary one, as the deflationary effects of the tightening of fiscal policies after the emergence of fears of a sovereign crisis began to be clear.

These are only part of the limits of European policies. They "are emblematic of the political difficulties that a lack of EU-wide institutions can present. The politics of shared burdens or of injecting capital into banks are often difficult, and trying to get the parliaments of 17 nations to ratify a change is immensely so" (Shambaugh, 2012: 196).

monetary policy is contractionary and is conducted irrespective of LTROs or not. The risk is that the ECB, while expanding the economy by LTRO, takes a contractionary stance in standard monetary policy actions, which partially neutralizes them. On this, see further Cahn et al. (2014).

A crucial shift in monetary policy stance began only in July–September 2012. Certainly, this followed a long period of falling inflation rates and the emergence of prospects of deflation. The negative effects of this fall have since been emphasized in papers by the ECB and the Bank of Italy at least (Neri, 2013; Neri, Notarpietro 2014), but were certainly predicted by President Draghi. Following his declaration in London that "within our mandate, the ECB is ready to do whatever it takes to preserve the euro. And believe me, it will be enough" (Draghi, 2012), monetary authorities decided to undertake a new program. Differently from the SMP, which was temporary, this measure – the Outright Monetary Transactions (OMT) – had no ex ante time limit and was geared to support bonds' demand in secondary markets of the sovereign states receiving official financial support from the EZ to an unlimited extent. This, again, was not true unconventional monetary policy similar to the American- or British-style QE for four reasons: first, OMT were limited to buying short-term public debt; second, the program was limited to a subset of European countries (those having an "appropriate" EFSF/ESM program designed to reduce the deficit and debt/GDP ratios), whereas QE in the United States and the United Kingdom targeted those countries' entire debt; third, the impact of the interventions of the OMT had to be sterilized in order to reabsorb the liquidity injected. Finally, even if the immediate targets of the ECB interventions resembled those of the Federal Reserve, i.e., driving down the interest rate on government bonds, the final objectives differed. For the Fed the fundamental aim was to lower long-term interest rates by FG and large-scale asset purchases so as to foster private investment. By contrast, the ECB was basically seeking to make up for the EMU's lack of a consistent and credible institutional architecture and, ultimately, to ensure the survival of the euro, which had emerged in the course of the crisis as the true issue at stake (on this point, see also Torres, 2013). In any case, criticism of OMT based on inflation risk, moral hazard, market efficiency, and fiscal

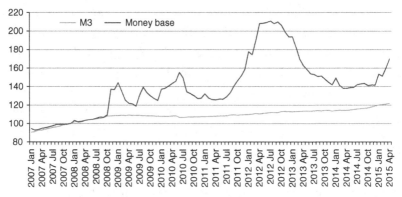

FIGURE 6.1 Growth of money base and M3, 2007–2015 (Source: ECB)

implication is unfounded (De Grauwe, Ji, 2013a). Figure 6.1 shows that the huge increase in money base did not transmit to M3, which implies that the credit multiplier did not work.

By contrast with the United States, true QE operations, under the form of an Expanded Asset Purchase Programme (APP), were introduced in the EMU only lately, in January 2015, persisting low or negative inflation and growth rates. These were targeted longer-term refinancing operations (TLTROs), which provided financing to credit institutions for periods of up to four years. In October 2017, the ECB's Governing Council decided to reduce net purchases from the monthly pace of €60 billion to the new monthly pace of €30 billion from January 2018 until the end of September 2018. In September 2019, the ECB cut the interest rate on money banks deposit with it for the first time since 2016, by a tenth of a percentage point to –0.5 percent, and will restart QE from November. These operations pursued multiple objectives: in particular, to reduce sovereign yields on long-term bonds and raise share prices of banks having more sovereign bonds in their portfolios; to expand credit supply. While the former can be said to have been obtained (Andrade et al., 2016),[3] the latter has not materialized indeed – at least in peripheral countries – as the true problem there is lack of credit demand.

---

3   Afonso et al. (2017) speak of a new bond-pricing regime in which spreads have weaker links with fundamentals.

With regard to FG, in 2013 the ECB introduced it in an "open-ended" form, but the simplicity of the ECB reaction function, which is tied to only one primary objective, made it possible for a member of the ECB Executive Board to speak of both Delphic and Odyssean features contained in this announcement (Praet, 2013).

Notwithstanding these profound differences with the US experience, the unconventional monetary measures adopted by the ECB before 2015 had beneficial effects. In fact, they contributed to liquidity management, lower bank funding volatility, and increased loan supply, similarly to what nonstandard measures did for the United States (ECB, 2011; Giannone et al, 2011, 2012; Eser et al., 2012; Carpenter et al, 2013). In addition, OMT stopped the speculative component of spreads between GIIPS countries' public debt and the German Bund. Unconventional monetary policies operated as indirect risk-sharing mechanisms improving EMU stability. They also improved the welfare of peripheral states by decreasing the cost of fiscal interventions but came to some extent at the cost of core countries (Canofari et al., 2019). This outcome has been confirmed and quantified by Neugebauer (2018) and Afonso et al. (2019) (see more in Section 10.1). Had the ECB decided to commit earlier to unlimited (indirect) support of sovereign debt, the crisis in the EZ might have followed a different course.

However, the impact on bank lending of cuts in the ECB official rates should not be overvalued, as the transmission mechanism of monetary policy did not work properly. In fact, interest rates of bank lending did not fall proportionally to the cuts in official rates (Illes, Lombardi, 2013; Gambacorta et al, 2014), thus showing opportunistic behavior of banks and an increase in their profit margins (ECB, 2013; Arestei, Gallo, 2014; Moro, 2016). This conduct could also have negatively influenced loan demand, partly explaining the low value of the multiplier, which caused a break in the transmission of monetary policy to the real economy (Neri, 2013; Van Rixtel, Gasperini, 2013), showing insufficiency of this policy for boosting economic recovery.

By contrast, the QE implemented since the beginning of 2015 might have contributed to the recent recovery in Europe, either because it implied an expansion of the ECB budget or for its direct positive impact on long-term interest rates, together with depreciation of the euro toward the dollar and reductions in raw material prices. Saraceno and Tamborini (2016) develop a model supporting the ECB official view, according to which QE reverses deflationary expectations, thus eliminating persistent output gaps. Success of QE – as opposed to conventional monetary policy operations – derives from its ability to overcome the limitations of the latter due to the zero lower bound (ZLB). Existence of this limit for short-term interest rates makes its fall below zero very difficult, facilitating also a fall in long-term rates, which would encourage investment.

Recent simulations expect QE to have significant effects from the point of view of both inflation and the GDP growth rates in Europe, whereas empirical evidence in favor of them is mixed. In Japan, they were unable to avoid deflation, until 2013, when the government launched its multifaced plan to revive the economy (see Section 5.5).

Simulations for Europe estimate QE to result in about a 1 p.p. increase in both the GDP and inflation in the first two years, as an effect of falling long-term interest rates and increasing liquidity, which support consumption and investment, and the depreciation of the nominal exchange rate (Cova et al., 2015). Similar nontrivial expansionary effects are found by Cova and Ferrero (2015) and Burlon et al. (2017b). Provisional findings by Gambetti and Musso (2017) suggest that QE gives a higher stimulus of GDP in the short run and has a higher impact on prices in the longer run. All these results contrast with previous studies that in general were not in favor of a significant positive impact of QE beyond the short term (see, e.g., Gambacorta et al., 2014, who estimated a vector autoregressive model (VAR) for the period 2008–11). However, the possibility is still there that late intervention by monetary authorities, the constraint on its maximum target inflation, nonconvergence of monetary and fiscal policy, and political uncertainty will push the EMU toward a "slow-moving debt crisis." In addition, there are limits properly linked to QE (Honkapohja, 2016).

As to fiscal policies, they were managed at the country level, having deflationary effects, due to the constraints and restrictions imposed by the initial institutional setup and the rules added to it after 2011. An additional component of their deflationary impact is due to the fallacy of composition effect. These effects were strengthened by the limit imposed on the operation of automatic stabilizers as a result of the boundaries imposed on the deficit/GDP ratio by the SGP and the fiscal compact.

6.4   WHY SO MANY DIFFERENCES? THE ROLE OF EMU INSTITUTIONS AND THE CRISIS

As we have seen, in the United States expansionary policies were adopted almost with no hesitation, even if there had been some mismanagement in policy attitudes before the financial crisis. In the EMU, only monetary policy has been – all in all – expansionary, with the exception of a premature exit policy adopted for a certain time, whereas fiscal policy has always been contractionary since 2010. The balance, as shown also by the different outcomes in macroeconomic terms, is clearly in favor of the United States.

Striking the proper balance between restoring normality and avoiding a protracted depression is the crux of the matter of exit policies. This has proved to be all the harder in a currency union like the EMU, which has a conservative central bank, is not a federal state (and thus has no common fiscal policy), and is composed of variegated local economies. In the current institutional setting, the exit strategies adopted within the EMU have derived from a bias toward being premature and have aggravated the risk and the costs of a prolonged depression, at least until the declaration by the new ECB president in July 2012 in favor of a firm active policy to stop the crisis. The bias stems from some deficiencies in the institutional architecture of the EMU, which have first acted to sustain crisis factors, thus making the pressure of markets prevail, and then imposed adoption of premature exit strategies and limitations to the use of some policies. In the following subsections, we deal further with gaps and biases in the ability of EMU institutions to counter situations of crisis.

6.4.1 The Role of Institutions in Sustaining Imbalances before the Crisis Started

In this subsection, we point out the specific EMU institutional features that explain the different steps of the EMU crisis, having an eye on US institutions. In the United States, we cannot speak of institutional failures properly. There have been wrong economic policies implemented before the crisis (e.g., financial deregulation and, more generally, an excessive role assigned to markets and neglect or improper treatment of distributional factors underlying the crisis; inaccurate supervision, etc.), which sustained its insurgence, and possibly some mismanagement of the crisis. However, overall, the American institutional setting was better able to fight the crisis than the European one.

Generally speaking and apart from fiscal policy, absence or weakness of a number of common institutions in the EZ concurred in nourishing the factors underlying the private debt crisis. We refer to absence of common and strong policies in fields such as financial regulation, wage policy, regional, and industrial policy. Financial regulation would have prevented accumulation of excessive credit and debt positions. Wage policy would have set appropriate price regulation and wage dynamics in relation to productivity growth for each country, which could have prevented, on the one hand, competitive real devaluations of the kind triggered by Germany and, on the other, continuous appreciations of the real exchange rate in peripheral economies. In addition, this sort of instrument could have avoided the conundrum generated by the current account balance, implying the difficult choice between internal and external devaluation faced by deficit countries (on this conundrum, implying for members of EMU also the possibility of an exit from it; see EEAG, 2013, Chapter

2). Some degree of wage and price control (i.e., an appropriately designed wage accord policy) or a deregulated labor market behaving as assumed in the NK model would have been necessary to avoid the need for stabilizing fiscal policy, as in Germany (Carlin, 2013). However, many would regard this as incompatible with a free-market economy. Common and strong regional policy together with industrial policy would have facilitated a growth of peripheral economies "sounder" and higher than that actually achieved, but would have required a more significant EU budget.

However, these policies were countered as an excessive expansion of "big" government contrary to the spirit of the Union and, for most countries, a surrender to the EU of the last effective policy instruments over which they had sovereignty. Thus, absence of a common and active government in the monetary union and persistence of a collection of diversified economic systems go a long way toward explaining the real imbalances that emerged. In addition, fiscal imbalances arose or increased as an effect of a generally deflationary environment and policies.

The asset price booms deriving from capital inflows in peripheral countries partially moderated the effects of this deflationary environment. They lasted or were not reduced up to 2007. This can at least partially explain why policymakers did not implement long-term policies for addressing imbalances in these countries, in particular gaps with the core countries in terms of productivity dynamics. The system of signals for local policymakers that had been implemented at a European level was an imperfect one, i.e., it did not make the signals of a possible crisis apparent to the agents involved, with the doctrine tending to justify absence of correcting interventions by national governments (Chapter 7).

Not only common or coordinated actions directed at overcoming structural differences and imbalances were (and are) absent from the EMU institutional setup. In addition, common agreed-on policies of a passive nature, such as the limitations to fiscal policy deriving from the SGP and the fiscal compact, have been introduced that have a negative impact on such differences and the ability of countries to overcome them. In fact, they constrained national governments in their reforms in a number of ways (references in Girardi, Paesani, 2008; Albonico et al., 2016[4]). It is true that fiscal policy constraints might tend to stimulate shortsighted governments to introduce reforms, as Buti et al. (2007) hold. However, reforms can be implemented only under some circumstances, e.g., availability of information by the constituency and proper working of the political process. In addition, such constraints are only a second-best substitute for proper common policies of the kind mentioned earlier (Girardi, Paesani, 2008) and can backfire on other countries, essentially those that have based their growth strategy on exports to other EMU countries. One can thus explain why Germany also suffered from the crisis, not only in 2009, but also later. The EMU institutions were a kind of straightjacket for implementing reforms by national policymakers, as they imposed constraints not only on monetary action, but also on fiscal deficits. As a result, in order to comply with such rules in times of crisis, as most of the current expenditures are difficult to cut in the short run, the only choice left was to reduce public investment expenditures, which lowered potential output.

6.4.2 The Role of Institutions in the Management of the Crisis

Mismanagement of policy instruments on both sides of the Atlantic is undeniable, as said. However, this has to do with current policies more than institutions. Insofar as the specific role of institutions as a factor constraining policy interventions is concerned, a parallel with the United States can again be useful. In this country, one can find few limitations on the side of institutions in a short- to medium-run perspective, as the Fed has no conservative mission and a fiscal union exists. However, also in

---

[4] Albonico et al. (2016) claim that simple recovery would not be sufficient to restore the relative income level that GIIPS had achieved before 2007, if they do not engage in long-ranging reforms, in particular with reference to the factors influencing productivity. In Italy, timid signs of an improved prospect in the productivity dynamics, due to the recent redesign of industrial policy, are found by Bugamelli et al. (2018).

this country some limits to an expansionary fiscal policy have derived from the ceiling on the absolute amount of debt, which President Obama found difficult to raise at least in two instances, in 2012 and 2013. The ceiling has limited the possibility of prolonging the fiscal expansionary stance, which made the discretionary impulse of the federal budget (moderately) negative or of an uncertain sign. It has its roots in the different visions dividing American society about the public agenda between a conservative and a liberal attitude, which could have a negative impact in a longer-run perspective. Even more important than the existence of a debt ceiling could be in the medium run the bubble-creating effect of unconventional monetary operations.

As to Europe, even more stringent limits to fiscal action derive from the SGP and the fiscal compact. EMU institutions have not only nourished the crisis, but heavily constrained current policies, making them unable to combat the crisis or even to reduce its effects. After the first signs of the transformation of the private debt crisis into a public debt one, the SGP – i.e., again, a passive rather than active fiscal policy – contributed too to the accumulation of public debt in most GIIPS countries and the ensuing speculative operations that aggravated it, soon after the first signs of the public debt crisis. A limited, but timely, intervention by a federal government such as in the United States would have avoided precipitating the financial position of those countries. Moreover, the fiscal compact has further limited expansionary fiscal action, as it requires compulsory debt reduction. Only the deep pockets of the ECB (and the IMF) avoided a significant increase in deficit and debt in Germany. However, the fiscal policies required from peripheral countries, deriving from absence of a common (and expansionary) fiscal policy – and confirmed by the core countries' attitude during the crisis – have overburdened the deficit and debt of the whole euro-area (EA).[5]

---

[5] On this, see also Mody (2015). A rather negative assessment of the assistance programs to the GIIPS countries is instead in Pisani-Ferry et al. (2013). In particular, these authors criticize the institutional defects of the EMU institutions and the action of the EU Commission and the ECB involved in these programs. Such defects lay behind the features of the intervention and the conflicts of interests that opposed the various subjects devising the programs.

In addition to formal institutions and specific policies, we should finally mention the value judgments underlying them, as these have certainly concurred to the actual attitudes of European policymakers vis-à-vis the crisis. Relying on punishment, especially by markets, in order to reduce moral hazard and to secure compliance to the rules, has been at the heart of the interventions to cope with the public debt crisis and the route actually followed for fixing EMU institutions, in particular for stiffening the mechanism of the SGP and imposing "bail-in."[6] The latter can even further aggravate it: in fact, bondholders will run for cover every time they fear the likelihood of a default, with the possibility of activating a self-fulfilling mechanism of illiquidity and crisis.[7] According to Messori and Micossi (2018: 2), "The (in)famous Deauville announcement by Merkel and Sarkozy in October 2010 that private sector participation in the losses on sovereigns would become a permanent component of the new crisis management procedures, prompted a run by investors that toppled Ireland and Portugal and spread contagion to Spain, Italy and even France." A system of stick and carrot together with restructuring of debt of countries like Greece would have been more effective, opening the door for a softening of the austerity program (De Grauwe, 2011a, 2015, 2016b; De Grauwe, Ji, 2013b). Another value judgment underlying the management of the crisis has certainly been that debt is equivalent to guilt, and not only that public deficits and debt should be avoided, but also that the burden of adjusting current account imbalances should be left mainly on

---

[6]   This requires that restructuring in banks that face difficulties should be borne by the creditors and the shareholders of banks, thus avoiding a government "bail-out."

[7]   De Grauwe (2011b, 2015a) explains self-fulfilling expectations as due to the bad design of the EZ institutions, notably absence of the central bank power as a lender of last resort for sovereign debt. This is also indicated as the typical cause of fragility of the EZ, differently from what happened in the EMS, where fragility derived from absence of a lender of last resort in the foreign exchange markets (De Grauwe, Ji, 2014). Tamborini (2015) presents a model showing that multiple equilibria arise when investors have no direct information and form heterogeneous rational beliefs about the government solvency. These can force government to default, even when the initial solvency conditions are satisfied. Passamani et al. (2015) explain the vicious circle between hard austerity plans in peripheral countries and rising default risk premia in terms of self-fulfilling beliefs.

"debtor" countries. This, together with the different bargaining power of deficit and surplus countries and vested interests, can easily explain in particular the asymmetric MIP.

Briefly, responsibility for the crisis in the EMU is thus largely attributable to the unsuitable institutions for an area too heterogeneous in terms of economic growth and inflation, in addition to the different orientations and interests among member countries. An area without a federal government and whose only common policy is that of a conservative central bank can face shocks of the kind and size that have hit Europe only at the cost of depression. The difficulty of facing the crisis in such an area had been recognized at an early stage of the crisis by the then president of the ECB himself. In fact, he said, "we must remain mindful that the EZ consists of 16 sovereign states. It is not a fully-fledged political union or a fiscal federation, within a unified government bond market" (Trichet, 2010). From an abstract point of view, at least the policies to tame the crisis should look for new institutions. This is not an easy task, however. Changing the institutions could be also in the interest of surplus countries, but only if one does not consider the value judgments we have referred to earlier.

Passing to the difficulties of managing a crisis where interest rates have hit the ZLB, one must consider that new issues arise in this case, as shocks, such as cost-push ones, driving "inflation and output in opposite directions when the interest rate is free to react can instead induce a fall in both variables at the ZLB. In addition, the combination of the ZLB with the debt-deflation channel amplifies the contractionary effects on economic activity" (Neri, Notarpietro, 2014: 12). Hence, the absolute need arises of driving the EZ economy out of the ZLB and the deflationary trap. To this effect fiscal policies and unconventional monetary policy are needed be needed (Neri, Notarpietro, 2015).

6.4.3   Faults in the Institutional Design

The faults in the institutional architecture of the EMU can be summarized as follows:

i. The institutional setup tends to be deflationary and incomplete.

ii. It is defective, due to the lack of proper mechanisms. In particular, reequilibrating institutional mechanisms are lacking, as they are entrusted to markets, which lack proper signals and are often highly imperfect. This is especially so for the markets that should primarily ensure readjustment of imbalances of a currency union in the absence of a fiscal union, i.e., labor markets; these are highly segmented between countries and convey the influence of different national rules. Differences in real interest rates and free capital movements across countries have also contributed to issuing wrong signals for national policymakers about the true state of the economy.

iii. Reequilibrating mechanisms of the kind operating even in the Gold Standard (where temporary and limited devaluations or revaluations were possible) are absent (Mills, 2015). For the reasons given under (i) and (ii),. these cannot be substituted by imperfect and segmented markets.

iv. In some cases, the existing rules have constrained the action of EMU bodies (this is the case of the ECB, because of its conservative nature) and countries (as for the SGP, the fiscal compact and the asymmetric MIP) in their policies both before and during the crisis ("a sin of commission"). In some others, they have not done so, as for structural and current account imbalances or financial regulation ("a sin of omission").

v. The policies adopted by EMU bodies seem to be guided and constrained not only by the inadequate institutional architecture, but also by the visions and interests of the dominant countries. Think of the risks related to the carry trade of German banks after mid-2008, when spreads began first to rise in a sensible way, and also of the strategy followed by Germany to tackle the Greek crisis, which could be interpreted as conveying the influence of the ties between the German government, banks, and nonfinancial enterprises, which form a true "vertically integrated industry" in that country.

In the following sub-section, we deal with the first issue more in depth. In Chapter 7, we will investigate the following four issues. In Chapter 3, we have deepened the study of the theoretical foundations of EMU institutions and the reasons why they tend to impress them a deflationary bias. Chapter 3 has also hinted at the practical interests for supporting those theories and complementing them.

6.4.4 The Deflationary Bias

This bias can be inferred from what we have said before about the ECB, the SGP, the fiscal compact, and, most importantly, the MIP (e.g., Marani, Altavilla, 2001; Acocella, 2011; Stockhammer, Sotiropoulos, 2014).

The target and nature of the ECB have already been dealt with at length in this book. Also its actual policy has been investigated to some extent, but other notations are in order. Overall, it acted well, consistently with its main target, i.e., preservation of both an inflation-free and deflation-free environment, even if the struggle against deflation faced strong opposition inside the Bank. In fact, monetary stability has been its overriding goal and the Bank interpreted this role very strictly (Bibow, 2006)[8] up to the crisis and even later for some years. From a point of view, in the first years of its existence, this conduct can be understood by reflecting on the need of the new bank to create a reputation which could not have derived only from the inheritance from the Bundesbank, its statutory goals, and Otmar Issing's (formerly chief economist at the Bundesbank, who took over the same position at the ECB until 2006) orthodoxy. As said, pending the crisis in 2011 it even overvalued the risks of inflation, moving back to an unjustified deflationary stance. In addition, only lately and with the fierce opposition of the Bundesbank, it faced the financial and sovereign crisis by means of the same unconventional monetary policies used elsewhere, years after the Fed and other central banks. Finally, the ECB has tended not to support national governments directly during the crisis (Gabor, 2014). This can be understood to a large extent, since direct aid to governments would have generated even deeper conflicts within its governing bodies, as shown by the opposition to the more limited help offered by QE. In addition, it might have violated the Bank's statute, leading to removal of the violators or even to legal procedures

---

[8] Bibow even contests that the ECB's design could be indicated as true inflation targeting, propending for the one of monetary targeting. However, the ECB has made it clear that it is a "medium term" inflation targeting similar to that of the Reserve Bank of New Zealand (Castelnuovo et al., 2003: 50).

against them. The true problem lies in the constraints imposed by the ECB mission, often resembling that of "a driver who is quick at slamming the brakes, but notoriously abstains from using the accelerator" (Bibow, 2006: 13).

In addition to the effects of a monetary policy that tends to be contractionary, fiscal policy also confirms this tendency, as we have underlined a number of times.

Finally, the existence of untackled asymmetries between different countries that nourished foreign imbalances, while moderating the deflationary environment in peripheral countries before the crisis (but issuing wrong signals on the state of their economies), translated into a very powerful deflationary bias, due to debt deleveraging after the crisis, as is well known since I. Fisher and Keynes (Fisher, 1933; Keynes, 1936). The mechanism is well illustrated by various authors such as Eggertsson, Krugman (2012), and Campos et al. (2018). A consumer or a firm that must reduce their debt will reduce consumption and/or sell assets. Increased saving will reduce demand, production, and incomes. Sale of assets will lower their prices, creating new insolvencies and the need for deleveraging. Both actions will frustrate the private sector's attempt to reduce its debt in a deflationary spiral, unless the public sector counteracts them by increasing its consumption and taking over private debt.

The deflationary rebalancing mechanism imposed on peripheral countries – practically negating or limiting the expansionary role of the public sector in these countries – could have been avoided indirectly, had core countries expanded their public budgets or raised their wages. The cost of not following this option has been very high. By using a Keynesian model, Stockhammer and Sotiropoulos (2014) estimate it to be as high as 47 percent of the peripheral countries' GDP, if they wanted to eliminate their current account deficits. Fitoussi and Laurent (2009) show that imposing deflationary macroeconomic policies has reduced both efficiency and equity in the EA. In particular, weakening the European social model, as an effect of these policies, has further reduced the ability to face the financial crisis, by limiting the action of automatic stabilizers. In addition, by imposing structural reforms directed at cutting wages and restricting public budgets, the solutions have tended, on the one hand, to cure (some) symptoms of the crisis, not its roots; in fact, imbalances within the EZ depend on both the contractionary demand and wage policies pursued by surplus economies and the structural inefficiencies of peripheral countries, reflecting specifically in their lower productivity growth. On the other side, imposition of supply-side reforms in some cases aggravated the crisis, as at a certain point this was due to lack of demand. In the short-medium run, the structural reforms advocated by the EMU for peripheral countries, i.e., increasing liberalization in the labor and product markets, can aggravate the crisis, as they act on the side of supply, and not only do they not support demand, but reduce it, thus adding to the issues of the interest rate stuck at its ZLB level (Eggertsson, Mehrotra, 2014;[9] Eggertsson et al., 2016).[10] These policies would also lower potential output (Campos et al., 2018). By contrast, only by boosting demand can some structural reforms be effective (De Grauwe, 2014a).

The risk envisaged by Gregory and Weiserbs (1998: 48) before the start of the Union about the "potential deflationary bias that the Maastricht criteria are likely to impose throughout the EU" has thus materialized. This bias has also caused a tendency to secular

---

[9]   They point out that one can easily understand that, in terms of the AD-AS apparatus, by considering that when the ZLB binds, higher inflation stimulates demand through lower real interest rates and then the aggregate demand curve becomes upward-sloping.

[10] It must be said that even if Lamo (2017) found a positive impact in Europe of a country's labor reform on its performance during the financial crisis, the IMF had found a large negative effect of reforms of the employment protection legislation (EPL) and unemployment benefits when implemented in a slump, even if they retain their positive effect in good times. Other labor market reforms, such as lower labor tax wedges and increased public spending on active labor market policies, have positive effects also in the short run, possibly because of their fiscal stimulus. Finally, product market reforms have instead a positive effect in the short term (IMF, 2016). For similar considerations, see OECD (2016). Blanchard and Giavazzi (2003) had already warned that the product market reforms should precede labor market reforms. Roeger et al. (2019) find that labor market reforms may be suboptimal in terms of distributional effects when there are rigidities in goods markets.

stagnation, resembling the situation that emerged in the 1930s as a consequence of the deflationary policies enacted by European countries trying to stay on the gold standard (De Grauwe, 2015b). In addition, implementation of the fiscal compact not only does not offer a solution to the problem of finding the appropriate budgetary-monetary policy mix in EMU – a problem already well identified in the Delors report – but may under certain circumstances contribute to increasing the conflict between various European institutions (Mortensen, 2013).

At this point, the roots of the deflationary bias of the EMU institutions and policies must be discussed. These are indeed numerous. One important factor is the preeminent role of Germany and its meme against inflation. Also the role of wrong theories predicating expansionary austerity, low fiscal multipliers, and the like must be stressed. Finally, the importance of vested interests, first in nourishing growth of the financial sector, then in influencing the action of the ECB, and finally in choosing policy solutions for the financial crisis and in particular the issue of Greek public deficit and deficit[11] (also Chapter 3).

6.5   NEW TENDENCIES AND OBSTACLES

In 2014–17 new tendencies – however contradicted by the 2018–19 slowdown of the largest countries – seem to have emerged in the EA. First, there has been a recovery that has affected the GDP growth of the main countries (although to a variable degree), and in some cases has been even more noticeable in some peripheral countries, such as Spain. For the first years since 2009 the process of GDP fall in Greece has stopped. Also employment has increased and unemployment has lowered in all major countries. These new tendencies are mainly the fruit of the expansionary monetary policy, as fiscal policy has instead remained – at best – neutral overall. Second, as a Janus face of the

[11]   Some of these notations are in Blyth (2013).

recovery, deflation has turned into inflation, partly pushed up in 2016 also by oil prices.

However, initiatives for strengthening EMU cohesion and decisional process are lacking, as a division still weighs between the countries (especially peripheral countries) that would like a larger sharing of macroeconomic risks and those (core countries) aiming to maintain a prudential conduct and to ensure compliance of the others, in particular in terms of sovereign debt. As an effect of this, the process of hardening the banking union is incomplete.

7 Asymmetries, Imbalances, Signals, and Incentives to Change

Both the founding fathers of the Union and the literature before the creation of the EMU as well as the Maastricht Treaty practically delegated most of the burden for integration, alignment, reforms, etc. to private institutions (markets), in a practical vacuum of other common institutions, except for the common currency and specific limitations to national action in the fiscal field, initially, through the SGP. The common currency and the common monetary policy can be conceived as a tie to the action of private and public agents, not only because of the constraint imposed by the single currency (the external constraint), but also for the conservative orientation of the ECB. Many economists and politicians saw this institutional architecture as imposing a strong network of ties in particular on the conduct of the agents in the countries with higher inefficiencies, which should – almost naturally – have compelled them to change their conduct and enact the needed reforms.

A number of theoretical considerations and catchphrases were advanced in practically all peripheral countries (Featherstone, 2001) to explain the virtues of these external ties and their capability to foster the necessary changes of conduct by local public and private agents. In particular, the role of the EMS, first, and the EMU, later, in imposing the necessary changes was asserted in various forms. These were: the "tying one's hands" or "scapegoat" mechanism (Giavazzi, Pagano, 1988; Begg, 2002),[1] the *"vincolo esterno"* or "external empowerment"

---

[1] The reason for the effectiveness of a fixed-exchange-rate agreement lays in the fact that operators recognize that this penalizes excess inflation and thus reduces "the public's

(Banca d'Italia, 1954;[2] Carli, 1993: 406; Dyson, Featherstone, 1999), and the "there is no alternative" (TINA) (Bean, 1998) or the "back against the wall" (Alesina et al., 2006) theses. Giving up the possibility of exchange rate variations would introduce an external constraint favoring virtuous conduct of both public and private agents in high-inflation countries. Governments of these countries would tie their (inflationary) hands by committing to a fixed exchange rate with lower-inflation countries (Sibert, 1999) and the ability of politicians to use macroeconomic policy for partisan or electoral gain would be limited (Berhnard, Leblang, 1999). Thus, monetary policy would credibly be delegated to an external entity and private agents would no longer expect their government to inflate the economy, thus acting consistently. Because of that, they would adjust their conduct and rely on instruments other than higher wages or markups to pursue their revenue or profit targets.[3] More generally, as Featherstone (2001)

mistrust of the authorities" (Giavazzi, Pagano, 1988: 1055). This is indeed an application of the time inconsistency argument: inconsistency of ex post monetary conduct with ex ante promises is then avoided. As Schelkle (2006: 677–8) points out, this argument, originally motivating participation in the EMS, was transposed to the EMU, with some notable (but contradictory, also in their effects) changes.

[2] The initial notion of *vincolo esterno* is due to the then Governor of the Bank of Italy, Donato Menichella, who introduced it in his annual report at the meeting of the Bank of Italy shareholders, in May 1954, as recalled by Gualtieri (2009). In Italy, the *vincolo esterno* argument was rather diffuse, beginning with participation in the EMS. An independent external monetary authority – or a tie, such as the EMS – could enhance separation of Italy's central bank from the government and make use of the "whip" available to monetary authorities. The passage to a common currency could make markets and foreign competition work better, ensure efficiency, and make the external constraints capable in due time of forcing politicians, businessmen, and trade unions to more efficient conduct (Dyson, Featherstone, 1999).

[3] However, a note of caution was offered by Ozkan et al. (2000). Previously, a similar caution was expressed by Walters (1990) with reference to the EMS. According to Walters's critique, the EMS tended to be dynamically unstable after capital controls were lifted. In fact, with freedom of capital movements and different inflation rates in the various countries, in the absence of expected exchange rate changes, arbitrage would reduce to zero the differentials of nominal interest rates, thus causing further divergence of inflation rates and pressure on exchange rates, finally leading to their changes. Even if it must be recognized that institutional ties were certainly more stringent and credible in the EMU, with respect to the EMS, this critique was too easily dismissed by Emerson et al. (1992) and Miller and Sutherland (1993), who argued that in a world with agents having rational expectations (REs) the monetary constraint would be internalized, thus preventing pressures for a real exchange rate appreciation.

pointed out, the argument of the external tie has been used differently within different institutional settings, as a strategic lever for reform and a stimulus to shift norms and beliefs affecting policy in both higher- and lower-inflation countries. Legitimization of reforms at the local level was thus largely devolved upon the EMU institutions, including the operation of markets.

However, this was a largely faulty argument. In fact, further political economy contributions have criticized various aspects of it. According to Schelkle (2006),[4] reneging on the promise of price stability cannot be solved by introducing additional costs or multiple veto players as reneging would still be in the government's hands. In addition, as Cukierman (1992) and Keefer and Stasavage (2002) underlined, the idea that this process can be governed by controlling growth of money supply is simplistic, since this instrument would be impaired as an effect of Goodhart's law (Goodhart, 1975; Chrystal, Mizen, 2001). Related to this is the notation that the possible positive effects on financial markets, through lower inflation expectations, do not transfer to labor markets, as to some extent lower interest rates make rising public expenditure easier (Giavazzi, Spaventa, 1990; Schelkle, 2006). The evidence in favor of the *vincolo esterno* is puzzling, as some studies would seem to support its effectiveness, whereas others do not.

As McNamara (1998) and Featherstone (2004) put it, the argument and the option of the *vincolo esterno* were indeed the fruit of a consensus among *élites* for redefining the role of the state.[5] Penetration among most sections of the population lagged or lacked altogether. Alternatively, the leverage from the external constraint argument was used by domestic groups in a variety of ways, mainly according to whether the norms and values to the EMU institutions were "internalized" by the different countries or simply accepted for instrumental reasons (Featherstone, 2004). We can also add that the consensus was fragile in many cases, each of the various sections of

4   See also Forder (1996), Lohmann (2000, 2003).
5   On this role of *élites*, see also Willett (2000).

the *élites* hoping to shift the burden of adjustment onto others. The consensus and reliance on the virtues of markets, the common currency, and the SGP deprived national governments' policies of much content or reduced their effective range of action. Moreover, the argument of the *vincolo esterno* convinced public opinion that everything was about to be settled, automatically, simply as an effect of participating in the Union. Public opinion did not really put much emphasis on the need for structural reforms and behavioral changes. The nature of the adjustment needed – with the possible exception of reducing the public debt – and the possibility of being exposed to shocks and crises were not clear to people and to policymakers. A similar effect of reducing the expectations of the need of adjustment at the national (or higher) level derived from the consideration that much of the necessary (or the whole) convergence of the higher-inflation countries had been obtained as an effect of complying with the Maastricht rules for admission. Admission was thus considered by many as the final act in the series of painful measures to be adopted by these countries. Further, in the first years of the Union, comparisons with the poor state of Germany tended to confirm this orientation and induced optimism.

On Europe's action relied even those who were conscious of the necessity of reforms and did not trust national governments or private agents for their will and ability to undertake such reforms somehow. However, as said, the EMU and other existing common institutions were not empowered with most of the necessary tools. This left enough room for dominant groups to further their interests.

Bean (1998) presented a rather balanced view of economic and political considerations favoring or being an obstacle to structural reforms at a national level. His *economic* arguments in favor seem to prevail over those against. The former include: notably, the TINA argument (or a variant of it); more importantly, the incentive to make the local environment more attractive for business; the increase in decentralized labor bargaining. The factors that were an obstacle to reforms were mainly the lower incentive for reforms in a monetary union, which derives from the fact that benefits of reforms in a country have spillover effects abroad. This was relevant from the point of view of time inconsistency and the absence of incentives to introduce rules for debt consolidation. Overall, the arguments sustaining *political* feasibility of reforms did not prevail. A decisive reason that was an obstacle to reforms was existence of short-run costs that these would impose on a rather wide group of people. Opposition to this policy could be easily overcome in a growing environment, but this was difficult to obtain at the Union level, as reforms were prevailingly an issue for a subset of countries and were not considered to be a common issue.

Begg (2002) too presented a balanced view and advocated participation of social partners in the process of reform, to avoid disruptive results. Participation was seen as necessary, since if guidelines were issued by "Brussels" which called for unpopular or controversial reforms, they risked being seen as unacceptable (Chassard, 2001). Nevertheless, the EU could be used also as a scapegoat in pushing through unpopular measures in order to circumvent lack of domestic support (Begg, 2002). A risk was that different levels of governance had roles that should be complementary, but in practice could be subject to competitive overlapping, originating confusion (the "too many cooks" syndrome), rather than leading to the ideal cooperation of the kind suggested by Wessels (1997). This is indeed necessary for establishing a single currency system. In particular, heterogeneity of employment and employment policies in the EMU called for the clarification of a model toward which change should be directed as well as of the agents that would push toward it at the various levels. In this sense too, see Begg (2002).

A mild version of the *vincolo esterno* is that coordination within the EMU is based on the principle of "horses for courses": each agent is tailored for a specific job. If everyone sticks to his duty, that creates trust and harmony, leading to positive outcomes (Ardy et al., 2005). In this respect, recent reflections by Heinemann and Grigoriadis on the way to make the expectations and conduct of different agents consistent with planned action can be useful. They say:

> A theory of reform resistance is severely flawed if it is simply based on the view of reform-resistance driven by narrow self-interest. The micro-evidence, in particular, underlines the role of considerations of (procedural) fairness. Voters need a minimum of confidence into their democratic institutions in order to accept the uncertainties involved in far-reaching institutional change. Interestingly, trust in European institutions can to some extent be a substitute for trust in national institutions.
>
> *(Heinemann, Grigoriadis, 2013: 38)*

Trust in Europe was in effect high, and this could compensate for the lack of trust in national government in many EMU countries. However, Europe was not empowered with the exact kind of policy instruments needed to reform labor markets and business structure and conduct public administration.

In the next two sections, we deal with national policymakers' attitudes toward reforms in terms of constraints and incentives. In Section 7.4, the incentives offered by signals to both policymakers and private agents deriving from the working of markets in general or from the constraints existing in a monetary union issue are discussed. Section 7.5 deals with the possibility that absence of proper signals can be associated with moral hazard or adverse selection. The final section draws a balance of the failures due to markets or governments.

7.2 IS MONETARY AND FISCAL DISCIPLINE EFFECTIVE?

This topic raises a number of issues. Adoption of a regime of fiscal and monetary discipline would generate mixed effects on efficiency, according to Coricelli et al. (2006), Acemoglu et al. (2008), and others. A regime of discipline was enforced both on the way to the common currency (at least in the higher-inflation countries, for which fulfilling the Maastricht criteria was more problematic and required contractionary action) and afterward (as the ECB had to establish a reputation and the SGP was in effect).

Acemoglu et al. (2008) present a model where reforms of the kind advocated in other contexts by the Washington Consensus (basically, contractionary fiscal and monetary policy, reforms that are supposed to be efficiency-enhancing, such as market liberalization, privatization, etc.) can be detrimental.[6] In fact, in their opinion such reforms induce politicians to adopt other instruments for furthering their redistributive action, patronage, etc., thus originating a kind of "seesaw" effect. An issue that is linked to contractionary fiscal policies and a reduction of government involvement in the economy is that of the effects on efficiency of the size of the government sector. Da Costa et al. (2017) find that, "contrary to what some authors have found when considering a single objective, typically economic growth, there is no discernible bell-shaped curve, sometimes called Armey curve or BARS curve (Barro, Armey, Rahn, and Scully), when visually confronting each country's classification in terms of government performance and size." There may be a floor, instead, around 35 percent of the public expenditure/GDP ratio, below which the performance deteriorates. Alesina et al. (2010) underline the transparency and constraining effects of market liberalization and monetary and fiscal discipline, even if they recognize that there are reasons to say that adoption of the euro may hinder structural reforms. They conclude that disciplinary factors prevailed, possibly because policymakers exploited the novel setting to justify implementation of structural reforms. However, these prevail in product markets,

---

[6] A critique of the Washington Consensus is also in Serra and Stiglitz (2008). As to the effects of the privatization, in particular of public services, in the EU, the neoliberal policy began to fade from the end of the 1990s, after the shortcomings of private-sector provision – especially in terms of quality and employment conditions – became evident and the Treaty of Lisbon of 2007 recognized the essential role of public authorities, also in terms of their discretionary action "in providing, commissioning and organising services of general economic interest as closely as possible to the needs of the users" (Article 1 of The Treaty on Functioning of the European Union). Most recently, in peripheral countries this reappraisal of public enterprises showed a setback, as some of these had to be privatized in order to reduce public debt (Wollmann, 2014).

whereas they are limited in labor markets. According to Coricelli et al. (2006) and Dalmazzo (2014), a stricter monetary policy has positive effects on both inflation and unemployment, as it imposes a discipline on trade unions. However, Dalmazzo notes that "commitment to price-stability may allow governments to persist in 'bad' fiscal policies and tolerance for low competition," as governments can trade part of the social gains deriving from it for distortionary taxation, redistribution, patronage, and the like (Dalmazzo, 2014: 4). Thus, a more conservative central bank tends to bring about a higher tax rate, thus raising doubts on the desirability of this type of monetary authority claimed by Coricelli et al. (2006). In addition, monetary discipline reduces market deregulation. This result weakens the argument in favor of resorting to an external constraint under the form of a conservative central bank in order to reform countries characterized by lax fiscal policies and scarcely competitive goods and labor markets.

Some of these implications can be accepted, with reference to the possibility that contractionary policies may not be efficiency enhancing and can induce politicians to adopt other instruments for furthering their redistributive action. Others can be accepted only after careful analysis. Not only because they derive from models admitting no trade-off between inflation and unemployment (at least in the short run), but also because external discipline can have mixed effects on reforms. In fact, to some extent implementing contractionary policies requires pressure, but it is hard to have support for them, due to the costs imposed in the short run (OECD, 2009). In addition, they do not consider that between the transition period and the period after admission to the Union there are similarities and differences. Similarities refer to adoption of rather strict monetary and fiscal discipline in the two periods. Other features can instead justify apparently different behavior of public and private agents in each period, in particular due to absence of a perceived prize to gain in the short to medium term *after* admission. In fact, the conclusion derived from the models used by these authors does not fully take account of the different incentives of policymakers and private agents before and after admission to the EMU. In addition, the incentives to reforms can change according to the clarity of the signals perceived by agents. In the next two sections, we discuss precisely these issues. All in all, both before and after admission incentives tied to contractionary policies worked, but the incentives in the first period were certainly higher than in the second, as we show more extensively in the next section.

7.3 THE INCENTIVES

7.3.1 *Incentives during the Transition to the EMU and After*

Admission to the EMU of the various countries implied a number of effects, which reduced the incentives to a more efficient conduct of private and public agents, etc. Some effects pertain to adoption of a stricter regime of monetary and fiscal discipline imposing this type of conduct. As said before, incentives were certainly lower after admission to EMU. Thus, the periods before and after 1999 have different specific features and consequences, as we explain now.

In the former period, as said earlier, some mitigation of the effects of contractionary policies in favor of conduct tending to reduce inefficiencies derived from lower real interest rates, due to the disappearance of the country currency risk. However, the prospect of a prize certainly affected the conduct of some agents, notably the government, big firms, and trade unions (at least those institutions with some degree of centralization), which were conscious of the stricter relation between their conduct and the possibility to earn the "prize" attached to admission to the Union (on this, see IMF, 2004: 114 and Acocella et al., 2009).[7] More questionable is the likelihood of similar conduct by small- and medium-size enterprises, due to their likely free-rider attitude and lower attitude and limited ability to acquire and

---

[7] In particular, the incentive of a prize could temper Dalmazzo's (2014) argument of governments trading part of the social gains deriving from a reduced interest burden on public debt for distortionary taxation and the like.

process information. In addition, as noted by Lindbeck and Niepelt (2006), when the exchange rate still acted as a signal, the foreign exchange market performed the role of a watchdog on domestic fiscal policies, tied to the possible depreciation of the domestic currency ensuing adoption of inappropriate policies.

By contrast, after admission to the EMU, there was no apparent prospect of a future prize tied to restructuring and eliminating inefficiencies. Hence, incentives for different conduct were absent. Instead, the negative effects of contractionary policies on private and public budgets were alleviated or removed by some kind of soft budget constraint. Strictness of the regime in existence after admission to EMU can in fact be – and has been – questioned, as credit availability increased in peripheral countries. This is really an effect that began to loom – along with reduction in real interest rates in these countries – during the transition period. However, it could gain momentum only after some time and especially after the formal admission to the EMU of peripheral countries. In fact, these countries commonly perceived admission as a signal of having finally crossed the finish line. When the EMU began to operate, current account imbalances and the associated capital inflows to higher-inflation countries from abroad, mainly from Germany, raised credit ratings and availability, especially to private agents, and created bubbles in these countries. This soft budget constraint, coupled with absence of a (further) prize related to EMU participation, could then have reduced incentives to enact structural reforms in higher-inflation countries. In terms of Dalmazzo's model, this would correspond to an exogenous rise in the weight put on redistribution of rents. However, differently from his model, this rise in the weight would derive from disappearance of incentives to a more efficient conduct.

In addition to this, after admission (and thus disappearance of the exchange rate with other EMU countries), the reactions to fiscal policy choices in terms of prices were confined to the bond market. As said, those deriving from the effects of such choices on exchange rate market expectations no longer existed, thus lowering the incentives for "responsible" fiscal policies (Lindbeck, Niepelt, 2006). Existence of bubbles made the reduced signals feebler or even led to wrong signals.

Then, on top of an issue common to the previous period, i.e., contractionary monetary and fiscal policies, the second period implied different outcomes for both public and private agents, due to the different incentives. In addition, after the admission the influence of the changed budget constraint deriving from low real interest rates and credit availability induced optimistic or "distorted" beliefs and expectations of future prospects in peripheral countries. We deal with the implications on incentives of the softer budget constraint in the next subsection.

7.3.2 The Government Budget Constraints and Incentives in Practice

According to Baskaran and Hessami (2013), the EMU did not imply a harder budget constraint of the kind advocated by the supporters of the argument for an external tie induced by fixed exchange rates. Instead, in accordance with the literature since Wildasin (1997), they find empirical support for the idea that the EMU itself created a soft budget constraint. In their opinion, this would derive from the failure in 2003 of the European Council to sanction France and Germany, which – together with Portugal – had violated the SGP. According to them, this failure reduced public and private agents' incentives for reforms in other countries. This explanation is insufficient or misleading, as the effect would have acted only after that date.[8] The

---

[8]   Also other countries might have violated the SGP fiscal rules, without incurring formal infraction procedures. This was certainly so for Italy. This is one of the countries for which moral hazard could have arisen out of the decision not to sanction France and Germany. This very decision, indeed, might have derived also from the attitude of the Italian government in favor of these countries at the meeting where the decision was taken, which could have been due to the awareness of a looming excess deficit in Italy's budget. In the period 2001–6, this country overshot the upper boundary of 3 percent for government net borrowing and disregarded the rule of budget parity over the medium run (also Bassanetti et al., 2014). However, this only emerged in 2004–5 due to a revision of national accounts. Improper monitoring facilitated the violation. Eurostat's power to monitor national statistics has been strengthened only more recently (in particular, as

additional issue arising from it is why in the following years the soft budget constraint, first inaugurated by France and Germany, operated in other countries only (those with a higher inflation), which cannot be explained unless these countries could be pretty sure to be exempted from behaving in accordance with the Pact in a way similar to these two countries. This expectation, however, would have been unwarranted, as no other country enjoyed the same status and decision power as France and Germany. Nor would it explain why, after the violation of the SGP, Germany – and to some extent also France, which was exempted – not Portugal (which was fined), inaugurated "virtuous" conduct.

A different explanation would be that the signal of a soft budget constraint could have come from the way the EMU was conceived and worked since its first years of existence, as the bubbles generated in the peripheral countries by capital inflows gave the impression that everything was right there (Fernandez-Villaverde et al., 2013). These authors basically suggest two reasons for the existence of a soft budget constraint:

(i) The public decision process can be assimilated to a war of attrition (Alesina, Drazen, 1991); this implies that free capital movements and capital inflows, like aid, have the effect of delaying reforms (Casella, 1996) by relaxing budget constraints;

(ii) Independently of that, when there are bubbles and booms it is difficult for "principals" to extract good signals as to the future. Easy borrowing has the effect of raising the rate of growth in the short to medium run, while leading to low long-run growth, as it multiplies future engagements for wrong or low-productive investments, which waste resources. Among a number of implications, it causes: a variant of the Dutch disease leading to misallocation of resources away from the tradable sector; a deterioration in policy and institutions, which are induced to resort to debt and to postponement of reforms; diffusion of low-quality agents and

a consequence of the financial crisis), and, in any case, this is not an independent institution, but is designed to serve the European Commission.

principals and reduction in incentives of agents tilt political-economic equilibrium against reforms (for this, see Section 7.5).

In particular, the explanation based on moral hazard created by the decision of the European Council not to sanction France and Germany does not account for the interaction between the bubbles and policies in peripheral countries. Bubbles were at the root of the incentive to adopt loose policies, which were "justified" by the apparently good state of the economy. In fact, bubbles induced public and private agents to choose "soft" policies, i.e., they gave the politicians an incentive to raise deficits while inducing private agents to increase their leverage and not to increase the efficiency of their concerns. Credit availability – which, according to Lane and McQuade (2013), is positively correlated with net capital inflows – made it easier for the government and the private sector to borrow, thus reducing their incentive to adopt "sound" policies. Reduced interest rates in the period before entry to the EMU didn't have similar effects, especially on politicians, as their conduct should have been "virtuous," pending admission. In addition, capital outflows from core countries had not yet materialized. By contrast, Germany, as a country with very low inflation rates, exported capital abroad and suffered from a kind of hard budget constraint, also as an effect of the policies following unification with Eastern Lander.

Looking at figures for a period including both the years before admission and the following ones until eruption of the crisis in 2007–8, government debt (as a percentage of GDP) lowered and then increased for some higher-inflation countries (for Greece, it rose up to mid-1990s and stayed almost constant until 2007; for Portugal, it certainly rose after 2000). In other countries, the reduction lasted (but proceeded at a slower rate than in the period up to 2000) until 2004 (in Italy) or 2007 (in Ireland and Spain). More uniform in all higher-inflation countries was the growth performance, which on average was strong or very strong until 1999 or 2000, slightly lower after, up to the financial crisis.[9] By contrast, growth was rather high in Germany until 2001, which reflected also on a current account deficit until 2002–3, but drastically dropped afterward up to 2005. Thus, with the only exception of Greece (which had a high rate of growth), there was no boom in higher-inflation countries after their inception into the EMU, as claimed by EEAG (2011) and Fernandez-Villaverde et al. (2013). However, growth certainly proceeded at a rather high rate there, at least with respect to Germany: the soaring asset prices relaxed credit and budget constraints in high-inflation countries, even if this did not propel a boom, at least in comparison with the pre-EMU period, exception being made for Greece (Eurostat, database). This is likely to have generated some misperception or a false assessment of fundamentals, which was "corrected" only when the crisis erupted in Greece in the second half of 2009.[10] Some constraints deriving from the new institutions, such as monetary policy, which was contractionary at least until mid-2001, but to some extent also later, ruled out any possibility of a true boom. This would suggest an explanation of the evolution of policies and the performance of higher inflation countries based on the absence of proper signals for the need of a change. We deal with this in the next section.

7.4 INCENTIVES AND SIGNALS. WRONG OR NOISY SIGNALS OF IMBALANCES

After accession, relaxation of the external constraint and a rather high growth rate caused the important signals of the balance of payments and the exchange rate to be forgotten (Michie, 2000; Tornell, Velasco, 2000), without being replaced by some common institution like the MIP, which was introduced after the crisis. In due course, this should

---

[9] However, one must consider that in the early 2000s growth rates lowered in the whole EMU. This was the consequence not only of the contractionary effects of the common monetary policies and fiscal rules, but also of the slowing down of the growth rate in the United States, after the burst of the financial bubble created by the crisis of the "new economy" and the 2001 terroristic attack.

[10] Even with reference to Italy, where the bubble was not so large as in other GIIPS countries, higher assets contributed to the GDP increase.

have a negative influence on peripheral countries' policy. The balance of payments, the current account as well as some indicators of competitiveness could still be calculated, but were not used in current policy action and the conduct of private agents. The moderately high rate of growth was reassuring for policymakers. For private agents, loss of competitiveness and cuts in the shares of foreign markets were at least partially substituted by the domestic market, made possible to some extent by the looming bubble, again implying that information was mixed and signals of a loss of competitiveness were noisy or practically irrelevant. Finally, reliance on temporary jobs as well as on relocation abroad of some industrial production lines implied that many firms could cope also in this way with reduced demand abroad, the impossibility of resorting to nominal currency devaluation, inefficiencies and rents, without suffering a substantive loss in their total competiveness, at least in the short or medium run.

More generally, the ability of private and public agents to perceive the right market information and signals can be debated. From this point of view, we spot two sets of issues:

(a) Can markets disseminate enough information and issue the right signals to policymakers and private agents and, in the affirmative, under what conditions? Symmetrically, what are the difficulties of information processing and signal extraction in market economies?

There are a number of reasons underlying difficulties in extracting signals from prevailing trends in any market economy. Some refer to markets and political institutions in general. First, information and signals coming out of market trends can be noisy, depending on existence of multiple equilibria. In addition, even if there were a unique equilibrium, mention should be made of shortsightedness of people and policymakers, which is particularly acute in financial markets and certainly acted in the EMU. Capital markets are plagued by beauty contests and bubbles, a point we develop under (b) in the following text. Moreover, the procedure followed by public and private agents for extracting the right signals is imperfect, because they do not know the right model, as the theory often offers a variety of contrasting positions.[11] In the end, there might be a few people able to apply correct methods of information collection and processing as well as of signal extraction. Most private agents perceive information and signals and adapt their expectations mainly based on the specific market where they operate, being specifically interested in the evolution of this market, as either this is more pressing or interrelations between markets are difficult to assess. Their ability to perceive imbalances looming elsewhere and ultimately having a reflection also on their own market is often scanty. This is not an issue of information dissemination – information can be available at no cost – but only one of perception and processing ability.

(b) Apart from these considerations, do markets in a monetary union issue the right signals for the use of policymakers and private agents or, at least, did the EZ markets release them before the crisis erupted? In case they do not or do that only conditionally, can other signaling systems and institutions help in correcting markets in a union in their informative and signaling role?

As for the signals existing in a currency union and their effectiveness, duration of current account imbalances depends not only on the extension of imperfections in the product markets and the size of imbalances, but also on the degree of wage flexibility and labor mobility. Labor markets are often characterized by more rigidities and tend to react to signals with a longer delay and in a different way, according to the specific characteristics of the various countries. Correctness and effectiveness of signals coming from current account imbalances imply the ability of markets – and even more of policymakers – to foresee both the size of imbalances and the strength of reequilibrating forces in action, including the lasting possibility to compensate them

---

[11]   This is obviously true also for choosing the best model for economic policy design. However, the ability to process the available information, including that on the economic interrelations provided by a suitable model, is higher for policymakers.

with capital movements, with no possible interruptions or reversals. Here, the point raised under (a) becomes even more relevant.[12]

Up to 2005 at least, the general conviction that the transition period had cleared all previous asymmetries and imbalances and the forces in action would avoid their reappearance derived, as said, to some extent also from the difficulties met by Germany (Wyplosz, 2006). This was commonly perceived as the best performer in the EMU and has always been a benchmark for countries like Italy, for some common features of their productive structure and for the efficiency of its private and public agents. This conviction was strengthened by mispricing of country risks, which is common for financial markets – partly due to the system of payments of fees to the rating agencies, but deriving also from this perception of a catching up in action between the periphery and the core.[13]

As to the possibility to find suitable institutions (and policies) for fixing the defective information and signaling capacity of markets in a monetary union, policy issues can be complicated by the different speed of adjustment between the different markets. In the case of the EZ, the common currency – in a situation of different country characteristics and mispricing of country risks – soon led to capital movements that compounded the effects of the absence of signals, nourishing bubbles and confusing them. Careful analysis of the composition of the balance of payments between the two accounts could have indicated existing or looming imbalances, but the policymakers

---

[12]   Blanchard and Giavazzi (2002: 186) tended to neglect the existence of an external constraint, as any imbalance in the current account would be cleared by free movements of capital, and concluded that, "although benign neglect may not be optimal, it appears to be a reasonable course of action." A few other authors held that this would imply too much flexibility, but could result in "enormous future burdens of adjustment" (Jones, 2003: 219).

[13]   With reference to the financial crisis, Pagano and Volpin (2010) indicate the determinants of mispricing. More generally, see Levich et al. (2002) and Schuck (2014).

    In the development of the crisis in Europe, rating agencies played an important role, propelled by an unfortunate decision of the ECB, which laid the ground for the role they played later, by subjecting to a minimum credit-rating threshold the eligibility of all assets, including government bonds, as collateral for the ECB financing (Orphanides, 2018).

often did not correctly interpret them and did not react in the right direction or with the right policies or acted only with some delay. In any case, even a correct interpretation of the existing mixed signals could not play the compulsory role that the balance of payments constraint has in a deficit country with independent monetary policy, as a mechanism to enforce adjustment policies. In addition to free capital movements, in the first years after 2007 other institutions could have implied some kind of incentive to accumulating imbalances. We refer to the TARGET2 payment system, where all the imbalances constitute claims or liabilities on or to the Eurosystem, with a deferred regulation.[14] Later, when the crisis erupted violently, TARGET2 imbalances were misinterpreted and country risks were overvalued.

Free capital movements were the immediate source of wrong signals. One could ask whether a monetary union can be conceived without completely free capital mobility. Possibly, it could not, but in this case specific common policies should be added to substitute for the signaling defects and to cope with the kind of asymmetric shock built in the EMU institutions (Krugman, 2013). A reform in this direction would have avoided imbalances in different areas or prevented their degeneration into a crisis.

There are many alternative ways to cope with excessive capital inflows and current account imbalances. Excessive net capital inflows can be regulated by proper direct control or taxes or, at least, by

---

[14] The alternatives suggested, such as that advocated by Sinn (2011) and Sinn and Wollmershäeuser (2011, 2012), are against this solution as these authors claim that accumulation of TARGET2 imbalances should be limited, by imposing their annual accommodation. This position comes from a "flow" interpretation of TARGET2 imbalances, as deriving from the current account, whereas Whelan (2011), Buiter et al. (2011), ECB (2011), and others maintain that their source lies in a capital reversal. Evidence for that is offered by the increases in TARGET imbalances arising after 2015, due to massive buying by the Italian and Spanish nonfinancial sector of shares, bonds, and mutual investment funds of institutions situated in Germany, Luxembourg, and the Netherlands. Hristov et al. (2018) use a counterfactual analysis and derive the conclusion that the system has contributed in a substantial manner to avoid deeper recessions in peripheral countries, while depressing to a smaller degree aggregate economic activity in core countries. On the controversy and for more references, see also Moro (2016).

financial regulation, in particular of banks. As to direct policy instruments, there are two different considerations especially addressed to their use: one is theoretical; the other is practical. As to the former, in the words of EEAG, "such proposals [are] naive and dangerous, because, by attempting to mimic through controls the outcome of market discipline, they are bound to confuse symptoms with causes and direct the attention to policy tools that are entirely inappropriate as remedies against long-term structural deficiencies of market economies" (EEAG, 2011: 82). The latter has to do with the Union's institutional architecture, which rules out capital controls and emphasizes market self-adjustment, practically banning other forms of common policy intervention. Both these considerations can be debated. As to the former, it is true that causes rather than pure symptoms should be removed. However, this requires time, as the causes are difficult to tackle and remedies need time to be implemented and to produce desired effects, the more so when this must be done unilaterally at the country level, in the absence of suitable common labor and industrial policies and in a deflationary environment. Arguments against the position expressed by the EEAG also derive from the critiques of the theoretical foundations of EMU institutions and the need to reform them (Chapter 8). As to the practical issue deriving from the use of direct controls, the recent creation of a banking union and introduction of macroprudential regulation can be considered as steps toward more (qualified) regulations and controls over financial flows. This shows that introducing some kind of direct control is possible within the EMU institutional design. However, some plans must still be implemented, as, e.g., in the case of the European bank deposit insurance (Chapters 2 and 8). Plans for common guidelines for labor markets are still to emerge.

In case of a current account imbalance due to competitiveness, wages should be lowered or raised according to the nature of the imbalance, also by means of incomes policies. Structural policies, in particular industrial policies, should try to remove the underlying determinants of the lack of competitiveness. Imbalances in the current account not due to competitiveness should be faced by symmetric policies for boosting or contracting aggregate demand.

7.5 MORAL HAZARD AND ADVERSE SELECTION OF POLICYMAKERS

7.5.1 Signals and Moral Hazard

Absence of a proper system of information and signals, if coupled with asymmetric information and conduct by an agent that is detrimental to the principal, implies moral hazard or adverse selection.[15] This does not seem to have occurred, except in some cases, whose analysis can offer additional interesting perspectives for understanding the implications of EMU institutions.

Let us refer to the different markets where moral hazard might have played a role. The main markets are those for goods, labor, and financial assets. There is no immediate way of devising some kind of asymmetric information relevant for our issues in the first two markets. However, institutional changes can act on the incentives usually existing in those markets. Take the case of the Hartz reforms in Germany: the situation of hard budget constraint existing there for the reasons already indicated induced the government to enact a series of reforms related to the labor market that according to many scholars had a positive impact on the workers' incentive to accept a job and possibly also to change the terms of wage bargaining.[16] A similar (and

---

[15] As is well known, moral hazard arises when the agent, who does not take the full consequences and responsibilities of his actions, has an incentive to act to his benefit, also by exercising less careful effort than he otherwise would, leaving the principal to bear some negative consequence of his actions. Asymmetric information protects him, as wrong or distorted signals cause the principal to find it costly monitoring the agent and to think that the outcome achieved by the agent is due to external circumstances. Adverse selection takes place when, due to asymmetric information, it is difficult to separate, with reference to our case, "bad" from "good" politicians – i.e., politicians incompetent or acting in their own interest or promising appealing, but unsound, policies – from those able or truly acting in the public interest, even if they promise tough policies.

[16] This is only an example. Institutions – and also their effective reforms – are very specific to each country: reforms similar to those enacted in Germany might not have been effective in other countries, especially if these lacked other German

even more manifest) kind of moral hazard could have interested financial operators and the governments, but, most likely, only after the onset of the crisis, when some kind of guarantees were expected under certain contingencies. As to the effects of the labor reforms, however, Bofinger (2017) shows that unemployment in Germany since 2005 reduced mainly due not only to cyclical factors but also to the petering out of the negative effects on employment that had been caused by the consequences of German unification.

7.5.2 Bubbles, Entry of Politicians, and Adverse Selection

Bubbles can act not only on incentives of agents in general, but also on adverse selection of politicians and other agents. Putting issues of partisanship aside, adverse selection is likely to occur because by necessity the program of future policy declared by each candidate before the election is always incomplete, cannot foresee possible shocks, and may not correspond to his real intentions and future choices. Thus, the orientation of a politician can only be inferred from his action, if and when in charge as a policymaker. This was especially important after admission of countries to the EMU. In fact, after 1999 the process of restructuring the economy of "peripheral" countries had still to be completed, but there was a prospect of continuing relatively high growth rates and gaining benefits from participation to the EMU without further reform. Then people were more inclined to opt for candidates – even the less able and/or those having a special interest in taking office – promising some relaxation of the restrictive policy experienced until then (Le Borgne, Lockwood, 2002). Some promises of a softer budget constraint to the core constituency were appealing while appearing credible, which could have positively influenced the probability of a poll success or political survival of a ruling government or a challenger (Robinson, Torvik, 2009).

Let us suppose, as an example, that all the assumptions for the validity of the median voter model hold. Each constituent will vote

institutions – in particular, the substantial powers of works councils at the workplace – to act as complements.

according to his preferences, under the constraint of his current and prospective budget. Let us assume also that current incomes have all been reduced by contractionary policies, which should be continued in the near future. Two parties offer different prospects for their policies: one, A, promises to continue the present contractionary policy; the other, B, promises to reduce taxes just as a way to prevail in the entry stage of the political process. The latter will be chosen, as the alternative prospect is no longer tied to the promise of a benefit like that of entering the EMU, an event thought to be fruitful of future gains. Whether this theoretical conclusion corresponds to stylized facts in "peripheral" countries is a matter of empirical inquiry, since not only does the median voter model have a number of limitations, but also different specific circumstances can operate in each country that cause nonpopulist politicians to prevail.

In addition to the issue of separating bad from good politicians, another problem arises whose relevance grows with asymmetric information: empowerment of some social classes or groups. The EMU introduced a system of beliefs and incentives (what Knill and Lehmkuhl, 1999, called framing integration – see Chapter 2). These were effective in peripheral countries before their admission to the Union. But their effectiveness was ephemeral, as they did not permeate public and private agents in a way to affect their conduct in the new institution, as people did not understand its implications. Failure of this kind of policy is also due, in a symmetric way, to the limited extent of positive integration policies. These policies should have been attributed a larger role, whereas negative integration policies prevailed in practice. Confidence in the action of limited positive integration, which was simply conceived as a complement to negative and framing integration (through the operation of free markets and the single currency as well as a change in beliefs and expectations due to the *vincolo esterno*), was too optimistic and destined to failure. This was probably due to the fact that a change in beliefs and expectations was "tied to the pattern of political development and state tradition; the compatibility of appropriate policy beliefs; support for 'Europe';

the record of economic discipline; and the will and capability of actors to engineer compliance" (Featherstone, 2004: 247).

7.6 IMBALANCES, MARKET AND GOVERNMENT FAILURES

The relative role of market and government failures must be recalled in this summary. As we have seen before, both kinds of failures were involved in nourishing the factors of the crisis that finally sprouted in the EZ as well as in the way this was tackled. Government failures were present first with respect to the way the Union was designed (pointing at an almost exclusive role of markets and the single currency). The original design of the EMU was flawed, since it did not consider the fragility of a monetary union in the absence of a common fiscal policy (and with limits to national fiscal action) and a banking union (Lane, 2012). This can explain the different performance of the economy with the United States, with respect, first, to the imbalances that were nourished between the various countries (having no correspondence with those among the various US states) and, then, to the absence of a federal state intervention to tame the crisis. Moreover, government failures derive from the way country governments tolerated the bubbles nourished by capital inflows and did not properly regulate markets (not to speak of misreporting of the state of public finance in Greece) and in the way the EZ authorities dealt with the financial crisis.[17]

Market failures consisted in the accumulation of financial imbalances and liability positions by banks and nonfinancial firms as well as improper conduct of investors before the crisis and after its

---

[17]   It is astonishing how policymakers, at the EU or the national level, took their tasks lightly. Pisani-Ferry (2013: 8) is very clear on this: "When drawing on the literature, European policymakers too often practised selective reading, with worries dismissed and the optimistic interpretation prevailing. There was, for example, too much confidence that EMU could develop into an OCA. Perhaps inevitably, selection criteria were set in nominal rather than real terms, thus making entry feasible also for countries with weaker fundamentals. Post-entry, however, and less inevitably, there was no mechanism (and, more importantly, little willingness) to ensure real convergence."

inception, when market forces produced a progressive destabilization of the EZ. In the former case, not only did debtors overcharge their financial exposure, but also creditors lent money without properly assessing the risks involved. In the latter case, the sudden reversal of the direction of capital flows caused external diseconomies and the crisis of sovereign debt. This is the reason why one can doubt the validity of those analyses saying that in progress of time, most (indeed, 65 percent) country-specific output shocks were smoothed by higher financial integration (as well as introduction of the EFSF and ESM), against only 40 percent at the beginning of the EZ (Cimadomo et al., 2018a). This integration could have smoothed some shocks, but has certainly produced others, in particular the extension of the financial crisis.

Thus, market failures were no less relevant than government failures and the two interacted in the origin and the evolution of the crisis. This implies that the position taken by a group of German experts (Feld et al., 2016a), insisting only on government failures, seems unbalanced vis à vis the more balanced position expressed by a majority of experts in their "consensus view" (Rebooting Consensus Authors, 2015; see also Bofinger, 2016b).

PART III Lines of Reform of EMU Institutions

8 How to Reform the EU and the EMU: Broad Outlines

The Great Recession has shown the invalidity of policies advocated for a long time by pro-market mainstream economics and international organizations as well as the fragility of European institutions, highlighted by an incomplete currency union, inflation as the primary goal, and unemployment less of a priority than it used to be.

The financial crisis has also shown that industrialized countries are not immune from contagion and that in the end international imbalances can have high costs for all countries. Moreover, regional agreements, such as the EMU, do not isolate countries from shocks, but, on the contrary, may exacerbate them if they are not ruled by appropriate institutions and policies.

The Great Recession, with its negative economic and political consequences, could be an incentive to change, but will not necessarily ensure strengthening the EMU governance in order to remove the negative institutional features.[1] In fact, the Recession has added to the factors determining the general crisis of the project that sustains the Monetary Union: "A worsening legitimacy problem, dysfunctional institutions, the limits of collective leadership and, not least, a decision-making system still largely based on the principle of 'one-decision-fits-all'" (Majone, 2014a: 211).

---

[1] Nordvig (2014: XV) has noted that European policymakers have let imbalances accumulate, "not recognizing the euro's weaknesses before it was too late. European policy makers have finally woken up to the reality, but they are still playing defense."

> In sum, both history and logic tell us that there are different possible modes of European integration. The depth of the present crisis strongly suggests that the approach followed since the 1957 Rome Treaty has reached, if not overstepped, its limits. Only a political culture of total optimism could induce European leaders to confuse process with actual results. What is needed today is more modesty, greater realism and, especially, clearly defined and popularly supported goals.
>
> *(Majone, 2015: 14)*

This is in clear contrast with the current situation, where "the EZ is ... in a halfway house – too afraid to move forwards to further integration where necessary, and not able to move back towards purely national policies lest the euro fail. ... The European project has been increasingly associated with crisis and austerity rather than with opportunities and growth" (Beck, 2017: 22–3).

The line of reasoning of this chapter is as follows: after having sketched in the next section achievements and shortcomings of the Union, we deal first with theoretical advances that entail the obsolescence of the EMU institutions and policies as well as the need for reforming them (Sections 8.3–8.6). Three sections follow that indicate some possible meta-objectives of reforms (Sections 8.7–8.8) and a new division of tasks between the different levels of European institutions (Section 8.9). Specific suggestions on new macro- and microeconomic policies – or amendments to existing ones – are deferred, respectively, to Chapters 9 and 10. Chapter 11 concludes with a few considerations about the prospect of a breakup of the EZ and the need to establish a really democratic Union.

8.2 WHAT HAS WORKED IN THE EMU, AND WHAT HAS NOT?

A number of lessons can be drawn from the experience so far about the Union's performance. Noneconomic benefits in terms of avoiding conflicts between the various countries must be accounted as a possible relevant benefit of the Union.[2] However, the deterioration of intercountry relations as an effect of its erroneous design and the way the financial crisis has been faced can be of detriment for their long-run development. The recent roots of rising populism and localism – a trend certainly not specific to Europe that is due to various factors, among which is neoliberalism – in the EZ derive also from the excessive austerity and the double-dip recession, which certainly led people to seek liberation from "euro shackles" (De Grauwe, Ji, 2013c)[3] or from "the Germans" (Michailidou, 2017). Eichenberg and Dalton (2007) had noticed a contrast between the pre- and post-Maastricht periods. In the latter, support for EMU and the EU dropped as a direct consequence of the austerity imposed by the institutions chosen as well as, possibly, of the pressure to harmonize or integrate countries' social security programs.[4] Guiso et al. (2016: 247) find a loss of confidence in the EU since 1992, even if "in spite of the worst recession in recent history, the Europeans still support the common currency. Europe seems trapped: there is no desire to go backward, no interest in going forward, but it is economically unsustainable to stay still."[5] However, this may be due simply to the high and uncertain costs of withdrawal.[6] The situation seems to disprove Jean Monnet's claim according to which a "chain-reaction" effect would have operated: a crisis would have triggered a jump forward to

---

[2] One must, however, consider that land grabbing by wars in developed countries may have lost its appeal, because there are other ways to pursue dominance, economic – such as foreign direct investment, export penetration, and the like – or political – such as a hegemonic role in regional or other international organizations, which can be instituted rightly for the purpose of controlling other countries' actions.

[3] More recently, the shocking impact of the wave of immigration has added to the demand for closing national borders and to populism.

[4] As to the negative impact of the crisis on the citizens' support for Europe, see also Braun and Tausendpfund (2014).

[5] This echoes Beck's notation mentioned in the previous section. As to the current support for the euro, see Hobolt and Wratil (2015) and CEPS (2019).

[6] Willett (1994, 2000) and Feldstein (1997) clearly anticipated this possible shortcoming of the EMU. Even if not pertaining strictly to the focus of this book, which is on the Monetary Union, the Great Recession has had a negative influence on the unity of the EU as a whole, as shown by the result to leave the Union of the referendum of June 2016 in the United Kingdom.

more integration.[7] Spolaore (2013) suggests reasons that can make Monnet's prophecy seem overoptimistic. Also optimistic has proved to be Habermas's (2012) prediction of a mobilization of citizens and development of democratic debate at the EU level (Baglioni, Hurrelmann, 2015).

On the side of the economic limits of the European construction, the issues are indeed numerous. Here we organize them for discussion by referring to a short- and a long-run aspect, not excluding the possibility that some issues pertain to both.

In relation to the former, two specific issues should be dealt with: the ways to prevent the next economic crisis in the EMU; the ways to cope with it, if it takes place. For both, desirable and realistic solutions should be compared. Both have to do with the design of European institutions (a long-term issue), in addition to the effects of the policies necessary for facing the crisis. As for the long run, the central issue is: Why has the EZ grown less than other countries or regions, even before the recent crisis?

Both the short- and the long-run issues are tied to the imbalances arising in a monetary union with pronounced asymmetries that have been studied at length in the previous chapters and absence of proper institutions to tackle them. In terms of the long-term performance, asymmetries allowed for uneven growth and nourished these imbalances, which generated or enhanced the conditions for an export-led economy growing in some countries, to the detriment of other member countries, in a generally deflationary environment. This, in turn, led to asymmetric shocks, as an effect of the financial crisis. In fact, Pasimeni (2014) argues that asymmetric shocks can be intrinsic to a monetary union characterized by structural divergences, which happens in the absence of a banking union and a mechanism for restructuring unsustainable debts, with a central bank that does not perform the role of a lender of last resort for sovereign institutions.

---

[7]   Guiso et al. (2016: 247) recall Monnet's "prophecy": "L'Europe se fera dans les crises et elle sera la somme des solutions apportées à ces crises." [Europe will be forged in crises, and will be the sum of the solutions adopted for those crises.] – Monnet (1976).

Conceptually, according to Rossi (2017), this runs counter to the idea of a currency union. Practically, it abolishes automatic and nonautomatic stabilizers. It leaves governments exposed to financial speculation, which leads to sovereign risk premiums and self-fulfilling crisis and debt overhang, thus making it impossible for national states to provide stabilization (Frenkel, 2012; De Grauwe, Ji, 2013b).

The recent crisis has alerted at least part of the public opinion in the EZ to the need to amend its institutional design.[8] As to this design, the need to balance rules-based policymaking with some discretion – when implemented – has turned out to be highly politicized, to the advantage of the most powerful countries (Feld, 2016), as shown by the experience of the decision to absolve France and Germany for their violation of the SGP in 2003–4. There is indeed a "German problem" in the design and management of the EZ, which largely derives from the crude version of ordoliberalism adopted especially by the Bundesbank, and the public at large in order to protect Germany's narrow interests (Wyplosz, 2017b, and the literature cited therein).

A kind of inconsistency has emerged rather clearly as a consequence of the crisis, implying the necessity to adjust: the final goals of the EZ institutions (in particular with respect to the concept of fairness inspiring them and the cooperative or noncooperative strategies to implement); the type of architecture governing the Union and the relations between the upper and the state level; macro- and microeconomic policies to make use of.

The path followed until now in the relevant political institutions has pointed to a direction almost opposite to a discussion of the soundness of the EMU institutional architecture, as shown by a few examples. First, the focus of the European Parliament until 2019 has not been on the institutional design, as this issue has often been mixed

---

[8]   This can be derived indirectly from the fact that, as Bastasin (2015: 5–6) says: "Throughout the crisis, national governments have acted as if their states were or had to become self-sufficient, live within their own means, and stand on their own two feet. [This goal] became the cornerstone of crisis management and of the European system of economic governance that later emerged."

with, or substituted by, that of national policies. Thus, the issue of prompting further integration has not been on the main agenda and a tendency has emerged "towards 'nationalizing' different policy options about the crisis management and the reform of the European institutions" (Farina, Tamborini, 2015: 16–17). In addition, the reform package suggested in recent years by the EU Commission led to the fiscal compact – almost a transposition of Germany's "debt brake" (*Schuldenbremse*) – and to an asymmetric MIP.

The diagnosis underlying the former is wrong, since public deficits and debts were not a determinant of the crisis, as said before. Instead, insisting on debt consolidation has at least negative short-run effects. Focus has been on the spending rather than the revenue side, also because this can avoid discussion of the issue of tax competition, which has not been addressed until recently. No special allowance is made in country budgets for those public expenditures that tend to raise potential output most, i.e., investment expenditures, which, as we have said, can be cut more easily, as the experience has shown, both in the phase of admission to the Union and after the fiscal compact.

As to external macro imbalances, the asymmetric constraint set for their value has been justified on the ground that deficits are worse than surpluses, which also implies that the burden for adjustment should be on deficit countries more than on surplus countries.[9] Certainly, both surpluses and deficits are the effect of a different price and demand dynamics in the various countries (a consequence of the existing asymmetries), but to cope with this the Macroeconomic Dialogue could be strengthened and expanded to help coordinate adjustments of nominal wage and price trends (Watt, 2010) as well as aggregate demand by surplus countries. According to Blanchard and Milesi-Ferretti (2012), these countries should be obliged to expand their economies and reduce their surplus. This would be not so much on the grounds of a repeated-game argument,

---

[9]   In addition, it is not even respected, as in practice current account surpluses go beyond the limit set by the MIP.

according to which a similar rule could also benefit them in the future. In fact, this argument appears less credible to those in the surplus countries who firmly believe in their ability to continue along the current path. Instead, the argument that running a current account surplus derives from beggar-thy-neighbor strategies appears more credible. At a more pragmatic level, expansion of their domestic demand and wages could be beneficial for growth not only to the rest of the world, but also to countries with a current account surplus, as expansion abroad would translate to some extent into higher demand for their goods. Especially so, we could add, if other countries could retaliate in some way. More generally, coordination of national macroeconomic policies should be improved, as required by the Maastricht Treaty (Blanchard et al., 2015).

8.3 RIP VAN WINKLE AND THE REBUTTAL OF THE THEORETICAL CONVICTIONS OF THE 1970S AND 1980S

Many economists and observers[10] warned about the fragility or the limits of the EMU project. Their number decreased as the Union proceeded and seemed to gain success. However, the theoretical bases of the project soon revealed their weakness. More than a decade ago, Alan Blinder claimed that "a sharp revision of the naively optimistic views (about the capacity of economic policy to control the economy) held by some economists circa 1966 was called for. But ... the pendulum may have swung just a bit too far" (Blinder, 2004: 26), producing similar naively optimistic views about the virtues of markets and asking for restraining government action.

[10] Eichengreen and Frieden (1994) offer an overview. For the practical absence of anticyclical policies and the limitation of the European budget, see Buiter et al. (1993). On the perverse incentives created by the Maastricht Treaty, leading to self-realizing speculative attacks, see Eichengreen and Wyplosz (1993). On the issue of coordination between monetary and fiscal policy, see also the largely or partly critical contributions by Bryson (1994), Dixit, Lambertini (2001), and Onorante (2006). For the position taken by US economists, before and after creation of the EMU, see Jonung and Drea (2009). On the compromises between different positions leading to the Treaty, see Bini Smaghi et al. (1994).

Blinder's words are even more relevant nowadays as economic theory has further questioned the system of analytical conclusions and beliefs that had emerged in the twenty years or so after 1966, a system that, however, still retains some assumptions that led to the propositions featuring that credo. Three decades later, Rip van Winkle's[11] faith in the credo would again be crowded out by the analytical developments (and some empirical findings) that intervened in these years. Think of:

- The limitations reemerged in the functioning of markets, especially capital markets, with specific reference to: herd behavior; realization of conditions subject to which freedom of capital movements and the mechanism of risk sharing can be justified (Cooper, 1999[12]);
- The limited practical relevance of the surprise effect, recognized by Lucas (1996: 679) himself;
- The disproval of the Lucas critique, e.g., with reference to changes in structural parameters as a consequence of a change in policy rules;[13]

---

[11]　Rip van Winkle is the character created by Washington Irvin and evoked by Gordon (1976). After sleeping for twenty years, he woke up in the republican America and made a terrible "environmental" mistake, by declaring himself a devoted subject of King George III.

[12]　Two aspects of this market failure should be underlined here. First, as Cooper – a convinced advocate of free market – warns, the basic justification for freedom of capital movements, i.e., their ability to ensure efficient allocation of resources, is subject to some conditions. Among them are: equal tax treatment of capital across countries, adequate information available to investors to avoid herd behavior (including the possibility of a sudden reversal of capital movements, as a consequence of a shock, new information, or simply a change in sentiment), existence of well-regulated capital markets. In addition, as said, the mechanism of risk sharing that would avoid asymmetric shocks refers to gross capital movements, in the absence of large imbalances, whereas also sizable net capital flows emerged. The evolution of the crisis in the Eurozone has shown that both reservations are founded (Chapter 6). These conclusions are strengthened by Williamson (1999), who adds that capital mobility can act as a "wrecking ball," à la Soros, against not only weaker countries, but also those countries whose fundamentals are in order. On similar grounds, see also Stráský and Claveres (2019). Evidence has been found of a massive increase in resource misallocation due to credit boom before the financial crisis, which was not lowered in the following phase of deleveraging (Banerjee, Coricelli, 2017).

[13]　Dreger and Wolters (2016) have shown the persistence of the EMU money demand function, even in case of a change in the monetary policy rule (in particular, a policy tending to keep interest rates at the ZLB, which could break down the function). This ensures that the evolution of M3 is kept in line with money demand.

- The irrelevance of many critiques of the "classical" theory of economic policy (in particular, to Tinbergen's "golden rule" about controlling the economy) based on REs (Blinder, 1998: 8; Acocella et al., 2013[14]);
- The theoretical and practical limits to time inconsistency – when policymakers have enough instruments – and thus to related prescriptions of the monetary and fiscal policy rules that should replace discretionary action (Blinder, 1998: 56; Acocella et al., 2013: ch.11);
- Existence of a long-run nonvertical Phillips curve (Hughes Hallett, 2000; Graham, Snower, 2008; Benigno, Ricci, 2011; Acocella et al., 2013);
- The need for a more active fiscal policy and regulation (especially of financial markets and institutions) once some unrealistic assumptions of current models are ruled out;[15]
- Critique by Posen (1994) and Hayo (1998) of the arguments put forward by Rogoff (1985) (and Bade, Parkin, 1978, before him) in favor of political independence of central banks;[16]
- Suboptimality of a conservative central bank in a monetary union with active trade unions, but benefits from fiscal coordination when a conservative central bank operates (Acocella et al., 2007a, 2007b);
- Critique of the Friedman rule and need for an inflation target well above zero (Di Bartolomeo et al., 2015) when due account is taken of the difference

---

[14] Public action can indeed be facilitated by REs. In what circumstances this can happen depends on the number of targets and that of the instruments available to the government and the private sector. With REs the government having a sufficient number of instruments available can overcome the Lucas critique. When the policymaker does not have a sufficient number of instruments available, he can make use of appropriate announcements of future policies (e.g., to exercise FG, for which see Woodford, 2007, 2008; Williams, 2011) and exploit REs in order to pursue his targets in a shorter period of time (Acocella et al., 2013; Hughes Hallett, Acocella, 2018, 2019).

[15] We refer to the assumptions leading to full intertemporal consumption smoothing – such as perfect foresight or REs, infinitely living agents, absence of liquidity constraints, etc. – and limiting the effectiveness of fiscal policy. As to the possible negative impact on real activity of imperfections in financial markets, see Bernanke and Gertler (1989, 1990), Greenwald and Stiglitz (1988, 1990, 1993), Kiyotaki and Moore (1997, 2002), Bernanke et al. (1999), and a lot more recent contributions.

Europe and the United States have slowly moved to introduce tough regulation in this field. Remarkable is the new position of the IMF, which now advocates exceptional (even if limited) direct controls of capital movements, reversing the *pro* free-market position adopted in the previous forty years (IMF, 2012).

[16] These authors highlight that both political independence and inflation are the outcome of structural, economic, and social factors that cause the central bank statutes to have no impact on inflation.

between the effects of public transfers and public consumption on consumer behavior;

– Empirical findings suggesting that: (1) reputation effects of tying one's hand through fixed exchange rates can be rather limited, whereas credibility depends on country policies and "fundamentals" (Gibson, 2003); however, in the case of Greece, credibility soon emerged as a result of its participation in the EMU and the anti-inflationary attitude of the ECB (with spreads significantly below those that would be predicted by fundamentals), whereas after May 2010 actual spreads have exceeded those predicted by some 400 basis points; this casts doubts on the ability of financial markets to make correct forecasts according to fundamentals and to be "wardens" of a proper policy conduct; (2) countries that adopt inflation targeting have not attained better monetary policy performance relative to a control group of highly successful noninflation targeters (Mishkin, Schmidt-Hebbel, 2007);

– Recent analytical developments about the validity of the OCA impinging on the overall foundations of European institutions. We have already said that the EMU, as such, does not respect the prescriptions of this theory. Whether or not the Union designers were conscious of this, some policies (mainly in terms of prescriptions to the national policymakers) have been implemented based on marginal adaptation of labor and product markets to the conditions prescribed for the existence of an OCA.

We will be selective and illustrate only some of these developments in the next sections.

8.4 THE NEED FOR REVISITING THE INFLATION TARGET

With specific reference to the optimality of the Friedman rule and thus to the very foundations of the ECB statute, consider a standard NK macromodel characterized by price stickiness (calling for zero inflation), augmented with transaction costs (calling for deflation, according to the Friedman rule) and tax distortions to finance public consumption expenditures set at 20 percent of GDP (calling for positive inflation according to Phelps's argument). In this model the optimal inflation rate is negative, but close to zero. Increases in public expenditures lead to significant increases in optimal inflation only for implausibly high levels of public spending (Schmitt-Grohé, Uribe, 2004). The rising labor supply increases the tax base and makes an increase in the distortionary tax rate unnecessary. However, if public transfers are also considered in addition to public consumption expenditures, conclusions change. Increasing these on the top of the 20 percent public consumption expenditures (the baseline calibration) pushes optimal inflation remarkably up. With the same ratio of public consumption to GDP (20 percent), but for values of public transfers to GDP of 10–15 percent, an inflation target between 2 percent and 4 percent (rather than price stability) becomes optimal, as shown in Figure. 8.1. In this figure the inflation rates and the amount of public expenditures are indicated, respectively, on the vertical and horizontal axis. Along the abscissa SGU stands for Schmitt-Grohé and Uribe. The reason is simply that transfers have a different impact on tax and inflation revenues, and there are thus different incentives for using taxes or inflation to finance them. In fact, as long as public expenditures increase, private consumption declines and labor supply increases, which raises the tax base and then also taxes, reducing the incentive to use inflation as a tax or to increase in the distortionary tax rate. By contrast, transfers have no impact on overall consumption and labor supply and thus do not favor ordinary tax financing of public expenditure vis-à-vis an inflation tax (Di Bartolomeo et al., 2015).

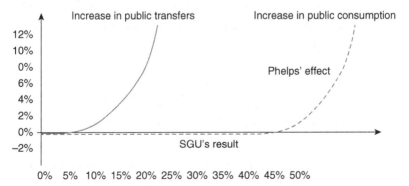

FIGURE 8.1 Optimal inflation rates with public transfers or public consumption (Source: Di Bartolomeo et al., 2015)

8.5   FISCAL MULTIPLIERS, CONSOLIDATION, AND EUROPEAN INSTITUTIONS

8.5.1   The Issue of Multipliers and Fiscal Policy

The initial fiscal institutional setup of the EMU assumed ineffectiveness or low effectiveness of fiscal policy. This had an influence on the management of the sovereign crisis.[17] More recently, the fiscal compact has followed the same route and this has certainly hindered recovery from the crisis and negatively affected reduction of the public debt. This section deals with the issue of multipliers. We defer to Section 9.3 discussion of the consequences of prescribing fiscal consolidation by contractionary policies.

Doubts with respect to some tenets of the assertion of very low spending and tax multipliers were first raised by Blanchard and Perotti (2002), who gave a substantially Keynesian answer to the issue of the effects of the tax increases and expenditure cuts needed for consolidation. In fact, they found that the former have a contractionary effect, while the latter are expansionary, thus disproving the doctrine of expansionary austerity. The authors did not engage in a discussion about expansionary debt consolidation strategies, but, accepting their arguments, one could hardly assert that a policy of expenditure reductions and (to a lesser extent) of tax increases, while certainly contributing to the reduction of the numerator of the debt/GDP ratio, would give an impulse to the denominator. Instead, their findings *might* support a Keynesian-type attitude of debt consolidation not based on a budget contraction, at least in so far as the direct effects on income are concerned.

Again, of specific relevance are some analyses that take account of open economies (in some cases, the EMU) and spillover effects. In order to quantify these effects, Coenen and Wieland (2002) constructed a small macroeconometric model of the United States, the EZ, and Japan. They found that international spillovers of domestic

---

[17]   Think of the conditions imposed on countries in need of financial assistance by the EMU and the IMF.

shocks turn out to be rather small when exchange rates are flexible and short-term interest rates are set according to policy rules that focus on stabilizing domestic variables. Beetsma et al. (2006) combined a panel VAR model in government spending, net taxes, and GDP with a panel trade model. They found that on average a public spending increase (tax reduction) equal to 1 percent of GDP implies 2.3 percent (0.6 percent) more foreign imports over the first two years. If Germany initiates such a budget change, the effect on the GDP of its trading partners is 0.23 percent (0.06 percent) over the first two years. These figures are likely to indicate lower bounds for the effects that will actually occur. Beetsma et al. (2008) found that a 1 percent public spending increase produces a 1.2 percent output rise on impact and a 1.6 percent peak response of output. In addition, rising imports and falling exports together produce an impact fall in the trade balance as a ratio of GDP of 0.5 percent and a peak fall of 0.8 percent. The public budget moves into a deficit of 0.7 percent of GDP on impact. Similar results are in Beetsma and Giuliodori's (2011)[18] estimation of the multiplier of government purchases on income in open European economies, which is higher than 1 on average in the short to medium run. The public and trade balance deteriorate. Existence of leakages strengthens the rationale for a concerted fiscal expansion between European countries and, by contrast, implies that decisions to introduce fiscal discipline – either independently decided by a country or imposed by some common rule – have cumulative negative effects that may impair reaching the target of a reduction in the debt/GDP ratio throughout the Union.

Recent analyses have shown that the value of multipliers is strictly dependent on the time of reference of the effects as well as on the state of the economy. A rather complete and detailed empirical analysis of the effects of fiscal consolidation is in International Monetary Fund (2010: 113), which takes account of numerous aspects of the effects of fiscal consolidation policies: in particular, their timing

---

[18]   This paper also offers a good review of the results of existing empirical tests.

(i.e., whether they are short or long term), the monetary policy stance, and the expansionary or contractionary nature of budget policies of other countries. Its conclusion is that, first, "the idea that fiscal austerity triggers faster growth in the short term finds little support in the data. Fiscal retrenchment typically has contractionary short-term effects on economic activity, with lower output and higher unemployment . . ., (but) fiscal consolidation is likely to be beneficial over the long-term." In addition, fiscal consolidation is likely to have more negative short-term effects if interest rates are near zero (as monetary policy has little room for partially accommodating its deflationary effects), the lower the likelihood of a currency depreciation and the less expansionary are the policies of other countries, which gives little scope for raising net export.

Of a similar nature is the result of more recent theoretical and empirical research. Some authors point out that smoother fiscal consolidations are more successful than stiffer ones (Batini et al., 2012). Other studies stress the efficacy of expansionary fiscal policy in severely depressed economies when central banks do not offset its effects (DeLong, Summers, 2012; Blanchard, Leigh, 2013). More generally, fiscal multipliers are shown to be asymmetric and regime-dependent, "being stronger in recessions than in expansions, in particular in presence of financial market stress, so that contractionary effects can become very severe when fiscal consolidations are pursued" (Semmler, Semmler, 2013: 2). This can be the effect either of some economies being locked in a bad equilibrium (De Grauwe, 2011a) or of macroeconomic non-linearities (Semmler, Semmler, 2013).[19] This result is confirmed by the analysis of seven structural dynamic stochastic general equilibrium (DSGE) models used for policy action as well as two academic DSGE models (Coenen et al., 2012). With specific reference to the ZLB constraint, Denes et al. (2013)

---

[19]   A new component of the value of multipliers has been added recently. In fact, Ercolani, Valle, and Azevedo (2018) consider a model where there can be substitutability between private and public consumption. This could lower the value of multipliers, even at the ZLB.

suggest that both cutting government spending and increasing sales taxes can increase the budget deficit at zero interest rates according to a standard NK model, calibrated with Bayesian methods. Thus, again, the effects of fiscal policy are highly dependent on the policy regime. However, a permanent fiscal stimulus implies lower values of the initial multipliers and a negative impact on income in the long run. Finally, Papadimitriou et al. (2013) find a multiplier of 2.5, capable of explaining the failure of the "Troika" expansionary contraction prescriptions for Greece – now recognized first by the IMF and then also by the European Commission and the ECB – and the deflationary bias of European institutions. However, Corsetti et al. (2013) show that, with a sovereign risk premium due to high debt, fiscal multipliers tend to be lower than during normal times or even to be negative in extreme scenarios.

8.5.2 *Institutions and Policies in Time of Crisis: Short- and Long-run Effects of Fiscal Consolidation*

As said, the low value of multipliers in open economies strengthens the rationale behind a fiscal expansion concerted among European countries. By contrast, it implies that decisions to introduce fiscal discipline – either decentralized or imposed by some common rule such as the SGP – have cumulative negative effects that may impair reaching the target of a reduction in the deficit and debt/GDP ratios, at least in the short run. By paraphrasing Auerbach and Gorodnichenko (2012: 17), coordinated "fiscal activism may be more valuable than previously thought."

In addition, the foundations of the SGP (and of the fiscal compact) are weakened when reconsidering the issue of the relationship between fiscal and monetary action in the Union in the light of progress in theoretical findings, adding to, and confirming, the practical failures of the EMU institutions and policies to face the crisis.

Variability and regime-dependency of multipliers make it necessary to distinguish between the different possible aims of fiscal action. If the aim is that of expanding the economy, a *short-run* multiplier larger than one is enough to suggest the need for an expansionary fiscal action. This should have no negative effect on the deficit- and debt-to-GDP ratios, *in the short run* at least. On the contrary, the effect on these should be positive. Thus, the "new" conventional wisdom of an expansionary fiscal consolidation (the doctrine of expansionary austerity) that inspired a number of policy attitudes and interventions in the last couple of decades, from Japan in 1996 to the EMU more recently, has been disproved. In the words of H. Rey, "the austerity policies put in place to deal with the crisis are self-defeating. More fiscal austerity, and especially the generalized, front-loaded fiscal austerity undertaken in a number of the peripheral countries, means weaker economies and possibly increases rather than decreases in debt-to-GDP ratios" (Rey, 2012: 221). Bénassy-Quéré et al. (2016) hold that fiscal adjustments during a crisis (in particular, those requiring fiscal consolidation) are self-defeating and restructuring of public debt requires proper reforms of the banking sector and strengthening of the ESM. In addition, in the short run, fiscal consolidations in one country have negative spillover effects, in addition to the negative impact on the GDP of that country. A fiscal consolidation of the order of 1 percent of GDP in ten EZ countries can reduce the combined output by 0.6 percent (Poghosyan, 2017), out of which half is driven by indirect effects from fiscal spillovers.

However, a high value of short-run multipliers does not guarantee that the effect of fiscal expansion is positive also in the long run. In this context, a necessary and sufficient condition for an expansionary fiscal action to lead to a reduced debt/GDP ratio in the long run is that the long-run multiplier is higher than the inverse of this ratio (Cozzi, 2013; Nuti, 2013). This is especially good news for highly indebted countries, as this condition widens the range of the values of multipliers that make for expansionary fiscal policy to reduce the debt/GDP ratio. For a country such as Italy, a value higher than 0.7 would be enough to suggest a fiscal expansionary action as an instrument of fiscal "consolidation." In any case, one must be sure that the multiplier considered is a *long-run*, not a short-run, one.[20] This condition may not be satisfied for Italy and – changing what needs to be changed – for other European countries as well. In such a case, a two-stage exit strategy could be followed within the EMU. In the first stage, a coordinated fiscal stimulus could raise the Union's GDP and alleviate the negative effects of the crisis. As the positive effects of the stimulus tend to fade away, a phase of smooth consolidation of public debt could follow, either through more traditional policies or by revising other aspects of the EMU institutional setup.[21]

8.6 THE THEORY OF OPTIMUM CURRENCY AREAS, THE FOUNDATIONS OF THE EMU, AND THE REASONS FOR REDUCED SUPPORT IN IT

The OCA theory has been criticized by Fratianni (1994), Cesarano (1997, 2006, 2013), and Bordo and James (2006), among others. In particular, Fratianni and Cesarano, in order to define the conditions for an OCA, take an approach radically different from the one of Mundell (1961) and his followers, who all define static conditions for the optimality. As said, some exogenous conditions or, at most, a few endogenous factors are assumed that facilitate the functioning of an OCA and avoidance of asymmetric shocks. Exogenous conditions satisfying requirements for the viability of an OCA, e.g., wage and price flexibility and labor mobility, can sometimes be addressed by policies tending to change them in a way to satisfy the requirements. Indeed, some recent prescriptions by European institutions for the member countries, especially the peripheral ones, tend to this end.

---

[20] On long-run multipliers, see De Boef and Keele (2008).

[21] Cugnasca and Rother (2015: 21) find that "countries ... in recession would benefit from initially reducing the speed of consolidation ... to avoid significant negative effects on output." Countries that are not in recession should frontload fiscal consolidation, as confidence effects would compensate the negative effects of possibly high multipliers. However, we can add, in expansionary times the value of multipliers tends to be lower, which reduces the negative impact of consolidations on the GDP. An issue different from that of the effects of the value of multipliers for the desirability of a contractionary or an expansionary fiscal stance concerns the effects of the debt/GDP ratio on optimal growth (Checherita et al., 2014).

Endogenous factors are indicated first, e.g., by Mundell (1973a). Fratianni and Cesarano's approach to OCAs shifts the focus from the static conditions to be satisfied before the union to the dynamic problem of the domestic mechanism of adjustment that can absorb shocks, in a way to pursue the target of internal balance. This is done in order to avoid the logical mistake of defining ex ante conditions for optimality of the area (such as labor mobility) existing at a certain time, but that could not resist changes due to the "natural" evolution of economic and social conditions (Cesarano, 2013).[22] Bordo and James's approach is only apparently different. They refer to the novelties induced by globalization. This continuously makes the relation between prices of tradables and nontradables to change, which challenges mature economies, thus requiring exchange rates to vary. In the absence of this mechanism, mature countries would go toward placing limits on foreign trade.

To explain the reasons on which the conclusions of these authors are based, one needs to reflect on the assumptions underlying Mundell's initial reasoning – shared by his followers – on both international and intra-national adjustment. As said, they make optimality depend on given exogenous circumstances, not on endogenous factors deriving from the optimal conduct of public and private agents. To be clear, also the assumption of wage and price inflexibility is an exogenous assumption contrasting with the hypothesis of optimal decisions by agents. In fact, as Mundell (1961: 663) underlines, it corresponds to the hidden assumption of money illusion by workers and firms, who could bear the consequences of flexibility through changes in the exchange rates, not via nominal wages or prices. Moreover, multiple solutions can derive from different exogenous conditions, representing a case of "degenerative problem-shifts"[23] (Lakatos, 1970). Among the essential elements that can hinder – or

---

[22]   Obviously, some factors assumed to be exogenous can change as an effect of the realization of the currency area. However, it does not seem that any such factor did change in a way to facilitate the functioning of the currency area in the EMU.

[23]   These are changes of the auxiliary hypotheses of a research program that do not succeed in producing new facts but only defend the "hard core" of the program.

favor – internal adjustment in a monetary union, of specific relevance are those related to the border effect (due to various kinds of "home bias"), which derives in particular from the fact that policies other than the monetary one are left to participating countries, as in the EMU.[24] The border effect is relevant, as it impinges on the factors influencing adjustment: information, institutional constraints, and policy tools, including not only monetary policy tailored to the problems of the country, but other instruments of macroeconomic and microeconomic policy (think of structural, labor, and regional policies). However, the border effect lies also in the existence in each country of a greater fluidity of information as well as of common institutions, laws, and languages, which all reduce the uncertainty of the environment. Only ex post can one know whether the border effect has operated in favor of, or against, persistence of the monetary union. In our case, it seems that the latter is the case, even if a favorable effect can have operated due to nonstrictly economic, but political, considerations, as a cement against conflicts between member countries, a case of "European," not national, border effect. How long it can last should, however, depend on existence of reforms of European institutions and policies, failing which reduced support to Europe will derive.

In order to get the desired economic adjustment, careful design of the currency area is needed. Money alone cannot ensure the needed adjustment and the currency area should be only part of a political union, and all the policy tools, both macroeconomic and microeconomic, should be at hand at the European level. Mario Draghi contends the view that the EZ is not a political union (Draghi, 2014).[25] It seems to us that this position has a feeble foundation. It is true that

[24] To be noted is Balassa's critical comment to Mundell's analysis, which seems to confound issues of international adjustment with those of interregional ones, in suggesting monetary unification without political unity (Balassa, 1973).

[25] He says: "A common misconception about the European Union – and the Eurozone – is that they are economic unions without underlying political union. This reflects a deep misunderstanding of what economic union means: it is by nature political ... Fiat money is a political construct and monetary union could not operate without adequate political structures."

a number of decisions in the Monetary Union – such as those on admittance to the EZ and appointments – are of a political nature. However, the issues of democratic accountability and parliamentary control are largely outside the EMU institutions.

In the historical experience until now, cases of a monetary union with no political union are limited to very specific situations, all characterized by economic (and political) disparity of power, like those of very small countries or former colonies, which tie their currency to that of a larger country or to the home country's (Fratianni, 1994). "Political integration ... appears as a necessary and inescapable accompaniment of monetary integration," according to Bordo and James (2006: 400).

All the findings mentioned in the present and the previous three sections have important consequences for our topic, in so far as both institutional and short-run policy implications are concerned. We will briefly deal with both in the next section. Here we would finally underline that all these findings lay the foundations for a modern revaluation of Keynesian theory and its application to the EMU, even if this latter consequence would not be an easy task. In fact, differently from the United States, where at least some improvements have been introduced, neither the theoretical progress of the 1990s and the following decades nor the depth of the crisis that has hit the EMU countries has produced a substantial change in the institutional architecture of EMU and current policy attitudes. The deflationary bias of the former has even been stressed by the fiscal compact.[26]

8.7 FOR A FAIRER EMU AT THE SERVICE OF CITIZENS AND NOT PRONE TO FINANCIAL CRISES AND STAGNATION

The design of the Union has proved to be conducive to divergence of the strategies of growth of the different countries as well as to

---

[26] From this point of view, Rip van Winkle would certainly not be hit by the institutional changes introduced in the EMU. He could still declare himself a convinced supporter of the theories asserted by Friedman or Barro, Lucas, Sargent Wallace, without repeating an "environmental" mistake.

financial speculation, crisis, and deflation. According to Bibow (2007), the Maastricht regime was built in a way to foster instability itself, as it features powerful built-in destabilizers nourishing divergences and fragility. These outcomes are unfair, as they not only add to inequality between countries, but also negatively influence static and dynamic efficiency. Proposals for rebuilding the system to make it exempt from such faults should start from these needs.[27]

Thus, the EA's institutional architecture should be designed anew, taking account of the novelties in economic analysis and the (scarce) achievements of the Union in the last decades. Mostly, a new contract between the member countries should be drafted, as new goals – or a redefinition of the previous goals and/or rebalance of their relative weights – must be agreed upon. If these new targets are accepted, with a reduction in the relevance of monetary stability, a higher weight on employment, growth, financial stability, and fairness, reasoning on the most appropriate reforms and instruments is easier.

More generally, a complete and satisfying redesign would require the following:

- Institutional reforms putting less emphasis on the virtues of the operation of markets and the common currency.

---

[27] Milone (2015, 2017) covers this issue, mainly by reviewing an extensive literature and dealing with problems often debated within public organizations such as the IMF and OECD. He refers specifically to reforms that appear necessary after the crisis, which to a large extent has stressed some urgencies already evident before. Necessary changes differ among the various countries, but should aim at increasing both static and dynamic efficiency, reducing excessive income inequality, and reforming structural political institutions.

Monastiriotis and Zartaloudis (2010) deal only with labor market reforms, in particular with flexibility. They argue that theoretical and empirical considerations show the existence of a variety of degrees and directions for (de)regulating labor markets. The agenda is then open for an active exploration of the most appropriate policy options. These should have been discussed and disciplined even before the crisis, which has simply aggravated the underlying issues. With reference to issues more general than labor market reforms, we must deal with the essential features of the "European model" and discuss also the role of rules versus discretion, of free markets, fiscal and monetary policy, to end with the relative weights of price stability and employment in the welfare function of the EZ policymakers.

- Institutions and policies allowing for the emergence of the conditions that
  ensure the validity of the OCA. They must be created not so much by states
  in terms of labor market flexibility (especially in times of crisis), but at the
  EMU level. This must be done by completing the union with federal
  institutions and policies that would make the EMU eventually fit the
  conditions for an OCA, such as a fiscal union and the central bank as
  a lender of last resort for governments (Handler, 2012; Savona, 2015).
- A change in the ECB goals and statute, starting – as said – from the
  redefinition of the inflation target, to set a higher ceiling, downgrading the
  predominant role of anti-inflationary policies in a way to leave more room
  for the employment and financial stability goals and, in addition, giving it
  the possibility of serving the government objectives. The model of the
  Bank of England could be followed, with no political independence and
  the goals of inflation, set, in our case, on an annual basis by the European
  Commission.
- An increased role of other common policies, in particular fiscal policy. The
  common budget should thus be increased in order to permit anti-cyclical
  action as well as to design common investment strategies to foster
  a uniform growth throughout the Union. The budget should perform
  a stabilization role proper (for symmetric shocks) and an insurance function
  (for asymmetric shocks). A common welfare system and other
  microeconomic policies should be devised to make structural adjustments
  of the economies possible in the direction of a higher efficiency and equity.
  This, again, requires an increase in the size of the common budget.
  Macroeconomic policies to reduce the existing asymmetric actions foreseen
  in the macroeconomic imbalance procedure devised in 2011 should also be
  enacted. The fiscal policy rules should be drastically changed, by
  introducing the golden rule of public finance.
- Introduction of a system of incentives to change, as the one suggested
  by Steinbach (2016). This author proposes to redesign treaties and
  statutes by introducing either contractual agreements between the EU
  and individual member states, underpinned by financial support
  offering an incentive, or mutual agreements concluded between
  member states for the implementation of structural reforms. According
  to Belke (2016), the Excessive Deficit Procedure does not offer
  incentives and sanctions to countries better than those of market-
  based interest rates. It must be added that incentives and sanctions

should be referred also to surplus countries. Some studies have even found a negative effect on yield spreads of announcements of excessive debt (Afonso et al., 2019).

- Enhancement of structural policies, avoidance of opposing strategies of growth by member countries, and reduction of the current account imbalances permitted.

Redesign of the EZ along these lines would not be an easy task. Political objections would be numerous to both their basic tenets and their specific structure and features. Recently, timid openings for a change of the current structure have emerged. These are contained in the documents, speeches, and declarations of the representatives of the ECB and the European Commission (Juncker Plan) and are proved to some extent by the practical implementation of some innovative policies, as in the case of unconventional monetary policies and a banking union. Most likely, the necessity of the reforms outlined above could be more widely recognized if reforms were diluted through time and a rather long path to their final realization were devised. This implies that their main body would be implemented only with the next generation or two. However, it would be important to realize their need and agree on a timetable right now.

8.8 A COMMON GROWTH STRATEGY INSTEAD OF COMPETITIVE STRATEGIES BY DIFFERENT COUNTRIES

In the previous chapters, we have seen the implications of various types of imbalances within the Union. These derive precisely from the adoption of different strategies of growth (export-led or credit-led) between the member countries. This dual strategy had a negative influence on imbalances and implied low growth and the possibility of crises in the Union as a whole. To avoid these negative effects, a program of reconstruction and redesign of the EZ institutions should be devised from a short-term, a medium-term, and a long-term perspective.

In the short run, the issue is to prevent a new financial crisis and stabilize peripheral economies. This requires a mechanism like the one suggested by Bofinger (2016a) and others. The mechanisms provided by the ECB might be insufficient to this end in the event of insolvency of a (rather) big country. Common policies of relief, in particular directed to the financial sector, together with its regulation, are required.

In the medium term, internal imbalances in both the current account and the public sector should be reduced. As to the current account, the MIP should be amended, by making imbalances symmetric and reducing their size. All policies on the side of costs and demand not shared with other member countries that trigger current account surpluses for one country are beggar-thy-neighbor and should then be avoided, also because the associated capital account surpluses impress a short-run expansionary impulse to other countries, leading there to bubbles and distortions in the structure of production. Rebalancing can indeed take place through either inflation and expansion of demand in the core or deflation and contraction in the periphery or both. This would have different implications on unemployment, which would rise in the periphery in case of deflation of wages and prices, whereas it would shrink with expansionary policies in the core. Expansion by Germany and other surplus countries might imply a public deficit and an increase in public debt, but would allow a reduction in the deficit and public debt of other countries.[28] In addition, a cut in demand in peripheral countries usually implies a cut in public investment, which worsens the gap in the productivity trend between the core and the periphery. It should then be avoided. The issue of excessive outstanding debt should be faced in the medium-long run through a redefinition of the EMU institutions (next section) and

---

[28]   The rise could also benefit Germany. In fact, the ratio of public investment to GDP in this country is a little higher that 2 percent, well below the EZ average, close to 3 percent, and the country badly needs public intervention for coping with decaying infrastructure (see, e.g., ECB, 2016; Fratzscher, 2017). One could also add that the private component of the formation of German capital stock has shown a very low growth profile, in comparison to other European countries (Roth, Wolff, 2018),

policies based on different goals and attitudes of monetary and fiscal policy, as indicated in the next sections.

In the long term, a new strategy should be implemented, based on a common program of investment and growth. However, this should be devised – or, at least, outlined – soon, in order to inspire short- and medium-run interventions, recognizing that "social investment can promote demand in a manner that sustains rather than drains the private sector" (Garofoli, Holland, 2017: 4).

The common growth strategy could be a way to address not only phenomena, but their underlying causes, which really derive from the past divergent growth strategies. In addition, it should be decided jointly. This common strategy should allow for getting rid of the numerous fiscal rules and lead to joint decisions, once its guidelines have commonly been accepted. It could be supported by Eurobonds, an initiative usually ascribed to Jacques Delors[29] – i.e., issuance of "Union Bonds" to finance infrastructure investment. They could be issued not only in order to mutualize part of the outstanding debt and stabilize financial markets,[30] but also to complement expansionary fiscal policy (Claessens et al., 2012). Muellbauer (2013) suggests all new EZ sovereign borrowing to be in the form of jointly guaranteed Eurobonds. Beetsma and Mavromatis (2014) are more cautious and propose limiting the EU guarantee, in order to induce the government to reduce debt, and make it conditional on the implementation of sufficient structural reformism, privatizations, opening up of product markets, more flexible labor markets, and increased efficiency for public good provision.[31] Finally, new financial instruments especially

---

[29] The proposal had already been suggested before, but received its official christening by the Delors Commission's White Paper (Delors Commission, 1993).

[30] Other proposals have also been advanced. For example, Depla and von Weizsäcker (2010) suggest issuance at a central level of "blue bonds" (up to 60 percent of GDP of each country) – which would be senior – and "red bonds" (above the mentioned threshold), which would be junior. Bofinger (2016a) suggests a mutualization of an order of magnitude of 10 percent for coping with the insolvency risk of member states. Favero and Missale (2012) argue in favor of Eurobonds if markets are considered to stay irrational longer than a country can stay solvent. See also Section 9.3.

[31] This should be balanced against the negative short-medium-run effects of product and labor flexibilization, as we have seen in Chapter 6. More recently, Duval and Furceri

dedicated to social infrastructure, such as social bonds, could be issued in order to finance EU-wide social investments (Fransen et al., 2017). In quantitative terms, a recent analysis (Burlon et al., 2017b) reestablishes a number of classic arguments in favor of an EA-wide public investment project,[32] as it finds that this would have a multiplier close to 2 (higher than 3) in case of a FG assurance offered on the short- (long-)run interest rate. The multiplier would be higher (in the short run) in case of investment for productive goods and debt- (rather than tax-)financed.

In practice, in November 2012 a framework for the issuance of "Project bonds" was approved. These are a financial instrument launched by the European Commission and the European Investment Bank as an innovative response to the needs for investment in large EU infrastructure projects, as a part of the Europe 2020 Project. "Stability Eurobonds" have been proposed in order to reduce and share the default risk, and the EU Commission has also suggested some guidelines for their introduction.

8.9   THE EMU, THE STATE, AND THE LOCAL LEVEL: MORE, STRONGER (AND MORE ACTIVE) COMMON INSTITUTIONS OR INSTITUTIONAL COMPETITION?

Institutional redesign and reforms of the EZ have long been debated, especially after the Great Recession, also in the light of the outcomes produced by those implemented more recently, such as the MIP, the fiscal compact, and the banking union.

Hooghe and Marks (2010) have noted that power and competencies have spread across multiple centres of governance. On the one hand, the legal impact on national and local authorities of decisions

---

(2016) emphasize the geographical distribution of reforms and their effects as well as the important role of complementary macroeconomic policy support. This implies that there is a problem of implementing these structural reforms, whose timing should be carefully devised together with simultaneously suitable macroeconomic policies.

[32]   The study warns that the literature leads to mixed conclusions on the effectiveness of public investment, with, e.g., the International Monetary Fund (2014a) in favor and Garin (2016) against.

taken at the EU level has risen continually, mainly for microeconomic policies. The EU level has to some extent increased its role in imposing its directives on the lower levels. A lesser role has been played by the EU level in enlarging the scope of its direct macroeconomic intervention. The motto guiding this level seems to have been: not acting, but forcing to act (by imposing constraints). On the other hand, the European Committee of the Regions has been empowered with some responsibilities and dialogues directly with the EU level (Guderjan, 2012), adding to the shift of balance toward this third level of governance, as already underlined by Jeffery (1997). We do not discuss this level of governance further and prefer to concentrate on the relationship between the EU and the country level, with the latter still having a dominant role in most fields. From our previous analysis the need arises to discuss this state of affairs and possibly suggest changes, in different fields. In what follows we mainly refer to some general issues, leaving a detailed discussion of specific macroeconomic and microeconomic policies to the next two chapters.

From some points of view we could say that the current state of the EU institutions still evokes an old debate which arose at the beginning of the European construction (e.g., Siebert, 1990): whether and how much to harmonize or to let competition play between different national institutions. Certainly, that debate must be updated in the light of experience, particularly after the Great Recession.

The current debate reflects partly the positions of the different countries about the relative roles of the two EU levels of government and partly ideological disputes and partisanship of the various government officials and the citizens. The "Euro-marketeer" or "Euro-socialist" role of EU top officials in the contention about the direction of EU policy is testified by the results of an empirical survey of their opinions offered by Hooghe (2000). Left-wing- (right-wing-) oriented officials are more (less) in favour of regulating the EU economy. According to these results, political orientation is more important than the country orientation which would tend to pursuit of national benefits when bargaining about EU policy.

Numerous benefits and costs arise from each level of governance. Curzon Price (2011) and Rodrik (2013) present a detailed list of both, but in some cases the same issue can be seen from different points of view. Let us consider fairness. One can say that the "level playing field" adds to it. However, one could also hold that different institutions should be maintained, if they correspond to differences in needs and preferences.[33] In addition, one can say that on the side of harmonization there are the economies of scale that can be gained, deriving from cuts in the transaction costs implied by diversity. An objection to this is that these economies favor big companies and monopoly[34] and that – echoing the argument already presented – rule diversity corresponds to different preferences inherited from history. Confidence can, however, be placed in the possibility that these preferences can evolve, as diversity can make people and governments learn from different experiences.[35] Similarly, in more specific fields, such as tax harmonization, there are gains in that this could avoid a race to the bottom of the state tasks (in particular of the welfare state), due to the competition, but there would also be costs, in neglecting the preferences of citizens in some countries for low state involvement.

As a general conclusion, institutional reforms are necessary in order to promote economic convergence (Papaioannou, 2016). In other terms, the former are in many ways (but not always) a precondition for the latter. In general, the best institutional solution is likely to be an

---

[33]   It is often the action of firms that pushes toward (somewhat artificial) differentiation of technical specifications of the product features. Take, for instance, the case of petrol's diversity. However, in most cases consumer preferences are precisely toward harmonized rules, at least in the area of consumer goods.

More generally, Sen (2009: 143) notes: "There is something of a tyranny of ideas in seeing the political divisions of states (primarily, national states) as being, in some way, fundamental, and in seeing them not only as practical constraints to be addressed, but as divisions of basic significance in ethics and political philosophy."

[34]   This is not true in at least one area. Think of tax-treatment diversity. This is fundamentally unfair, as it favors big transnational companies and richer people who can devise tax-elusive solutions. But also in other fields, such as environment or technical standards, smaller firms can support too high costs to face diversity.

[35]   This is the position expressed by Wohlgemuth (2007).

intermediate one between differentiation and harmonization (see, e.g., Curzon Price, 2011; Rodrik, 2013). With specific reference to the EMU, most of all it is important to change some existing links between the EU-EZ and the country level. In fact, as noted recently by Papaioannou (2016: 222), "it is hard to imagine an 'ever closer' union in Europe with the currently large institutional gap in courts, public administration, red tape, corruption, and fiscal capacity. The asymmetries in national institutions across the EZ are destabilising both because they impede real economic convergence and because EU-EZ policies depend crucially on local institutional structures, disparities and imbalances." Possibly, peripheral countries should be helped in reforming their malfunctioning institutions. The Great Recession has somewhat changed the picture of the best solution with respect to the one that could be devised before. In fact, it has indicated the need for some policies to be implemented at the EU level – such as active fiscal coordination and/or raising the size of the EU budget, issuing Eurobonds or Union bonds or similar types of bonds[36] – which should enter the stage. At the same time, common regulation, especially in the financial field, should be strengthened, together with creation of a common social welfare system and structural intervention.

A more complete perspective can be gained if, in addition to discussing harmonization versus institutional competition, we deal with multilevel governance. In fact, the different levels can be complementary: there can be areas where decisions ought to be taken at the EU level and others where a lower level is more productive. Or, for the same area some decisions – possibly, on criteria and lines of conduct to follow – should be taken at the former level, while others should be decentralized. Scharpf (2001) suggests four different types of multilevel interaction: "mutual adjustment," "intergovernmental

---

[36]   EuroUnionBonds have been suggested by Prodi and Quadrio Curzio (2011). These should be issued by a European Financial Fund, which would receive gold reserves, bonds, and shares conferred by member states. Quadrio Curzio had also made a number of proposals on this topic, and Quadrio Curzio (2011) suggests a type of bonds slightly different from the EuroUnionBonds.

negotiations," "joint-decision making," and "hierarchical direction." Choice among them can be made with reference to the problem-solving capacity and institutional legitimacy of each type, which somewhat go back to our previous discussion. We will deal with the issue further below in the two following chapters.

9 How to Reform the EU and the EMU

Macroeconomic Policy Instruments of the Common Strategy

9.1 MONETARY POLICY

The points to discuss refer to the following issues, which are strictly interrelated one to another: the assessment of the ECB action in the recent crisis, as a premise to suggestions of institutional and policy changes; the role and mission of the ECB, including its objectives; the kind of independence and the status to be given to the Bank; the instruments to use and the effects of each; the limits of monetary policy. Let us deal with each in turn.

(a) Assessing ECB Action in the Recent Crisis

The risk of possible losses deriving from the ECB intervention in secondary markets of sovereign debt has been first underlined. However, the main concern here is that, according to the current institutional architecture of EMU, the Central Bank should not be drawn into bailing out a national government with an unsustainable public debt. The Eurozone has nineteen countries sharing the same currency, but none has legal or political authority to ask the central bank to create liquidity in an emergency – even for banks facing a genuine liquidity crisis. Nevertheless, the ECB has found it necessary to bail out illiquid, possibly insolvent, financial institutions in member states, repeatedly since 2007; and continues to do so. Examples would be the following: bank loans in the ECB's short-term lending program; debt of distressed sovereigns held by banks and bought on the secondary markets; and loans made against collateral in order to lower borrowing costs. Since financial institutions have traditionally been the largest purchasers of domestic sovereign debt, this informal facility has been deemed by some authors and institutions as a way of bailing out an illiquid or insolvent sovereign (e.g., Sinn, 2018), possibly by the backdoor.[1] According to this interpretation, the ECB has been instrumental in converting private debt into public debt, or public debt into private debt. By intervening in order to stabilize EZ sovereign debt markets, or to stabilize privately held debt and shore up the banks and banking system, the ECB can be thought of as having stretched its mandate and violated the separation principle (Bordes, Clerc, 2013) requiring no interference between monetary policy aiming at the goal of price stability and credit and interest rate policies directed to the objective of financial stability. However, as Bordes and Clerc recognize, interpreting the implications of the current policies of the ECB is a difficult and debatable issue. Four arguments can be raised here.

First, the risk incurred in intervening in secondary markets is connected to any open-market operation. Second, as we said, fiscal deficits and public debt are often the result of "sudden stops" or reversals in financing, or private-sector deleveraging after a period of debt, or capital leakages caused by institutional or private debts or liquidity shortages (e.g., Calvo et al., 2002). All these situations make the expected value of a unit of the common currency different in different places, which is difficult to accept. The third argument has to do with counterfactuals: absence of ECB intervention for stabilizing the sovereign debt markets may be deemed to be unfair, as the ECB would help financial markets to force the sovereign governments into default. In addition, think of the possibility that it is the financial sector that, based on unfounded expectations, originates a self-fulfilling crisis. By financing the private sector, while being forbidden to finance governments, the ECB can fuel the crisis, without being timely aware of that, and make the government deviate from its original targets, to increase the burden of its debt (as a consequence of higher interest rates) or even to default. The fourth and most important argument runs as follows: one could argue that the ECB's

---

[1]   Conditions for insolvency should take account of the intertemporal budget of the government and of implicit taxes and subsidies as well as of seigniorage.

conduct is justified by the overriding goal of this institution, i.e., to ensure viability of the EZ and to avoid precipitating it into an even deeper crisis. This goal is preeminent also with respect to the ECB's mission of keeping price stability. And what the ECB has not agreed to do is to intervene directly in the primary debt markets for distressed sovereigns, including the all-important refinancing operations of those sovereigns, to reduce borrowing costs or keep domestic financial markets operating. All the same, unconventional policies have produced beneficial effects. In fact, counterfactual analysis shows that in their absence, there would have been a cumulative loss of output of about 19 percent with respect to its precrisis level (Mouabbi, Sahuc, 2018). Unconventional operations have also been beneficial in terms of a reduction in financial market stress in the short run, even if their effects are, instead, negative in the medium run (Lewis, Roth, 2017).

(b) The Role of the ECB and Its Mission

Two considerations are in order here: the size of the inflation target and the range of the ECB goals. As for the goal of inflation, it has been shown that the maximum target level of the inflation rate allowed so far by the statutes of the ECB (below, but close to, 2 percent) is nonoptimal, being too low and contractionary (Section 8.4). On different grounds, this policy of an inflation rate (temporarily) higher than the 2 percent upper limit is advocated also by Corsetti et al. (2016a: 157). Moving toward a higher target can expand the policy space to escape liquidity traps as well as "re-anchoring longer-term expectations around the desired level." Among the benefits of a higher inflation target, we must consider not only the direct impact of a more expansionary monetary action on other targets, but also the indirect benefit that derives from reducing the value of extant public and private debt (even if after 2007 the private debt of nonfinancial institutions did decrease in the EA; see BIS, 2012, 2018).

In advocating a higher inflation rate, one should consider that it can have not only benefits (of the kind of those already indicated), but also shortcomings (Acocella, 2018). As for dissent on the opportunity to raise the inflation rate, Mishkin (2011) argues that very deep recessions like the one begun in 2007–8 are very rare and then the risk of easily reaching a constraining ZLB is not very relevant. Then the benefits from a higher inflation target (in terms of a larger reduction in the real interest rate) would not be very large. In addition, he fears that people's expectations on future inflation will keep on rising. Similarly, Piketty (2013) holds that the initial positive effect can partly disappear over time, as people's expectations can change. Woodford (2009), Bernanke (2010), and Mishkin (2011) are skeptical on targeting higher inflation, say at 4 percent, since people would think that going to 4 percent is only a first step to going to 6 percent or more and it would be very difficult to tie down expectations at 4 percent. After thirty years of successful anti-inflationary action by central banks, the advantages of anchoring the expectations of firms and workers to price stability should not be lost (e.g., Kohn, 2010).

Accepting the argument of the beneficial effects of anchoring inflation expectations, however, does not rule out choosing a moderately higher inflation rate target than the ECB's. In Ball's opinion (Ball, 2014b: 14), the "central bank should determine its optimal policy, explain this policy to the public, and carry it out. We have learned from recent experience that 4% inflation is better than 2%, because of the zero bound problem. Why can't policymakers explain this, raise inflation to 4%, and keep it there?" This seems to us a very reasonable argument: raising the target would not impair expectations anchoring. In fact, Blanchard et al. (2010: 11) provocatively ask: "Is it more difficult to anchor expectations at 4 percent than at 2 percent?"

Another possible shortcoming of a higher inflation rate target can derive from the possibility that bubbles in the asset markets can derive from the inappropriate timing in its implementation (Wolff, 2014). This is really a relevant point, but cannot be overemphasized. The true problem is that policymakers should be well aware of this possibility and introduce additional tools, such as macroprudential policies, to counteract the risk. It has also been noticed that higher inflation can cause distortions. These are of two kinds at least. First, there are distortions on money holdings: their "taxation" can reduce the use of currency. In addition, a strong anti-inflationary policy mitigates the adverse effects of uncertainty on aggregate demand, as hiring decisions play a significant role in transmitting uncertainty (Guglielminetti, 2016). A final objection to a higher inflation rate is that a rise in this rate can reduce the purchasing power of fixed-income earners, if there is no protection against it. All these distortions cannot be denied. The real issue is to compare them with those of higher taxation. In all probabilities, the net costs of an inflation target of 4 percent rather than 2 percent are not significantly higher, while the benefits are certainly higher. We discuss other targets to add to inflation under point (c) in the following.

The range of operations to be performed by the ECB to pursue its targets should include not only issuing money, but also being a lender of last resort to sovereign states, and monitoring the financial sector in order to avoid financial crises. By contrast, regulating or monitoring issuance of sovereign debt is a task to be performed by an authority different from the Central Bank, e.g., the European Commission (EC).

If a direct role of lender of last resort is not accepted, a second-best option could be at least to maintain and formally christen the indirect role that the ECB has performed in supporting government debt through interventions in secondary markets, overcoming the critiques addressed to it. This solution, however, would not guarantee a rapid and positive reaction to negative shocks by markets, as these could cause doubt about the will and/or ability of the central bank to face them.

More generally, what would really be needed is revising the whole European institutional architecture. The separation principle would be less of an obstacle, if the original mission of the ECB were reconsidered, not only with regard to the quantitative value of the price stability target, but also the relative priority of this target with respect to others (employment, financial stability). The European institutional architecture would certainly gain if a model of a central bank like that of the US Federal Reserve, allowing for multiple targets, were adopted (on this also Stiglitz, 2016). The positive experience of the type of policies implemented by the Fed and other central banks shows that there can be successful interpretations of the principles of charging a policymaker with multiple, conflicting targets.

(c)   Goal and/or Instrument Independence?

Our position with respect to independence is that it should be limited to the use of instruments. There are many justifications for that. From a practical point of view, goal independence is not a necessary condition for price stability, even if it can be judged as being an appropriate solution for some countries. On the empirical ground, some studies find a high positive correlation between independence and monetary stability, but others contradict this result.

On the side of those finding a positive effect of monetary policy independence on inflation and macroeconomic performance, Berger et al. (2001) corroborate robustness of the negative correlation between the degree of goal independence and inflation. Arnone et al. (2007) find an increasing trend in the autonomy of central banks in the almost two decades after the end of the 1980s, with a positive influence of this trend on reduction of inflation. On the side of critics of independence, according to Hayo and Hefeker (2010), central bank independence does not serve to attain a better monetary policy performance, as it is a condition neither necessary nor sufficient for monetary stability. Besides all, many central banks are only instrument independent or it is very difficult to define whether instrument or political independence holds. In general, recent papers have confirmed the previous dichotomy in the orientation of the theoretical literature, with a prevalence of skeptical views on the advantages of independence. A recent finding is that, at least in advanced countries, political independence is not significantly related to inflation, whereas it is for emerging economies (Balls et al., 2016). Instrument independence has instead a positive influence on price stability. As a general comment on these empirical studies, one could say that correlation gives no indication about causality. Proper tests – corroborated by historical analysis – should be devised in order to give more reliable results. Anyway, political independence does not come at a cost, as it can involve a lower inflation rate, but a higher unemployment rate. After all, political independence was supported by the financial sector, which has a low preference for inflation (Santoni, 1986).[2]

Hartmann and Smets (2018) notice that the ECB action evolved in various ways in response to the challenges of the time and the Bank now resembles more other central banks. However, the distance to these is still long from various points of view, mainly targets and accountability. A possible indication would be to adopt a solution for the ECB similar to that of the Federal Reserve. After all, this institution can show a remarkable positive impact on the US economic performance. In 1951, the Fed and the Treasury agreed that the Fed got back the power to run a monetary policy independent of fiscal policy, whereas during World War II it had supported government bonds by pegging interest rates. While both are politically independent, the main difference with the ECB lays in that the European institution is constrained to a maximum inflation target by its statute, whereas it is the Fed's Federal Open Market Committee (FOMC) that decides the inflation target to pursue, together with other targets, i.e., employment and financial stability. This implies that the Fed can be somewhat open to the influence of the government and to the needs deriving from the path actually followed by the economy, which has actually been the case. Its accountability is ensured both by testimonies of its officials before the Congress and by submitting to this twice a year an extensive report on recent economic developments and of its plans for monetary policy as well as by ensuring transparency through publication of the minutes of its governing bodies. Finally, while the Congress can censor its operation and modify its statute, the ECB's statute can

---

[2]   Hayo and Hefeker (2010) note that the influence of other interest groups should be the object of more extensive analysis.

be modified only by reforming the Maastricht Treaty (De Grauwe, 2016, Board of Governors of the Federal Reserve System, n.d.). In fact, some authors have questioned formal (de jure) independence of the Federal Reserve arguing that in practical terms its action is influenced by politics (Cargill, 2016). Cargill and Driscoll (2013) hold that the "myth" of the Fed independence cannot be accepted in the absence of a price or inflation rule.

On a quite different side, the big issue of political accountability of the ECB arises, as a consequence of its political independence. Whatever the impact of political independence on price stability, an even more compelling argument against it refers to the ECB as consisting of unelected officials, in contrast to governments, where elected officials decide policy actions, even when they can resemble a - Leviathan.[3] In particular, it is inconceivable that unelected people could undo what governments try to do in order to avoid the EZ being pushed into insolvency. It must be recognized, however, that on the occasion of the Great Recession it is the ECB that has faced it since 2012 in a rather successful way, partiality of success being due to the limited effectiveness of monetary action to relieve the economy from recession.

(d)   The Instruments

The ZLB and the liquidity trap have strained conventional instruments of monetary policy. As said in previous chapters, new instruments have been implemented also in the EU to circumvent some of the effects of short-term interest rates hitting the ZLB. From this point of view, the ECB has introduced no novelty. It can prolong the situation of negative interest rates and still have the opportunity to resort to issuing "helicopter money" or a "fiscal currency,"[4] but the limits of monetary action should be reckoned.

---

[3]   Harashima (2007) develops a model explaining that an independent central bank is necessary, simply because it guarantees that inflation does not accelerate, thus protecting against governments which are not weak, foolish, or untruthful, but simply corrupt (true economic Leviathans).

[4]   Helicopter money was suggested by Haberler (1952) and, paradoxically, also by Friedman (Friedman, 1969). It consists in distribution of money to all citizens or to

(e) The Limits of Monetary Policy

These derive first from its feature of being more able to create a recession than to obtain (full and fast) recovery. In particular, monetary policy tends to overreact to cost-push shocks, showing a kind of stabilization bias (Woodford, 2003); this bias arises when monetary policy is the only policy tool to react to shocks (Albanesi et al., 2002). A second limit of monetary policy derives from its long-known limit to transmit expansionary impulses to the real economy, partly due to the behavior of banks, which do not lower deposit rates, in order not to negatively influence their funding sources, raising their lending rates instead (Eggertsson et al., 2019).

Another limit of monetary policy has to do with its different country impact in an area so variegated as the EZ. Unemployment and prices are less reactive in the South than in the North (Barigozzi et al., 2014), which raises the need for fiscal and microeconomic policies to correct them (Saraceno, Tamborini, 2016). The main justification for fiscal action is that monetary policy cannot act on the output gap of each country, while fiscal action can. Demertzis et al. (2004) find that pursuit of different targets by the independent central bank and elected governments generates a conflict and both authorities will be unable to reach their respective objectives, the more so the larger the difference between their preferences. The endogenous voting extension of the model shows that, on the one hand, existence of a conservative central bank encourages the public to favor more expansionary policies. On the other, these conflicts can cause fiscal policy to become more expansionary than is appropriate because of the need to offset/overcome the effects of more conservative monetary policies. This has consequences for efficiency and the long-run debt position. Benigno and Woodford (2004) also underline the need for complementarity of monetary and fiscal policy. Di

specific categories of agents, under various forms. Fiscal currency is the instrument of payment devised by Galbraith (2016). It could be issued and freely distributed by the government, which would guarantee its acceptance for future tax payments and other payments to the state allowing for some discount. This currency could circulate among people similarly to the euro.

Bartolomeo et al. (2015) strengthen Benigno and Woodford's (2004) argument that the optimal fiscal and monetary stabilization policies should be seen as complements, by referring to a different, novel mechanism, that offered by a higher inflation rate, which would relieve the fiscal burden. A final reason for coordinating fiscal and monetary action derives from the mixed nature of some innovative unconventional monetary policies. Arestis (2015) suggests coordination of fiscal policy not only with monetary policy but also with financial stability policies in order to reduce unemployment and income inequality.

9.2 THE NEED FOR STRENGTHENING FINANCIAL REGULATION AND SUPERVISION: MACROPRUDENTIAL POLICY

9.2.1 *The Specific Issues to Deal With*

The recent financial crisis has highlighted the need for strengthening financial regulation and supervision, going beyond a purely microeconomic approach. The literature searching for proper financial regulation has soared, involving the foundations of macroprudential tools, their nature, implementation, and effectiveness, together with the need for coordinating it with monetary and credit policy also internationally. As to the relations with monetary policy, in particular, the need has been shown for monetary policy to change its attitude – by not trying to prevent a financial crisis through a "leaning against the wind" attitude (in particular, in deflating demand in case of a boom) – and to substitute it with macroprudential policy. In fact, the economy could be hit by a policy that keeps the interest rate too high: rather than lowering the probability and severity of a future financial crisis, it could instead weaken the economy, thus raising the prospect and the cost of financial instability (Svensson, 2016).[5] Macroprudential

---

[5] Evidence also shows that financial instability can develop even in a low-inflation environment, which is likely to be the case of the EZ (possibly, not of the US), but a "leaning against the wind" policy is certainly inappropriate and financial stability

policy would avoid this prospect, by dealing directly with the risk of financial instability.

The framework of macroprudential action in Europe and other countries has emerged recently and evolved incrementally; this piecemeal approach has created a number of weaknesses in the framework, and an overlapping toolset, of macroprudential instruments, more in Europe than elsewhere. The incremental evolution of macroprudential policy makes it necessary to deal with existing rules more extensively, before turning to proposals for changes and additions.

In this subsection, we deal with the following specific issues that have been the object of study. In the next subsection we analyze in more depth some policy issues arising from them. Objects of the study have been:

1. Identifying the sources of asset price bubbles and financial instability;
2. Defining macroprudential policies beyond micro action to counter instability;
3. Implementing macroprudential policies;
4. Finding out the consequences and the effectiveness of these policies;
5. Coordinating macroprudential policies at an international level to meet cross-border spillover effects;
6. Outlining some aspects of the European financial regulation;
7. Suggesting a framework for macroeconomic policies in a currency union.

We deal with each in turn.

1 Identifying the sources of asset pricing bubbles and financial instability

Galati and Moessner (2013) illustrate the reasons that can explain some of the roots of the financial crisis. Overconfidence in the self-adjusting ability of financial markets – causing improper policies of financial deregulation – led to underestimating the consequences of a growing financial sector, increasing indebtness and financial

should be addressed with other instruments than the interest rate fixed by central banks (Blot et al., 2015).

innovation, reduced risk premia, and soaring asset prices and bubble formation.

The theoretical reasons underlying these bubbles can be traced back in particular to limited market participation, as in this case even small shocks cause relevant asset price volatility and multiplicity of equilibria (Allen, Gale, 1994). Interbank loans can transmit and amplify shocks and cross-border spillovers and transmit them from one country to another (Allen, Gale, 2000; Nocciola, Zóchowski, 2016). The size and extension of unconventional policies implemented for taming the crisis, which have sharply increased liquidity, put emphasis on the risk of new financial booms and asset bubbles and, thus, on the need to devise a proper regulation.

2 Defining Macroprudential Policies: Beyond Micro Action

Asset bubbles justify macroprudential regulation. Microprudential regulation – e.g., quality/quantity of capital, leverage ratio, liquidity requirements – aims at forcing banks to internalize possible losses on their assets to protect deposit insurance funds and reduce moral hazard. This kind of regulation – even if of general application to all banks – does not consider the links between the various financial institutions as well as the procyclicality of the operation of the financial system. These can lead to financial imbalances and systemic risk that cannot be counteracted by simple microprudential regulation (Brunnermeier et al., 2009). In fact, this improves the resilience of individual financial institutions, but disregards the issues of the financial system as a whole deriving from the externalities that arise from the conduct of financial institutions, and can even have procyclical negative effects. Macroprudential regulation has exactly the objective of coping with these externalities and thus increasing the resilience to *systemic* risk. It consists in many cases of the same tools as the microprudential one, e.g., of ceilings on credit, applied to specific sectors or to the whole economic system, or deposit insurance. To act in a systemic way, macroprudential regulation should have countercyclical effects. This can be achieved by introducing different requirements (e.g., of capital) according to the state of the economy and to the likelihood of an asset bubble formation. Requirements should then be higher in times of expansion, lower during contractions. The change in the strictness of the regime can be discretionary or rule based (i.e., automatic), in case it is linked to some indicator of economic activity, exactly for the purpose of smoothing out cyclicality. The various macroprudential policies can be combined in order to better correct systemic risk, but capital requirements are likely to play a crucial role (De Nicoló et al., 2012).

3 Implementing Macroprudential Policies

Both in the implementation of macroprudential policies and in the adoption of the banking union, an important role has been played by the Bank for International Settlements (BIS), an institution created in 1930 by some European central banks and those of Japan and the United States, for facilitating the reparations imposed on Germany by the Treaty of Versailles – a task that soon became obsolete when reparation payments were suspended. The institution survived, by fostering cooperation between its shareholders. After the early 1970s exchange rate turmoil and bankruptcy of some banks, the Basel Committee on Banking Supervision (BCBS) was created and the BIS became active in fostering supervision and regulation rules according to international standards.

Basel III (i.e., the Third Basel Accord) is a global, voluntary agreement for regulation developed by the members of the BCBS. It was reached in 2010–11 and focuses on enhancing the stability of the financial system. It does so by requiring an increased quantity and quality of regulatory capital and liquidity. In addition, it tends to increase the instruments at the supervisors' disposal to reduce bank risks, while ensuring that financial institutions have sufficient loss-absorbing capacity, and to safeguard the stability of the financial system. Thus, it is particularly useful as a guide for the ECB in its new role as a supervisor of the banks under the Banking Union. Due to banks' reactions, amendments aimed at making the accord milder,[6] going under the name of Basel IV,[7] were decided in December 2017. They also incorporate the methodology for calculating the risks associated with the various assets (*risk-weighted assets*, RWAs) and overcome the previous impasse that had divided the members of the committee and experts. The beginning of a five-year stepwise implementation of the Basel III agreement, originally planned to take place by March 2019, has been deferred to 2022. Basel IV increases bank liquidity and decreases bank leverage, by strengthening capital requirements (European banks will need a 40 billion capital rise). In particular, it deals with systemic risk in stating the possibility for national financial regulators to introduce "discretionary counter-cyclical buffers," as an extension of the capital conservation buffer. This can be done by requiring up to 2.5 percent of additional capital during periods of high credit growth.

4   Finding Out the Consequences and Effectiveness of these Policies

When macroprudential policies of the kind required by the Basel IV agreement are implemented, the risk arises of their effectiveness being impaired due to Goodhart's law. Rational agents can, in fact, react to the rules and make them ineffective or even dangerous. Actually, the effects of macroprudential policies are still largely unproven and some unconventional monetary policies, such as asset purchases, look similar to macroprudential policy. The consequence, according to Smets (2014), would be that monetary authorities also should "keep an eye on financial stability." Moreover, rational agents could anticipate that the regulators – in particular, in the case of discretionary macroprudential regulation – will tend to be lenient in their countercyclical policies, as an effect of pressures from the financial industry and politicians, thus creating ex ante moral hazard (Horvàt, Wagner, 2016). Finally, some macroprudential policies may hit profitability of banks (Bank of

---

[6]   Even so, a McKinsey report warned that its effects on banks could be much deeper than anticipated, as these will need to raise more capital (McKinsey&Company, 2017).

[7]   On Basel IV, Nelson and Roth (2017) can be usefully consulted.

Slovenia, 2015). This can imply that they might even be counterproductive, if they induce banks to get involved in riskier projects. However, in general macroprudential policies should reduce risks and the negative effects of capital flows volatility (e.g., Başkaya et al., 2016).

5 Coordinating Macroprudential Policies at an International Level to Meet Cross-border Spillover Effects

Cross-border financial operations raise international spillovers, whose sign and magnitude depend – inter alia – on the ownership structure of financial institutions and their linkages. This raises a number of issues about how to coordinate national macroprudential policies in a way to avoid excessive negative spillovers and reduce their impact. In particular, existence of a common prudential standard and supervisory body can be useful (Cecchetti, Tucker, 2015; Kara, 2016). Even if cooperation appears to generate sizable gains, it could be difficult to implement it (Agénor et al., 2017). In any case, bilateral agreements for stronger reciprocity arrangements between countries, or some notification of the looming bubbles and policy actions, are necessary for mitigating leakages. An (un)intented consequence of monetary and regulatory policies can be banking deglobalization (Forbes et al., 2016b).

6 Outlining Some Aspects of the European Financial Regulation Policy

In Europe, both national authorities and EU-level institutions operate in this field (Margerit et al., 2017). The former are the national banks in some countries, such as in Belgium, Ireland, and the United Kingdom, or different special institutions set up for this purpose only (as in Germany, France, and Italy) coordinating the action of other institutions entrusted with micro- or macroprudential regulation in specific areas (banks, other financial institutions).

As said, also at the Union level different institutions operate for microprudential regulation and under the impulse of the financial crisis, new institutions for macroprudential regulation and monitoring were agreed upon in 2009–10 and later: the EBA and the European

Systemic Risk Board (ESRB). Without changing the principle of national supervision, centralized boards or authorities have been created for surveillance of systemic risk and coordination of national regulation of the different sections of financial markets.

The EBA must ensure the orderly functioning and integrity of financial markets and the stability of the financial system in the EU. To this end, it monitors and assesses market developments, trends, and potential risks or vulnerabilities stemming from the microprudential regulation. In cooperation with the ESRB, it can perform EU-wide stress tests on financial institutions, in order to assess their resilience to adverse market developments, as well as to contribute to the overall assessment of systemic risk in the EU financial system.

The ESRB, created in 2010, is an independent body of the EU chaired by the president of the ECB. Together with EBA and other institutions it is part of the European System of Financial Supervision (ESFS) and is responsible for macroprudential oversight of the financial system of the Union in order to contribute to preventing or mitigating systemic risks to financial stability. It does so in a number of ways, ranging from collection of data for identifying systemic risks, to issuance of nonbinding warnings to countries and cooperation with all the other bodies within the ESFS. It also coordinates member states' macroprudential policies.

In 2012, a report (Liikanen Report, 2012) prepared by a group of experts was published containing a number of proposals. These mainly addressed the following issues: bank bigness (creating the need for governments to intervene and bail them out, related to the position of some of them being "too big to fail"); the confusion of different-risk operations in the activity of banks, typical of most European ones.

The report contained two main proposals: first, the separation of the trading business from other parts of the banking business for large banks (the Separation Proposal), in order to divide the risk of insolvency and facilitate continuation of activities by its solvent parts, while submitting the others to resolution; second, the mandatory issuing of subordinated bank debt thought to be liable (forming the strict "Bail-in Proposal").

Separation of banks' activities has both benefits and costs. The former derive from reduction of risks and protection of the shorter-term investors, as well as improvement of resolvability of ailing activities, in connection with the reduction of the "bank bias" that is a feature of the European financial system (Langfield, Pagano, 2016; Radojičić, Krstić, 2017). The latter include: the costs of implementation and supervision; the reduction of the diversification benefits due to economies of scope, which have been found to be positive and not negligible in many cases, at least on the side of revenues (Rossi, Beccalli, 2018); and possibly the risk of migration to the shadow banking system or abroad (Radojičić, Krstić, 2017). Resistance to the implementation of the report has been found to be diffuse, in particular among German banks (Goldback, Zimmermann, 2015; Spendzharova et al., 2016). Possibly due to this resistance, implementation of the Liikanen proposals has failed. In October 2017, after confirmation of the previous position of the Council, the Commission withdrew its proposal, officially due to the lack of progress and foreseeable agreement, also recognizing that the objectives pursued by the proposed rule have already been achieved by other regulations.

The Single Supervisory Mechanism (SSM), created in 2014, entrusts the ECB with new binding *microprudential* powers (whereas the powers of the ESRB are nonbinding) within the Banking Union that we will be dealing with below. It adds banking supervision and microprudential policy at the EU level to monetary policy. The respective roles of the ESRB and the SSM, however, are not very clear and the two bodies lack some coordination, as the ECB is not even officially represented in the ESRB.

Some macroprudential rules have also been lifted from the country to the European level. Now the ECB has the ability to implement macroprudential measures and is responsible together with the national authorities competent for macroprudential policy in the EZ and the other countries participating in the SSM. For addressing

systemic or macroprudential risks, the ECB can apply higher requirements for capital buffers, systemic risk buffers, capital surcharges for
systemically important financial institutions, sectoral capital leverage ratios, and other measures.

In 2013, a deepening of the financial crisis led European
authorities to create a route toward a banking union. The Banking
Union establishes the principle of unitary supervision to partially
replace national monitoring and regulation. It was created in order
to rule banking operations, restructure banks in difficulties, break
the sovereign-bank loop that had caused a prolongation of the
crisis, and share risks at the EU level. In 2014, these principles
were applied to the 150 largest "systemically important" EZ banks.
Following the EC roadmap for the creation of the Banking Union,
the EU institutions agreed to establish the SSM. The Banking
Union applies to countries in the EA, but countries outside the
EZ can also join. The supervision entrusted with the ECB must
comply with the rules established by the EBA. At the same time,
the ECB issued in 2017 an addendum to its rules for minimum
levels of prudential provisions referred to new nonperforming
loans (NPL) requiring full coverage for the unsecured portion of
new loans.

In 2014, new rules for bank resolutions have been decided (bail-in),
in order to reduce moral hazard of the managers and the costs of resolutions to taxpayers due to state bailouts, shifting their burden on to shareholders, bond holders, and depositors having a deposit higher than
€100,000. In fact, most EU countries have already introduced a national
Deposit Guarantee Scheme, entirely funded by banks, up to €100,000 or
to a value equivalent in national currency (for countries outside the EA),
as required by an EU Directive in 2014. In addition to that, creation of a
common resolution mechanism for banks could relieve sovereign states
of the need to rescue their national banking system.

As a further step to a fully fledged banking union, in November
2015, the Commission put forward a proposal for a European Deposit
Insurance Scheme (EDIS), which would provide a stronger and more

uniform degree of protection for all retail depositors in the banking union. The Scheme, however, has not been implemented, and in October 2017 the Commission presented a Communication to the European Parliament and other EU institutions whereby sharing the risks was postponed to a final stage that was set for 2024 (but recently this specific date has been substituted by a generic expression: "the final stage"), and in a first phase the EDIS would only provide reinsurance. In suggesting to defer implementation of EDIS, the EC accepted the position of the German government and the Bundesbank. The justification is that "the Banking Union can only function if risk reduction and risk-sharing go hand in hand" (European Commission, 2017c: 6). The Communication envisages that

> in case of a default of a bank, national Deposit Guarantee Schemes would have to deplete their funds first before a possible intervention by the EDIS. This Scheme would only provide liquidity to the national Deposit Guarantee Schemes (which is in reality a loan, since it should be fully recovered from the banking sector afterwards) and would cover up to 30% of liquidity shortfall in the first year (2019), 60% in the second year (2020) and 90% in the third year (2021). The rest would be covered by national Deposit Guarantee Schemes with the resources not transferred to the EDIS during this phase or via ex-post contributions from banks. By leaving losses to be covered nationally and providing liquidity assistance for national schemes if needed, this solution would on the one hand ensure depositor protection from the beginning (for which liquidity is needed) and, on the other hand, take into account legacy and moral hazard concerns.
>
> *(European Commission, 2017c: 10)*

The extant national system of deposit insurance has two main shortcomings: it can create a bank run and capital outflows; it implies the likely intervention of the national government to guarantee repayment of bank deposits in case of a systemic bank crisis that cannot be faced by the fund created at the national level to repay deposits, thus possibly originating a sovereign crisis. The EDIS would create a European system, i.e., a system finally supported by European tax-payers, to be used in case of bank difficulties in refunding deposits and for bank resolution.

Apparently, the EDIS would avoid the bank crisis-sovereign state crisis loop, what has been defined as the "deadly embrace" between the banks and the sovereigns (Obstfeld, 2013). In fact, there could be a two-way feedback between them (e.g., Acharya et al., 2014), since, on the one hand, high shares of sovereign debt owned by the banking system in countries with a high sovereign debt can make banks suffer from a sovereign crisis and lead to bank crises; and, on the other, the more risky and undercapitalized banks tend to purchase more sovereign debt, the more likely are bank crises. This would lead to government intervention to save ailing banks and, possibly, to sovereign crises. The EDIS would be a useful institution for cutting both links. However, a number of critiques have been made about this proposal, not only because in some countries banks have accumulated high exposures against the sovereigns and in terms of NPL (which implies that banks in other countries could unduly be burdened and possibly be involved in cross-subsidization of such banks), but also due to the possibility of moral hazard arising from the facility.

As to the first issue, one can say that risk-sharing refers, and should refer, to the future and extant positions, which should be settled in a different way. As to the second, according to Carmassi et al. (2018), moral hazard would be tackled by risk-based contributions, which can internalize the specificities of banks and banking systems. On the other hand, a contribution equal to 0.8 percent of the insured funds would be sufficient to cover payouts also in a systemic crisis.

A recent proposal of a group of French and German economists (Bénassy-Quéré et al., 2018) has two components relevant from the point of view of the loop: one aims at reducing the risk incurred by banks that hold sovereign bonds; the other refers to risk-sharing. As to the former, risk weights should be applied on sovereign bonds held by

European banks for the calculation of their prudential capital. The proposal referring to risk-sharing would tend to avoid funding by the EU budget: each country participating in the Scheme should be charged with a premium proportional to its country-specific risk, a reinsurance approach would be applied and intervention by EDIS would be admitted only after exhaustion of national funds. In November 2019, the German Federal Finance Minister Olaf Scholz proposed a "European Reinsurance System" for bank deposits very similar to that suggested by Bénassy-Quéré et al., according to which losses exceeding both the national and the European guarantee fund should be borne by the member state concerned. These proposals would offer an incentive to the diversification of banks' portfolios, avoiding their concentration in terms of government securities in some countries. However, technically the reinsurance mechanism would not be able to cut the links. Both components of the proposals could produce a result exactly opposite to the one desired, "by raising fears that sovereign debts might not be honored" and thus augmenting market risks (as the Greek experience shows) and possibly leading to a self-fulfilling crisis, also in cases when there is a situation of illiquidity, not of insolvency (SEP Economists, 2017: 2). This effect is even more likely as Bénassy-Quéré et al. would also remove the financial stability exceptions in state intervention (i.e., those exceptions that would allow for it in case of a possible threat to systemic risk) in the activation of bail-in rules (Messori, Micossi, 2018). Finally, the solutions proposed would also be unfair with respect to the huge responsibilities of EU institutions and policies for the accumulation of public debt by banks.

Obviously, together with policies at the EU level, macroprudential policies for each member state are also necessary. As noted, these macroprudential policies, implemented after 2012, are primarily in the hands of either the central banks or other microprudential supervisors or new multi-institutional authorities. They are responsible for both the macroprudential powers shared with the ECB and not harmonized instruments, e.g., caps on loan-to-value ratios (LTVs), debt-service-to-income ratios (DSTIs). National macroprudential authorities are not represented as such in the ESRB governing bodies.

7 Suggesting a Framework for Macroeconomic Policies in a Currency Union

Macroprudential policies can be helpful when highly indebted agents suddenly do not feel safe with the amount of their debt and try to deleverage and reduce their spending sharply. A slump can be avoided only if someone spends more to compensate for the fact that debtors are spending less. If this is not so, a liquidity trap can arise, as even a drop to zero of the nominal interest rate may not be enough to induce the needed spending. In other terms, the decline in the interest rate that may be needed in order to avoid a fall in the aggregate demand may be prevented by the ZLB (or other impediments to a negative interest rate) and the economy would enter a liquidity trap (Hall, 2011; Eggertsson, Krugman, 2012; Guerrieri, Lorenzoni, 2012). Ex ante macroprudential policies – such as debt limits – can help in being targeted toward reducing leverage, thus improving social welfare. Contractionary monetary policy would be less effective (Korinek, Simsek, 2016).

In a monetary union, macroprudential policies are useful at a union level, unless the probability is low that financial imbalances arise at – or transmit to – that level, which can happen if integration of national banking sectors is incomplete and there are heterogeneous financial cycles across countries. If financial cycles are common to the union area, application of the Tinbergen principle states that in order to ensure two targets – price and financial stability – monetary policy should be complemented by macroprudential policy at the same level and their coordination would equally be desirable, given synergies between instruments and trade-offs between the targets (Boeckx et al., 2017). Macroprudential policy at a union-wide level is particularly necessary in the present situation, where a prolonged expansionary monetary policy could feed common financial imbalances.

Macroprudential policies at the country level in a monetary union can help monetary policy and reduce changes in the nominal interest, partially substituting for the lack of national monetary policies (Brzoza-Brzezina et al., 2013; Quint, Rabanal, 2014). They can deal with local risks, avoiding the formation of asset bubbles, without the need to alter the expansionary stance of monetary policy (Visco, 2015; Burlon et al., 2017a).

9.2.2 An In-Depth Analysis of Some Policy Issues

Many issues arise from this policy. We deal here only with the following four: (a) the need to complement monetary policy in the attempt to strike a balance between attempting to pursue full employment and avoiding financial instability, as underlined by Summers (2014b); (b) after the principles on which the institutions operating this policy should be based (c) how to implement macroprudential regulation; (d) the need to reduce current account imbalances within the EZ also in order to avoid stresses to the TARGET2 (Trans-European Automated Real-time Gross Settlement Express Transfer 2) system.

(a) As to the *first* issue, many tools could be implemented to reduce real interest rates, ranging from further pursuit of low nominal interest rates to the increase not only of current but also of target inflation rates. However, since the risk of asset bubbles arising in the EZ or elsewhere could increase as a result of these policies, the need for a specific policy, i.e., proper macroprudential policy, arises for avoiding financial instability.

(b) As to the *second* issue, the principles on which macroprudential policies should be based are worth discussing. According to Constâncio (2016), from whom we freely draw part of what follows, the *ultimate* aim and the principle on which the policy should be based is to prevent and mitigate systemic risk. This includes strengthening the resilience of the financial system and smoothing the financial cycle, in order to preserve the effective provision of financial services to the real economy. In shaping the macroprudential policy framework, *seven* aspects can be identified as guiding principles.

First, macroprudential policy should be preemptive and strongly countercyclical, which requires early identification of risks by early warning indicators and models to predict potential sources of systemic risk as an essential first step in the policy-setting process. Macroprudential policy should then act forcefully to smooth the financial cycle preventing it from reaching a dangerous peak.

Second, and related to the first, macroprudential policy should rely and be calibrated on the concept of the "financial cycle" (Borio, 2012) at a national scale in order to assess the position of the economy, predict its development, and appropriately calibrate the use of macroprudential instruments, devising instruments that are adjustable over the cycle (e.g., countercyclical capital and liquidity requirements) (Merler, 2015).

Third, the prices of real estate and financial assets are of paramount importance for the financial cycle and should be included as a relevant indicator, leading – at least for taming real estate prices – to adoption of borrower-side tools to influence the demand for credit (such as loan-to-value or debt-service-to-income ratios), in addition to capital-related measures conditioning bank credit supply.

Fourth, stress tests of the banking and financial system must have a macroprudential dimension. Such comprehensive assessments need to be embedded in a macrofinancial environment. They entail an assessment of the position of a specific economy in the financial cycle, since, for example, the adequate level of capital requirements cannot be dissociated from a country's position in the cycle. Existing stress tests are based on simplistic logics that envisage the representation of "what-if scenarios." These are "completely inadequate for a complete assessment of the risks borne by the banking system, although it must be said that they brought to light the excessive revaluation of certain assets" (Minenna, 2016: 349).

Fifth, macroprudential policy is complementary to monetary policy and should share the same status as a policy area. Central banks must have responsibilities in both policy areas even if they are not involved in micro-prudential supervision. Several reasons justify such a setup. Both areas need to work in close cooperation; central banks are more sensitive to macrofinancial stabilization goals; they possess more information about financial markets and the economy. Separation of the institutions charged with micro- and macroeconomic regulation can add to the effectiveness of supervision. However, since supervisors have to look at various microeconomic and macroeconomic indicators in order to implement the most appropriate tools, the mandate to be conferred to them is necessarily of the kind of an incomplete contract. Then, an issue of principal–agent arises, which has consequences for the effectiveness of macroprudential policies and requires choice of proper incentives for supervisors (Masciandaro, Quintyn, 2016).

Sixth, macroprudential policy should go beyond the banking sector and encompass market-based finance institutions and products. As the interlinkages of the latter sector continue to expand, thus increasing its role in lending to the real economy, nonbanks are clearly gaining in systemic importance. Moreover, the more policymakers are effective in using macroprudential tools to constrain excessive leverage and credit growth in the banking sector, the more likely it becomes that there will be excessive adjustments in the nonbank sector through leakages. For these reasons, the coverage of the macroprudential framework needs to be extended to the shadow banking sector.

From this point of view, some authors hold that Europe has a bank-biased financial structure, which derives also from regulatory favoritism for banks that only recently has been partly re-addressed by requiring higher bank funding (and of a higher quality) as well as tighter prudential supervision and improved resolution of insolvent banks. This structure is associated with greater systemic risk and implies a lower growth performance (Langfield, Pagano, 2016). These authors also underline the need for reducing the complexity of the bank resolution mechanism, getting rid of its insufficient funding together with absence of a centralized deposit insurance mechanism, still on its way.

They finally ask for a more aggressive anti-trust policy and separation of the lending and security trading activities of banks having a global systemic importance, in order to limit their risk exposure and control systemic risk.

We agree with these suggestions, which can be useful also from different perspectives. Think, in fact, of the usefulness of a Europe-wide deposit insurance scheme from the point of view of its ability to prevent substantial capital outflows from any country where a bank or some banks face difficulties. On another plane, however, a larger role of financial markets vis-à-vis bank activity, no matter how useful, would not be a panacea and the issue of a more extensive and penetrating regulation should be applied also to these markets, as the US experience has taught us.

Seventh, macroprudential policies must be geared also to breaking the sovereign-bank loop. To some extent, this can be done by different devices, such as by increasing capital requirements in proportion to the concentration of sovereign debt in banks' balance sheets (Dell'Ariccia et al., 2018).

(c) The *third* issue to discuss is that of the practical implementation of macroprudential regulation.

In November 2016, a consultation among stakeholders (companies, also international, and public bodies, mainly national central banks and the ECB), promoted by the EU Commission, reviewed the current EU macroprudential framework, with the aim to ensure the right balance between national flexibility and union control. The point of departure of the review was the recognition by the Commission that the existing set of rules had evolved incrementally over recent years, and that "this piecemeal approach has created a number of weaknesses in the framework," which may involve "streamlining the toolset of instruments, changing the activation procedures, enhancing the role of the ESRB as a macro-prudential hub and clarifying the role of the SSM in the framework." To sum up the responses of the consultation, there was broad support amongst stakeholders for some revisions to the macro-prudential framework. In particular, stakeholders supported simplifying the use of certain macro-prudential instruments, for example, by amending the activation mechanisms. Some stakeholders also supported extending the macro-prudential toolset beyond the banking sector. Some support was also expressed for amending the role and functioning of the ESRB.

(European Commission, 2016a)

An important role should be played by the Asset Quality Review for European Banks derived from the consultation among stakeholders just indicated, in order to determine the quality of bank credits and to find proper solutions. This review should distinguish between "bad" credits, i.e., credits toward insolvent firms, and "good" ones, in favor of firms illiquid, but solvent. The solution for the former could be the institution of a European "bad bank" to securitize them, thus relieving banks of their weight, which could add to their lending ability, while the other types of credit could survive through the action of the ESM and still perform their role (Minenna, 2016).

EU-level supervision must be complemented by national supervisory policies. The only problem with these is to ensure their homogeneity and consistency in order to avoid loopholes. In any case, we have now a case of incomplete banking union, as there is yet no risk-sharing and the stability of the banking system of each country depends on the financial stability of that country as well as on the ECB intervention.

Research promoted by the European Parliament has estimated the costs of a possible financial shock, finding that an increase in the "equity ratio" target to 9 percent or more for the banking sector and lower dividends could partly protect against the shock (Giraud, Kockerols, 2015).

A potential limitation of macroprudential tools – as for the implementation of the separation principle – is that they can be subject to regulatory arbitrage, provoking either greater cross-border borrowing (Cerutti et al., 2017) or migration of activities from banks to the shadow banking sector. This loophole derives from the prevalence of cross-border lending in the EU coupled with the fact that the macroprudential rules implemented by member countries apply to domestic banks and subsidiaries of foreign banks, not to the branches of foreign banks (ESRB, 2017). Therefore, reciprocity would be required by applying uniform rules. Clearly, this raises an issue of coordination over the whole EZ, which should be simplified.

In particular, macroprudential policy can be improved by a simplification of the authorities in charge of it and their coordination, clarifying the roles of the ESRB and the SSM and ensuring the ECB representation in the ESRB. Coordination is essential to avoid spillovers, but macroprudential regulation should be country-specific, due to possible asymmetries of financial cycles over the Union. This makes coordination more difficult. The considerable complexity of the rules involves a cumbersome and lengthy process for arriving at a decision and, possibly, implies an

> inaction bias or ... the possible use of instruments that are suboptimal for the purpose ... In addition, the overlap of powers between the European and national levels may give rise to contrasting goals. In the EZ, the instruments available for domestic macroeconomic management are often perceived to be too limited. There is a risk, in this situation, that macroprudential tools may be used as substitutes for "missing" instruments, notably monetary policy. For example, limits on bank credit (in the form of capital surcharges) could be imposed at the national level to compensate for a single monetary policy that is perceived to be overly expansionary in relation to national conditions. This could give rise to distortions in credit markets and fuel the development of the unregulated sector.
>
> (Angeloni, 2016)

However, the role of macroprudential policies should not be overemphasized as other factors act in nourishing asset bubbles; in addition, other policies, of a microeconomic type, should be implemented to get rid of these (Jones, 2015). On this, see further Section 10.1.

(d) As for solutions to excessive TARGET imbalances, it has been noted that deposit insurance would not solve radically one of the problems of capital movements (Westermann, 2012). The only comprehensive and durable solution would be to find ways to avoid structural asymmetries and lasting imbalances between EZ countries. In addition to what we have already said with reference to the MIP, a partial solution would be to redirect German current account surpluses to the rest of the world by establishing a German Sovereign Wealth Fund, possibly with the support of the public sector in order to face exchange rate risks. This would lower the euro exchange rate, with benefits also for EZ deficit countries (Gros, Mayer, 2012). One might of course object that this proposal presents a typical "Germanic" mercantilist view, which transfers the burden of adjustment to the rest of the world. But under the current circumstances one has to choose the lesser evil: a strong euro combined with ever-increasing internal tensions which also threaten global financial stability, or a weaker euro without the internal tensions. We believe that the global economy will be better off under the second scenario, even if the need arises of avoiding excessive current imbalances also at the world level.

9.3 FISCAL POLICY

For a long time, only a few economists have been in favor of fiscal policy as a powerful tool for dealing with crises (Arestis, Sawyer, 2010). In Section 8.5, we dealt with the rather recent revision in the literature regarding the value of multipliers. This implies a negative assessment of the austerity imposed in the EMU, especially to peripheral countries. In a nutshell, according to Illing and Watzka (2013: 269), "austerity measures across Europe seem to have actually amplified the decline of depressed economies, endangering the stability of political institutions and social cohesion, particularly in the periphery of the continent." The damages of fiscal austerity measures in deferring adoption of new technologies, with ensuing negative consequences for productivity and growth in the medium run, must be accounted together with their possible benefits if they succeed in reducing borrowing costs for private and public agents (Bianchi et al., 2019).

Time has come to introduce a new design for fiscal policy. Some of the measures needed refer to contingent choices (usually designed for stabilization purposes) and operate within the current institutions, possibly being part of a medium- and long-term plan tending also to change institutions, whereas others involve changes in the Union's institutions.

In what follows, we have suggestions for both types of policies (Sections 9.3.1 and 9.3.2) and distinguish introduction of federalism (Section 9.3.3) from other institutional changes; we also discuss proposals for dealing with debt (Section 9.3.4).

9.3.1 Stabilization Policies within Existing Institutions

The most important issue refers to the choice of countries that should bear the cost of adjustment. Within existing institutions, the burden is borne by deficit countries, which are asked to implement deflationary actions, such as complying with the Stability and Growth Pact (SGP) as well as the fiscal compact, thus implying the risk of accelerating an economic crisis. The institutional implication is evident that the existing rule should be reversed or, at least, made more balanced. We deal with this further under (b) in the following.

Remaining within the existing institutions – possibly only with a few amendments – the issue can be raised of supporting individual countries facing an asymmetric shock. Funding for stabilization can derive from the ESM – which is an intergovernmental organization not deriving from the treaties – or some right to issue a predetermined amount of Eurobonds (Holland, 2016;[8] Pisani-Ferry,

---

[8] Holland notes that Eurobonds should be considered as a means for reviving the economy, rather than for mutualizing the debt, as Matthijs and McNamara (2015) do. Along similar lines, according to Bordo (2012) Eurobonds can be used in the case of large asymmetric shocks for transferring revenues between member states.

2016). The ESM facility is now separate from the EU budget, but in progress it should be integrated into it or at least some kind of linkage should be devised, in a way similar to the EFSM. Alternatively, it could be established as an independent – adequately funded – institution (Alcidi et al., 2017).

The revision of the ESM, to take place in 2020, will draw a legal basis for the new tasks assigned to the mechanism. The current version of the revision includes: introduction of the common backstop for the SRF (to be in place by January 1, 2024, or earlier, if banks reduce their exposure to risks, notably NPL) as well as further development of the financial assistance instruments and the role of the ESM also in terms of demand for public debt rescheduling; in addition, precautionary credit lines working like an insurance policy – with eligibility criteria, limited to ESM members having a fundamentally strong financial situation, and a sustainable government debt, which are respectful of the fiscal compact – available for the EZ members affected by an adverse shock beyond their control. This latter condition would limit the range of countries eligible for the ESM assistance, as not all of them have been or are in a position to respect fiscal compact requirements. The impossibility to fulfill the conditions required for assistance would have negative effects on speculation, starting already at the time when the revised ESM Treaty is accepted, in a way to make it almost impossible to respect the conditions in the future.[9] Think of the increased deficit and debt burden due to the higher interest rate spreads ensuing from acceptance of the revision. This would also be the effect of any announcement of debt rescheduling that could derive from the other requirements of the new Treaty, according to which the ESM members should commit to introducing into the new sovereign bonds issued, starting from January 1, 2022, Collective Action Clauses (CACs)[10] of

---

[9] Balassone and Visco (2019: 3–4) note that "the small and uncertain benefits of a debt restructuring mechanism must be weighed against the huge risk that the mere announcement of its introduction may start a perverse spiral of expectations of default, which may turn out to be self-fulfilling."

[10] These clauses allow in general only a qualified majority of bondholders to change the terms of a bond even against the position of other bondholders. They should facilitate

a type allowing only the majority vote of all the series of the bonds issued for restructuring of any single series of bonds to take place at the level.

Some sensible policies within the existing institutions are suggested by Bénassy-Quéré et al. (2016): avoiding fiscal adjustments by countries in crisis that can be self-defeating, which requires making sovereign debt restructuring feasible; strengthening the banking sector and enlarging the role of the ESM; enhancing fiscal coordination, especially under exceptional contingencies; increasing the role of automatic stabilizers, in particular through federal unemployment insurance for large shocks (see also Section 10.1) or a common pension scheme.

Some other reforms could require changes in the treaties.

9.3.2 *Institutional Changes*

In suggesting them, one must first properly assess the existing institutions. Many critiques can be raised against the current fiscal rules. First, a shortcoming of the fiscal constraints imposed on countries derives from the procyclical effects of the corrections required to comply with them, what De Jong and Gilbert (2018) call the "corrective arm procedure." These effects have certainly operated, as shown by these authors. In order to avoid them and the ensuing limitations of the operation of automatic stabilizers, the preventive arm should operate, trying to avoid in good times future violations of the limits due to the negative state of the economy. The limitations could work especially in countries that already keep deficits at a level below 3 percent or even at a lower value, in order to fulfill the fiscal compact, in case of a debt higher than the 60 percent ratio of the GDP (e.g., Eichengreen 1998b; De Grauwe, Ji, 2015b).[11] In

---

debt restructuring, but can also make it more difficult, if the restructuring meets the opposition of creditors. In the case of the EU, the clause applies to new securities with a maturity of over one year, issued after January 1, 2013.

[11] In other countries, especially Central and Eastern European Countries (CEEC), they are very low, due to the scarce relevance of provisions such as unemployment benefits or progressive taxation.

contrast with these positions, according to Buti and Sapir (1998), the limit of 3 percent is sufficient to make automatic stabilizers work. An agent-based model shows that the SGP makes the economy more volatile, raises unemployment, and is likely to produce deeper crises and have depressing effects also in the long run (Dosi et al., 2014). However, this model does not discriminate between the effects of the corrective and the preventive arm of fiscal policy constraints. Summing up, the procyclical effects of the fiscal rules in a situation of slow growth in global demand, such as that prevailing at the turn of the millennium and later, have prompted scholars, politicians, and EU officials to call for the strictures to be eased or the adoption of measures to attenuate their impact.

As to the variable currently chosen for expressing the constraint on national governments, the deficit is an endogenous variable very sensitive to the state of the economy. Its increase may simply be due to the effect of a contractionary phase, not of the government's profligacy. Sticking to the ceiling of the deficit would imply to impress a further negative impulse to the economy. From this point of view, having a debt target, instead of a deficit one, can at least reduce this sensitivity.[12]

Since the net effect of these constraints may be unclear on a theoretical side (Lindbeck, Niepelt, 2006), the controversy about benefits and costs of the SGP can only be settled by proper empirical analysis. Most such analyses show an important contribution of automatic stabilizers in the EU, even if of a differing exact amount, due to different definitions and methodology (more recently, Dolls et al., 2014). Results are even accentuated if one considers the counterfactual to automatic stabilizers, i.e., the state of the budget without automatic stabilizers, which can be expressed in a fixed nominal value of expenditures and taxes – or, alternatively, as a ratio to the GDP. If this is the case, empirical analysis shows that the relevance of automatic stabilizers is much higher than the constraint imposed by

[12] On the ground of greater simplicity, the shift to the sole anchor of a debt rule is supported by Andrle et al. (2015).

the SGP (in 't Veld et al., 2012). As a matter of fact, in line with the recent empirical evidence (e.g., De Grauwe, Ji, 2013b), the SGP austerity policy appears to be self-defeating, as the public debt to GDP ratio has skyrocketed, while under Keynesian fiscal policies it would have remained low and stable.[13]

As a further argument for dropping reference to fiscal deficits, it must be considered that they can only be calculated with reference to structural balances, i.e., cyclically adjusted budget balance indicators, net of one-off and temporary measures.[14] Assessment of the nonaccelerating wage rate of unemployment (NAWRU) is crucial to this end and that requires the calculation of structural indicators of the potential growth. Problems derive from the difficulty of measuring potential output accurately, which is necessary to indicate the cyclical budget deviations. Rules of this type can thus be manipulated, or be the object of quarrels, and lack credibility. In addition, the NAWRU, as estimated by EC, is not stable over time and is not independent of the economic cycle. Problems also arise in the estimation of the hysteresis effects, which can lead to different output gaps. The higher this estimation, the higher is the structural effect and, then, the lower is the need to adjust current imbalances as violating "fundamental" disequilibria (Cottarelli et al., 2014).[15] Finally, it should be noted that the method leading to the estimation of potential output in Europe leads to its undervaluation with respect to the computation of the IMF and the OECD, who make use of the nonaccelerating inflation rate of unemployment (NAIRU).[16] This implies a procyclical effect on structural balances, affecting peripheral countries more than core countries

[13] This depends on the size of multipliers, on which we said more in Chapters 4 and 8.

[14] The original function of the concept of a cyclically adjusted budget balance indicator as well as its application in the EU are the subject of Costantini (2015).

[15] The rule is somewhat exposed to criticism, as recognized by Larch and Turrini (2009). For many other critiques, one can see Costantini (2015) and references therein. In practice the Economic Commission considers various factors when assessing the violation of this rule.

[16] For example, the IMF indicates an output gap of –1.7 percent for Italy for the year 2017, of – 1.2 percent for 2018, and of –0.3 percent for 2019, whereas for the Economic Commission, the figures are, respectively, –1, –0.3, and .3 percent. With reference to the three years, the cumulative difference is of 2.2 p.p. of GDP.

(Fantacone et al., 2015). In addition, it implies an emphasis to be placed by countries on structural policies, which implies a supply-side adjustment. This kind of adjustment, however, can aggravate the demand problems that certainly hit the EZ during the Great Recession and should be deferred until the demand problems are solved (Chapter 5).

The SGP and, even more, the fiscal compact, despite the formulation of this that could be passed by the EU Parliament (see (c) in the following), show a bias against public investment, as recognized by the IMF (International Monetary Fund, 2014b). In fact, cuts in public investment expenditures have been the usual consequence of fiscal consolidation and the attempt to pursue a deficit constraint, due to their greater flexibility.

Therefore, some authors have suggested that in calculating the deficit public investment expenditure should be excluded, thus implementing the "golden rule of public finance."[17] The proposal of adopting it emerged in the early 2000s (e.g., Fitoussi, Creel, 2002; Blanchard, Giavazzi, 2004), as it would have been a true implementation of a pact, the SGP, whose alleged targets include not only stability, but also growth. According to Bofinger (2019), the German Council of Economic Experts also suggests implementation of the golden rule, in particular as leading to a more balanced current account. However, as noted by Creel and Saraceno (2010), the SGP reform of 2005 stated that no expenditure item could be removed from the 3 percent limit of deficit. Certainly, the rule needs to be defined with accuracy and to conform to some desirable features, in order to ensure countercyclical conduct and growth, while guaranteeing financial sustainability (Creel, Saraceno, 2010). Among such features, rules not only allowing for the operation of automatic stabilizers but also defining the content of public investment can be devised. This should be made by applying the rule to a cyclically adjusted measure of the overall deficit and by

---

[17] A variant of the deficit rule that is easier to implement prescribes that current revenues must match current spending over the cycle. Borrowing is permitted only to fund public investment.

ensuring, in the long run, that physical assets do not increase to the detriment of other capital expenditures that certainly have a high(er) positive impact on growth, such as education.[18] A similar rule could require a zero ceiling on the ratio to GDP of the cyclically adjusted deficit (net-of-public-investment), as suggested by Creel and Saraceno (2010), who depart from the definition given by Blanchard and Giavazzi (2004).[19]

This rule is not considered by the EMU institutions (Section 2.3).[20] A justification for it is that the debt issued for investment implies both a burden and a future yield, since investment is productive (e.g., Abiad et al., 2015), as it adds to public assets more – if properly devised – than to public liabilities, thus increasing gross debt, but decreasing its net counterpart. As a consequence, growth could be enhanced and both stability of public finances and a fair distribution of the fiscal burden would be ensured if certain conditions are met. One of these conditions is that public investment should generate a rate of return at least equal – or in any case similar – to the private rate. This condition is satisfied depending, on the one hand, on the monetary policy reaction and the crowding-out effect and, on the other, on the human capital and the externalities created by public investment. The golden rule was implemented in the United Kingdom in 1997, was suspended in November 2008, and has not been practiced any more since the March 2009 budget (Truger, 2015).

Going further on the issue of the nature of the SGP and its aims, Lindbeck and Niepelt (2006) clarify that if it wants to keep in check the spillover effects of some countries having excessive deficits, instead of the SGP's legalistic approach based on deficit and debt ceilings, with punishments in case of their violations, the policy

---

[18]　On the implementation of remedies to avoid manipulation of the rule (e.g., increasing current spending by relabeling it as capital spending), see De Grauwe (2017b).

[19]　In favor of adopting the golden rule is also OECD (2016: 89).

[20]　A skeptical view on its implementation in the EZ was held by Balassone and Franco (2000). More recently, Truger (2015) has written in favor of it. Dervis and Saraceno (2014) have proposed an "augmented" golden rule, whereby not only investment, but also some current expenditures could be deficit-financed.

outcomes considered to be at the source of the most important spillovers to other countries could be taxed or subsidized. As an example of these spillovers, we could mention expansionary fiscal policy in one country that increases the average inflation rate in the EMU area to an extent that induces the ECB to raise interest rates with consequences for all member countries.

Taxing and subsidizing spillovers would tend to improve both efficiency and enforceability. A shortcoming of this solution derives from its possible addition to procyclicality. If the objective is instead to correct for domestic policy failures, "procedural" rules and limited delegation of fiscal powers to fully accountable committees may help resolve the fundamental conflict between policy flexibility and the ambition to counteract policy failures.

As to debt ceilings, while their positive effects in the long run can be debated, one of the arguments sustaining them is based on the idea of consolidation brought about by keeping a lid on expansion of expenditures also in the short run, due to the role of expectations (Giavazzi, Pagano, 1990, 1996). However, this idea seems to be devoid at least of empirical validity. An early criticism was expressed by Farina and Tamborini (2002). More recently, the IMF Economic Outlook of 2010 concluded that, first, the idea that fiscal austerity triggers faster growth in the short term finds little support in the data. "Typically, fiscal retrenchment has contractionary short-term effects on economic activity, with lower output and higher unemployment ..., (but) fiscal consolidation is likely to be beneficial over the long term" (International Monetary Fund, 2010: 113). In addition, a budget cut is less expansionary the lower the interest rate (as monetary policy has little room for partially accommodating its deflationary effects), the lower is the likelihood of a currency depreciation and the less expansionary are the policies of other countries, which gives little scope for raising net exports. Also critical of the expansionary effects of fiscal consolidation is Perotti (2013), who shows that – at least in the episodes referred to by Giavazzi and Pagano in their paper on the expansionary virtues of fiscal consolidation – the expansion derived from either external demand or other factors. Similar results hold for consolidations implemented by Belgium, Finland, and the United Kingdom. An important ingredient of the success of consolidation was incomes policy, even if it offered only temporary beneficial support (see Chapter 3).

From an abstract point of view, expansionary policies coordinated between the different countries could be designed to help the higher-debt countries comply with the fiscal compact rules. There are, however, two contrasting factors. First, the visions, strategies, and interests of member countries differ. Thus, the "German view" calls for respect of rules (really after having breached them). In addition, Germany is pursuing export-led strategies, and, in the more recent years, can finance its public bonds at zero interest rates. Some other countries (Belgium, Luxembourg, the Netherlands, and the United Kingdom) enact – or enacted[21] – true "beggar-thy-neighbour" policies, by lowering ordinary taxation in favor of foreign investors and adopting "tax rulings." These to some extent protect them from deflationary impulses outside and within the Union. Finally, the expansionary effects of a coordinated fiscal policy could be frustrated by restrictive monetary policies on the argument that it would likely increase the average inflation rate in the EZ. This raises the issue of coordination between the two macroeconomic policies, which will be the object of Section 9.6.

In devising new rules, the burden of adjustment would also be more evenly spread if fiscal discipline in peripheral (more generally, deficit) countries were, at least, balanced – or, better, substituted – by expansionary fiscal policies in core (surplus) countries. The budget balance to aim at could be linked to the current account position (Bénassy-Quéré, 2016; Pasimeni, 2016). In particular, Bénassy-Quéré (2016) suggests adoption in exceptional times of a "top-down" solution, managed by the Commission, based on a fiscal stimulus by countries with lower inflation and current account surpluses. By

---

[21]   This is the case of the Netherlands, which reduced its low-tax treatment in 2017.

contrast, in "normal" times the usual "bottom-up" approach of fiscal policy should be maintained, whereby the EC assesses whether the national budgets presented by each country are sustainable and stabilizing. This solution for exceptional times would certainly be of help. In our opinion, an even better solution would be a generalized anticyclical conduct in both groups of countries, surplus and deficit countries, possibly in a differentiated measure in order to take account of the different situations of each country. This, however, would be the object of an even more difficult policy agreement.

In fact, even within existing rules, coordinating a common response to the crisis runs into difficulties, and Bofinger (2016a: 235) suggests that the coordination process through the European semester

> could be considerably improved if the recommendations define a concrete value for the aggregate fiscal policy stance. Based on this aggregate fiscal policy stance, specific target values for the structural budget balance of each member state should be derived taking into account the divergences in terms of "fiscal space." In case of a severe crisis like the Great Recession additional fiscal space could be created by increasing the ceiling for debt mutualisation if such a scheme was ... already in place.[22]

The indicated measures would tend prevailingly to avoid crises. Other policies can be devised in order to cope with different emerging negative occurrences. These usually go under the heading of some kind of fiscal federalism, which we deal with in the next subsection.

A different, but related, issue refers to the possibility of self-fulfilling fluctuations. In fact, multiple equilibria can arise when monetary policy is stuck at its ZLB and inflation is below the ECB target, in the case agents are pessimistic, due to the likelihood of the emergence of a sovereign default. In this situation, Jarociński and

---

[22]   Fiscal space can be defined in various ways, e.g., as the difference between the debt target and the estimated limit of debt allowing its sustainability or, as seems more likely in the context of the paper cited, the difference between the current debt ratio and the estimated limit of sustainable debt.

Maćkowiak (2017) show that even a rather modest degree of centralization of fiscal decision-making would avoid the probability of the default.

A final issue has to do with the independent assessment of the fiscal conduct of the member countries and the EU as a whole. Some authors (Asatryan et al., 2017) have suggested strengthening the independence of the European Fiscal Board. One way to do so is by separating it from the EC, into which it is now integrated. In addition, the Board should avoid discretionary assessments of the fiscal stance, i.e., assessments not based on the strict implementation of existing rules, even if it can recommend changes to them. It is true that sometimes the Commission's assessment of compliance with rules is based on political considerations. However, some space for discretion should be left, in order to avoid outcomes that can be disastrous in economic and political terms.

In the medium and long run, other prescriptions can also be devised in order to improve the EZ's capacity to prevent crises or to cope with those that might occur. One can think of: limits to debt, rather than to deficit;[23] reinforced common supervision, as a way to prevent crises hitting specific countries that possibly transmit to the others; absence of "overambitious" deflationary policies and of cuts to deficit and debt, especially during a crisis (Obstfeld, 2013); higher inflation rates that could moderate the size of debt, both in its extant level and its future formation.

9.3.3 Fiscal Federalism

In order to indicate both feasible policies, i.e., actions within the constraints of current rules, and new and more effective institutions, we suggest simultaneous pursuit of strategies with different time horizons. In the long run, it is clear that the objective is reaching a fiscal union, but the path to be followed in the near future is also important. Timid steps in this direction can actually be seen, e.g., for

---

[23] Acocella et al. (2016), Acocella (2018), and Bénassy-Quéré et al. (2018) suggest the preferability of debt rules rather than deficit rules, among others.

some suggestions contained in the so-called Five Presidents' Report (Juncker et al., 2015: 14) in order to implement common stabilization interventions – in cases of shocks that "cannot be managed at the national level alone" – and to work on a fiscal union.[24] However, there are fierce oppositions to a prospect like this. Consider that at the beginning of 2018, a common position expressed by both EZ and other EU countries (what we call the "New Hanseatic League," i.e., the Netherlands, Estonia, Finland, Ireland, Lithuania, Latvia, as well as Denmark and Sweden) opposed transfer of new powers to the EC, asking also that all decisions concerning the EZ should be discussed within the EU.

In devising the tasks of the common budget, the theory of fiscal federalism (Musgrave, 1959; Oates, 1972) is useful. These tasks should include: (a) stabilization at the level of the EZ as a whole and of countries hit by asymmetric shocks; (b) growth, with a destination of part of the expenditure to common investment; (c) redistribution and allocation, in particular through a common welfare system, of structural and regional funds.[25] This should be guaranteed by deficit spending – also deriving from enhancement of automatic stabilizers at the level of the EZ as a whole when this is hit by a symmetric shock (Dolls et al., 2014) – and by transfers for counteracting idiosyncratic crises (especially systemic financial crisis, and banking and sovereign debt crisis), thus introducing risk-sharing.[26] The total level of the EU

---

[24]   See Section 8.8. See also European Commission (2016b).

[25]   For recent suggestions on the implementation of a federal reform of the European institutions see Dhéret et al. (2012), Pissarides (2016), and Tabellini (2016). A similar proposal, advocating an enlargement of the EU budget for carrying out the same roles as those indicated in the text, has been suggested by Andor et al. (2018).

[26]   Regional coinsurance was initially advocated by Ingram (1959), later by Bajo-Rubio and Diaz-Roldán (2003), and more recently by the IMF (2013a). The simulations of this latter study indicate that annual contributions averaging 1½ –2½ percent of GNP per year would provide significant stabilization for country-specific shocks and that all countries would benefit over the long term.

    In the words of Van Parijs (2017): "A Transfer Union is needed in order to provide a macroeconomic stabilizer essential to the survival of the euro. It is needed to provide a demographic stabilizer essential to the political survival of Schengen. It is needed to provide a firm common floor essential to protect the generosity and diversity of our national welfare states against tax and social competition. It is needed to make

budget as a percentage of GDP should be raised. In the short run, it should be increased to 2–3 percent, to have a minimum expansionary push,[27] but in the medium or long run it should reach levels of the order of magnitude of those of federal states, Germany and the United States, i.e., around 15–20 percent of GDP. Just to begin, the increase could be devoted to financing EU-wide projects for developing infrastructures, to stimulate growth.

As an alternative, in case of opposition by the non-EA members of the EU, an EZ common budget layer should be created, overcoming the opposition of those in the EZ and the EU that are in favor of all decisions – also those pertaining only to the EZ – to be taken at the EU level, as noted earlier.

A proposal more credible than the Juncker Plan – in terms of both the assumed multipliers and the amounts invested – should be implemented. As said in Section 8.5.1, public investment in the EZ could be very effective, especially if the stimulus is common to the various countries. The stimulus will be higher, the more accommodative is monetary policy (with forward guidance (FG) and quantitative easing (QE) continuing), the higher is its share of public investment financed by debt (at least in the short run) and the more it is directed to productive goods (Burlon et al., 2017b). In addition, on the one hand, the European Investment Bank (EIB) and national development banks could be used to help catalyze private investment; on the other, the pace of fiscal consolidation should be reduced (Griffith-Jones, Cozzi, 2016). As to this second proposal, one way to resume public investment is to introduce the golden rule of public finances.

tangible to the stay-at-homes that the EU cares for them too, and not only for the movers. Is this a radical proposal? Of course it is. But it is no more radical than what Bismarck did when he created, under the pressure of violent protests, the world's first national social security scheme. And do you really think that the EU will be able to survive without radical changes?"

[27] Aglietta and Leron (2017) suggest the rise be financed by a financial transactions tax and a carbon tax, which could raise some €500 billion, a bit more than 3 percent of the EU GDP. Fiorentini and Montani (2014) show that just raising it by .19 percent could ensure an increase in the growth rate.

As to income redistribution, Dolls et al. (2013) analyze the effects of an EMU tax and transfer system replacing the existing national systems by 10 percent and of a fiscal equalization mechanism that compensates for different taxing capacities across countries again by 10 percent, but find these proposals unlikely to receive political support. By contrast, a system of transfers limited to countries in times of crisis might be feasible.

On the way to introducing a federal design a number of these reforms would be in order, such as: (i) substituting the existing SGP constraints with new fiscal rules that allow for countercyclical spending and, in any case, introduction of the golden rule of public finance; (ii) reforming the ESM, with a change of its governance (to allow for some kind of majority rule, possibly involving the EU Parliament), an increase in its resources by extra transfers from member states, and a change in its role, in order to allow for making the ESM resources available also for unsustainable debt.[28]

A federal design can have a number of advantages, in addition to those deriving from performing the traditional functions of a budget. It would guarantee a true political union and common decisions made by the representatives of the different countries, rather than by unelected people and markets; it would also prevent destabilizing capital movements within the EZ; moreover, it could avoid unsustainable immigrant pressure, by promoting effective agreements with the countries of origin of immigrants and devising common investment projects in those countries.

However, the prospect of a federal union has raised fierce opposition. Some opposition arose even before the institution of the EMU. Someone noticed that common fiscal action to counteract asymmetric shocks is scarcely needed in Europe, since each country has powerful enough fiscal capacity to do that, contrary to what happens in the

---

[28] On this and complementary reforms, see, in particular, Bénassy-Quéré and Giavazzi (2017), Tabellini (2017a), and Arnold et al. (2018). Balassone et al. (2018) suggest, in any case, increasing the lending capacity of the ESM and the necessity that it provides timely and predictable finance.

United States. Countries should only be encouraged to do their part in counteracting the shock. The crisis has shown that this has not been the case in reality, since there is no well-developed transfer mechanism to be used in episodes of distress (Bordo et al., 2013). We can say, instead, that the countries mostly hit have found limits to their action due to the SGP and the fiscal compact. Thus, even this milder requirement has proved to be unfeasible. Later, the idea of creating a stabilization capacity was criticized first as it could create moral hazard problems discouraging countries from implementing necessary structural reforms and thus leading to a situation of a transfer union and an increase in taxes also in countries not hit by shocks. These critiques are dismissed by the analysis of Carnot et al. (2017), whose simulations show that they are unfounded.

As a matter of fact, not many countries have expressed their favor for – or have really implemented – an active anti-cyclical policy. Nor have core countries shown any sign of doing their part in counteracting the crisis, even less of making transfers to peripheral countries. One likely explanation is that they do not want to feed moral hazard of national policymakers in peripheral countries and in particular in those that are deemed to behave "irresponsibly."[29] This may indicate that the way forward is a reform of existing institutions, not trying to make them more effective, but this is certainly a hard way. Therefore, while striving for the first best federative solution, we must be ready for second-best alternatives that start from the existing setup. Four of them have been suggested so far. The first one, whose qualification as a second-*best* alternative can be doubted for what we will say, is from the former German minister of finance Wolfgang Schäuble, who in a famous "non-paper" suggested that "as long as there is little

---

[29] Beetsma et al. (2018) recognize the existence of moral hazard as a consequence of common stabilization facilities and suggest as an alternative relatively exempt from it the possibility of financing the countries that are hit by an exogenous decline of the world demand of the goods in whose production they are specialized. However, this solution could hardly solve other problems of coordination in the Union. In fact, fiscal policies would be locked into a prisoner's dilemma in case of technology shocks; on the other hand, multiple coordination equilibria would arise as an effect of cost-push shocks. A supranational authority would avoid such outcomes (Kirsanova et al., 2018).

willingness for treaty changes, we should follow a pragmatic two-step approach: an intergovernmental solution now, to be transposed into EU law later on ... (and) the ... ESM ... (are the) right vehicle for this solution" as it provides "temporary financial support under strict reform conditionality" (Schäuble, 2017: 1). This solution, while adding to the deflationary institutional setup, would keep all the institutional faults unaddressed, since no guarantee is offered that the necessary structural roots of the imbalances are eradicated and also countries with a budget and a current account surplus do their part in the adjustment. In other terms, this proposal would not only keep these institutional faults in place, but even harden them.

A second solution could be to devise some way to mimic the action of a rise in the EU budget, even if this is not significantly increased. One should start from the consideration of the asymmetry of the SGP, since it can compel fiscal consolidation, but does not force fiscal expansion. An appropriate fiscal stance compels expansion by countries having fiscal space. In addition, the suggestion by Bénassy-Quéré (2016) could be appropriate. national fiscal policies should be coordinated in "exceptional" times in order to reduce fiscal spillovers and mimic the action of a federal budget. This solution is certainly more reasonable, as it could solve, at least in a pragmatic way, the issues arising from the preceding solution.

A third solution would be that under exceptional circumstances the constraints of the SGP and the fiscal compact are softened (Fazi, Iodice, 2016)[30] and that each country is in a position to run its own

[30] We can add that the prospect of embodying fiscal compact rules into the European Treaties seems to have disappeared. In fact, in December 2017 the EU Commission proposed simply to include the fiscal compact in EU law in a milder form that allows for some flexibility according to the rules of the SGP, also delegating national institutions to control observance of rules. Its directive will be submitted to the EU Parliament for approval. The EU Commission (2017g: 4) hopes that the necessary steps toward incorporating its substantive provisions in the Union legal framework be taken within five years after its entry into force (that is, by 1 January 2018). "Such incorporation would bring greater democratic accountability and legitimacy across the Union. It would also allow for a consistent evolution of the European and national fiscal rules and for more effective monitoring of their implementation." However, also this prospect should be resisted, as it entails some ambiguity (e.g., will the fiscal

fiscal stabilization (Balassone et al., 2018). The possibility for some European democratic institution to declare the need for an even sizable fiscal accommodation, potentially falling outside the limits of the SGP, is suggested by Corsetti et al. (2016b). This institution could also buy national sovereign debt by issuing bonds like Eurobonds, guaranteed by the ECB. In this perspective of devising short- and medium-run second-best solutions to the issue of federalism, a way of also compelling surplus countries to act in case of a crisis should be found, which could be of the kind suggested by Bénassy-Quéré et al. (2016), who recommend distribution of fiscal policy expansions between all member states. Certainly, one must be sure that this discretion is properly used, which should be done by appropriate rules (Balassone et al., 2018). A partial way of reducing discretion could be that in these exceptional circumstances, instead of having to agree on the degree of flexibility, this is ensured by the golden rule of public budgets. The issue of ensuring not only restraint by deficit countries, but also expansionary action by surplus countries would remain and should be the object of an additional rule.[31] Moreover, discretion would also arise when the state of exceptional circumstances may be declared. If we wanted to totally avoid discretion, we should introduce a general provision in favor of the golden rule, independently of the assessment of a condition of exceptional circumstances. This would offer a solution, certainly partial (due to the asymmetry with surplus countries), but better than that proposed by the European Economic Advisory Group (EEAG). This suggests that

> the European integration process should replace the opacity of deals between national political leaders with pragmatic, explicit, and accountable compromises between socio-economic conflicts of

compact remain in force?). As a matter of fact, till October 2019 the issue had not been settled and the EU Parliament had not passed the proposal.

[31] Consider that in 2018 Germany had a budget surplus equal to 1.7 percent of its GDP. However, expansionary action in this country could enter into a collision course with the more restrictive internal rules (the debt limit, Schuldenbremse, and the budget rule, Schwarze Null). The issue of consistency between EU and country rules should then be settled.

interests that do not necessarily occur across national boundaries. It should accept the limitations that this approach implies for the scope and character of common policies and institutions, but also focus on the policy dimensions that do need to be harmonized.

(EEAG, 2014: ch. 2)

A fourth second-best solution could be to create a "rainy day fund" with common resources "allocated inter-temporally and across member participants according to the economic cycle" (Balassone et al., 2018: 140). An issue arises with such a fund, as some authors suggest the creation of a nonmutualized one, having a saving loan structure where each country should accumulate its savings in a national compartment to be used in case of need, with only limited borrowing from the rest of the fund. This kind of fund would thus exclude permanent transfers by other countries, thus avoiding moral hazard (Lenarčič, Korhonen, 2018). Other authors, while recognizing the need for sharing the impact of shocks recognized by the Five Presidents' Report, suggest creation of a Financial Stability Fund (FSF) as a long-term partnership allowing for risk-sharing, but with precautions in order to avoid persistence of situations of need and moral hazard problems, as well as taking account of existing "debt overhang problems" (Ábrahám et al., 2018).

As to the body governing the common budget, views differ, with someone asking for an independent body similar to that governing monetary policy (Tabellini, 2016) and others in favor of a single Treasury minister for the EMU, as suggested recently by the governors of the Bundesbank, Weidmann, and of the Bank of France, Villeroy de Galhau (Villeroy de Galhau, Weidmann, 2016).[32]

Some authors (Gros, Belke, 2016) show that the US "banking union" provides a very tangible insurance system against local financial shocks, without major involvement of the "fiscal union." They find, in particular, that the union-wide extension of banks and the

---

[32] On the theoretical side, this proposal is supported also by Semmler and Young (2017). However, it was rejected by the then French minister of finance, Sapin, and his German homologue, Schäuble. In Chapter 11, we will deal further with this proposal.

relevance of securitization in the United States helped to share at the level of the union or even internationally the losses incurred in specific states. However, these authors should have considered that it was some features of this system, such as the union-wide extension of many banks and their size, that caused the problems of the 2007–8 financial crisis, at least in so far as they made it difficult to let them go bankrupt, with the exception of Lehman Brothers. The features of the US financial system might have helped the system to share the losses of the crisis, but were certainly not irrelevant determinants of it.

In any case, one of the authors we have just cited – while being still very critical of the Fiscal Compact and the Excessive Deficit Procedure – recognizes that fiscal federalism should be implemented in the EMU, together with an incentive-compliant banking union: "The way towards a sustainable 'Economic Governance' of the EZ and the EU can only lead via a consistent fiscal federalism combined with an incentive-compatible Banking Union" (Belke, 2016: 150).[33] However, not only is fiscal federalism not there in the EZ, but currently the EU misses one of the three necessary components of a banking union, the EDIS (Section 9.2.1).[34] The relevance of this mechanism should be emphasized as a way to reduce speculative capital movements deriving from the appearance of a possible bank default and their negative implications in terms of sovereign crises. Some authors (Feld et al., 2016b) in reflecting the position taken by the German Council of Economic Experts express the fear of a possible danger of risks being transferred from the country facing bank difficulties to other member states. This explains – or mirrors – the opposition of the German government and the Bundesbank to introducing the mechanism. However, some measure of mutualization of risks must be implemented in an economic union. Absence of such a system would lead to repatriation of capital and the transformation of a private debt crisis into a sovereign one, with negative effects also on other member states, as has occurred recently.

[33]   On indicators of sustainable governance, see Bertelsmann Stiftung (2018).
[34]   We dealt with these schemes in Section 2.3.

As a conclusion to the issue of fiscal federalism, we can recall Pisani-Ferry's (2012) "trilemma," deriving from the association of three features of current EMU institutions, i.e., strict nonmonetary financing, the national character of banking systems, and no co-responsibility for public debt. In order to avoid EZ fragility, the missing requirements should be met. Strict nonmonetary financing together with the national character of banking systems would require a fiscal union. Strict nonmonetary financing and no co-responsibility for public debt would require a financial union and, finally, the national character of banking systems and no co-responsibility for public debt would need monetary financing for sovereigns. Different policy solutions are available to avoid this trilemma. Each of them implies abandoning one of the three tenets of the EMU institutions, which can be done by a broader ECB mandate allowing for either monetary financing of governments, or a banking federation, or a fiscal union with the possibility of issuing common bonds. A recent contribution applying a well-known NK micro-founded model has confirmed the advantages of fiscal unions having various federal revenues and transfers in terms of risk-sharing in providing macroeconomic stabilization across countries (Farhi, Werning, 2017). Fiscal integration is one of the suggestions contained in a study within the IMF (Allard et al., 2013), together with a system of fiscal risk-sharing by temporary transfers or joint provision of common public goods by a centralized budget. Finally, Furceri and Zdzienicka (2015) show that a relatively low-cost mechanism for risk-sharing, requiring a contribution of around 2 percent of the GNP of each country, could provide the same kind of stabilization as that achieved in Germany and other federal states. Introducing the principles of temporary transfers, being a function of serially uncorrelated shocks, would avoid moral hazard issues. These proposals are not easy to implement. Possibly, two solutions are more feasible: first, implementing the EDIS; second, taking some steps on the way to a federal fiscal policy, such as increasing the level of the EU budget. Both could help to rebuild trust in the Union (Dustmann et al., 2017). But the obstacles they meet are quite the same. In fact, both would require raising revenues at the EU level and enlarging the size of the EU budget, which is in contrast with the route followed after 2013.[35]

9.3.4 Policies for Debt

These should aim at lowering the risk of default of governments that derives from excessive public debt and enhancing its capacity to deal with large economic shocks. This can be done by various policies, trying to:

(i) avoid debt increase or lower its extant level;
(ii) reduce the amount of debt possessed by banks, in order to avoid their bankruptcy;
(iii) limit the risk of a government default and make the debt safer.

We deal in turn with each type of policy:

(i) Certainly, limits to increasing debt can have a role and must be taken into consideration. To this end the concept of "fiscal fatigue" has been suggested. Fiscal fatigue refers to an endogenous limit to the debt/GDP ratio beyond which primary balances cannot keep pace with rising debt, due to interest payments. This depends on the fiscal reaction function (i.e., the way governments react to the accumulation of debt) and can be computed (e.g., Ghosh et al., 2013; Berti et al., 2016).

On reflection, such a limit should be taken into account because policymakers must cope with financial markets, which often show a dangerous bias in considering liabilities only – and not assets – pertaining to public institutions, whereas what really matters is net debt. They do not seem to have a similar bias vis-à-vis private institutions. At least, their concern with illiquidity problems is very different from that for (even apparent) insolvency. Consideration – by both financial markets and, in any case, governments – of net debt would be the counterpart to acceptance of the golden rule of public finance.

---

[35] Marzinotto et al. (2011) suggest funding the insurance system by levying taxes of the order of magnitude of 1–2 percent of GDP.

Future debt will really be alleviated when the government invests in productive assets and issues debt to finance them, if productive assets have a rate of return higher than the cost of borrowing. Whatever this bias may be, if financial markets are to continue to have more or less the same role as today, some solution should be found for sovereign debt.

Two issues arise here: how to avoid its increase in the future and how to absorb its extant value. We have earlier dealt with both. As to the latter, solutions must be found for absorbing debt in a short time. Many proposals have been suggested to deal with it in a different way (a large and updated review is in Cioffi et al., 2019). We refer to a few such proposals. A more or less limited redistribution across countries derives from the proposal to absorb the existing debt by means of some European solidarity tax, suggested by Corsetti et al. (2015). Other proposals would imply either a higher control by other member states over the economic policy of a country and/or internalization of the risk to the country involved, with no negative external effects for, or contribution to, the indebted country by the others.

(ii) Rather than suggesting some solution for reducing the debt level, the Bundesbank president Jens Weidman demanded in 2013 a cut in bank holdings of government bonds and a rise in their capital requirements to reflect their riskiness. This proposal would have the effect of an immediate rise in interest rates for public debt and possibly a financial crisis in more indebted countries.

(iii) According to Andritzky et al. (2016), every ESM program should allow for a maturity extension if the debt burden is high, and debt restructuring should follow if the debt proves unsustainable. Countries should be compelled to issue debt with Creditor Participation Clauses, similar to the CACs , which would make clear the risk of bonds to their subscribers, thus introducing a kind of bail in for sovereign debt. This would limit the risks of aid from other countries. However, issuance of new public securities would be drastically cut and/or interest spreads would rise in high-debt countries, again with possible negative implications for financial stability and sovereign solvency.

A market solution to the issues of extant debt could be offered by official rating of the debt of each country that took account of the prospective debt evolution and proper corrective fiscal policies. This proposal should push domestic policies of the most indebted countries to reduce debt, but has shortcomings. One is the ability to make reliable predictions. If official rating leads to predictions similar to those of private rating agencies, this ability could be doubted, even if the former might not have the same bias as the latter. In addition, either official or market rating, in case of an uncertain outlook that led to downgrading of some sovereign bond, would aggravate the problems of debt, at least in the first years, by increasing the interest burden. If, in order to reduce this weight, the countries involved implemented a strong deflationary policy, the outcome could well be a further increase in the prospective burden of debt. In other words, the risk is one of self-fulfilling prophecies operating in a direction contrary to the stated purposes of the solutions.

Some authors have argued instead for the transformation of the ESM into a European Monetary Fund, to be financed by countries breaching the EMU rules. As seen in Chapter 2, this is part of the EU Commission proposals of December 2017 for completing the EMU. The Fund would conditionally lend its resources to each country up to the amount this contributed to it and would control the economic policies of that country (Mayer, 2009; Gros, Mayer, 2010, 2011).[36] From one point of view, this proposal is to be welcome, as it could overcome the limits of the ESM, which represents an underutilized facility. However, at least three problems would arise: the first one derives from the fact that some countries would like it to result from an intergovernmental agreement, which is indeed a very dangerous prospect, as the opposition of some countries could block or delay its activity, even in situations of crises that need prompt intervention. In addition, the finances provided to the Fund by undisciplined countries

---

[36] The German finance minister Wolfgang Schäuble made a first proposal for an EMF in 2010: see www.spiegel.de/international/europe/greek-debt-crisis-proposal-for-european-monetary-fund-wins-eu-support-a-682296.html.

could be limited. In order to have a meaningful capacity to intervene for financing the Fund, the EU budget should intervene, but this is extremely limited. In addition, the Fund would inherit other ESM rules, one of which implies veto powers by countries having a share higher than 20 percent (really, only France and Germany). This would imply giving a right to these countries to govern other countries' policies.

This solution has been criticized by a number of scholars: apart from one of its authors (Gros, 2017a), who now partially moderates his previous standing, Wyplosz (2017a) suggests many reasons against it, mainly that it would cause moral hazard, due to the laxer conditions usually imposed by a fund like the IMF with respect to those of the ESM, which lends on the basis of a memorandum of understanding that involves very strict conditions on the borrowing country. Sticking to an attitude like that of the ESM would most likely reduce moral hazard, but, if the experience of Greece (cited by Wyplosz) teaches anything, it is that the conditions imposed on it were indeed very hard and counterproductive. Consider also that the possibility would still be open that the policymakers of a country – possibly a rather big country, such as Italy – are induced to choose a strategy of heavy indebtness, bearing in mind that the conditions that could be imposed on the country by the EMF in case of insolvency cannot be so hard, due to the consideration of the deep implications in terms of austerity and, possibly, the negative externalities for other member countries. This, however, was not the case for Greece: the EMU has taken an attitude even harder than that of the IMF and the threat of a contagion has arisen, as even a small country has been able to transmit dangerous external effects to other countries. Then, at least if one assesses the European attitude toward debtors from the past, this can hardly be considered as lenient. Nor can one think that there are signs that this attitude could change in the future.

The decision by the EU Commission and the other proposals just mentioned would indeed exacerbate the existing structural defects of the EZ institutions. A more brilliant proposal (Minenna,

2017) is to reinforce the existing stability mechanism by instituting a true State Saving Fund, which should substitute the CAC with a repayment guarantee of all countries' public debt, against the contribution of an annual premium, thus favoring reduction of spreads. In a few years, the extant public debt would be completely guaranteed by the new Fund, being transformed into Eurobonds.

Supply of safe assets can be increased though mutualization of at least a part of the existing debt and/or future debt issuance. Many proposals have been suggested in addition to those of Eurobonds and the others discussed in Section 8.8 (e.g., see European Commission, 2011c; Doluca et al., 2012,[37] and, for a review, Cimadomo et al., 2018b). Three different systems of Stability Bonds, having different degrees of risk-sharing of the public debt issued by each country, were envisaged in a Green paper issued in 2011 by the EC, but no action has been taken until now. Creation of a system of "stability bonds" supported by EU tax revenues (either shared VAT proceeds or a new EA-wide tax) has been suggested by Ubide (2015) to partially finance EZ debt up to 25 percent of GDP. However, Ubide is very critical of Eurobonds. According to Jarociński and Maćkowiak (2017), the creation of a nondefaultable public debt instrument of the Eurobond type would avoid the probability of the default. Van Aarle et al. (2018) perform numerical computations on the impact of issuing Eurobonds. They find that debt mutualization would reduce risk premia for high-debt countries, while somewhat increasing them for those having a low debt, with a sensible net gain.

Other possible solutions for debt are consolidation, restructuring, transfer of country debt to the EU level, and a higher inflation rate.

[37] This proposal is of particular relevance, as the German Council of Economic Experts had suggested in 2011 adoption of a European Redemption Pact as an exit strategy from the debt crisis. This strategy is based on a binding commitment of the participating countries to reduce debt ratios below the value of 60 percent in the next twenty to twenty-five years. According to the Council, this objective could be reached with realistic primary balances, if the participating countries transfer the excess of their debt over the 60 percent threshold to a redemption fund for which they are jointly liable. We ignore what happened to this proposal, in particular whether it has been accepted by the German government.

Consolidation, i.e., public expenditure cuts and/or tax rises, has negative short-run implications, since it implies an immediate reduction in GDP. Longer-term effects can be beneficial. Both short- and long-run effects differ according to the instruments chosen for consolidation. Expenditure cuts are more detrimental in the short run, whereas they – or, at least, some of them – can be more beneficial in the long run. Then, in choosing the form of consolidation, the government should balance short- and long-run considerations (Alesina et al., 2012; Attinasi, Metelli, 2016). Another trade-off refers to the equity-efficiency implications of alternative fiscal consolidation strategies. Those based on spending are associated with more limited output losses but greater inequality and a reduction in the likelihood of achieving a successful consolidation with respect to those based on taxes. From the point of view of this trade-off, the best consolidation strategy can be achieved through a reduction in public consumption and temporary targeted transfers and tax reductions (Ferrara, Tirelli, 2017). This stabilizes consumption of the poorer part of the population even if it causes some limitation in the slow down of the pace of debt reduction.[38]

In our opinion, these trade-offs may be arguments in favor of alternative ways for coping with both short- and long-run problems deriving from debt. In fact, other solutions are available for lowering the size of the debt held at a country level, such as trimming or rescheduling the debt or transferring part of it to the EU level.

Restructuring options, in the most indebted countries or in all the EZ countries, can take different forms (for a review, see Committeri, Tommasino, 2018). One such solution would be a haircut (Mody, 2015), which, however, is unlikely to be successful from other points of view. In fact, it would bankrupt the banking sector, given the high share of their total assets represented by public debt, especially in some countries (e.g., Italy), or would risk violating the monetary financing prohibition of the Maastricht Treaty, due to

---

[38] The effects on income distribution of consolidation plans are the subject of Alari et al. (2017).

the high percentage of public bonds being held by the ECB as a consequence of QE (Ubide, 2015).

Another solution would be tranching sovereign bonds and making some tranches defaultable or spreading the debt obligations over a longer duration. However, a CAC could protect against restructuring and redenomination of bonds in currencies different from the euro (in case of return to national currencies), as we will see better later in this book. In practice, in May 2016 the IMF suggested spreading out the Greek debt.[39]

There are different options for transferring country debt to the EMU level. Schäuble (2017)[40] and various economists have suggested that the ESM should supply financial assistance only under clear rules allowing an extension of maturities or a debt restructuring mechanism that ensures fair burden-sharing by private creditors. These, on their side, would contribute to restructuring in case of sovereign difficulties. Tabellini is fiercely critical of this kind of restructuring. He rightly says that

> markets are an imperfect mechanism to discipline sovereign debtors. Markets react too late, and then when they finally do, their reaction is too sudden. Given the size of legacy debts in several countries, automatic restructuring or maturity re-profiling as a precondition for ESM assistance would raise global instability. Illiquidity risk would be transformed into insolvency risk, and self-fulfilling debt runs would become more likely.
>
> *(Tabellini, 2017b: 2)*

The so-called Politically Acceptable Debt Restructuring in the Eurozone (PADRE) plan foresees that an institution like the ECB acquires the debt of each EZ country by its own share of the Bank, swapping it into zero interest perpetuities. The institution

---

[39] Already in 2012 it advised smoothing debt obligations over a longer time period (International Monetary Fund, 2012).

[40] See also Sapir and Schoenmaker (2017) and Bénassy-Quéré et al. (2018). All these proposals go beyond an initial suggestion by Gianviti et al. (2010) to condition restructuring to a previous agreement between creditors and the sovereign on its terms.

will finance itself by borrowing at low interest rates on the financial markets. In return for debt relief, the various countries will give up the seigniorage revenues that would accrue to them in the future from the ECB (Pâris, Wyplosz, 2014). This would be a quiet way of paying off public debt. QE has to some extent performed the function of the PADRE plan, as central banks have acquired the public debt of various countries, thus earning interest on that, which will be devolved to the respective governments. Brunnermeier et al. (2011) suggested creating European Safe Bonds (ESBs), a Union-wide safe asset without joint liability, issued by a European Debt Agency (EDA), whose issue would fund buying of sovereign bonds of the European states in fixed proportion to the size of member countries. ESBs would be composed of a *senior* and a *junion tranche*. Sovereigns would remain responsible for repaying their own bonds. Then, these bonds do not imply shared responsibilities among Union countries for their repayment. If one sovereign defaulted, losses would be borne first by holders of the *junior tranche*.[41] Simulations show that the senior tranche of these Bonds would be at least as safe as German Bunds. A similar proposal to create sovereign bond-backed securities (SBBS) has been put forward recently by an ECB Committee chaired by Phillip Lane (European Systemic Risk Board, 2018).

ESBs have been criticized[42] as being "fake Eurobonds without any real risk-sharing between Member countries" and posing "more problems than they solve" (Minenna, 2018).[43] The perceived benefit of this approach, which echoes the structuring of the notorious "collateralised debt obligations" (CDO) in the years leading up to 2008, is that it breaks the so-called doom loop between the banking sectors in the EZ's periphery and their country's government bonds. However, the

---

[41]　See also Brunnermeier et al. (2016a), who calculate that they would almost double the supply of euro safe assets with respect to the status quo, weakening the loop between bank and sovereign crisis.

[42]　And in our opinion the critique also applies to SBBS.

[43]　In fact, Standard & Poors (2017: 2) holds that they would "probably reduce the supply of 'AAA' rated assets."

bonds "would give a signal to the market that the EZ accepts two different interest rate term structures," and any bonds not included in the structures "would become junk bonds," making them much harder to refinance (Hale, Allen, 2017). Minenna suggests a solution different from that of the ESBs, which would face the issues of both sovereign and banking debt, through some kind of mutualization of the former. We will deal with it in Section 10.3.

Another solution to rapidly reduce sovereign debt is a buyback through commitment of future revenues (seigniorage, VAT, or a wealth tax) or a "debt-equity" exchange with GDP-indexed bonds (Corsetti et al., 2015).

Finally, in order to reduce the extant debt, the inflation target could be raised, an option that we have already advocated in the previous pages. Since this solution would be fiercely opposed, some second-best solutions are in order. A partial solution consistent with the current EMU institutions would obviously be to raise the current inflation rate to its target level (Buti, 2014). However, success of this is not guaranteed, and the instruments used until now are under attack in some countries. Also the wage policy of surplus countries could serve the purpose and help in pursuing competitive rebalance of the member countries, but this policy certainly meets strong opposition (see the next section).

Another issue to deal with is the existence of the bank-sovereign "diabolic loop." The Great Recession in Europe was caused by the transmission of a bank crisis to a public debt crisis. The possibility is now open for a reverse causation of a financial crisis, due to the high percentage of bank assets invested in public bonds. Some authors and countries have required that this percentage should be reduced. Obviously, this would require some time to avoid a fire sale of public debt and allow for its absorption. However, Corsetti et al. (2015) have noted that this proposal can lead to banks having an incentive to invest in the highest-risk bonds. An alternative could be to implement a reduction of the sovereign debt held, together with restructuring of the debt. The share of public debt held by banks could be required to be partly invested in its senior tranche. Another alternative has been suggested by Corsetti et al. (2015), who propose to combine an attribution of risk weights on sovereign debt by the ESM/ECB together with a diversified basket of EZ bonds carrying a zero risk weight.

As a conclusion, the issue of rebalancing and attenuating the EZ problems, also from the point of view of financial stability and debt, is one of profound divergences about the visions and the interests moving the various countries, citizens, and authors. However, a solution must be found, possibly under the form of some mix of the different proposals we have indicated earlier.

As to the risk that restructuring can be damaging for the country implementing it, the past experience teaches us that this risk is very low, as tested, e.g., by the cases of Russia and Argentina.

9.4 WAGE POLICY

Any discussion of this topic should deal with at least the following three aspects, somewhat related one to the other: (i) the adjustment of wages required to face the crisis, both in peripheral and core countries, (ii) the adjustment of wages between countries to face existing structural asymmetries between them; (iii) wage policy in normal times in the Union.

(i) With reference to the first aspect, wage setting in peripheral countries – and a lower profile of productivity – have contributed (together with other factors, such as asset bubbles) to produce in these countries high inflation, high domestic demand, imports from abroad, and, according to some analyses, lower employment (Marotzke et al., 2017). In core countries, the opposite trend of both variables has led to low inflation, high savings, and an export-led economy. During the crisis, peripheral countries have been forced to pursue painful austerity measures that have reduced inflation and increased unemployment. EU authorities, e.g., former president Barroso (Barroso, 2012), asked for real wage cuts and structural reforms in countries facing a lack of competitiveness as the biggest problem for growth in Europe.

In the present situation, characterized by a kind of liquidity trap, this recommendation could fuel expectations of a prolonged deflation and thus of an increase in the expected real interest rate. This would further depress aggregate demand, as the nominal interest rate is stuck at its lower bound (Eggertsson, 2011; Eggertsson et al., 2014). In a similar way argues Shambaugh (2012), who underlines the usefulness of structural reforms in the long run, but their possible shortcomings in the present situation where an increase in supply can further depress an economy suffering due to a lack of demand. More recently, Blanchard (2018) has added to the discussion on wage policy, starting from a distinction of the roots of imbalances, which can be due to a demand shock or to an issue of competitiveness. A negative demand shock should not be faced by wage cuts, which would add to the lack of demand. Defects of competitiveness are instead to be cured through wage cuts. However, as to this situation, one should also ask whether scarce competitiveness derives from low productivity and/or structural factors. We will deal with this more in a few lines.

In fact, wage moderation can boost external competitiveness, but has negative effects because lower nominal wages and lower inflation, or deflation, can lower domestic demand and increase the burden of debt in real terms. The net outcome depends on the number of countries pursuing that policy and the monetary policy stance.

In contrast with prescriptions addressed to peripheral countries, the EMU core countries have not been required to correct their excessive wage moderation, even if imbalances, rather than being attributable only to peripheral countries' wage rise, derived also from core countries' wage moderation. As also Bofinger et al. (2016a: 236) show, it was the German wage moderation of the years 2000–7 that created serious imbalances in the EU. Now, higher wage increases would be needed in Germany, "leading to unit labour cost increases above the 2% threshold, at least for some years." In addition to what Bofinger et al. say, consider that low-wage workers as a percentage of total workers have increased from about 15 percent in 1998 to 20 percent in 2008 and even more in the following years.

Responsibility for wage policy in the EU is to some extent to be attributed to the EU Commission. Its Broad Economic Policy Guidelines have favored a policy of promoting company-level wage settlements and wage differentiation. This has enlarged wage differentials and "actually undermines the social parties' ability to act strategically in order to ensure wage trends that meet macroeconomic requirements, however these may be defined" (Hein, Niechoj, 2005: 14).

Horn and Watt (2017) and Horn et al. (2017) have studied the impact of wage policy on Germany's and other countries' current accounts. Both studies show that wage policy per se, in particular a rise that follows the wage norm of productivity growth plus the ECB target inflation rate, cannot do much to eliminate Germany's nominal surplus, while reducing its real value, due to the effects of higher export prices. More can be done by complementing wage rises with an expansionary fiscal policy, the more so as wage rises could fuel growth and increase fiscal surplus. Fiscal expansion in Germany should be very significant in order to allow compliance with the 6 percent "boundary" to current account surplus set by the MIB. Needless to say, wage rises and expansionary fiscal policy would be all the more necessary in the (unlikely) case the current account surplus permitted were lowered.

More generally, real wage cuts and further deregulation of OECD labor markets would not ensure the conditions for a viable, sustained economic recovery but are likely to be a recipe for prolonged stagnation of output and productivity growth. This is so especially now that there no longer exists an escape route through carefree borrowing like the one taken by the peripheral EZ countries as well as the United States before the crisis, also because households, firms, and governments are still burdened by debts (Palley, 2009; Palma, 2009).

(ii) Moving to the second aspect of the issue sketched at the beginning of this section, the need arises to manage wage and productivity growth (as well as domestic demand) in a way to ensure compatibility of the different country models that have developed until now[44] and thus to avoid the "incompatibility of national varieties of capitalism" claimed by Johnston and Regan (2016).

Then, coordination of wage policies throughout the Union, together with incentives for raising productivity in the peripheral countries, would be a fairer way of sharing the burden of adjustment in the long run and, thus, contributing to economic and political integration. In normal times, the EZ certainly needs less heterogeneity from the point of view of wage setting and bargaining systems. Obviously, to avoid increasing country inequalities, public investment and structural policies should be implemented too, in particular in those countries, such as Italy, where the dynamics of productivity has been lagging behind in the last twenty years or so (Sapir, 2016).

(iii) As to wage policy in normal times, the EMU has not encouraged an active role of trade unions in the process of wage determination, but has sometimes hosted suggestions for a weakening of collective bargaining institutions (Moschovis, Servera, 2010). The underlying idea is that union bargaining privileges wages of some groups of workers and determines a level of wages so high as to imply structural unemployment that hits other groups of workers. According to Jaumotte and Osorio Buitron (2015),[45] this has been the case in some South European countries. We dissent from this statement, at least if the authors refer to Italy, where a rather rigid wage and incomes rule was enforced starting 1993 and was somewhat relaxed only about mid-2000s. The true problem of some countries like Italy is that they had a low productivity profile, which does not depend mainly – or only – on union bargaining, although some forms of this can influence the productivity profile.

---

[44] We refer to the export-led and domestic-demand-led (or credit-led) growth models highlighted in Chapter 2.

[45] Jaumotte and Osorio Buitron have also shown that there is a direct correlation between the intensity of union bargaining and the lower income share. Absence of union bargaining might even have contributed to the European stagnation. To this end one must consider, in fact, the negative effect of inequality on growth, as shown in general by Ostry et al. (2014) and Lagarde (2015).

The ideal solution would be coordinating national bargaining across the EZ or, better, establishing a European institutionalized collective bargaining system. This could be *part* of a strategy alternative to that of a conservative central bank for ensuring low inflation and higher growth at the same time.

Coordinated wage bargaining oriented to productivity would contribute to achieving the policy goals of an equitable distribution of income as well as to stabilizing demand and guaranteeing price stability (Stockhammer, 2011). In addition, wage rises in the EU economy as a whole could generate good-quality employment and growth (Lavoie, Stockhammer, 2013; Storm, Naastepad, 2017). Wage policy and bargaining could in any case play a larger role also in the short-medium run, as countries lack macroeconomic tools for directing their economy (Driffill, 2006). Wage agreements would be needed that take account of both their impact at the country level and their Europe-wide effects. They can take into consideration current or past asymmetric shocks, establishing a wage dynamics for a specific country different from other countries. This can certainly benefit or damage that country's unions with respect to the solution of a uniform wage dynamics across the EZ, but would help in addressing the situation in that country.[46] In particular, German wages should be raised above productivity and the inflation target for a number of years.

Storm and Naastepad (2012) suggest an articulated policy package aimed at protecting both wages – by ensuring that they share gains from productivity growth – and profits, in order to guarantee investment and technological progress. A commitment to providing employment security at a microeconomic (firm) and a macroeconomic level should also be provided.

---

[46] Borghijs et al. (2013) hold that international wage coordination can hamper the absorption of asymmetric shocks in the EMU, since wage bargaining should take place at the level at which shocks occur (Pissarides, 1997; Calmfors, 2001). However, this consequence depends on the weights placed on the different targets of the preference function of unions.

The issue of the labor market in the EZ can be tackled not only from a macroeconomic but also from a microeconomic point of view. This will be the object of analysis in Section 10.8.

9.5 EXCHANGE RATE POLICY

In empirical terms, the trend in the overall EZ current account balance with non-EU countries has been close to zero since its inception until recently, but this reflects a very different contribution by the different countries over time. Up to 2010, Germany emerged as the country with an increasing surplus, compensated by deficits of other countries. These changed moderately for France and increased (in absolute terms) rather significantly for Italy, Ireland, Spain, and Greece, while remaining at a high level for Portugal. Negative imbalances in these countries derived also from rising Chinese competition and rising oil prices. As said, as an effect of intra-EA financial integration, they were financed by net lending from the core countries in the EZ (and, to some extent, also from external countries). After 2010, while the overall surplus position of Germany and a few other countries remained pretty unaltered, the deficit of other countries shrank notably or turned into a surplus.

Obviously, these imbalances were linked to changes in exchange rates. Within the EZ the only possible changes refer to real rates. Their appreciation or depreciation through price and wage inflation or deflation could help rebalance current accounts, together with suitable aggregate demand changes. However, di Mauro et al. (2016) are skeptical on their effectiveness, or on an equal effectiveness for all EZ countries, because of the emergence of global value chains, into which EZ economies are tightly integrated. In these circumstances, trade imbalances are largely the result of the international organization of production at the firm level. Transnational corporations assign production tasks of components or phases of the final product to different countries.

The implication is that imbalances within the EZ tend to be increasingly less affected by the adjustment of relative prices and demand vis-à-vis EZ trade partners ... a large part of value added crosses international borders multiple times before being absorbed in final demand.... This means that relative price changes can have complex effects. For example, a loss in competitiveness of a surplus country might drag down the exports of a deficit country, whose value added is indirectly being exported by the former.

(di Mauro et al., 2016)

Other studies (Horn, Watt, 2017; Horn et al., 2017) – while confirming, but for different reasons, the scarce effects of wage and price changes alone – show that a joint rise in wages and demand can be more effective. In addition to the argument of value chains, a problem of possible negative effects of price deflation on domestic demand, notably investment, arises, as noted by Keynes himself. Finally, the political and social feasibility of wage and price deflation should be checked, as unions and firms usually resist it. Wage rises are certainly more feasible, even if price inflation can be less popular in some countries, such as Germany.

As for the exchange rate of the EZ vis-à-vis the Rest of the World, the topic of the external imbalances at a world level is relevant. The overall EZ current account has been positive since 2012, after being almost balanced. Outside Europe, the surplus of oil exporters remained constant on the whole, and China's surplus shrank. The United States has maintained a deficit position. Thus, looking at the EZ imbalances in foreign accounts from a global perspective, the need for an adjustment of excessive positions arises in both deficit and surplus countries. Lane and Milesi-Ferretti (2014) advocate a combination of policies of less expenditure in deficit countries, together with higher demand in surplus countries, a suggestion in perfect agreement with the position we expressed earlier with respect to the perspective internal to the EA. However, following this recipe seems to be extremely difficult for the EZ, due to inexistence of a common fiscal policy. Also an alternative policy such as an exchange rate variation of the euro is difficult to implement. In fact, there is some disagreement about the institution in charge of setting the exchange rate, since Article 119 of the Consolidated version of the EU Treaty seems to assign exchange rate policy to the ECB, whereas Article 291 assigns this task to the unanimous decision of the European Council. As a matter of fact, the nominal exchange rate is influenced by monetary policy more than it would be by a decision of the Council of Ministers.[47] In any case, any such decision would cause problems for the monetary policy decisions, as it might require an interest policy rate by the Bank in contrast with its overriding target, i.e., monetary stability.

9.6 COORDINATION OF MACROECONOMIC POLICY

As a conclusion to the discussion on macroeconomic policy instruments we could refer to James Tobin's (1986) "funnel" theory about how best to calibrate monetary and fiscal policy in a region. Corsetti et al. (2016a: 157) draw the specific conclusion that "monetary policy cannot achieve stabilisation objectives without stronger mechanisms for fiscal burden-sharing and risk-pooling." We can extend this suggestion to all macroeconomic policies, which must certainly be geared in a way to reach the set of different targets indicated earlier, an application of the classic theory of economic policy, asking for simultaneous choice of multiple instruments directed at various targets.[48] To be more specific, interactions between the effects of different policies, in particular of a macroeconomic type, must be recognized in devising them, for a number of reasons: all policies interact one with the other; some policies have a double nature, both of a monetary and a fiscal policy type; no clear distinction can be drawn between

---

[47] Cecioni (2018) has found a visible influence on the euro exchange rate of both conventional and unconventional policies by the ECB after 2012.

[48] An ideal policy would require coordination of all the instruments available to the EMU and member countries. Since this would be a difficult task in practice – given the practical inexistence of comprehensive models, not only of models having both a macroeconomic and microeconomic specification, but also of comprehensive macroeconomic or microeconomic models – we limit ourselves to dealing with coordination of couples of the different macroeconomic instruments, hinting sometimes at some possible coordination between a macroeconomic and a microeconomic tool.

these two policies at the ZLB; there exist information problems (King, 2014; more generally, Acocella et al., 2013).

There can be either substitutability or complementarity between the various policies that only a general model of the economy can account for.[49] Policies are substitutes if each has a similar type of effect on some objective. This is the case, e.g., of monetary, macroprudential, and fiscal policy directed at raising employment and income. Policies are instead complementary if they are more effective when operating together. In both cases, if the different instruments are geared by different policy authorities, each instrument can be preferentially directed at one objective, which requires a kind of assignment of each tool to some preferential target. A recent example of this kind of "appropriate assignment" of instruments to targets has been derived by Menna (2016): in a dynamic stochastic general equilibrium (DSGE) model with non-Ricardian consumers monetary policy can stabilize inflation, while fiscal policy can cope with the effects of productivity shocks on income distribution. In any case, the use of each instrument must be calibrated, as certainly all of them have an influence on all targets.

Here, we deal in this order with (a) coordination of monetary and macroprudential policy; (b) coordination of monetary and wage policy; (c) coordination between monetary and fiscal policy; (d) international coordination with countries outside the EMU. We already hinted at the problems of coordinating monetary and exchange rate policies.

9.6.1 Coordination of Monetary and Macroprudential Policy

Both policies affect real economic variables. They are not mere substitute, as in some cases they can be complement.

Economic outcomes are superior if monetary and macroprudential policy are closely coordinated, especially when economic

---

[49] Difficulties in devising a model that is comprehensive of all possible tools usually constrain to analyze coordination only for either macroeconomic or microeconomic policies at a time.

fluctuations are driven by financial or housing market shocks, as both macroprudential and monetary policies have an influence on financial imbalances, inflation, and output (Angelini et al., 2011; Guibourg et al., 2015). From this point of view, the decision to involve the ECB in both policies is useful. Galati and Moessner (2013) note that, even if superiority of coordination should be recognized, when the two policies are charged with different authorities, practical problems, such as the lower frequency of macroprudential decisions, imply that the authority governing them should be the Stackelberg leader, similarly to what happens when dealing with monetary and fiscal policy coordination, for which fiscal policy should lead the other policy. A problem arises if macroprudential regulation targets not only financial imbalances, but also stability of the real economy. In this case, even if the gains from coordination with monetary policy are high, the instruments can be kept separated, each policy being assigned to the target for which it is more effective: monetary policy should target inflation and the output gap and macroprudential regulation should address financial stability (Svensson, 2012).

The sources of financial imbalances together with policies to deal with them are particularly relevant for small open countries such as emerging market economies. If these sources are large foreign borrowings, typically financial imbalances can ensue that could explode after a financial shock. Coping with them by monetary – rather than macroprudential – policy is likely to aggravate financial instability. In fact, "the greater the size of foreign borrowing the greater the benefits from macroprudential measures" (Ozkan, Unsal, 2014: 7).

As said, in a monetary union macroprudential policies at the union level are useful, if the probability is high that financial imbalances arise at this level.[50] As to coordination with monetary policy, application of the Tinbergen principle states that in order to ensure reaching two targets – price and financial stability – monetary policy

---

[50]　We have already dealt with the reason why they can serve also at a country level.

should be complemented by macroprudential policy at the same level, given synergies or trade-offs between the targets (Boeckx et al., 2015). Macroprudential policy at a Union-wide level is particularly necessary in the present situation, where a prolonged expansionary monetary policy could feed financial imbalances.

In summing up our considerations about coordination of monetary and macroprudential policy, we can say that the present institutional situation in the EZ seems worth preserving, even if the content of the Banking Union should be extended.

9.6.2 Monetary and Wage Policy Coordination

As said, wage and income policy has practically no role in the current EZ setting. It should have one instead, in particular in being implemented together with monetary policy. In fact, it could be a complement to this policy, remedying the nature of the latter as a policy acting on the EZ as a whole only. Internal imbalances deriving from wage and price trends could thus be reduced, especially if wage policy at the country level is correctly designed and complemented, in turn, by structural policies having an effect on productivity. This could be enhanced, on the one side, by decentralized wage negotiations and, on the other, by public and private investment, especially in education.

9.6.3 Monetary and Fiscal Policy Coordination

We deal, in turn, with: (a) the double nature of some monetary actions in general and in a monetary union specifically; (b) persistence of the motives behind separation of monetary from fiscal policy, again in general and in a union like the EMU.

(a) Some policies, such as helicopter money, have per se a double nature, both of a monetary and a fiscal policy type. Other policies, such as QE, can have fiscal effects, first because in general at the ZLB there is no clear distinction between these two policies (King, 2014). In addition, subtle reasons of this double nature may arise in a currency union. According to some authors and policymakers (mainly the president of the Bundesbank and some German economists), introduction of QE has changed the nature of the two policy tools under examination, since QE has a fiscal impact. Let us look at this claim in more detail. We will then deal with the respective tasks and the separation of monetary from fiscal policy.

In a country that is not a member of a currency union, when implementing permanent QE operations, the central bank replaces government bonds promising an interest rate with a monetary liability paying no interest. In a consolidated public-sector account, there would be no change. The government obligation toward the citizens is substituted by a (fictitious) central bank obligation toward them. Bonds really cease to exist, even if they may still appear in the balance sheet of the central bank. Something has changed, however, as the government (and, ultimately, the taxpayer) is relieved of interest (tax) payments. Consider, in fact, that the ECB profits deriving from the interests paid by the governments are distributed back to them. By contrast, the taxpayer could run the risk of inflation, but this risk is immaterial in a deflationary situation. Then, there seems to be a win-win situation. However, in a currency union like the EMU, QE can imply some intercountry transfers, if the purchases of individual countries' bonds are not distributed according to their respective equity shares in the ECB. In addition, if the highly indebted country defaults, interest payments stop, and this could be a case in which "virtuous" countries are penalized, unless proper solutions are devised. Also in case of only temporary QE operations (some of the bonds bought are sold on the market), there would be intercountry transfers. These remarks could then be relevant. However, all transfers could be avoided by appropriately devising the countries being the object of such operations and their amounts, i.e., if the sales are in proportion to the equity shares used for the purchase (De Grauwe, Ji, 2015a).

(b) We turn now to the persistence of the motives behind the separation of monetary from fiscal policy, with the creation of independent central banks, again first in general and then in a union like the EMU. The need to fight time inconsistency and inflation led some authors (not only, as said,

Sargent, Wallace, 1981, and Rogoff, 1985, but also Walsh, 1995) to require separation of monetary and fiscal policies as well as monetary leadership and commitment. A consensus gradually emerged on a similar position. This has lasted for almost three decades.

With the emergence of the crisis the primary objective of economic policy has changed from one of noninflationary expansion to higher employment and income growth. The resilience of the crisis to policy measures (monetary action, in most cases after 2009–10) has produced a rise in private and public debt, not only in absolute terms, but also with respect to GDP (Alcidi, Thirion, 2016). This again has required some kind of strict coordination between macroeconomic policies, discarding especially in the EU – or putting aside, given the deflationary environment – the very strict target of a noninflationary monetary policy (as this was stuck to the ZLB) and the requirement of a complementary tight fiscal policy.

As a parallel – but to some extent autonomous from contingencies – development, the "Old View" of the 1980s and the 1990s about the role of monetary and fiscal policy has lost ground from a number of points of view. It must be said, however, that the new orientation can lead to various different conclusions, highly dependent on the models and the underlying assumptions of each. We will be selective in our review and mention only some results of apparent interest. One of the reasons for doing so is that, given the high dependence of results on the kind of model used, the choice of the proper assumptions and model should be deemed to be very relevant, while being largely an open issue.

Referring to the issue of leadership of monetary or fiscal authorities, Dixit and Lambertini (2001) had found that leadership by either monetary or fiscal authority leads to better outcomes than Nash equilibrium, if there is a conflict of preferences or priorities between the authorities. Hughes Hallett (2008) has challenged the then prevailing view about leadership, by pointing out that – in a world of independent institutions in charge of the different instruments – fiscal leadership leads to better outcomes, not only for output, but also for inflation and fiscal balances. Hughes Hallett and Weymark (2007) and Hughes Hallett et al. (2014) have shown, first, debt targeting to be a natural way to provide the required (dynamic) fiscal leadership and to create a capacity for monetary policy to discipline undisciplined fiscal policymakers. In addition, they have extended this argument by showing how a Pareto-efficient outcome can be selected in situations with multiple equilibria. Leitemo (2004) also supported government commitment in a neo-Keynesian model of fiscal and monetary interaction. More recently, it has been shown, however, that in a situation of separate fiscal authorities fiscal leadership can have negative consequences. Chortareas and Mavrodimitrakis (2017) derive the result of a negative influence of isolated fiscal leadership in a currency union: in a three-stage game, with two fiscal authorities, fiscal authority of one country as a leader makes the other worse off when there are demand shocks.

As to the risk of time inconsistency, this can be avoided by well-designed and coordinated economic policies, if governments have a long enough time horizon and sufficient instruments to control the economic system. Time inconsistency and the need for a commitment technology may thus appear only in certain cases (Acocella et al., 2013).

Interesting innovative results have emerged mainly in the way to arrange coordination of the two policies. Onorante (2006) analyzed fiscal coordination from the point of view of stabilizing output and inflation and found that the form of fiscal cooperation is relevant: a mix of informal cooperation and rules can better preserve inflation control by the central bank. In addition, a revised version of nondiscretionary, but rule-based, fiscal coordination can also stabilize output. Bordo et al. (2013) suggest several conditions for implementing a fiscal union, notably, commitment to no bail out, well-functioning transfers to countries hit by a shock, ability to adapt to changes, but also a central tax authority and Eurobonds – whose service is ensured by taxes collected by the European tax authority – that can be used to make transfers to the members that are hit by asymmetric shocks.

Bajo-Rubio and Díaz-Roldán (2017) derive the result that, if fiscal authorities have fiscal deficit as their target, a fiscal union is beneficial only for common shocks. We can, however, question this condition for a couple of reasons. First, it does not correspond to reality, since in practice asymmetric shocks can lead to symmetric ones, due to interdependencies. In addition, the target of fiscal deficits is a consequence of the current EZ institutions, really a constraint imposed by them, which in theory could or should be removed, in favor of other targets. As to asymmetric shocks, automatic stabilizers would be available, according to Bajo and Díaz-Roldán.[51] However, these stabilizers should be enabled to fully operate, in order to be able to cope with asymmetric shocks, which would call into question the limits to deficits stated by the SGP and the fiscal compact. A solution suggested by Cole et al. (2016) could be choice of government consumption to stabilize the net exports gap procyclically, instead of acting counter-cyclically with respect to the output gap. This would provide stabilization even in a condition of distortionary taxation.

Hughes Hallett et al. (2011: 20–1) find that the first-best outcome can be achieved through some form of coordination, even simple exchange of information on the target output rate of each authority, rather than negotiation over the details of the policy actions of each. But even when the first-best outcome cannot be achieved, if the policymakers coordinate on an output target that differs from the socially optimal one, "such coordination can still improve social welfare relative to an uncoordinated Nash outcome. This is because coordination prevents the two policies from perpetually trying to offset each others' actions, i.e., engaging in a tug-of-war." In other words, there are often significant gains to be obtained through even limited coordination, but there can be no general result that incomplete coordination always leads to gains over no cooperation, given the theory of the second best. Orphanides (2017) recognizes that the current fiscal

---

[51]   A result already obtained by Galì and Monacelli (2008) through an NK model with many countries is that stabilization of country-specific shocks requires each country to be free from external constraints.

policy framework leads to "suboptimal" policies, due to positive spill-overs. This would suggest establishing common fiscal action, under the form of a fiscal union. Implementing this solution, however, would require a revision of the Treaty, which is not politically feasible, even if it has gained new supporters.[52] As a substitute to common expansionary action, according to Eichengreen (2017), "more investment in infrastructure, health, and education would be good for Germany itself" and also for other countries.

A final notation has to do with coordination of economic policies, not only from a short- but also a long-run point of view. One should consider that solutions to the short-run lack of demand and increases of current production can also improve potential output and avoid the prospect of secular stagnation. From both points of view, helicopter money would be an optimal candidate for relieving lack of demand in the short and the long run, given also the limitations of other monetary and fiscal policies, due, on the one hand, to the ZLB and, on the other, to the high level of public debt.

9.6.4   The International Dimension of Coordination

With reference to the EZ, one can speak of international coordination not only internally to it, as done above, but also with external countries.

International coordination of monetary policy is a difficult task, which is likely to occur mainly in exceptional circumstances, as happened in 2007–8. In more normal times, according to Obstfeld and Rogoff (2002), there can be little gain from coordination if monetary policy is directed at domestic targets, as each economy may be in different conditions and each central bank is under a specific mandate, especially so when we compare the EU to other countries. Instead of coordination, one can hope to establish some milder form of cooperation in order to try to add to stability of the

---

[52]   Rodrik (2017) claims that also the former German finance minister Wolfgang Schäuble is now convinced of the necessity of a fiscal union, as reported by his former Greek homologue, Yanis Varoufakis.

international environment. Thus, instead of aiming to equalize interest rates or other aspects of the policy, some weaker form of international collaboration can be feasible and useful. Cooperation can consist in foreign currency swap agreements for the case of crises, common preventive communication of current economic trends and the respective reaction functions of each central bank (Cœuré, 2014). According to this author, coordination is also a way of insisting on the role of markets. "Specifically, to ensure that Obstfeld-Rogoff findings hold even in a world of integrated financial markets, we must ensure that capital markets are indeed effective in delivering risk-sharing. Thus, the less we believe in formal coordination, the more we should strive to make international capital markets work."

We agree on the difficulties of international monetary cooperation, sharing many of the aforementioned considerations. However, we doubt that capital markets can be more effective than monetary authorities in delivering risk-sharing even after policy interventions, as claimed by Cœuré, for their fundamental shortcomings due to asymmetric information.[53] Writing after the many disruptions arising from the action of capital markets in the United States and Europe, this appears really a misleading statement.[54] Certainly, the operation of financial markets draws on existing structural differences as between different countries and government inaction or deregulation. But this is rightly the reason to react to the current situation by insisting on the coordination of action of monetary authorities.

International coordination of other policies takes place in a loose form, as in the case of fiscal policy, which is to some extent coordinated in international forums and a European level, but would need to be strengthened. In Europe, in fact, fiscal coordination is more

---

[53] However, according to some sources, in the United States around 60–80 percent of state-specific shocks are smoothed by risk-sharing channels, whereas this happens for no more than 20 percent in the EMU (Alcidi et al., 2017).

[54] In saying so, we do not want to disregard the role of government failures, which added to those of the markets, in particular for the deregulation of financial markets.

of a negative kind, with a number of constraints imposed on the activity of each country. In the specific realm of taxes, coordination is at the bottom, as the cases of tax havens within the Continent abound. Also in other macroeconomic fields the case of noncoordination is the rule at an international level.

10 How to Reform the EU and the EMU
Microeconomic Policies of the Common Strategy

10.1 MACROECONOMIC AND MICROECONOMIC POLICIES

Microeconomic policies are normally complementary to macroeconomic ones (the two are seldom substitutes) and therefore must be implemented in addition to, or in conjunction with, them. No analysis of macroeconomic policies can do without a parallel study of the microeconomic ones. The complementarity between microeconomic and macroeconomic instruments implies that implementation of microeconomic tools can make macroeconomic policies more effective. Think of regional, structural, labor, and industrial policies and their impact on how the European economy can react to symmetric and asymmetric shocks or nourish imbalances.

Microeconomic policies could pursue multiple objectives, such as sustaining social welfare and cohesion, also through higher employment and growth, reducing distortions and structural asymmetries and imbalances within the Union, including regional ones, and thus also avoiding symmetric or asymmetric shocks or reducing their size and impact, favoring sustainable growth, regulating the credit and labor markets, ensuring public services.

Some reforms do not involve costs for the EZ as a whole and only require law amendments or regulation for coordinating different policies. This is the case, e.g., of antitrust and tax policies. EU antitrust legislation tends to avoid distortions due to unfair country competition or fiscal dumping and is strictly implemented. However, antitrust legislation and formal tax harmonization policies can be – and are – circumvented through fiscal preferences. As already said earlier, there

341

are true tax havens in the EU, as the cases of Luxemburg's tax rulings and Irish tax preferences show.[1]

Pursuance of many microeconomic targets requires availability of funds. From this point view, the scope of these policies is severely limited currently at the EZ level. In fact, the overall budget is very low, being completely inadequate for the wide range of goals assigned to it, even simply those declared (Chapter 2). In addition, the Commission has recognized that funds are spread over too many programs and instruments and proposes to reduce their number by more than a third and to bring fragmented funding sources together into new integrated programs.

The need arises that the new budget overcomes the current failure to distinguish between economic, social, and territorial cohesion and between the intermediate steps necessary to guarantee each. Mixture of the final objectives can only cloud the assessment of each project and make checks of its implementation difficult. Some improvement would derive from the indication of fixed targets for each goal. More decisive improvements would require further enlarging the EU budget and focusing on specific targets. We will deal with these later in the chapter. Finally, the need for structural policies would be enhanced as a consequence of the possible transformation of the ESM into an EMF. Completion of the Banking Union would also require availability of a much higher budget (Sections 10.3 and 10.4).

Heinemann (2019) suggests ten priorities for the reform of the EU budget: primarily financing policies that genuinely produce a "European added value," which happens when the EU can perform a task at a lower cost or can achieve something exceeding the capabilities of the individual members; phasing out direct payments to farmers; improving the preconditions for successful cohesion policies; increasing own resources in proportion to their gross national income and expanding national cofinancing; retaining current unanimity rules on taxation and budgetary policy; cutting the nexus between

---

[1]   As to Ireland, in August 2016 the European Commission stated that in the decade 2003–14 it had granted undue tax credits for a total of €13 billion to Apple.

national banking systems and member states; establishing an insolvency procedure for EZ countries; introducing insurance against severe recessions as part of a comprehensive package; depoliticizing the SGP by expanding the role of the EU fiscal board; allowing more scope for a European identity to emerge. Most of these suggestions appear to be meaningful. One can instead dissent from the proposal of expanding the role of the fiscal board. In our opinion, fiscal policy is an essential trait of a political entity and cannot be delegated to a technical body. Fiscal boards can instead play an important role in counseling policymakers.

The timing of each microeconomic policy must be carefully devised. In fact, even if it can add to growth and the other indicated targets, it is often painful in the short run, the more so if implemented in the downturn phase of the business cycle. If a country is implementing a fiscal consolidation plan, its negative short-run impact could be offset by enacting structural reforms. The IMF's Global Integrated Monetary and Fiscal model has shown that it would take several years before the short-term negative impact of consolidation can be offset by structural reforms in peripheral countries, whereas reforms would be much easier for core countries (Anderson et al., 2014). In any case, as said before, the short-run negative effects of consolidation plans are expected to be aggravated. We have already indicated in Chapter 6 the need to defer implementation of most structural reforms to "good times" or at least to associate them with expansionary macroeconomic policy. This is the so-called two-handed approach (Blanchard et al., 1985; Draghi, 2014; Banerji et al., 2017).[2] Priority should then be given to reforms being beneficial also in the short run. Of this kind are those that,

> besides increasing productivity and improving labour utilization in the long run, can also boost demand in the near term ... [such as] policies aimed at restructuring government expenditure for

[2] However, account should be taken of the very long gestation of their growth effects (Marrazzo, Terzi, 2017).

> strenghtnening and modernizing public infrastructure ... [and]
> active labour market policies that ... aim at accelerating the
> unemployed's search for a new job ... [or to reforms that] reduce the
> taxation of labour incomes and transfer the tax burden on to other
> revenue items of the budget. ... Priority should be given also to
> reforms aimed at liberalizing product markets for their capacity to
> stimulate aggregate demand in the short term.
>
> (Milone, 2017: 10, 12)

Other reforms in both the labor and the product market can hit some groups in the short term, even if they are beneficial to others. Then, they may be unfeasible from a political economy perspective, either because they do not meet the government targets aiming at favoring the groups that they instead hit or due to the obstacles and reactions of the people who would be worse off. Solutions are, however, possible under different forms: first, by enacting simultaneously a number of reforms hitting and benefitting different groups, with a net gain for the society as a whole;[3] second, especially if there are administrative obstacles to enacting a large reform program, by staggering them over time and implementing each time only some reforms of the whole packet, in a way to hit only some small sections of the population; third, by granting compensation to those that are damaged.[4] Also synchronizing them throughout the Union can add to each country's benefits positive spillovers from other countries, by lowering transition costs in the short run and generating synergies in the long run (Everaert, Schule, 2008).[5] Synchronization, obviously, finds some obstacle in the absence of centralized institutions. However, the scope for common reforms is restricted by the

---

[3] See, e.g., more recently Barkbu et al. (2012) and Fiori et al. (2012).

[4] Obstacles arise for governments facing deficit or debt constraints. In this case, from a political point of view, a trade-off arises between the government's increased electoral chances deriving from compensation of the individuals hit by reforms and the cost of violating the deficit restriction (Ribeiro, Beetsma, 2008).

[5] Gomes et al. (2011) suggest that cross-country coordination of the reforms implemented by each country produces larger and more evenly distributed positive effects.

specificities of the various countries, as each one of them requires different reforms.

10.2 SOCIAL AND POLITICAL VIABILITY

In addition to the negative effects of the cuts in social spending mentioned in the previous section, other actions implemented at the EMU or country level have had a negative impact on social conditions and viability, causing increasingly serious social distress and wider inequalities. In the long run, this is destructive in both economic and social terms (e.g., EuroMemo Group, 2015).[6]

The economic policies adopted in the EU over at least the past two decades have been characterized by austerity, which has been imposed throughout the EU but mostly in the weakest economies, leading to drastic cuts to public services and unequal distributional effects,[7] which have seriously aggravated social problems.

Austerity and fiscal consolidation have caused negative effects on distribution. These have two aspects. One refers to past actions, the other to future policies. As to the past, a report by the European Commission holds that the distributional consequences of consolidation have been regressive in the ten countries under examination (European Commission, 2012). A more recent analysis shows that, even if in some countries the poorest sections of society were protected from some actions, the generalized increases in VAT had the opposite effect (Figari et al., 2015). In any case, the different effects in the various countries depend on the implementation of different fiscal instruments (public pensions, means-tested benefits, contributory benefits, noncontributory nonmeans-tested benefits, direct taxes, tax allowances, tax credits and worker insurance contributions), as shown by Avram et al. (2014).

This has far-reaching implications: "since our welfare model is a central safeguard of social cohesion, failure to seize reform

---

[6] The negative effects on growth of higher inequality are empirically found by Berg et al. (2018).

[7] A testimonial of these effects is Galbraith (2016).

opportunities will, by extension, risk undermining an important element of the inclusive European social market economy. Besides, social cohesion is a pre-condition for political viability of more integration. Therefore, ambitious structural reforms are the EMU-friendly resolution of ... (the) trilemma" ... between .... "conducting sound fiscal policies and achieving sustainable welfare systems while pursuing unambitious structural reforms that will keep EU economies locked in a 'stagnation trap'." An ambitious agenda of structural reforms should be pursued with policies focusing on competitiveness gains within sustainable and inclusive growth models. Balanced growth will require an acceleration of reforms in the core and semi-core countries, not only in the vulnerable countries that have shown greater "reform responsiveness" (Buti, 2014: 2).

Thus, the need arises for a change in priorities by addressing the problem of inequality at both the Union and the country level, in a way to revert all the negative consequences of austerity policies on inequality and social inclusion. This can be done by implementing not only direct actions to alleviate inequality and enhance social conditions through the EU budget, but also all the actions that we have indicated earlier tending to stop austerity.

The Great Recession has had a negative impact on the policies that can now be implemented, because it worsened the government budget and debt. The various countries have been overburdened by public debt; and the need to repay it or to serve interests on it will restrict the room for social expenditures. Thus, the position of the poor sections of the population will be sacrificed to feed the rent positions of the richer, who mostly own government bonds.

This introduces the issue of the future of the European social welfare system, which will be conditioned by this burden. All the same, some recommendations could be implemented along the route of protecting the European Social Model:

(1) Coordinating EU policies in a way not to endanger existing social welfare standards, in particular by using the tools of the European Semester to

ensure that the existing provisions for the more disadvantaged are saved when implementing economic policies.

(2) Setting common minimum social standards to be guaranteed all over the EU – or, at least, in the EA.[8] This is certainly a feasible policy, even if the ample diversity of standards existing in the different countries might imply a low level of the minimum. However, plans can be devised to raise this minimum over time.

(3) Raising the level of direct EU involvement in social policies, by pursuing common social policies, such as minimum levels of unemployment insurance or other social guarantees (Balassone et al., 2018; Dullien et al., 2018).

Arranging a common scheme without losers and at low cost would face a number of issues, due to the diversity of national welfare systems (Jara, Sutherland, 2014) and the limited capacity of common interregional systems to absorb regional shocks (Gros, 2014). Gros cited a recent IMF study (International Monetary Fund, 2013a) finding that in the United States about 20 percent of shocks to state income are offset by the federal fiscal system, while financial integration has done so to a much greater extent.

Suggestions of positive actions could be more fruitful than defense of the status quo. As an example of this kind of suggestion, the negative impact of austerity can be partly alleviated by promoting integrated programs in the social welfare provisions that exploit information and communication technology (ICT) innovations (Misuraca et al., 2016). In addition, pooling some welfare provisions, such as a partial pooling of unemployment benefit schemes, would directly connect the citizens to the problems arising from austerity and the possible occurrence of a state of need (Andor, 2014; Dullien, 2014; Beblavy, Lenaerts, 2015; Alcidi, Thirion, 2016; Beblavy et al., 2017). At the same time, this would offer an opportunity to endow the EZ with an effective fiscal stabilizer (Dullien, 2014).

---

[8] Rinaldi (2016) suggests a wide range of social policies, involving specifically human capital, social rights, and labor mobility.

Gros (2014) underlines first that the existing EZ mechanisms, such as the ESM, do not provide an insurance function. In fact, this mechanism only grants loans, to be repaid with interest. In devising a system of fiscal transfers, more than a system "that offsets all shocks by some small fraction, ... a system that protects against shocks that are rare, but potentially catastrophic" should be chosen. In particular, he suggests introducing a system of unemployment (re)insurance with a deductible, say 1 percent of GDP, such that the country hit by such a small shock would receive nothing. A similar proposal is in Andor (2014, 2015), Dolls et al. (2015), and Ábrahám et al. (2018), who suggest establishing a system of unemployment insurance that should enhance automatic stabilizers and help countries hit by relevant asymmetric shocks (i.e., rises in unemployment above a certain threshold and higher than the EZ average), for example under the form of a European Unemployment Benefit Scheme. This proposal was endorsed by the German finance minister, Olaf Scholz, in June 2018. Also reinsurance channels to allow transfers to countries hit by unemployment above a certain level have been devised (e.g., Dolls, 2018), which would absorb 15 to 25 percent of the income losses deriving from deep recessions.

10.3 CREDIT REGULATION

Some authors have noted that many policy actions in the EZ have been "in the banks' narrow interest ... and it is high time for a change" (Haidar, 2015: 567). They also ask for intervention of the European Stability Financial Mechanism (ESFM) if banks cannot be recapitalized by their shareholders. Regulating the institutions and policies that govern credit is indeed a very intricate matter. It involves a number of issues, such as: the need to avoid banks becoming "too big to fail," which would nourish moral hazard; the confusion of operations having different risk in their activity; excessive expansion of banks and other financial intermediaries and the need for their supervision; bank bail in; the tasks of the ECB; deposit insurance.

As for the first two issues, failure to implement recommendations of the Liikanen Report (Section 9.2.1) due to the opposition of banks should be overcome. The other issues are strictly linked one to the other.

With reference to risk-taking and supervision of financial intermediaries, proper regulation should tend to avoid excessive use of derivatives, which played a crucial role in fueling the financial crisis. This justifies – as being necessary, even if not sufficient, due to the need for more extensive regulation – the decisions taken, as said, in 2013 and the years after, when European authorities, led by the fear of a deepening of the financial crisis, decided to create a route toward a Banking Union and established the principle of unitary supervision to partially replace national monitoring and regulation. The Banking Union was created in order to rule banking operations, restructure banks in difficulties, break the sovereign-bank loop that has caused a prolongation of the crisis, and share risks at the EU level. Apart from the European Deposit Insurance Scheme (EDIS), it has two pillars, the Single Supervisory Mechanism (SSM) and the Single Resolution Mechanism (SRM), that apply to banks covered by the SSM.

The system of restructuring banks that face difficulties is organized in a way to reduce moral hazard and the costs of resolutions to taxpayers. As said earlier, these should be borne by the creditors and the shareholders of banks, reducing the moral hazard in the conduct of bank management. However, the possibility of asking for use of public funds would not be ruled out, in case of a threat to financial stability. Apart from this possibility, charging creditors and shareholders for the bail-in burden could depress share values, with possible negative repercussions on financial stability (Micossi, 2016).

Other solutions should instead be sought to reduce the concentration of the extant sovereign debt and its amount in banks' portfolios in a fair way. Such solutions could be of the European Safe Bonds (ESBs) type suggested by Brunnermeier et al. (2011) (Section 9.3). However, one must be very careful in devising ways for cutting the link between bank debt and sovereign debt. In fact, the risk might persist that a severe-enough financial shock in the EU will affect all the other borrowers in the same country in a self-fulfilling manner. Pretending that we can separate private from public finance may exacerbate, rather than moderate, financial boom-and-bust cycles. Reduction of sovereign bonds in banks' portfolios could not be a shortcut to full political union. It could instead be a way to aggravate not only public finances, but also financial institutions, since the market would receive a signal of bank possession of NPL or junk bonds, which would aggravate banks' burden. Thus, this pretense should be resisted unless some solution is found to transform part of the sovereign debt into Eurobonds or some guarantee is offered to face through the EU budget the risk of generating a financial crisis, which is a highly unlikely prospect, or intervention by the ECB is allowed. The standing issues of the present situation (i.e., the fear that any mutualization of risks, with reference to both sovereign and private debt, would encourage moral hazard, particularly in peripheral countries) could be dealt with by some solution coupling a degree of burden sharing of debts and disincentives to moral hazard with incentives to public investment. Dosi et al. (2018) and Minenna (2018) suggest that the ESM should be funded by the various countries, which would pay an insurance premium proportional to the amount of sovereign bonds issued by each country. The bond issues of each government coming to maturity should be substituted with new tranches of a common guaranteed EZ debt, issued by the ESM. This operation of risk sharing could be completed in no less than ten years. After this period, each EZ country would "give up its fiscal autonomy in exchange for a full mutualization of its past government debt" (Minenna, 2018).

Other authors hold that any attempt to separate private debt crises from sovereign crises through EDIS[9] would exacerbate rather than moderate financial boom-and-bust cycles (Rodrik, 2017).

[9] Separation could also be achieved by requiring a rigorous system of financial regulation and imposing very rigid fiscal rules, with a system of debt limits or targets and effective sanctions to rule out the chances of a sovereign default in the public sector.

According to this author, finance "is irrevocably politicized – for good as well as bad reasons." The way out could only be a complete political union.[10]

A road toward this should be opened by the recent European Commission plan for completing the Union. This not only foresees adoption of the EDIS, but has also a number of other proposals on Banking Union, including risk reduction, a common backstop for the Single Resolution Fund, and a scheme in favor of an enabling framework for European Sovereign Bond–backed Securities for the EZ, following the work of the European Systemic Risk Board (ESRB) (European Commission, 2017c). However, inadequacy of the EU budget would again undermine the plan.

An additional issue derives from the dual task assigned, on the one side, to the European Banking Authority (EBA), established in 2009 and operating since 2011, which develops technical standards for the whole EU, and, on the other, to the ECB, which is in charge of the SSM, for monitoring the financial stability of banks of the EZ (and other countries that decide to be part of it). This duality should some how be overcome to make the system more effective (Hüttl, Schoenmaker, 2016).

Also, the attribution of supervisory powers to the ECB, in addition to the typical function of a central bank, has been criticized, since it may influence liquidity management by the central bank and have a negative consequence on government debt financing in terms of moral hazard. According to Strassberger and Sysoyeva (2015), by acquiring supervisory powers the central bank is informed on the solvency of banks. This can influence its attitude in the field of monetary policy and, in particular, for providing liquidity to an extent that may conflict with its monetary policy objectives. However, it is only one of the papers cited by these authors in support of their argument that can contradict it (Dalla Pellegrina et al., 2013).

---

[10]   Notwithstanding this shortcoming, EDIS could be useful in making centralization of bank supervision consistent with the actions to be undertaken in case of a bank crisis (Wolff, 2016).

Empirical research has actually shown that the degree of supervisory unification in the hands of the central bank is likely to be higher the higher its reputation. In fact, the latter can be considered as a solid defence against the possibility that the central bank is too lenient, favoring provision of liquidity to insolvent banks.

10.4   INDUSTRIAL POLICY

As said, after the 1980s industrial policy turned from a vertical to a horizontal orientation (becoming a policy of "factors of production," rather than of industrial sectors). The new orientation started from full acceptance of the market logic, neglecting its failures, and was characterized by use of modest resources. By contrast, in some cases it consisted in removing some constraints on the operation of market forces. Over time, industrial policy played a minor role, practically no role at all, in the EU.

The European stagnation and the prolonged years of the recent crisis have reduced much of the production capacity in the industrial sector, especially in the Southern periphery. Other features of the European model, such as the bank-based nature of the financial system and scarcity of finance for small and medium-sized firms, start-ups, and innovative enterprises, may have contributed in the same direction (European Investment Bank, 2016). Reduced investment and productivity growth in comparison with the United States and South-Eastern Asian economies have led to a two-decade-long decline in competitiveness. The meager dynamics of productivity is the true factor behind the issue of competitiveness that makes wage rises seem too high.[11] Europe has lost most of the benefits of the digital revolution. Thus, the competitive position of manufacturing in most peripheral and Eastern Europe economies must specifically be improved (Stöllinger et al., 2013).[12] In fact, as we have seen, the high

---

[11]   Thimann (2015) underlines the high level of wages, together with existing barriers to job creation in the labor market, in particular in peripheral countries.

[12]   The "Industrial Compact," launched in 2014, is intended to revive the industrial sector, setting for it the target of 20 percent of GDP by 2020 and granting EU firms funding of €150 billion.

inflation dynamics and current account deficits which characterize these countries were at the roots of the imbalances that nourished the crisis. The need arises not only to offer incentives to small and medium-sized firms and to innovative investment, but also to get rid of the existing institutions and policies, such as differences in corporate taxation and preferential treatment that give undue incentives to big firms, especially transnational corporations. We can add that industrial policy should target not only manufacturing, but also other sectors of the economy, being systemic.

The reduction in the industrial productive capacity has been a loss for Europe, but the possibility is now open to substitute the capacity lost with new capacity incorporating new technologies, i.e., knowledge and ICTs. These can be useful for developing social infrastructures, especially for efficient and sustainable mobility and logistics, environment-friendly and energy-saving projects, as well as health and welfare services.[13] In this respect, industrial policy should indeed be able to promote "high-road competitiveness," as a way of achieving "beyond-GDP" goals or – better to say – goals going beyond short-term growth (as suggested, e.g., by the EU Commission, 2010 – which reproduces the Europe 2020 program – and Aiginger, 2014). Also social infrastructures in relation to the aging population should be financed at the EU level (Fransen et al., 2017).

Public policy can play a major role, not only in indicating the targets to pursue (including the privilege to be given to social services, education and human capital formation, research, and physical infrastructures), but also in implementing effective policy tools. These can range from incentives, particularly those having an impact on technical progress, to direct involvement in education and research (Aiginger, 2014). An important part of incentive policies should be directed to avoiding "rational herding" motivations behind institutional

---

[13] "Without selective and sustainable areas of meaningful economic growth, Europe as a whole could be stuck with sluggish markets, a heavy environmental burden, cosmetic attention to climate change, and growing inequality" (EuroMemo Group, 2015: 19).

investment behavior, e.g., through proper principal–agent contract designs (Jones, 2015).

Economies of scale and processes of market aggregation should also be favored by temporary incentives, but exploitation of the ensuing market power can thwart innovation. In this respect, the link between industrial policy and antitrust action must be stressed. In fact, the strategy of pointing to corporate giants in Europe or even at a national level (a renewed strategy of national or EU "champions") can be held to be responsible for its scarce dynamism, as oligopolistic or monopolistic corporate firms often tend to implement scarce innovative investment and to spend large amounts on advertising, in order to reshape consumers' preferences and to boost demand. Antitrust action and action in favor of small and medium enterprises can temper big firms' predominance and increase growth (Bailey, Cowling, 2006). At the same time, the integration of European markets for network industries should be completed together with Europe-wide regulatory authorities (Buigues, Meiklejohn, 2011). Then, public action is essential in terms of anti-monopoly regulation, together with a policy favoring the birth of new firms and their growth. Regional environments favoring clusters of firms and a macroeconomic policy tending to create a large market and a growing system are also useful (Pitelis, Kelmendi, 2011).

This kind of industrial policy should be pursued at both the EU and the country level. In fact, some of the projects at country level in these fields have a Union-wide extension and need to be implemented at this level, because of both their cost and, mostly, the externalities they can create for the Union. Vice versa, Union-wide projects need to be complemented by specific country-level ones. One relevant aspect of industrial policy should be the geographical orientation of foreign trade and investment. A large share of European manufacturing now has strong ties with East Europe, due mainly to German strategies of delocalization (Simonazzi et al., 2013), but also to those followed by other countries such as Italy, whereas the Mediterranean Basin only plays a minor role. One can ask whether industrial policy should be directed at rebalancing this geographic orientation, as a way to reduce the asymmetries behind the imbalances that have heavily hit Europe as well as to further political goals of increased stability in this region.

The need to revive the industrial policy strategies not only in Germany, but all over Europe, has recently been stressed by the German economy minister, Peter Altmaier, by supporting European industrial and technological sovereignty and capacity, in particular in order not to lose key technological competencies in the struggle with America and Asia.

As said, an important aspect of industrial policy refers to company legislation, in order to contrast the prevailing incentives of managers induced by the asset management industry. The diffusion of institutional investors and the incentives to asset managers (who earn performance fees), together with the principal–agent relationship relating them to savers (looking for short-term returns), encourage the search for short-term and high-risk investment and the formation of financial bubbles. These incentives are shaped by "large shifts in risk premia owing to the 'rational herding' motivations of asset managers (even in the absence of leverage)" (Jones, 2015: 38). From this point of view, industrial policy should complement countercyclical monetary and macroprudential policy. These can better counteract asset booms (in financial assets and real estate markets) driven by leverage, but can hardly deal with the issues deriving from challenges related to the growing asset management industry, which can also raise systemic risk, due to the rational herding motivations of asset managers and, thus, shifts in risk premia, far from the formal banking sector. According to Stiglitz (2016), reform of corporate governance is a key instrument for fostering growth, through, e.g., encouragement to long-term investment, in terms of loyalty shares giving special voting rights.

10.5 STRUCTURAL AND REGIONAL FUNDS

A currency union like the EU includes countries in very different structural conditions: some of them have very advanced economies, with a high per capita income, and are endowed with a well-functioning industrial structure as well as tertiary sectors. Some others have lower per capita incomes, a low-productive manufacturing sector, and an inefficient tertiary sector. All countries are exposed to competition also from countries that are not part of the Union. However, it is the more backward countries that might suffer more from the competition of emerging countries, given the affinity of their specialization with the latter's.

Our previous analysis has pointed out the inexistence of automatic forces leading to uniform growth and development, in particular to growth of backward regions. All countries – but in particular the more backward ones – face situations where market forces should be helped in implementing structural changes. The rationale for the EU policy intervention thus exists. Some authors have concluded that the gap between higher- and lower-income countries has narrowed, which would imply that EU regional and cohesion policies have been effective (Monfort, 2012). However, it is not sufficient to look at convergence between countries, considering each as a whole. In fact, in addition to national disparities, a problem arises as some countries suffer not only (or mainly) from relative backwardness, but also from internal regional imbalances. Italy's Mezzogiorno, Spain's Extremadura, and Greece's Makedonia – just to take a few examples from countries that have long been members of the EMU – are also plagued by decades-long states of backwardness, due also to the inefficiency of their governing bodies. A recent analysis underlines the relevance of this factor also in the exploitation of EU facilities (Arbolino, Boffardi, 2017). Based on a panel data model for the period 2007 to 2015, they find that the quality (efficiency) of regional governments in the Italian Mezzogiorno is a key determinant of their ability to make use of European regional funds for investments in these regions suffering from structural delays.

Looking at the EU directly from a regional perspective, convergence seems to be taking place with respect to some regions, whereas other regions are diverging further (Goecke, Hüther, 2016). The regions favored by European funds are those in the EU cohesion-fund countries, i.e., Ireland, Greece, Portugal, and Spain (Ramajo et al., 2008). However, it seems that EU funding can have a negative effect on regional convergence as a whole, as funding can cause a competition effect among neighboring regions (Breidenbach et al., 2016).

A number of issues arise, such as the objectives of intervention, the tools to be used, and the subject that should intervene. With reference to the former, there could be two possible such targets: maximizing the EU GDP growth rate as a whole or promoting higher growth in less developed regions. If the former is the case, regional income disparity would not be reduced, i.e., there would not be higher convergence, since agglomeration should be fostered. In the alternative case, regional policies should be very different from those actually devised by the EU (Boldrin, Canova, 2001).

Differences in the economic structure of the different countries/regions are certainly the culprit of economic and social disparities and need to be changed. The issue then arises whether the desired structure should be uniform and the countries should have competing industries or whether the different countries should somehow specialize in different sectors. Specialization has its advantages and also possible shortcomings. Benefits can accrue from complementarity, but also dangers can derive from the dynamics of innovation for certain branches. Competing industries in different member countries can be responsible for the apparently reduced (or negative) effect of EU funding mentioned before. Anyway, decisions about the kind of industrial structure to choose are strategic choices pertaining either to the Union or to countries or to a concerted action of the Union and the countries[14] that cannot be left to the action of market forces. In both this and the previous case, a fiscal union would provide funds to face structural change, through the allocative and growth tranches of its budget. In what follows, we will focus on the first goal.

---

[14] The risk arises of decisions taken by the EU that are biased in favor of the leading countries, exploiting their hegemonic power. But this is an issue of general relevance for all policies.

If the overriding target of regional policy is that of narrowing the per capita income gap at least between countries (but possibly also within each of them, as we will see), we could repeat the words of Shambaugh (2012: 157): "A currency union may not need a fiscal union, but it does likely need both a financial union and some way to adjust for unbalanced economic conditions across countries." This statement can be interpreted as saying that suitable structural and regional policies together with a financial union can be a substitute for a common fiscal policy.

The subjects to be charged with implementing structural and regional policy are either the national (and subnational) governments or the EU authorities. In some cases, regional policies have long been implemented by countries, sometimes with no appreciable positive results. Government intervention has at most avoided worsening the situation, but in some cases has generated moral hazard, addiction, and corruption, as in the Italian Mezzogiorno.

This is no outright justification for EU intervention as a substitute. However, arguments in favor of intervention at this level can be multiple. One is of a redistributive kind: it is fair for the Union to fund projects for the advancement of underdeveloped regions. The relative backwardness of the countries facing regional problems, often coupled with the high public debt burden inherited from the Great Recession, makes it difficult for them alone to provide funds for upgrading their structural situation, and requires EU intervention, possibly through structural and regional funds tied to adoption of such reforms. And it seems that these problems can be alleviated by the EU cohesion policy. In fact, it has been found that, "in the main beneficiary Member States, each euro of funding will generate an estimated return of EUR 2.10 in the countries' GDP" (Monfort, 2012: 9). Sometimes the EU intervention is justified by the possibility that vested interest and bias can operate at the local level, but, as said, this can be so also at the EU level. In any case, technical assistance from the Commission can be useful, especially for more backward countries.

An argument against EU intervention is the complexity of issues of regional development, requiring knowledge of a sophisticated nexus of links between firms having different roles (as suppliers or customers or providers of services) and other agents (Porter, 1990). One can doubt whether better knowledge of both the real situation and the desired one resides in Brussels offices rather than at the country level.

Until now, we have discussed regional policies in relation to structural problems. Regional issues, however, can also derive from the fact that countries – or regions within them – are hit by a negative shock, possibly as an effect of their specialization. If a country as a whole is hit, on the one hand, labor mobility may be low enough to provide the compensating market forces that operate in other situations (e.g., in the United States). On the other hand, an internal devaluation through price and wage containment is absolutely difficult, for well-known reasons. Finally, a country might be unable to face the effects of the shock, due to its fiscal conditions, especially when fiscal policy faces constraints such as the SGP and the fiscal compact. The need for some kind of support from the Union then arises. In the case of a fiscal union, this could be provided by the stabilization branch of the common budget, but the available facilities in the current EMU setting, again, are too low.

With reference to all regional issues, as pointed out by the Barca report (Barca, 2009), reform of the cohesion and regional policy should derive from a high-level strategic debate: (i) concentrate on fewer priorities;[15] (ii) be supported by a stronger evaluation system and a reinforced role for the Commission; (iii) have a clearer focus on performance. Possibly, as added by Monfort (2012), a simpler and more transparent management system should be adopted.

Thus, a fiscal union could certainly cope with the structural and regional issues arising in a composite Union such as the EMU. However, the likelihood that this can be fulfilled to a satisfying extent

---

[15] However, an issue of "collective learning" – then a diffuse task – arises as a way of enhancing local competitiveness (Camagni, Capello, 2011).

in the current situation is very low, even if the aforementioned proposals are implemented, unless the EU budget is reasonably raised
with a specific destination to structural and regional policies and some
other conditions of the kind just mentioned are met.

10.6 OTHER STRUCTURAL REFORMS: LABOR AND PRODUCT MARKET POLICIES

The benefits of the Single Market are undeniable and have been measured recently, by simulating a counterfactual scenario in which tar-
iffs and nontariff barriers are reintroduced. The benefits can, in fact,
amount to 8–9 percent of the average EU GDP in the long run (in 't
Veld, 2019). However, a number of features of the European national
labor and product markets are still an obstacle to having a true
European Single Market. As said, labor mobility is low, partly due
to: existence of different languages, scanty recognition of national
diplomas, poor retraining facilities and assistance in job searching,
difficulties found in the housing market, different work rules (e.g., as
to working time and overtime, job protection, job duration), not to say
wages (including minimum wages), and social protection. Some kind
of uniform rules (such as limited use of precarious contracts,
a minimum wage and a minimal level of protection of workers,
a system of vocational training, and common rules for a single
European labor market such as full portability of workers' rights)
could be introduced at the EZ level, especially if associated to EMU
funding. Higher flexibility of the labor market can damage workers.
Apart from implying higher inequality if it entails lower wage rates –
as said in Section 10.2 – it could damage growth if it is not accompanied by product market reforms (Estevão, 2005).[16] As to the higher
inequality, there are possible compensations, such as appropriate tax
and transfer measures. A "flexicurity approach" could also be followed, e.g., by providing higher unemployment benefits, even if this
approach can have severe shortcomings (e.g., Heyes, 2013).

[16] On the complementarity between labor and product market deregulation, see also
Nicoletti and Scarpetta (2005) and, more recently, Fiori et al. (2012).

These reforms could be complemented by reforms of other structural policies that are under the authority of member countries (Bénassy-Quéré, 2017). As to product market reforms, these include guaranteeing more competition and reducing barriers to entry of new firms (International Monetary Fund, 2016, which also deals with labor market reforms). We can add that this would be especially important for small and medium firms and startups. Finally, structural reforms of both product and labor markets can raise the long-run growth rate both in advanced and relatively backward EU countries according to Gomes et al. (2013). However, a note of caution is expressed by Gros (2016).

10.7 ENVIRONMENTAL POLICY

As seen in Chapter 5, the Europe 2020 environmental targets seem rather close to being achieved. This certainly reflects the negative effects of the crisis on the level of production and, thus, of pollution. However, econometric estimations have checked that the EU will achieve its Europe 2020 targets even as growth resumes, certainly to a different degree for the different targets.

A different challenge derives from the objectives originating from the 2015 Paris agreement (Liobikien, Butkus, 2017). This indicates the need to strengthen the EU environmental strategy, in particular by increasing renewable energy sources (RES-E). At a general level, the issue arises of improving implementation of existing rules for environmental protection, possibly making them more effective. This lack of implementation refers to most environmental sectors and can be found in almost all member states to different degrees, but with wide differences between them. A review of some years ago (European Commission, 2011b) found existence of implementation gaps. Even for the year 2013, with reference to Germany, a country that as a whole has recorded a good implementation level, the European Environment Agency has estimated about 76,000 premature deaths attributable to concentrations of fine particulate matters or ozone. Such gaps cause high costs, which could be around €50 billion per year. This figure does not account, however, for the costs saved due to nonimplementation. In fact, full implementation would create additional costs, e.g., for enforcement, but would give a net benefit, especially in terms of sustainable growth, and is then a valuable objective to pursue.

Remaining at a general level, integration of environmental policy into other policies is an important principle to obey (Liberatore, 1997), in order to implement sustainable development, i.e., a model of development that respects ecological sustainability. This principle, however, has been poorly implemented. Even if in 2001 the European Council committed to the EU Sustainable Development Strategy, providing long-term information on the environmental costs and benefits of all major Commission proposals, policy coordination and integration should still be improved. In practice, difficult issues arise, as there are few "best practices" that can be shared by different jurisdictions (Jordan, Lenschow, 2010). Finally, problems can arise in practical implementation of European policies, since the capacity to enforce rules is *a conditio sine qua non* to control pollution and this depends on the state of the rule of law, which is rather weak in certain countries (Castiglione et al., 2014).

In terms of more specific issues, one of the most relevant fields for environmental policy is reduction of CO_2 emissions. This needs a European energy policy, addressed in particular to the development of renewable energies, which requires in turn both national policies and more coordination between the member states, including the formulation of an effective bargaining strategy to ensure a global reduction of CO_2 emissions in order to make the ETS more effective (Gawel et al., 2014). In addition, while recognizing the validity of the economic principle of a single wholesale price, the repercussions of a low CO_2 price on market uncertainty and the discouragement of innovative efforts to develop renewable energies should be considered. To cope with these issues, establishment of a range for the CO_2 price has been suggested, with a max and a min. This should reduce market uncertainty and increase the dynamic efficiency of the ETS (Knopf et al., 2014). However, it has been noted that the linear reduction factor in the emissions will gradually lead to a higher carbon price, even without a short-term reform (Wettestad, 2014). The ETS has been reformed in 2017, partly introducing changes of the kind requested by the literature.

In fact, on the one hand, the cap on the total volume of emissions will be reduced annually by a linear reduction factor of 2.2 percent, which will raise the CO_2 price. The same effect would derive from the creation of a market stability reserve, in which to allocate the backlog of allowances unused due to the crisis, with the number of allowances to be placed in the reserve temporarily doubled until the end of 2023, when a new mechanism will become operational to limit the validity of allowances in the reserve above a certain level.

On the other hand, ETS policies supporting renewable energies – which have already increased the share of electricity produced by renewables from 7 percent in 2000 to 27.8 percent in 2014 (and should increase it further to 80 percent by 2050) – would lower the allowance price for emissions above caps, therefore making lower emission caps easier to negotiate (Gawel et al., 2014). This would facilitate implementation of the system, but has shortcomings: first, it is a costly system, whose desirability should be judged on the basis of the bargaining strength of the different subjects in real situations; moreover, the lower CO_2 price deriving from support for renewable energies would favor "dirty" production processes. To this argument, the objection has been made that the negative interactions between deployment of electricity from renewable energy sources "and the carbon price in the EU ETS have likely been exaggerated and they can be mitigated through appropriate coordination and/or instrument choice and design" (Del Rio, 2017: 825). Our position is that appropriateness of coordination is rather simple to assess ex post, as the author advocating it does in Section 6 of his paper, but more difficult in an ex ante evaluation. Then, also in this case, the situation must be evaluated case by case, having in mind the pros and cons of each solution.

In any case, a more decisive insistence on environmental policy could be a way to relaunch European economies and avoid their tendency to stagnation. Investment projects related to environment are required that are financed by government–private partnerships, as many investments are too long term to be of interest to the private sector only. However, the issue arises of the financial feasibility of the needed investments, and proper ways for connecting financial stability and the green economy should be found (Esposito et al., 2019).

IO.8   PRIVATE AND PUBLIC SERVICES

According to some authors (Unison, n.d.: 23), over the coming years "public services will be a key battleground between the forces of private capital and the principles of a non-marketised public realm." In fact, a general issue arises with reference to the need to revise the mix of private and public components in the provision of public services, exploiting the experience that shows the shortcomings and the benefits of privatization. Among the recent contributions, some have found a negative trend of employment and work conditions in privatized sectors (Hermann, Flecker, 2012). This may have different implications. On the one hand, one could hold that privatization and liberalization increased the efficiency in the specific field of provision of public services. On the other, the implication can be drawn that the positive effects in terms of employment claimed by supporters of privatization are unfounded, unless they should be referred to the general system, which is rather difficult to check. In addition, in general the quality of services has been reduced, even if in some cases there have been improvements.

In addition, three specific issues are relevant here. First, the peripheral countries that had to privatize their public enterprises in order to face mounting public debt should be relieved of this burden and be able to acquire their public enterprises back in due course. Second, given the varied effects of the privatization of public services, the need arises to regulate the services offered by private agents – and, more generally, public services – in order to ensure their quality, affordability, and accessibility, together with satisfactory employment conditions. Third, common EU services should be provided.

An area open to sharing public services in Europe is that of information technology provision, through possibly uniform rules throughout the continent. As an example, in Section 10.2 we dealt with two such common public services: on the one hand, pooling some welfare provisions, on the other, developing common EU projects for social infrastructures by exploiting ICTs. There are, however, also other fields open to cooperative action.

11 **Conclusions**
The Future of the Union

11.1 INTRODUCTION: THE EMU AT A CROSSROADS

By contrast with the diffuse skepticism of the 1990s, as said, after the first decade of functioning of the EMU optimistic views prevailed. Eichengreen (2010a) suggested that the rumors of some years earlier about the possibility of one or more members of the EZ leaving it in the next ten years were largely unfounded and that its breakup was even more unlikely. However, Nordvig (2014) rightly speaks of a (premature) celebration, as the fathers of the euro did not realize that the shaky institutional foundations of the EZ would soon lead to sustained "homegrown" instability. The crisis soon showed this sad reality and skepticism came back. In fact, after 2009, numerous authors, policymakers, or political parties have advocated exit of peripheral countries from the monetary union, especially as an effect of the policies implemented in the EMU in order to tame the crisis. A debate on the various prospects – and, in particular, of the pros and cons for exit, together with the discussion of the different ways to implement it – has then arisen, involving economists, politologists, political parties, and laymen.

The EMU is now really at a crossroads. A number of differences divide the various countries and make amendments to its institutions very difficult to devise and, even more, to implement. The Union needs now more common institutions, notably a fiscal union, but there are a number of obstacles to its implementation. These derive from structural differences between the countries that have even been exacerbated by the effects of the crisis. In addition – and maybe mainly – the obstacles derive from political differences that find their roots in both cultural and material differences.

Let us briefly deal with political diversities. These basically originate in history, but are enhanced by a number of objectively different current situations. In fact, on the one hand, the nature of political institutions and the current conduct of politics in countries like France and Germany are more solid and self-reliant than those of many peripheral countries. On the other, the plague of populism and localism has spread out, to some extent as an effect of (i) the heavier negative consequences of the financial crisis for more peripheral countries and (ii) the higher exposure of some countries, such as Italy, to the recent immigration waves, also coupled with the reduced need for migrants in these countries compared to Germany and other countries.

Section 11.2 deals with the different possible ways out of the current situation. Section 11.3 concludes our analysis by suggesting some lines of reform for building a democratic institution that ensures absence of significant influences of sectional or country interests. It also indicates some possible reforms to implement in the short-medium run with the aim of increasing efficiency.

11.2 THE MAIN ALTERNATIVES: A BREAKUP, A MANY-SPEED UNION, EXIT OF SOME COUNTRIES, STRUCTURAL REFORMS OF THE EMU INSTITUTIONS AND POLICIES

As said, as an effect of negatively assessing not only the competitive position of some countries in the EMU, but also the performance of the whole Union, the prospect of a future crisis arises. The four possibilities indicated in the title of the present section are open. Let us deal with them in turn.

(a) A *breakup* of the Union, even more than exit of one or a few countries, can occur in an orderly or a more or less chaotic way. It might derive from exit of a country (either a weak or a strong country), especially following a crisis of the kind of the Great Recession. This can cause a domino effect on other countries that are in a similar position, which can practically be forced to follow the first country, by speculation or other factors. A breakup was a rather likely outcome in the worst days of the Greek crisis, which could have reduced the EZ to a handful of countries.

To avoid the prospect of a chaotic breakup, plans must be prepared in advance, as we will say in more detail with reference to simple exit. This can explain the usefulness of discussing this topic also in the case of Finland, which is certainly a country belonging to the core, not to the periphery, of the EMU, as Malinen et al. (2017) do. Belke and Verheyen (2013) describe both the genesis of a doomsday scenario and its impact on domestic debt, the domestic banking sector, EU membership, the freedom of trade, as well as the social and political costs of the social disorder that would follow. As said, a breakup of the EMU is advocated by Rossi (2016).

The prospect of a breakup is now fading out, after exit from the crisis, even if rising concerns have now arisen with respect to the situation of Italy. A breakup seems not to be in the interests of either the core or the periphery: the glue that led to the formation of the EMU seems to be still strong also after the outcomes of May 2019 elections of the European Parliament.

(b) Various forms of *differentiated integration* aim at introducing elements of flexibility recognizing heterogeneity within the EU and may involve the EMU too. There are many classifications of differentiated integration, according to the principle inspiring them.

From the point of view of its pace, the main types of differentiated integration are: (i) *variable-geometry* integration, which is already a reality now, as almost one-third of the EU members have not joined the EZ and some of them do not take part in Schengen Agreements or a series of intergovernmental agreements; (ii) à la carte integration, such as the permanent right given to Denmark and the United Kingdom to remain outside the EMU (Stubb, 1996); (iii) *multispeed* integration, such as provision of transition periods and temporary derogations from formally accepted common objectives (Demertzis et al., 2018); (iv) *multispeed integration with "parallel currencies*," such as a new drachma or a new lira (Meyer, 2012). Stiglitz (2016) suggests a smooth transition out of the euro, with an amicable divorce and possibly adoption of a two-tier monetary union, i.e., a "flexible-euro" system – having a northern euro and a southern one – and flexible exchange rates. With specific reference to this latter type, also Rossi (2017) has suggested a two-speed EMU, starting from the consideration that a number of different euros are already circulating now in the Union. The two-speed union would acknowledge this situation, while ensuring stability of the EZ. Each country would reintroduce its former currency for its domestic payments and the euro could circulate as a truly international currency.[1]

With respect to the primary law from which differentiation could derive, two types have been indicated by Schimmelfennig and Winzen (2014): "instrumental" and "constitutional" differentiation. With the former, originating from the EU treaties, the new member states are temporarily excluded from some policy areas, for two reasons: the fear of old members of some kind of competition from the new members and the (in)ability of the latter to meet some policy requirements.

Here we are interested in constitutional differentiation, originating from the revision of the EU treaties. It transfers new competences to the Union, thus "deepening" the process of integration in some areas. This has already developed to some extent through the instrument of intergovernmental cooperation. The need for closer cooperation, but also for the policy differentiation that it can involve, first arose with the Treaty of Amsterdam in 1997, which introduced this kind of cooperation, a deliberate legitimatization of variable geometry.[2]

Among the most relevant recent steps, we should mention:

– The Rome Declaration, signed by the leaders of twenty-seven EU member states (absent the United Kingdom) on March 25, 2017, on the occasion of

---

[1] For other types of differentiated integration see Leruth, Lord (2015).
[2] On the underlying rationale, see Philippart, Edwards (1999).

the sixtieth anniversary of the Common Market and the Rome Treaty, stating that they "will act together, at different paces and intensity where necessary, while moving in the same direction" (European Commission, 2017a);

- The Agreement of June 2017 reached by the EU Council of Bruxelles to set up Permanent Structured Cooperation in defense (EEAS, 2017);

- The Proposal in September 2017 by the EU Commission president to create an EU minister of economy and finance as well as an EU monetary fund, by "graduating" the existing European Stabilisation Mechanism (European Commission, 2017b; Asatryan et al., 2018).

Differentiated integration seems in any case to pursue different strategies for different countries. It is a pragmatic way to integration, which can, however, really lead to widening the current differences. It could indeed turn into exit of some countries from the EMU. Independently of this prospect, it is a way to integration that negates the possibility of devising a common growth strategy, a course of action we strongly reject (Chapter 8).

(c) *Exit* from the EZ of a less competitive country[3] can be the result of the unilateral decision of one country. It can derive from some kind of speculative attack or be prepared in normal contingencies as a result of a reflection about its benefits and costs.

An automatic exit is suggested by Ritzen and Haas (2016), who, while criticizing the Five Presidents Report as based on unrealistic assumptions, suggest a New Deal between the highly indebted countries of the EZ and the other EZ countries. This would mutualize debt, but also lead to automatic exit in case of noncompliance with the agreed rules.

The pros and the cons of exit must be discussed in more detail. The difficulties encountered in building the EZ with the contribution of countries having different institutions and histories – better to say, countries that had been engaged in some

---

[3] Exit of more competitive countries is in any way a possibility suggested by some authors and politicians.

cases in ferocious conflicts and wars – have been enormous. These differences certainly had an influence on the choice of policies for coping with the crisis. The different course of the crisis in the various countries, with a high price paid by the periphery in terms of GDP, employment, and debt burden, has implied understandable requests of exit from the EA, in particular in peripheral countries. But doubts have also been raised as to its benefits and costs mainly with reference to the effects of exit on competitiveness and the path that would follow from it, given some crucial features of the economies of peripheral countries. We deal with both in turn. The effects are different according to whether there is a "disorderly" or an "orderly" and consensual exit. While this distinction is important, for reasons of brevity we do not go into detail and address the reader to Meyer (2012) for an in-depth discussion. In any case, it must be said that the benefits and costs of exit are primarily assessed by national policymakers, in a way that reflects not only "objective" determinants, but also popular consensus and/or the interest of lobbies (Masciandaro, Romelli, 2018).

Exit is advocated with many justifications. First, it has been argued that the economic advantages of participation in the monetary union have been meager (Dreyer, Schmid, 2016). Some authors have noted a negative impact of the financial crisis on the members of the EZ, due to fixed exchange rates, which tend to accentuate the negative effects of the crisis (Bohl et al., 2016). In exiting, a country would, first, regain control over monetary and fiscal policy and be freed of the constraints on their use deriving from the reduced inflation target as well as the SGP and the fiscal compact that limited its action while a member of the EMU. It would thus have the possibility to cope with asymmetric shocks and its specific problems, such as a high debt burden. In addition, by exiting it would (re)gain control also of the exchange rate as a way to improve its competitiveness: countries no longer tied to the euro would adopt a flexible or fixed (but adjustable) exchange rate, allowing for a depreciation or a devaluation of their new currency (Feldstein, 2012).[4] In fact, an increase in competitiveness would ensue from that, and the country would bridge the gap with Germany, which enjoys a competitive advantage deriving from an undervaluation of its real exchange rate of the order of about 20–24 percent with respect to Italy (Sapir, 2017).[5] According to this author, there is no other alternative open to France, Italy, and Spain and permanence in the EMU would mean the death of the economy, due to impoverishment and deindustrialization. Bagnai et al.'s (2017) stochastic simulations show that, after some initial stress in terms of their balance of payments, appropriate countercyclical policy measures could cause Italy's growth to resume in five years' time, "at a reasonable pace," with lower unemployment and a reduced public debt-to-GDP ratio. Apart from the nominal adjustment channel, the persistence of real exchange rate misalignments would be reduced by an improvement in the quality of regulation and institutions (Fidora et al., 2018).

Critics of exit remark that the relief deriving from exit would be of short duration, as the external depreciation would fuel wage and price inflation. The inflationary process could be so high as to have a negative impact on distribution and social cohesion, as happened in the past when national currencies were either tied by adjustable fixed exchange rates or not pegged at all as an effect of some international agreement (e.g., after 1992, for the Italian lira and the English pound as well as in the EMS, especially before 1985–7).[6] Moreover, Eichengreen (2010a) notes that a country would experience a significant rise in interest rate spreads and debt-servicing costs as an effect of its

[4]   Obviously, in the event of exit of a hard-currency country, the problems could be opposite. This prospect is investigated by Meyer (2012).

[5]   The order of magnitude of the devaluation is debated, as some authors think that it may be rather low (Durand, Villemot, 2016), while others hold that it may reach a peak of 60 percent, at least at the beginning (Minenna, 2016). Obviously, it depends on a number of factors referred to the country involved, such as its financial and real exchanges reserves as well as the degree of overvaluation of its real exchange rate with respect to the rest of the EMU, the secrecy of preparation for exit and the time required for the new payment system to be implemented.

[6]   In the case of Italy, it was only the extremely cooperative attitude of social partners that allowed putting a halt to depreciation in 1992.

departure from the EA. The public and private debts that are euro denominated would increase in terms of the new local currency. Credits toward foreigners would instead appreciate in terms of the new currency. If the *lex monetae* – whereby a sovereign state can decide the currency of denomination of its debts – is called into question, there will be no such appreciation, unless a CAC is to be applied, which is the case for the majority of Italian government bonds, as from 2017 on. In 2022, almost all these bonds will be under the CAC, whereas almost none were at the end of 2013. This would imply a net loss of €381 billion, assuming a 30 percent devaluation of the new currency (Figure 11.1).

As to private debt, the prevailing interpretation is that it cannot be redenominated in the new currency, which would imply a loss related to the devaluation of the new currency. Most likely, it would be firms would be mainly hit by this loss. The balance could then show that the costs from the devaluation would prevail. All in all, there could be a fall in GDP, which is estimated – possibly overestimated – by Deo et al. (2011) as high as 40–50 percent of GDP, for the first year after exit. Even if this estimate is "greatly exaggerated," various famous economists have written against exit (e.g., Feldstein, 2017).

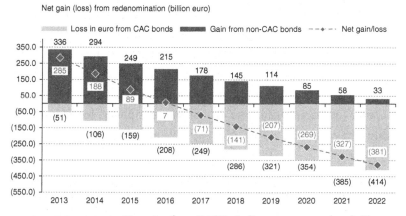

FIGURE 11.1 Net gains from CAC in Italian government bonds (Source: Mediobanca, 2017)

Really, an analysis of the effects of exit could be superficial and lead to prescriptions of a dubious foundation, if not complemented by a study of the determinants of the scarce competitiveness underlying the need to resort to it. Only the latter could indicate the true roots of imbalances and give advice on how to avoid them. These roots can originate not only from the low productivity profile (ascribable – in turn – to different growth models, private- and public-sector inefficiencies, and a different stage of development), but also from the austerity and stagnation imposed by the EMU institutions and policies, which act differently, given such diversity. To the latter determinant, one should add the negative impact on resource allocation and productivity of the low real interest rates existing in the EMU as an effect of expansionary monetary policy after 2010, which has been found by Gopinath et al. (2015) and Cette et al. (2016).[7] As one can see, there are cases of a low competitiveness endogenous to the participation of a country in the monetary union. Obviously, they would be removed in case of exit. Coping with factors of backwardness or slow growth of peripheral countries not endogenous to their participation in the EMU would entirely remain on the shoulders of the exiting country, which should weigh its chances to effectively steer its economy. In any case, use of available instruments for coping with low competitiveness will be effective only in the medium-long term, which implies the need for the country to reduce the short-term negative effects, such as inflation, redistribution, and unemployment.

In addition to the pros and the cons of exit for the exiting country, an issue of the beneficial or costly consequences for the remaining countries arises. As an example, a benefit (cost) in terms of higher (in)stability, in case of exit of a peripheral (core) country would derive to the latter. Most likely, all countries, both those

---

[7] According to Gopinath et al., firms with a higher net worth increase their capital in response to the decrease in the real interest rate, thus lowering their marginal productivity of capital, while more productive firms with lower net worth remain financially constrained. A lower sectoral total factor productivity ensues. The negative effects on the efficiency of the public sector of the softer budget constraint deriving from a reduction in the real interest rates have already been discussed (Section 7.3).

exiting and the remaining ones, would suffer from financial turmoil if the exiting countries are not small ones and if there is no preliminary agreement for exit.[8]

Going to the path that peripheral economies would follow for the exit, one may first ask whether exit is the real target to pursue, given a positive balance of its benefits vs costs, or whether it is simply a threat to other countries directed at pursuing other benefits through some kind of concession. If the latter is the case, the threat, even if not desired per se, should be credible. Thus, exit requires in any case a favorable review of economic benefits and costs.[9] In addition, it should be carefully prepared. Many authors have noticed that it could be particularly disruptive, as speculative capital outflows would arise even before exit, due to expectations (Dobbs, Spence, 2012). This can even happen when simple fears of exit – not followed by it – arise in a country, as it happened after 2010 in some countries. Bank failures could follow from capital outflows. Certainly, capital controls (notably, under the form of taxes on foreign capital) could be implemented, but one can doubt their effectiveness when adopted by countries having an inefficient public administration and in an era where electronic money and transfers are available. In any case, capital controls have not only direct effects (i.e., those due to taxes), but also indirect effects that influence investors by signaling the likelihood of future policies, especially action that will negatively affect their investment (Forbes et al., 2016a).[10]

The need to keep plans for exit secret would thus arise and this way of implementing exit is advocated by many authors (see, e.g.,

---

[8] In the case of the EZ it would be difficult to repeat the positive experience of the numerous cases of exit, almost exclusively of LDCs, from currency unions enquired by Rose (2007: 121). He finds inexistence of "sharp macroeconomic movements before, during, or after exits."

[9] If this is the case, exit would be chosen. However, political factors could advise not to do so.

[10] These conclusions refer to cases of capital controls in political and economic environments such as that of Brazil's tax on capital inflows implemented from 2006 to 2013. They can only be indicative of some indirect effects of such measures that are not easy to devise and assess.

Sapir, 2011; Bootle, 2012; Tepper, 2012). However, it seems difficult to respect secrecy, not only for possible malfunctions in the administrative path to follow, but also because exit would imply complex accomplishments for converting means of payments from the euro to the new money. In addition, the possibility of capital flight and speculation arises, since financial integration is extensive and controls would be scarcely effective even in well-organized countries. To reduce the associated costs, it could be useful to prepare a kind of backup domestic payment system, "using as an argument the eminently sensible (and truthful) need for national economic security" (Malinen et al., 2017: 14). An even more powerful argument against secrecy in the preparation of exit is the need for democratic control over government decisions by the national Parliament, in addition to the need to inform the governments of other countries and the EZ institutions. Thus, also counterarguments to secrecy are relevant or even more relevant than those in favor.

In addition to these possible outcomes, one should consider that exit from the monetary union might require exit from the EU (Section 1.1). Some authors think it possible to exit only from the EMU, without this implying exit also from the EU (Marelli, Signorelli, 2017). Cooperation with European institutions like the ECB, EBA and the European Commission is important in case of exit as it can decrease its costs, e.g., in terms of the extent and length of the capital controls and the costs of economic and political retaliation by other member countries (Malinen et al., 2017). If exit from the EMU also requires exit from the EU, an unclear and potentially complex process would be required (Nicolaides, 2013) (as the case of Brexit teaches us). In addition, exit from the EU is not really desired by some of those who favor exit from the EZ. Permanence in the EU, even in case of exit from the EZ, could be sought not only for political, but also for economic, considerations. Remaining only on the economic ground, Dreyer and Schmid (2016) empirically find positive effects on growth from the EU membership, but not from the EZ, during the first fifteen years of the euro.

Even if exit seems appealing to some authors and political parties, some of its effects for the exiting country would tend to discourage it. Thus, presently it seems to be a very unlikely prospect.

(d) The need for reforms in the EU derives from persistent structural divergences and aims, compounded by new divergences originating not so much from its enlargement, but mainly from the financial crisis, as shown earlier.

Policies in a broad sense – as including both institutions and current measures – can be imagined that do not imply exit or the other alternatives indicated at the beginning of this section. The current policy most favored by some researchers and countries could derive from an internal devaluation strategy in peripheral countries, implying deflation of wages and prices. Apart from considerations of fairness, this might not be an easy way out, however. The simple prospect of price deflation would create a "fundamental contradiction" that makes the internal devaluation strategy impossible or very hard to pursue. In fact, the more countries reduce wages and costs, "the heavier their debt load inherited from the past becomes. And, as the debt burden becomes heavier, public spending must be cut further and taxes increased to service" the debt of the government. Banks may be in a situation similar to the government. "This, in turn, creates the need for more internal devaluation, further heightening the debt burden, and so on, in a vicious spiral downward into depression" (Eichengreen, 2010c). One way out would be debt haircut and restructuring of debt, e.g., conversion of bank debts into equity or their writing off, if banks are insolvent. Similar haircuts or restructuring or a prolongation of maturity might be necessary for public debt. However, this route would also not be an easy one. As an effect of such operations being implemented in a country, a contagion to other countries being in a similar position – and, at the same time, a flight to "quality" or to "safety" toward sound countries – could ensue. While contagion is certainly dangerous for the countries interested, flight to quality would mainly benefit the country toward which investors direct their capital, by relieving its public debt financing. This country, however, could be endangered by the reduction of exports to the country experiencing a crisis.

Other policies could be devised that can, instead, consolidate the Union. Rather than deflationary policies by peripheral countries (or debt restructuring), expansionary ones could be implemented in core countries. As said, some authors note that this route neglects the interconnectedness of the various German institutions, specifically of those in the labor market and corporate governance, which behave rationally and make fiscal stabilization unnecessary (Carlin, 2013). However, requirements of a reflation in the surplus countries can even go beyond what is also obtained otherwise, especially if expansion is consistent with reducing other imbalances, such as the export surplus. In addition, fully implementing the banking union, moving to a fiscal union, and introducing Eurobonds or similar common financing instruments could help in avoiding exit or the other policy options mentioned at the beginning. All these policies would require the assent of core countries acting as hegemon or leaders. German leaders should convince their constituents that these policies can be in their longer-run interests. In fact, they could even be a premise of more cooperative policies, leading to completion of the union and more rapid and uniform growth. Rodrik (2015) argues in a similar way.

Finally, all the other policies that we have suggested in the previous two chapters, including structural policies, should be considered. From the point of view of the latter, as said, the EU Commission president in September 2017 proposed to double the EU budget for structural reforms, which would be a very promising prospect. This appears to be the most likely and practical solution to the current EMU impasse, but needs to be executed. Some of the policies indicated, instead, are unlikely to be implemented and, by contrast, those reforms that are unlikely to reduce the existing tensions and could even enhance them – such as the fiscal compact and, most importantly, the asymmetric MIP – have been preferred.

11.2.1   A Summing-up

All countries should make a benefit–cost analysis, albeit a difficult one, in order to evaluate both the short- and long-run implications of any action (mainly, implementing structural reforms and one or another policy, exiting or staying within the union, favoring or hampering other countries' action). In many cases, such an analysis would lead to a cooperative attitude. However, a significant obstacle can arise, because the short- and long-run costs and benefits deriving from the various alternatives are differently distributed over time. In many cases, the alternatives most profitable in the longer run imply also higher short-run costs. In addition, costs and benefits are also unevenly distributed across the various sections of the constituency in each country. Time preferences of different people and, in any case, of each country's governing body are then different. This compounds the difficulty of finding a common position of the governments of different countries. Divergences in the positions within the EMU will thus emerge.

The opinions on the future of the EZ widely differ. Gros (2017b) is optimistic on the outlook of the European economy, as it appears to be exiting the crisis with fundamentals better than other countries, especially in terms of the debt/GDP ratio, which is really not the case at least for peripheral countries. By contrast with Gros, De Grauwe (2017a) judges that a budgetary and political union in Europe would be needed, but is far away, since the willingness to move today in this direction is simply nonexistent, which will continue to make the EZ a fragile institution. One could add that this prediction is consistent with persistence of asymmetries and imbalances inside the EZ, which, together with weaker institutions and policies, could imply a sinking of the whole boat, due to the specific faults of its stern (i.e., peripheral countries). Even so, we can add that some possibilities of adopting structural changes are still open and should be explored further.

11.3 FOR A DEMOCRATIC EMU NOT PRONE TO COUNTRY OR SECTIONAL INTERESTS

An important preliminary clarification is needed about the meaning of the term "democratic institution." Democracy can be seen from a "collective" or an "egalitarian" perspective. The former emphasizes the possibility for a people – in this case, the entire EZ constituency – to elect its governing institutions. The latter is less demanding, as it preserves self-government of countries, but also suggests integration of policies and accountability of international institutions (Eleftheriadis, 2014). According to Eleftheriadis, the EU is only a union of peoples, which can become more democratic, even if it cannot become a democracy. If in the short run we can accept this position, it must be said that the dream of the founding fathers of Europe tended certainly more to the goal of a European people. This dream may require time, but it is important to have in mind some kind of path that can lead to its implementation.

The EU Commission has introduced a system of contacts with various stakeholders, trying to develop a method of consensus. However, this has involved mainly the élites and has not ensured the necessary transparency (Newman, 2006).

Chiti and Teixeira (2013), and Majone (2014b) speak of a kind of "democratic default" in the Union, which arose over time, starting with the failure of the Common Agricultural Policy (CAP) (as it became a cash cow from big landowners), continuing with that of intergovernmental agreements (implying a reduction in the relevance of the general interest and democratic legitimization ensured by the European Parliament), and ending with the misconduct of the EMU governing bodies in the prevention of, and response to, the financial crisis. Then the issue arises of how to combine democracy with other requirements of a heterogeneous Europe and the different positions and abilities of each country. Only from solutions respecting all these requirements can a viable and democratic Europe spring (Featherstone, 2016).

It must be said that responding to the demands of people and countries has become very difficult in Europe after the crisis, as this has implied a return of the primacy of narrow national economic interests in the European governance, together with a good dose of confusion. In the words of De Wilde et al. (2016: 15), now "different 'Europes' are demanded by different people, in different settings, different countries and even by the same people at different times." This implies that political unification as a premise to fiscal unification and complete pursuance of the dream of Europe's unity cannot be realized.

Possibly, a change of some institutions and the attitude of some countries could help. To this end, going beyond what Chiti, Teixera, and Majone say, democracy would require less hegemonic positions by any country and less involvement in policy decisions and in the ability to punish of unelected people, such as those governing the EU Commission and the ECB, and markets (De Grauwe, 2010). It is true that the European Parliament has some powers in nominating the European Commission, but this does not put these institutions in the same position as national parliaments and governments. De Grauwe (2010: 173) notes.

> (w)hen the Commission starts an excessive deficit procedure which aims at forcing national governments to cut spending and/or increase taxes, it bears no political responsibility for these decisions. In fact, the national governments do. When these follow up on the Commission's procedure, by cutting spending and raising taxes they are the ones who will be judged by their national electorates, and who face the threat of being punished by the voters at home. In contrast, the European Commission at no time faces the prospect of being voted away. Thus from a political point of view, the European Commission, which initiates the control and sanctioning procedure of the SGP, lacks democratic legitimacy, because there is no mechanism to make the Commission accountable before an electorate for its actions.[11]

---

[11] This can be partially tempered by the possibility of voting against some policies required by the Commission on the occasion of the EU Parliament polls.

De Grauwe (2011) says that

(n)either the European Commission nor the other members of the Council face political sanctions for the measures they impose on one member country. The principle of "no taxation without representation" lies at the heart of democracy. The SGP has been an attempt to short-circuit this principle, by giving powers to individuals and institutions that do not face the political consequences of their actions. Such an attempt has to fail and happily so.

As to the ECB, in Chapter 9 we have underlined some differences with the status of other central banks, such as the Fed, that aggravate the democratic deficit of an institution that is independent from the democratic institutions of the EU. Finally, as to markets, their power to punish, to favor, or in any case to indicate directions to follow should be more decisively balanced by fiscal responsibility (on this, see also Bénassy-Quéré et al., 2016). On the various aspects of the democratic deficit and the ways to cope with it, one can see Hoskyns (2018).

Also according to Schelkle (2006), there are issues of democracy in the EU. In fact, against the position that has led to "keeping politicization out" there are good arguments in favor of "bringing politics back in," as this would "halt growing apathy or outright hostility toward the emerging European polity" (Schelkle, 2006: 681) or, at least, contribute to that. Schelkle's reasoning seems to be even more relevant facing the growing populism and localism in European countries. To overcome apathy and populism, more transparency of the process leading to decisions is also needed.

In sketching the lines of a democratic reform of Europe's institutions, some kind of "deliberative supranationalism"[12] (at least in

---

[12]   This is the application of the concept of deliberative democracy to the EU case. Deliberative democracy holds that a democratic decision is legitimate, if it is preceded by authentic deliberation – not merely the aggregation of preferences obtained by voting – keeping aside the distortions deriving from unequal political power and economic wealth or the support of interest groups. As to the influence of the latter,

the transitional phase before a federation or the goal of a European people can be established) would be required in order to face conflicts between countries. In fact, both country and sectional (often conflicting) interests now play a relevant role in EU governance. We have briefly dealt with the latter in Chapter 3. Here we can add that policymakers' personal preferences or the sectoral interests influencing them fill in the space between input participation by the people and output, in terms of policy effects in favor of people. This can be hindered by people's participation in governance, which can ensure transparency, accountability, and inclusiveness, thus contributing to a better outcome (Schmidt, 2013). However, in the words of Nicoli (2017: 399),[13] the EU misses the necessary "convergence of identities."

This generates a number of problems of governance in the EZ, which are at the root of the pains related to the crisis. In a nutshell, the missing "convergence of identities" makes it difficult to build a federal entity.[14] Almost as a reflection of this, the Union "is ... not equipped with a government, but with a series of partial powers" (Pisani-Ferry, 2014: 165):[15] the ECB, the EU Commission, more or less powerful national governments, and markets. And the more recent steps for reforms have aggravated the deficit, by creating a number of intergovernmental bodies and strengthening the role of

---

it must be recalled that most likely also in Europe, as in the United States, it is the rich that largely control the political process. In fact, it has been shown that most forms of participation in the EU are suitable for organized interest and expert communities more than for ordinary citizens (Russack, 2019).

[13] On this, see also Schmidt (2009).

[14] Absence of a convergence of European identities is documented by Alesina et al. (2017: 206), even before the financial crisis, as most Europeans "became prouder of their national identities" between 1980 and 2009.

In the absence of this convergence, "the EU risks facing the emergence of a dysfunctional system, hostage of minority blockages in national or even regional parliaments and characterised by recurrent instability on the financial markets. Ultimately, such sub-optimal solutions may not be sustainable and also may end up provoking the collapse of the EMU" (Nicoli, 2017: 401).

[15] According to Pisani-Ferry, Europe, is "reminiscent of Blaise Pascal's definition of the universe: 'a sphere whose centre is everywhere'" (Pisany-Ferry, 2014: 166), except, perhaps – we can add – under the command of a European people.

the Eurogroup, the Economic and Social Committee, and, in some cases, the European Council. As to country interests, one case may be of particular significance:

> (w)hile EMU's domestic demand-led models are forced to pursue painful austerity measures that have reduced inflation and increased unemployment, no attempt has been made to correct the excessive levels of wage moderation in the EMU north, specifically Germany, which undermined the periphery's lack of competitiveness in the euro's first decade. The result of the EU's policy response, which has been shaped in the shadow of German hierarchy, has been to establish an asymmetric low-growth equilibrium within Europe that exclusively penalizes its southern rim.
>
> *(Johnston, Regan, 2016: 333)[16]*

The different size of countries and the asymmetry of power between "creditor" and "debtor" countries in the management of the EZ crisis as well as the ongoing institutional reform process of EMU have brought the issue of German dominance in Europe back to the forefront of scholarly debate. Germany has pursued the interests of its savers by shifting on debtor countries the burden of adjustment deriving from the financial crisis (Steinberg, Vermeiren, 2016), as is clear from the policies imposed on Greece.[17] Also in the case of the policies to relieve the EZ from the ensuing recession, the Bundesbank and, to some extent, the German government have pushed against unconventional policies, expansionary fiscal policy, and rising inflation, in order to protect the interests of German savers. In this circumstance, the ECB has taken a firm position, favored by its independence.

---

[16]   According to Kollmann et al. (2015), the effects on German current account surplus of German expansionary consumption and investment would be meager. They do not consider, however, the effects on the surplus of a simultaneous increase in wages and public expenditures, notably public investment, as done by Horn and Watt (2017), and Horn et al. (2017), cited before.

[17]   Cramme and Hobolt (2015) describe the pressures deriving from the financial markets on the EU governance.

However, this situation is no longer tolerable and a more balanced governance should be implemented. Creating a common finance minister for the whole EZ could to some extent increase the coordination of macroeconomic policies, even if institutional issues would arise. One of these refers to the powers of such a minister and the goals to pursue. In our opinion, this minister should have, in addition to the general task of better coordinating country policies, the authority to declare the existence of the exceptional circumstances that allow the possibility to make available to member states some flexibility in their budget policies (also Balassone et al., 2018). Alternatively, a Fiscal Council could be charged with this task (more in Pisani-Ferry, 2014), but it should be remembered that such a Council should not undertake decisions that in their essence are of a political nature.

Some steps for pursuing over the next years not only economic and political goals, but also democratic accountability and effective governance, are indicated in the paper recently prepared by the EU Commission (EU Commission, 2017d). It covers issues such as banking and capital markets unification, economic and social convergence, preparation of the new MFF, the fiscal stabilization function, in addition to issues of accountability and effective governance. There are different projects for the periods 2017–19 and 2020–5.

Cramme and Hobolt (2015) call for proper solutions to the democratic deficit of the EU.[18] The situation could be improved by implementing some minimal rules, such as more transparency about the motivations and effects of decisions, with specific reference to the categories of people that would benefit and those that would be hit. Hix (2015) suggests a range of reforms oscillating between a minimalist and a maximalist perspective. To exemplify, let us refer first to governing bodies. The European Commission could be elected either indirectly via the European Parliament or directly by the

---

[18]   Moravcsik (2002) finds little evidence in favor of the existence of a democratic deficit in a comparative perspective. Only the ECB looks like somewhat departing from the case of other countries, but this is justified by its position of particularly pronounced independence. However, the warning by Follesdal and Hix (2006) about the need for more democracy is still valid at present, even after some small improvements.

EU citizens. As to the ECB, in confirming its independence one can think of subjecting it to oversight, either by the EU Parliament and the Eurogroup and/or by national parliaments of member countries. Finally, bailout funds and austerity programs can be subject to approval and scrutiny by national parliaments or referendums ratifying them.

A solution to the democratic deficit would thus require not only a change in the orientation and the modes of current decisions, but also and mainly a radical change in the institutional setting of the EMU (Pisani-Ferry, 2014). This would be difficult to implement in the absence of a process of

> re-envisioning of the EU's socio-economic policy, ... in concert
> with the people, through pluralist processes, and by the
> representatives of the people at both national and EU level, through
> more politics ... In addition to the political and economic
> reforms, ... the EU needs to re-envision its identity and change its
> decision rules ... [in particular] by eliminating the unanimity rule.
> (Schmidt, 2009: 38)

Alesina et al. (2017: 207) also suggest searching for institutions in charge of European policymaking in a way that can make them accountable and "accelerate the formation of European identities and the emergence of a European (as opposed to national) public forum, where European policy issues are discussed in a European perspective."

A democratic state must respect the will of its citizens, but also be efficient both in their interests and in order to preserve it from attacks by supporters of some kind of dictatorial solution. From this point of view, a number of reforms of the EZ are also in order. We should recall all our suggestions of the previous pages. From a methodological point of view, a starting point is offered by existing institutions, in the process of changing them in the directions we have traced. Key elements can be: reinvigorating the Broad Economic Policy Guidelines and the framework that guides economic policy.

Horn and Watt (2017) suggest also extending the EU Macroeconomic Dialogue, in particular by setting up meetings at the EZ level, by involving the Eurogroup (including the president of ECB), the peak European social partner organizations, and – at the level of member states – the participation of national central banks, fiscal authorities, and national social partners. Other essential steps in the process of implementing all the reforms we have suggested are as follows:

- Extending to other financial sectors than banking the macroprudential toolset, together with simplifying its command under one authority only;
- Enlarging the EU budget and possibly creating a separate EZ budget; this is preliminary to other actions, such as implementing the Macroeconomic Dialogue guidelines, when they recommend "boosting investment by making the most of the opportunities provided by EU funds, including the European Fund for Strategic Investments and the Structural Funds to finance investment in key growth areas" (Council of the European Union, 2015). This recommendation seems to ask for "getting blood out of a stone," given the current size of the EU budget, which, as we suggest, should be raised substantially;
- Creating a common minister of the economy and finance is indeed a reform complementary to creating some kind of fiscal union, but implementing the proposal can help as one of the first steps toward such a fiscal union; in fact, a common minister may at least detect some preliminary and feasible actions that can facilitate it in due time;
- The European Semester should be more focused on some objectives and its conclusions should be mandatory, subject to fines or some other kind of penalty;
- Making steps in amending fiscal rules in a way to ensure they are anticyclical and symmetric between surplus and deficit countries; EU Commission warnings should be addressed to Germany and other surplus countries saying that sanctions will be adopted in case they do not reduce to the upper boundary their export surplus as a percentage of the GDP as required by the MIP; this would help in suggesting a way able to lead to a common growth strategy together with suggestions for common wage rules; this is indeed a very important step in reducing all the factors behind monetary imbalances and asset bubbles;

- Nominal wages should not show huge differences in the various countries (being too low in "core" countries and excessive in the others); and they should change following the norm of the rate of change in productivity plus the ECB target inflation rate;
- In order to raise the low productivity trend of some countries, like Italy, in addition to structural policies (in particular, reform policies referred to product market) and incentives to innovation, proper incomes polices rules should be implemented; a number of EU provisions could be tied to implementation of this target;
- Amending the monetary rules to make the ECB more accountable and adding new targets to inflation containment. This is really a very difficult reform to implement; however, at least some steps in this direction could be taken by reforming the Maastricht Treaty in a way that the European Parliament can at least censor its operation – as it is for the Fed – and possibly modify its statute in order to attribute more importance to employment and growth targets.

Most of these proposals have some likelihood of being implemented only if they are backed by enough political support from the member countries. In particular, this should be the case, on the one hand, of some core countries (the "New Hanseatic" league, in addition to Germany) and, on the other, of peripheral countries, which must not only implement necessary reforms, but also get rid of spreading populist orientations.

References

Abiad A., D. Furceri, P. Topalova (2015), The macroeconomic effects of public investment: Evidence from advanced economies, IMF W. P. No. 15/95

Ábrahám Á., J. Brogueira de Sousa, R. Marimon, L. Mayr (2018), On the design of a European Unemployment Insurance System (EUIS), ADEMU W. P. No. 2018/106

Ábrahám A., E. Carceles-Poveda, Y. Liu, R. Marimon (2018), On the optimal design of a Financial Stability Fund, ADEMU W. P. 2018/15

Acemoglu D., P. Restrepo (2017), Secular stagnation? The effect of aging on economic growth in the age of automation, MIT Dept of Economics W. P. No. 17–02, January 12

Acemoglu D., S. Johnson, P. Querubin, J. A. Robinson (2008), When does policy reform work? The case of Central Bank independence, *Brookings Papers on Economic Activity*, 39(1): 351–418

Acharya V., I. Drechsler, P. Schnabl (2014), A Pyrrhic victory? Bank bailouts and sovereign credit risk, *Journal of Finance*, 69(6): 2689–739

Acocella N. (2005), *Economic Policy in the Age of Globalization*, Cambridge: Cambridge University Press

Acocella N. (2011), The deflationary bias of exit strategies in the EMU countries, *Review of Economic Conditions in Italy*, 2–3: 471–93

Acocella N. (2014), The theoretical roots of EMU institutions and policies during the crisis, Annali della Fondazione Einaudi 2013, Turin

Acocella N. (2015a), A tale of two cities: The evolution of the crisis and exit policies in Washington and Frankfurt, in B. Dallago, J. McGowan, eds.

Acocella N. (2015b), Towards a fairer economic and monetary union. How to institutionalise fairness in the EU? Memotef, W.P. No. 142/2015

Acocella N. (2016), Signalling imbalances in the EMU, in B. Dallago, G. Guri, J. McGowan, eds., *A Global Perspective on the European Economic Crisis*, London: Routledge, Ch. 2, pp. 48–67

Acocella N. (2018), *Rediscovering Economic Policy as a Discipline*, Cambridge: Cambridge University Press

Acocella N., A. Hughes Hallett (2018), Forward guidance policy announcements: How effective are they? Mimeo

Acocella N., P. Pasimeni (2018), Uncovered inflation rate parity condition in a monetary union, Forum for Macroeconomics and Macroeconomic Policies W. P. No. 28, IMK 2018, ISSN: 2512-8655

Acocella N., G. Di Bartolomeo, P. Tirelli (2007a), Fiscal leadership and coordination in the EMU, *Open Economies Review*, 18(3): 281-9

Acocella N., G. Di Bartolomeo, P. Tirelli (2007b), Monetary conservatism and fiscal coordination in a monetary union, *Economics Letters*, 94(1): 56-63

Acocella N., G. Di Bartolomeo, P. Tirelli (2009), The macroeconomics of social pacts, *Journal of Economic Behavior & Organization*, 72(1): 202-13

Acocella N., G. Di Bartolomeo, A. Hughes Hallett (2013), *The Theory of Economic Policy in a Strategic Setting*, Cambridge: Cambridge University Press

Acocella N., G. Di Bartolomeo, A. Hughes Hallett (2016), *Macroeconomic Paradigms and Policies. From the Great Depression to the Great Recession*, Cambridge: Cambridge University Press

Afonso A., J. Tovar, J. M. Kazemi (2019), The effects of macroeconomic, fiscal and monetary policy announcements on sovereign bond spreads: An event study from the EMU, REM W. P. 067-2019, January

Afonso A., M. G. Arghyrou, M. D. Gadea, A. Kontonikas (2017), "Whatever it takes" to resolve the European sovereign debt crisis? Bond pricing regime switches and monetary policy effects, Cardiff Economics W. P. No. E2017/12 September

Agénor P.-R., E. Kharroubi, L. Gambacorta, G. Lombardo, L. A. Pereira da Silva (2017), The international dimensions of macroprudential policies, BIS W. P. No. 643, June

Aghion P., E. Caroli, C. Garcia-Peñalosa (1999), Inequality and economic growth: The perspective of the new growth theories, *Journal of Economic Literature*, 37 (4): 1615-60

Aghion P., J. Cai, M. Dewatripont, L. Du, A. Harrison, P. Legros (2012), Industrial policy and competition, NBER W. P. 18048, May

Aglietta M., A. Leron (2017), *The Double Democracy: A Political Europe for Growth*, Paris: Seuil

Aiginger A. (2014), Industrial policy for a sustainable growth path, in D. Bailey, K. Cowling, P. Tomlinson, eds., *New Perspectives on Industrial Policy*, Oxford: Oxford University Press, pp. 365-94

Alari P., F. Figari, H. Sutherland (2017), The design of fiscal consolidation measures in the European Union: Distributional effects and implications for macro-economic recovery, *Oxford Economic Papers*, 69(3): 632-54

Albanesi S., V. V. Chari, L. J. Christiano (2002), Expectation traps and monetary policy, *Review of Economic Studies*, 70(4): 715-41

Albonico A., A. Paccagnini, P. Tirelli (2016), PIIGS in the EZ. An empirical DSGE model, September 24, DEMS W. P. No. 331, March

Albonico A., R. Cardani, P. Tirelli (2018a), Debunking the myth of Southern profligacy. A DSGE analysis of business cycles in the EMU's big four, University of Milano Bicocca, DEMS W. P. No. 373

Albonico A., A. Paccagnini, P. Tirelli (2018b), Limited asset market participation and the EZ crisis. An empirical DSGE model, Center for European Studies, University of Milano, Bicocca, No. 391, November

Alcidi C., G. Thirion (2016), Assessing the EZ's shock-absorption capacity risk sharing, consumption smoothing and fiscal policy, CEPS Special Report No. 146, September

Alcidi C., D. Gros, J. Núñez Ferrer, D. Rinaldi (2017), The instruments providing macro-financial support to EU Member States, CEPS Research Report No. 2017/06, March

Alcidi C., N. Määttänen, G. Thirion (2015), Cross-country spillover effects and fiscal policy coordination in EMU, FIRSTRUN Project Funded by the European Union No. 649261

Alcidi C., P. D'Imperio, G. Thirion (2017), Risk-sharing and consumption-smoothing patterns in the US and the EZ: A comprehensive comparison, CEPS Working Document, No. 2017/04, May

Alesina A., S. Ardagna (1998), Tales of fiscal adjustments, *Economic Policy*, 13(27): 489–545

Alesina A., A. Drazen (1991), Why are stabilizations delayed? *The American Economic Review*, 81(5): 1170–88

Alesina A., F. Giavazzi (2010), eds., *Europe and the Euro*, Chicago: University of Chicago Press

Alesina A., R. Perotti (1995), Fiscal expansions and adjustments in OECD countries, *Economic Policy*, 10(21): 207–48

Alesina A., R. Perotti (1997), Fiscal adjustments in OECD countries: Composition and macroeconomic effects, *IMF Staff Papers*, 44(2): 210–48

Alesina A., S. Ardagna, V. Galasso (2010), The euro and structural reforms, in A. Alesina, F. Giavazzi, eds., pp. 57–93

Alesina A., S. Ardagna, F. Trebbi (2006), Who adjusts and when? On the political economy of reforms, NBER W. P. No. 12049

Alesina A., C. Favero, F. Giavazzi (2012), The output effect of fiscal consolidations, NBER, W. P. No. 18336

Alesina A., G. Tabellini, F. Trebbi (2017), Is Europe an optimal political area? Brookings Papers on Economic Activity, Spring, pp. 169–213

Alessandrini P., M. Fratianni, A. Hughes Hallett, A. Presbitero (2014), External imbalances and fiscal fragility in the EZ, *Open Economies Review*, 25(1): 3–34

Allard C., P. Koeva Brooks, J. C. Bluedor, F. Bornhorst, K. Christopherson, F. Ohnsorge, T. Poghosyan, and an IMF Staff Team (2013), Toward a fiscal union for the EZ, September, IMF Staff D. N./13/09

Allen F., D. Gale (1994), Liquidity preference, market participation and asset price volatility, *American Economic Review*, 84(4): 933–55

Allen F., D. Gale (2000), Financial contagion, *Journal of Political Economy*, 108 (1): 1–33

Altavilla C., D. Giannone, M. Lenza (2014), The financial and macroeconomic effects of OMT announcements, ECB W.P. Series 1707, August

Alter A., A. Beyer (2013), The dynamics of spillover effects during the European sovereign debt turmoil, February, ECB W. P. Series 1558, June

Alvaredo F., A. B. Atkinson, T. Piketty, E. Saez (2013), The top 1 percent in international and historical perspective, *Journal of Economic Perspectives*, 27 (3): 3–20

Amendola A., M. Di Serio, M. Fragetta (2017), The government spending multiplier at the zero lower bound: Evidence from the Euro Area, Università degli Studi di Salerno, Celpe, D. P. 153

Anderson D., B. Hunt, S. Snudden (2014), Fiscal consolidation in the EZ: How much pain can structural reforms ease? *Journal of Policy Modeling*, 36(5): 785–99

Andor L. (2014), Basic European unemployment insurance. The best way forward in strengthening the EMU's resilience and Europe's recovery, *Intereconomics*, 49 (4): 184–9

Andor L. (2015), Shared unemployment insurance. Helping refocus the EZ on convergence and cohesion, http://static1.squarespace.com/static/541ff5f5e4 b02b7c37f31ed6/t/563a2231e4b0c3bc9ae46643/1446650417384/Shared+Une mployment+Insurance.pdf

Andor L., L. Bini Smaghi, L. Boone, S. Dullien, G. Duval, L. Garicano, M. A. Landesmann, G. Papaconstantinou, A. Roldan, G. Schick, X. Timbeau, A. Truger, S. Vallée (2018), Blueprint for a democratic renewal of the EZ, Il politico, 28 February

Andrade P., J. Breckenfelder, F. De Fiore, P. Karadi, O. Tristani (2016), The ECB's asset purchase programme: An early assessment, ECB D. P. No. 1956, September

Andréasson H. (2014), The effect of decentralized wage bargaining on the structure of wages and firm performance, Ratio W. P. No. 241

Andreozzi L., R. Tamborini (2017), Why is Europe engaged in an interdependence war, and how can it be stopped? Trento University, DEM W. P. No. 2017/06

Andritzky J., D. I. Christofzik, L. P. Feld, U. Scheuering (2016), A mechanism to regulate sovereign debt restructuring in the EZ, German Council of Economic Experts, W. P. 04/2016, July

Andrle M., J. Bluedorn, L. Eyraud, T. Kinda, P. Koeva-Brooks, G. Schwartz, A. Weber (2015), Reforming Fiscal Governance in the European Union, IMF, Staff Discussion Note 15/09

Angelini P., S. Neri, F. Panetta (2011), Monetary and macroprudential policies, Bank of Italy, Temi di discussione (W.P.) No. 801, March

Angeloni I. (2016), Macroprudential policies to contain systemic risks, Keynote speech, Member of the Supervisory Board of the ECB, SUERF/Deutsche Bundesbank/IMFS Conference on "The SSM at 1", Deutsche Bundesbank, Frankfurt am Main, 4 February 2016, www.bankingsupervision.europa.eu/pre ss/speeches/date/2016/html/se160204.en.html

Arbolino R., R. Boffardi (2017), The impact of institutional quality and efficient cohesion investments on economic growth evidence from Italian regions, *Sustainability*, 9, 1432, doi:10.3390/su9081432

Ardy B., I. Begg, D. Hodson, I. Maher, D. G. Mayes (2005), *Adjusting to EMU*, London: Palgrave Macmillan

Arestei D., M. Gallo (2014), Interest rate pass-through in the EZ during the financial crisis: A multivariate regime switching approach, *Journal of Policy Modeling*, 36(2): 273–95

Arestis P. (2015), Coordination of fiscal with monetary and financial stability policies can better cure unemployment, *Review of Keynesian Economics*, 3(1): 233–47

Arestis P., M. Sawyer (2004), On the main ingredients of the European Economic and Monetary Union, *International Journal of Political Economy*, 34(2): 5–18

Arestis P., M. Sawyer (2010), The return of fiscal policy, *Journal of Post Keynesian Economics*, 32(3): 327–46

Armstrong M., J. Taylor (2000), *Regional Economics and Policy*, 3rd ed., Oxford: Blackwell

Arnold N., B. Barkbu, E. Ture, H. Wang, J. Yao (2018), A central fiscal stabilization capacity for the Euro Area, IMF SDN/18/03, March

Arnone M., B. Laurens, J. Segalotto, M. Sommer (2007), Central bank autonomy: lessons from global trends, IMF W. P. 07/88

Asatryan Z., X. Debrun, F. Heinemann, M. Horvath, Ľ. Ódor, M. Yeter (2017), Making the most of the European Fiscal Board, ZEW Policy Brief No. 3, May 04th

Asatryan Z., X. Debrun, A. Havlik, F. Heinemann, M. G. Kocher, R. Tamborini (2018), Which role for a European minister of economy and finance in a European fiscal union? EconPol Policy Report 05/2018 Vol. 2 May

Asonuma T., C. Trebesch (2016), Sovereign debt restructurings: Preemptive or post-default, *Journal of the European Economic Association*, 14(1): 175–214

Atkinson A. B. (2009a), Economics as a moral science, *Economica*, 76(s1): 791–804

Atkinson A. B. (2009b), Factor shares: The principal problem of political economy? *Oxford Review of Economic Policy*, 25(1): 3–16

Atkinson A. B., A. C. Guio, E. Marlier (2017), eds., *Monitoring Social Inclusion in Europe*. 2017 edition, Eurostat

Atkinson A. B., B. Cantillon, E. Marlier, B. Nolan (2002a), Indicators for social inclusion, *Politica Economica-Journal of Economic Policy (PEJEP)*, 18 (1): 7–28

Atkinson A. B., B. Cantillon, E. Marlier, B. Nolan (2002b), *Social Indicators: The EU and Social Inclusion*, Oxford: Oxford University Press

Attinasi M. G., L. Metelli (2016), Is fiscal consolidation self-defeating? A panel-VAR analysis for the EZ countries, European Central Bank W. P. No. 1883, February

Auerbach A. J., Y. Gorodnichenko (2012), Fiscal multipliers in recession and expansion, in A. Alesina, F. Giavazzi, eds., *Fiscal Policy after the Financial Crisis*, NBER, Chicago: University of Chicago Press, pp. 63–98

Avdikos V., A. Chardas (2016), European Union Cohesion Policy post 2014: More (place-based and conditional) growth – less redistribution and cohesion, *Territory, Politics, Governance*, 4(1): 97–117, http://dx.doi.org/10.1080/21622 671.2014.992460

Avgouleas E., C. Goodhart (2015), Critical reflections on bank bail-ins, *Journal of Financial Regulation*, 1(1): 3–29, doi:10.109 3/jfr/fju009

Avram S., H. Levy, H. Sutherland (2014), Income redistribution in the European Union, *IZA Journal of European Labor Studies*, 3: 22 27 November

Bachtler J., C. Mendez, F. Wishlade (2016), *EU Cohesion Policy and European Integration: The Dynamics of EU Budget and Regional Policy Reform*, 2nd ed., London: Routledge

Bachtrögler J., C. Hammer, W. H. Reuter, F. Schwendinger (2019), Guide to the galaxy of EU regional funds recipients: Evidence from new data, *Empirica*, 46 (1):103–50

Bade R., M. Parkin (1978), Central bank laws and monetary policies: A preliminary investigation, in M. Porter, ed., *The Australian Monetary System in the 1970s*, Monash University

Baglioni S., A. Hurrelmann (2015), The EZ crisis and citizen engagement in EU affairs, *West European Politics*, 39(1): 104–24, doi:10.1080/ 01402382.2015.1081507 1

Bagnai A., B. Granville, C. A. Mongeau Ospina (2017), Withdrawal of Italy from the EZ: Stochastic simulations of a structural macroeconomic model, *Economic Modelling*, 64(C): 524–38

Bailer S., M. Mattila, G. Schneider (2015), Money makes the EU go round: The objective foundations of conflict in the Council of Ministers, *Journal of Common Market Studies*, 53(3): 437–56

Bailey D., K. Cowling (2006), Industrial policy and vulnerable capitalism, *International Review of Applied Economics*, 20(5): 537–53, doi:10.1080/02692170601005481

Bajo-Rubio O., M. D. Montávez-Garcés (2002), Was there monetary autonomy in Europe on the eve of EMU? The German dominance hypothesis re-examined, *Journal of Applied Economics*, 5(2): 185–207

Bajo-Rubio O., C. Diaz-Roldán (2003), Insurance mechanisms against asymmetric shocks in a monetary union: A proposal with an application to EMU, *Recherches Economiques de Louvain, Louvain Economic Review*, 69(1): 73–96

Bajo-Rubio O., C. Díaz-Roldán (2017), The scope for a budgetary union in the European Monetary Union, in N. da Costa Cabral, J. R. Gonçalves, N. Cunha Rodrigues, eds., *The Euro and the Crisis*, Heidelberg: Springer, Part IV, pp. 357–66

Bajo-Rubio O., S. Sosvilla-Rivero, F. Fernandez-Rodriguez (2001), Asymmetry in the EMS: New evidence based on non-linear forecasts, *European Economic Review*, 45(3): 451–73

Baker S. (2006), *Sustainable Development*, London: Routledge

Balassa B. (1964), The purchasing power parity doctrine: A reappraisal, *Journal of Political Economy*, 72(6): 584–96

Balassa B. (1973), Comment on R. Mundell (1973b), A plan for a European currency, in H. Johnson, A. Swoboda, eds., Brookings Papers on Economic Activity, 43(1): pp. 173–7

Balassone F., D. Franco (2000), Public investment, the Stability Pact and the 'Golden Rule', *Fiscal Studies* 21(2): 207–229

Balassone F., I. Visco (2019), The Economic and Monetary Union: Time to break the deadlock. OMFIF-Bank of Italy seminar "The future of the Euro area", Rome, 15 November

Balassone F., S. Cecchetti, M. Cecioni, M. Cioffi, W. Cornacchia, F. Corneli, G. Semeraro (2018), Economic governance in the EZ: Balancing risk reduction and risk sharing, in G. Eusepi, R. E. Wagner, eds., *Debt Default and Democracy*, Cheltenham: Edgar Elgar

Baldock D. (2016), Retaining the center stage, in N. Haigh, ed., *EU Environmental Policy. Its Journey to Centre Stage*, London: Routledge

Baldwin R., C. Wyplosz (2006), *The Economics of European Integration*, 2nd ed., London: McGraw-Hill

Baldwin R., F. Giavazzi (2016), eds., How to fix Europe's monetary union. Views of leading economists, Vox CEPR's Policy Portal, 12 February, http://voxeu.org/a rticle/policies-and-institutions-managing-aggregate-macroeconomic-stance-EZ

Ball L. (2014a), Long-term damage from the great recession in OECD countries, NBER W. P. 20185, May

Ball L. (2014b), The case for a long-run inflation target of four percent, IMF W. P. 14/92

Balls E., J. Howat, A. Stansbury (2016), Central bank independence revisited: After the financial crisis, what should a model central bank look like? Harvard Kennedy School, M-RCBG Associate W. P. No. 67, November

Banca d'Italia (1954), Relazione Annuale. Considerazioni Finali, Rome: Banca d'Italia

Banerji A., V. Crispolti, E. Dabla-Norris, R. A. Duval, C. H. Ebeke, D. Furceri, T. Komatsuzaki, T. Poghosyan (2017), Labor and product market reforms in advanced economies: Fiscal costs, gains, and support, IMF Staff D. N. SDN/17/03, March

Banerjee A. V. (1992), A simple model of herd behavior, *The Quarterly Journal of Economics*, 107(3): 797–817

Banerjee B., F. Coricelli (2017), Misallocation in Europe during the global financial crisis: Some stylized facts, in B. Banerjee, F. Coricelli, eds., *Crisis, Credit and Resource Misallocation: Evidence from Europe during the Great Recession*, London: Cepr Press

Bank of Slovenia (2015), Macroprudential policy for the banking sector, Strategic framework, 24 September

Barca F. (2009), An agenda for a reformed cohesion policy. A place-based approach to meeting European Union challenges and expectations. Independent Report, European Parliament, April

Barigozzi M., A. M. Conti, M. Luciani (2014), Do countries respond asymmetrically to the common monetary policy? *Oxford Bulletin of Economics and Statistics*, 76(5): 693–714

Barkbu B., J. Rahman, R. Valdés (2012), Fostering growth in Europe now, IMF Staff D. N. SDN/12/07, 18 June

Barkin J. S. (1996), Hegemony without motivation: Domestic policy priorities and German monetary policy, *German Politics and Society*, 14(3): 54–72

Barrell R., E. P. Davis, O. Pomerantz (2009), The impact of EMU on real exchange rate volatility of EU countries, *National Institute Economic Review*, 208(1): 101–8

Barrell R., S. Gottschalk, D. Holland, E. Khoman, I. Liadze, O. Pomerantz (2008), The impact of EMU on growth and employment, European Economy, Economic Papers 318, April

Barro R. J. (1974), Are government bonds net wealth? *Journal of Political Economy*, 82(6): 1095–117

Barro R. J. (2000), Inequality and growth in a panel of countries, *Journal of Economic Growth*, 5(1): 5–32

Barro R. J., D. B. Gordon (1983), Rules, discretion and reputation in a model of monetary policy, *Journal of Monetary Economics*, 12(1): 101–21

Barroso J. M. D. (2012), State of the Union Address, 12 September, http://europa.eu /rapid/press-release_SPEECH-12-596_en.htm

Bartalevich D. (2016), The influence of the Chicago School on the Commission's guidelines. Notices and block exemption regulations in EU competition policy, *Journal of Common Market Studies*, 54(2): 267–83

Baskaran T., Z. Hessami (2013), Monetary integration, soft budget constraints, and the EMU sovereign debt crises, University of Konstanz, Department of Economics, W. P. 2013/3

Baskaya Y. S., J. di Giovanni, S. Kalemli-Ozcan, J.-L. Peydro, M. Ulu (2016), Capital flows, credit cycles and macroprudential policy, BIS Paper No. 86j, September, https://ssrn.com/abstract=2844247

Bassanetti A., M. Bugamelli, S. Momigliano, R. Sabbatini, F. Zollino (2014), The policy response to macroeconomic and fiscal imbalances in Italy in the last fifteen years, *PSL Quarterly Review*, 67(268): 55–103

Bastasin C. (2015), The euro and the end of 20th Century politics, LUISS School of European Political Economy, Policy Brief No. 10

Batini N., G. Callegari, G. Melina (2012), Successful austerity in the United States, Europe and Japan, IMF W.P. 190, July

Baun M. J. (1995–1996), The Maastricht Treaty as high politics: Germany, France, and European integration, *Political Science Quarterly*, 110(4): 605–24

Baun M. J., D. Marek (2014), *Cohesion Policy in the European Union*, Basingstoke: Palgrave Macmillan

Bayoumi T., B. Eichengreen (1997), Optimum currency areas and exchange rate volatility: Theory and evidence compared, in B. J. Cohen, ed., *International Trade and Finance: New Frontiers for Research, Essays in Honor of Peter Kenen*, Cambridge: Cambridge University Press

Bean C. (1998), Monetary policy under EMU, *Oxford Review of Economic Policy*, 14(3): 41–53

Beblavy M., K. Lenaerts (2015), *Feasibility and Added Value of a European Unemployment Benefit Scheme*, Brussels: Interim Report, CEPS

Beblavy M., K. Lenaerts, I. Maselli (2017), Design of a European Unemployment Benefit Scheme, CEPS Research Report 2017/04, 21 February

Beck T. (2017), Looking back at lost decade: Avoiding a second one, in A. Bénassy-Quéré, F. Giavazzi, eds.

Becker S. O., P. H. Egger, M. von Ehrlich (2018), Effects of EU regional policy: 1989–2013, *Regional Science and Urban Economics*, 69: 143–52

Beetsma R. M. W. J., A. L. Bovenberg (1998), Monetary union without fiscal coordination may discipline policymakers, *Journal of International Economics*, 45(2): 239–58

Beetsma R. M. W. J., X. Debrun (2004), Reconciling stability and growth: Smart pacts and structural reforms, *IMF Staff Papers*, 51(3): 431–56

Beetsma R. M. W. J., M. Giuliodori (2010), The macroeconomic costs and benefits of the EMU and other monetary unions: An overview of recent research, *Journal of Economic Literature*, 48(3): 603–41

Beetsma R. M. W. J., M. Giuliodori (2011), The effects of government purchases shocks: Review and estimates for the EU, *The Economic Journal*, 121(550): F4–F32

Beetsma R. M. W. J., K. Mavromatis (2014), An analysis of eurobonds, *Journal of International Money and Finance*, 45(C): 91–111

Beetsma R. M. W. J., H. Uhlig (1999), An analysis of the stability and growth pact, *The Economic Journal*, 109 (458): 546–71

Beetsma R. M. W. J., S. Cima, J. Cimadomo (2018), A minimal moral hazard central stabilisation capacity for the EMU based on world trade, ECB W. P. Series 2137, March

Beetsma R. M. W. J., M. Giuliodori, F. Klaassen (2006), Trade spillovers of fiscal policy in the European Union: A panel analysis, *Economic Policy*, 21(48): 639–87

Beetsma R. M. W. J., M. Giuliodori, F. Klaassen (2008), The effects of public spending shocks on trade balances and budget deficits in the EU, *Journal of the European Economic Association*, 6(2–3): 414–23

Begg I. (2002), EMU and employment, W. P. No. 42, ESRC 'One Europe or several?' Programme, University of Sussex

Begg I. (1995), Factor mobility and regional disparities in the European Union, *Oxford Review of Economic Policy*, 11(2): 96–112

Begg I. (2016), The economic theory of Cohesion policy, in S. Piattoni, L. Polverari, eds., pp. 51–64

Begg I., G. Gudgin, D. Morris (1995), The assessment: Regional policy in the European Union, *Oxford Review of Economic Policy*, 11(2): 1–17

Beirne J., M. Fratscher (2013), The pricing of sovereign risk and contagion during the European sovereign debt crisis, *Journal of International Money and Finance*, 34 (C): 60–82

Belke A. (2016), The fiscal compact and the excessive deficit procedure: Relics of bygone times? in N. da Costa Cabral, J. R. Gonçalves, eds., *The Euro and the Crisis*, Heidelberg: Springer, pp 131–52

Belke A., F. Verheyen (2013), Doomsday for the EZ: Causes, variants and consequences of breakup, ROME D. P. Series, No. 13–11

Bénassy-Quéré A. (2016), EZ fiscal stance: From theory to practical implementation, August 16, CESifo W. P. No. 6040, https://ssrn.com /abstract=2845283

Bénassy-Quéré A. (2017), A jobs union, in A. Bénassy-Quéré, F. Giavazzi (2017a), eds.

Bénassy-Quéré A., F. Giavazzi (2017a), eds., *Europe's Political Spring. Fixing the EZ and Beyond*, A VoxEU.org eBook

Bénassy-Quéré A., F. Giavazzi (2017b), Introduction, in A. Bénassy-Quéré, F. Giavazzi (2017a), eds.

Bénassy-Quéré A., X. Ragot, G. Wolff (2016), Which fiscal union for the Euro Area? Notes du Conseil d'analyse économique No. 29

Bénassy-Quéré A., M. Brunnermeier, E. Farhi, M. Fratzscher, C. Fuest, P.-O. Gourinchas, P. Martin, J. Pisani-Ferry, H. Rey, I. Schnabel, N. Véron, B. Weder di Mauro, J. Zettelmeyer (2018), Reconciling risk sharing with market discipline: A constructive approach to Euro Area reform, CEPR Policy Insight No. 91, January

Benedetto G. (2017), How the EU Budget has developed and changed in the last 10 years? European Parliament, PE 572.713, February

Benigno P., L. A. Ricci (2011), The inflation-output trade-off with downward wage rigidities, *The American Economic Review*, 101(4): 1436–66

Benigno P., M. Woodford (2004), Optimal monetary and fiscal policy: A linear-quadratic approach, in M. Gertler, K. Rogoff, eds., *NBER Macroeconomic Annual 2003*, Cambridge, MA: MIT Press, pp. 271–364

Benigno G., N. Converse, L. Fornaro (2015), Large capital inflows, sectoral allocation, and economic performance, *Journal of International Money and Finance*, 55(C), 60–87

Berg A., J. D. Ostry (2011), Inequality and unsustainable growth: Two sides of the same coin? IMF Staff D. N. 11/08

Berg A., J. D. Ostry, J. Zettelmeyer (2012), What makes growth sustained? *Journal of Development Economics*, 98(2): 149–66

Berg A, J. D. Ostry, C. Tsangarides, Y. Yakhshilikos (2018), Redistribution, inequality, and growth: New evidence, *Journal of Economic Growth*, 23(3): 259–305

Berger H., J. den Haan, S. C. W. Eijffinger (2001), Central bank independence: An update of theory and evidence, *Journal of Economic Surveys*, 15(1): 3–40

Bernanke B. S. (2010), Testimony before the Joint Economic Committee of Congress, 14 April

Bernanke B. S., M. Gertler (1989), Agency costs, net worth and business fluctuations, *The American Economic Review*, 79(1): 14–31

Bernanke B. S., M. Gertler (1990), Financial fragility and economic performance, *Quarterly Journal of Economics*, 105(1): 87–114

Bernanke B. S., M. Gertler, S. Gilchrist (1999), The financial accelerator in a quantitative business cycle framework, in J. Taylor, M. Woodford, eds., *Handbook of Macroeconomics*, vol 1C, Amsterdam: North Holland

Bernhard W., D. Leblang (1999), Democratic institutions and exchange-rate commitments, *International Organization*, 53(1) 71–97

Bernoth K., B. Erdogan (2012), Sovereign bond yield spreads: A time-varying coefficient approach, *Journal of International Money and Finance*, 31(3): 639–56

Bernoth K., J. von Hagen, L. Schuknecht (2012), Sovereign risk premiums in the European government bond market, *Journal of International Money and Finance*, 31(5): 975–95

Bertelsmann Stiftung (2018), Policy performance and governance capacities in the OECD and EU, Sustainable Governance Indicators 2018

Berti K., E. Colesnic, C. Desponts, S. Pamies, E. Sail (2016), Fiscal reaction functions for European Union countries, European Commission, Directorate-General for Economic and Financial Affairs, D. P. 028, April

Bhattarai S., A. Chatterjee, W. Yong Park (2018), Effects of US quantitative easing on emerging market economies, Asian Development Bank Institute W. P. Series 803, January

Bianchi F., D. Comin, T. Kind, H. Kung (2019), Slow recoveries through fiscal austerity, mimeo

Bibow J. (2006), Europe's quest for monetary stability, *International Journal of Political Economy*, 35(1): 24–43

Bibow J. (2007), How the Maastricht regime fosters divergence as well as fragility, in P. Arestis, E. Hein, E. Le Heron, eds., *Monetary Policies – Modern Approaches*, Basingstoke: Palgrave; originally published in July 2006 as W. P. 460 of The Levy Economics Institute of Bard College Skidmore College

Bibow J. (2012), The euro debt crisis and Germany's euro trilemma, Levy economics institute of Bard College, W. P. 721, May

Bibow J. (2013), On the Franco-German euro contradiction and ultimate euro battleground, Levy economics institute of Bard College, W. P. 762, April

Bini Smaghi L. (2015), What the history of the Bundesbank might teach the ECB, http://sep.luiss.it/news/2015/01/22/lorenzo-bini-smaghi-what-history-bundesbank-might-teach-ecb

Bini Smaghi L., T. Padoa-Schioppa, F. Papadia (1994), The transition to EMU in the Maastricht Treaty, Essays in International Finance No. 194, Dept of Economics, Princeton University, November

BIS (2015), *Statistical Bulletin*, Bank for International Settlements, Basel, December

BIS (2018), *Statistical Bulletin*, Bank for International Settlements, June

Blanchard O. J. (2007), Adjustment within the euro: The difficult case of Portugal, *Portuguese Economic Journal*, 6(1): 1–21

Blanchard O. J. (2018), The missing third leg of the euro architecture: National wage negotiations, Peterson Institute for International Economics, February 28

Blanchard O. J., F. Giavazzi (2002), Current account deficits in the Euro Area: The end of the Feldstein-Horioka puzzle? *Brookings Papers on Economic Activity*, 33(2): 147–209

Blanchard O. J., F. Giavazzi (2003), Macroeconomic effects of regulation and deregulation in goods and labor markets, *The Quarterly Journal of Economics*, 115(3): 879–907

Blanchard O. J., F. Giavazzi (2004), Improving the SGP through a proper accounting of public investment, CEPR D. P. 4220, February

Blanchard O. J., D. Leigh (2013), Growth forecasts and fiscal multipliers, IMF W.P. 13/1, January

Blanchard O. J., G.-M. Milesi-Ferretti (2012), (Why) should current account imbalances be reduced? *IMF Economic Review*, 60(1): 139–150

Blanchard O. J., R. Perotti (2002), An empirical characterization of the dynamic effects of changes in government spending and taxes on output, *Quarterly Journal of Economics*, 107(4): 1329–68

Blanchard O. J., G. Dell'Ariccia, P. Mauro (2010), Rethinking macroeconomic policy, IMF Staff Position Note No. 2010/03

Blanchard O. J., G. Erceg, J. Lindé (2015), Jump-starting the Euro Area recovery: Would a rise in core spending help the periphery? NBER W. P. 21426

Blanchard O., R. Dornbusch, J. Drèze, H. Giersch, R. Layard, M. Monti (1985), Employment and growth in Europe: A two-handed approach, Report of the

CEPS Macroeconomic Policy Group, Economic Papers 36, Brussels: European Commission

Blinder A. S. (1998), *Central Banking in Theory and in Practice*, Cambridge: MIT Press

Blinder A. S. (2004), The case against the case against discretionary fiscal policy, CEPS W.P. 100

Blot C., J. Creel, P. Hubert, F. Labondance, F. Saraceno (2015), Assessing the link between price and financial stability, *Journal of Financial Stability*, 16(C): 71–88

Blyth M. (2013), *Austerity: The History of a Dangerous Idea*, Oxford: Oxford University Press

Board of Governors of the Federal Reserve System (n.d.), What does it mean that the Federal Reserve is "independent within the government"? www .federalreserve.gov/faqs/about_12799.htm

Boeri T., M. Castanheira, R. Faini, V. Galasso (2006), eds., *Structural Reform without Prejudices*, Oxford: Oxford University Press

Boeckx J., P. Ilbas, M. Kasongo Kashama, M. de Sola Perea, Ch. Van Nieuwenhuyze (2017), Interactions between monetary and macroprudential policies, Economic Review, National Bank of Belgium, issue ii, pages 7–29, September

Bofinger P. (2015), German wage moderation and the EZ Crisis, VoxEU, 30 November, http://voxeu.org/

Bofinger P. (2016a), The way forward: Coping with the insolvency risk of member states and giving teeth to the European Semester, in R. Baldwin, F. Giavazzi, eds., pp. 227–39

Bofinger P. (2016b), Two views of the EZ Crisis: Government failure vs market failure, VoxEU, 8 April, http://voxeu.org/

Bofinger P. (2017), Hartz IV: The solution to the unemployment problems in the EZ? *Intereconomics*, 52(6): 353–7

Bofinger P. (2019), Time for a red shift from Germany's 'black zero', *International Politics and Society*, 6 March

Bofinger P., E. Mayer (2007), Monetary and fiscal policy interaction in the Euro Area with different assumptions on the Phillips curve, *Open Economies Review*, 18 (3): 291–305

Bohl M. T., P. Michaelis, P. L. Siklos (2016), Austerity and recovery: Exchange rate regime choice, economic growth, and financial crises, *Economic Modelling*, 53 (C): 195–207

Böhm-Bawerk E. (1924), Unsere passive Handelsbilanz, in F. X. Weiß, ed., *Gesammelte Schriften von Böhm-Bawerk*, Vol. I, Vienna and Leipzig: Hölder-Pichler-Tempsky

Bokan N., A. Hughes Hallett (2008), The impact of tax and market distortions on the Phillips curve and the natural rate of unemployment, *Economics – The Open-Access, Open-Assessment E-Journal*, 2, pp. 1–28

Bolaffi A., P. Ciocca (2017), *Germania/Europa. Due Punti di Vista sulle Opportunità e i Rischi dell'Egemonia Tedesca*, Rome: Donzelli

Boldrin M., F. Canova (2001), Inequality and convergence in Europe's regions: Reconsidering European regional policies, *Economic Policy*, 16(32): 205–53

Bolkestein Report (2001), Company taxation in the internal market, COM (2001), 582 Final, Bruxelles

Bologna P., M. Caccavaio (2014), Euro Area (cross-border?) banking, Questioni di Economia e Finanza (Occasional Papers) 228, Bank of Italy, Economic Research and International Relations Area

Bootle R. (2012), Leaving the euro: A practical guide, Lecture Winner of the Wolfson Economics Prize MMXII by Capital Economics, London

Bordes C., L. Clerc (2013), The ECB's separation principle: Does it "rule OK"? From policy rule to stop-and-go, Oxford Economic Papers, 65 (suppl_1):i66-i91

Bordignon M., S. Scabrosetti (2016), The political economy of financing the EU budget, SIEP W. P. 708, May

Bordo M. D. (2012), Whither the euro: Some lessons from the history of fiscal unions, remarks prepared for cigi-inet conference "Sovereign Debtors in Distress", Waterloo, Ontario, February 25

Bordo M. D., H. James (2006), One world money, then and now, *International Economics and Economic Policy*, 3(3): 395–407, doi:10.1007/s10368-006-0070-4

Bordo M. D., L. Jonung, A. Markiewicz (2013), A fiscal union for the euro: Some lessons from history, *CESifo Economic Studies*, 59(3): 449–88

Borghijs A., S. Ederveen, R. De Mooij (2013), European wage coordination: Nightmare or dream to come true? Enepri W. P. 20

Borio C. (2012), The financial cycle and macroeconomics: What have we learnt? BIS W. P. No. 395, December

Borsi M. T., N. Metiu (2015), The evolution of economic convergence in the European Union, *Empirical Economics*, 48(2): 657–81

Börzel T., T. Risse (2000), When Europe hits home: Europeanization and domestic change, Paper presented to the Annual Convention of the American Political Science Association, August 31 – September 3, Washington, D.C.

Bottero M., S. Lenzu, F. Mezzanotti (2015), Sovereign debt exposure and the bank lending channel: Impact on credit supply and the real economy, Bank of Italy, Temi di discussione W. P. 1032, September

Bourguignon F. (2018), World changes in inequality: An overview of facts, causes, consequences and policies, *CESIfo Economic Studies*, 64(3): 345–70

Braun D., M. Tausendpfund (2014), The impact of the Euro Crisis on citizens' support for the European Union, *Journal of European Integration*, 36(3): 231–45

Breidenbach P., T. Mitze, C. M. Schmidt (2016), EU Structural Funds and Regional Income Convergence. A sobering experience, Ruhr Economic Papers 608

Brennan G., J. M. Buchanan (1980), *The Power to Tax: Analytical Foundations of a Fiscal Constitution*, Indianapolis: Liberty Fund, Inc.

Brunazzo M. (2016), The history and evolution of Cohesion policy, in S. Piattoni, L. Polverari, eds., pp. 17–35

Brunnermeier M. K., A. Crocket, C. Goodhart, A. D. Persaud, H. Shin (2009), *The Fundamental Principles of Financial Regulation*, Geneva Reports on the World Economy 11, Princeton University and CEPR, Arlington, VA

Brunnermeier M. K., L. Garicano, P. R. Lane, M. Pagano, R. Reis, T. Santos, S. Van Nieuwerburgh, D. Vayanos (2012), *European Safe Bonds*, The euro-nomics group, mimeo, https://personal.lse.ac.uk/vayanos/Euronomics/ESBies.pdf

Brunnermeier M. K., S. Langfield, M. Pagano, R. Reis, S. Van Nieuwerburgh, D. Vayanos (2016a), ESBies: Safety in the tranches, ECB W. P. Series 21, September

Brunnermeier M. K., J. Harold, J. P. Landau (2016b), *The Euro and the Battle of Ideas*, Princeton: Princeton University Press

Bryson J. H. (1994), Macroeconomic stabilization through monetary and fiscal policy coordination: Implications for European Monetary Union, *Open Economies Review*, 5(4): 307–26

Brzoza-Brzezina M., M. Kolasa, K. Makarski (2013), Macroprudential policy instruments and economic imbalances in the Euro Area, ECB W. P. 1589, September

Buchanan J. M., G. Tullock (1962), *The Calculus of Consent: Logical Foundations of Constitutional Democracy*, Ann Arbor: University of Michigan Press

Bugamelli M., F. Lotti, M. Amici, E. Ciapanna, F. Colonna, F. D'Amuri, S. Giacomelli, A. Linarello, F. Manaresi, G. Palumbo, F. Scoccianti, E. Sette (2018), Productivity growth in Italy: A tale of a slow-motion change, Bank of Italy Occasional Paper 422, January 29

Buigues P.-A., R. Meiklejohn (2011), European economic integration and network industries, in M. N. Jovanović, ed., pp. 45–76

Buiter W. H. (2002), The fiscal theory of the price level: A critique, *The Economic Journal*, 112(481): 459–80

Buiter W. H., G. Corsetti, N. Roubini (1993), Excessive deficits: Sense and nonsense in the Treaty of Maastricht, *Economic Policy*, 8(16): 57–90

Buiter W. H., E. Rahbari, J. Michels (2011), The implications of intra-European imbalances in credit flows, CEPR Policy Insight 57, August

Buiter W. H., E. Rahbari, J. Seydl (2015), Secular stagnation: The time for one-armed policy is over, Vox CEPR's Policy Portal, 5 June

Bundeszentrale für politische Bildung und dem Wissenschaftszentrum Berlin für Sozialforschung (2013), Datenreport 2013, Ein Sozial-bericht für die Bundesrepublik Deutschland, Bonn

Burlon L., A. Gerali, A. Notarpietro, M. Pisani (2017a), Macroeconomic effectiveness of non-standard monetary policy and early exit. A model-based evaluation, International Finance, 20(2): 155–73

Burlon L., A. Locarno, A. Notarpietro, M. Pisani (2017b), Public investment and monetary policy stance in the Euro Area, Bank of Italy, Temi di discussione (W. P.) 1150, December

Buti M. (2003), ed., Monetary and Fiscal Policies in EMU. Interactions and Coordination, Cambridge: Cambridge University Press

Buti M. (2014), A consistent trinity for the EZ, Vox CEPR's Policy Portal, 8 January, www.voxeu.org/article/consistent-trinity-EZ

Buti M., A. Sapir (1998), eds., Economic Policy in EMU, Oxford: Clarendon Press

Buti M., N. Carnot (2018), The case for a central fiscal capacity in EMU, VoxEU, 7 December

Buti M., D. Franco (2005), Fiscal Policy in Economic and Monetary Union. Theory, Evidence and Institutions, Cheltenham: Edward Elgar

Buti M., W. Röger, A. Turrini (2009), Is Lisbon far from Maastricht? Trade-offs and complementarities between fiscal discipline and structural reforms, CESifo Economic Studies 55(1): 165–196 DOI:10.1093/cesifo/ifp001

Cacciatore M., G. Fiori (2016), The macroeconomic effects of goods and labor markets deregulation, Review of Economic Dynamics, 20(1): 1–24

Cacciatore M., G. Fiori, F. Ghironi (2016), Market deregulation and optimal monetary policy in a monetary union, Journal of International Economics, 99 (C): 120–37

Cahn C., J. Matheron, J.-G. Sahuc (2014), Assessing the macroeconomic effects of LTROS, Banque de France W. P. 528

Calmfors L. (2001), Wages and wage-bargaining institutions in the EMU – A survey of the issues, Empirica, 28(4): 325–51

Calmfors L., J. Driffill (1988), Bargaining structure, corporatism, and macroeconomic performance, Economic Policy, 3(6): 14–61

Calvo G. (1998), Capital flows and capital-market crises: The simple economics of sudden stops, Journal of Applied Economics, 1(1): 35–54

Calvo G., A. Izquierdo, E. Talvi (2002), Sudden stops, the real exchange rate and fiscal sustainability: Argentina's lessons, Inter-American Development Bank, W. P. 469

Camagni R., R. Capello (2011), Spatial effects of economic integration: A conceptualization from regional growth and location theory, M. N. Jovanović, ed., pp. 148–68

Campos N. F., P. de Grauwe, Y. Ji (2018), Structural reforms, growth, and inequality, in N. F. Campos, P. de Grauwe, Y. Ji, eds., *The Political Economy of Structural Reforms*, Oxford: Oxford University Press, pp.1–44

Canofari P., G. Di Bartolomeo, M. Messori (2109), Sovereign debt crisis, fiscal consolidation, and active central bankers in a monetary union, Luiss, School of European Political Economy, W. P. 14/2019

Cargill T. F. (2016), The myth of central bank independence, Mercatus Working Paper, Mercatus Center at George Mason University, Arlington, VA, October

Cargill T. F., F. P. O'Driscoll (2013), Federal reserve independence: Reality or myth, *Cato Journal* 33(3): 417–35

Carli G. (1993), *Cinquant'anni di Vita Italiana*, Bari: Laterza,

Carli G. (2003), *Lacci e Lacciuoli*, Rome: Luiss University Press

Carlin W. (2013), Real exchange rate adjustment, wage-setting institutions, and fiscal stabilization policy: Lessons of the EZ's first decade, *CESifo Economic Studies*, 59 (3), 1 September

Carmassi J., S. Dobkowitz, J. Evrard, L. Parisi, A. Silva, M. Wedow (2018), Completing the Banking Union with a European Deposit Insurance Scheme: Who is afraid of cross-subsidisation? ECB Occasional Paper Series 2018, April

Carnot N., M. Kizior, G. Mourre (2017), Fiscal stabilisation in the Euro-Area: A simulation exercise, Université Libre de Bruxelles, W. P. CEB 17–025

Carpenter S. B., S. Demilrap, J. Eisenschmidt (2013), The effectiveness of the non-standard policy measures during the financial crises: The experiences of the Federal Reserve and the European Central Bank, Federal Reserve Board, W. P. 34, January

Casella A. (1989), Letter to the Editor, *The Economist*, 22–28 July

Casella A., B. Eichengreen (1996), Can foreign aid accelerate stabilization? *The Economic Journal*, 106(436): 605–19

Castelnuovo E., S. Nicoletti-Altimari, D. Rodríguez Palenzuela (2003), Definition of price stability, range and point inflation targets: The anchoring of long-term inflation expectations, in O. Issing, ed., *Background Studies for the ECB's Evaluation of its Monetary Policy Strategy*, Frankfurt am Main: European Central Bank

Castiglione C., D. Infante, M. T. Minervini, J. Smirnova (2014), Environmental taxation in Europe: What does it depend on? *Cogent Economics & Finance*, 2: 967362, http://dx.doi.org/10.1080/23322039.2014.967362

Cecchetti S. G., P. M. W. Tucker (2015), Is there macroprudential policy without international cooperation? Presented at the 2015 biennial Asia Economic Policy Conference (AEPC) on Policy Challenges in a Diverging Global Economy at the Federal Reserve Bank of San Francisco, 19–20 November 2015

Cecioni M. (2018), ECB monetary policy and the euro exchange rate, Bank of Italy Temi di Discussione (W. P.) 1172, May 3, https://ssrn.com/abstract=3176930

Cecioni M., G. Ferrero, A. Secchi (2011), Unconventional monetary policy in theory and in practice, Banca d'Italia Occasional Papers, 102

CEPS (2019). Twenty years of the euro, www.europarl.europa.eu/committees/en/econ/monetary-dialogue.html

CER (2015), *Better in than Out? Economic Performance Inside and Outside the European Monetary Union*, Rome: CER

Cerutti E., S. Claessens, L. Laeven (2017), The use and effectiveness of macroprudential policies: New evidence, *Journal of Financial Stability*, 28(C): 203–224

Cesarano F. (1997), Currency areas and equilibrium, *Open Economies Review*, 8(1): 51–9, repr. in F. Cesarano, *Money and Monetary Systems*, Cheltenham: Elgar, 2008

Cesarano F. (2006), The origins of the theory of optimum currency areas, *History of Political Economy*, 38(4): 711–731

Cesarano F. (2013), The optimum currency area puzzle, *International Advances in Economic Research*, 19(3): 259–71

Cesaratto S. (2013), The implications of TARGET2 in the European balance of payments crisis and beyond, *European Journal of Economics and Economic Policies: Intervention*, 10(3): 359–82

Cesaroni T., R. De Santis (2015), Current account "Core-periphery dualism" in the EMU, London School of Economics, "Europe in Question" D. P. 90, March

Cette G., J. Fernald, B. Mojon (2016), The pre-Great Recession slowdown in productivity, *European Economic Review*, 88(C): 3–20

Chari V., P. J. Kehoe (2008), Time inconsistency and free-riding in a monetary union, *Journal of Money, Credit, and Banking*, 40(7): 1329–55

Chassard Y. (2001), European integration and social protection. From the spaak report to the open method of co-ordination, in D. G. Mayes, J. Berghman, R. Salais, eds., *Social Exclusion and European Policy*, London: Edward Elgar

Checherita-Westphal C., A. Hughes Hallett, P. Rother (2014), Fiscal sustainability using growth-maximising debt targets, *Applied Economics*, 46(6): 638–47

Chen H., V. Curdia, A. Ferrero (2012), The macroeconomic effects of large-scale asset purchase programs, *The Economic Journal*, 122(564): F289-F315

Chiti E., P. G. Teixeira (2013), The constitutional implications of the European responses to the financial and public debt crisis, *Common Market Law Review*, 50: 683–708

Cho D., C. Rhee (2013), Effects of quantitative easing on Asia: Capital flows and financial markets, ADB Economics W. P. 350, June

Chortareas G., C. Mavrodimitrakis (2017), Strategic fiscal policies and leadership in a monetary union, *European Journal of Political Economy*, 47: 133–47

Chrystal K. A., P. D. Mizen (2001), Goodhart's law: Its origins, meaning and implications for monetary policy, Paper prepared for the Festschrift of Charles Goodhart, Bank of England, November

Christodoulakis N. (2009), Ten years of EMU: convergence, divergence and new policy priorities, London School of Economics, GreeSE Paper 22, January

Cimadomo J., O. Furtuna, M. Giuliodori (2018a), Private and public risk sharing in the euro area, ECB W. P. Series 2148

Cimadomo J., S. Hauptmeier, A. A. Palazzo, A. Popov (2018b), Risk sharing in the Euro Area, ECB Economic Bulletin, No. 3

Cingano F. (2014), Trends in income inequality and its impact on economic growth, OECD Social, Employment and Migration W. P. 163, OECD Publishing

Cioffi M., P. Rizza, M. Romanelli, P. Tommasino (2019), Outline of a redistribution-free debt redemption fund for the euro area, Bank of Italy, Occasional Papers 479

Claessens S., M. Ashoka, V. Shahin (2012), Paths to Eurobonds, Bruegel W. P. 2012/10

Coen D., J. Richardson (2009), *Lobbying the European Union: Institutions, Actors, and Issues*, Oxford: Oxford University Press

Coenen G., V. Wieland (2002), Inflation dynamics and international linkages: A model of the United States, the Euro Area and Japan, European Central Bank, W. P. Series 181

Coenen G., C. G. Erceg, C. Freedman, D. Furceri, M. Kumhof, L. Lalonde, D. Laxton, J. Lind, A. Mourougane, D. Muir, S. Mursula (2012), Effects of fiscal stimulus in structural models, *American Economic Journal: Macroeconomics*, 4(1): 22–68

Cœuré B. (2014), The global and European aspects of policy coordination. Speech at the Global Research Forum on international macroeconomics and finance, Washington D.C., 14 November, www.ecb.europa.eu/press/key/date/2014/ht ml/sp141114.en.html

Cole A. L., C. Guerello, G. Traficante (2016), One EMU fiscal policy for the EURO, LUISS Guido Carli, W. P. CELEG 1602, September 28

Coley T., B. Griffy, P. Rupert (2015), A tale of three Europes, European economic snapshot, January 26, http://europeansnapshot.com/

Collignon S., S. Diessner (2016), The ECB's monetary dialogue with the European Parliament: Efficiency and accountability during the euro crisis? *Journal of Common Market Studies*, 54(6): 1296–312

Commission of the European Communities (1977), Report of the study group on the role of public finance in European integration, 2 voll., Brussels

Committee for the study of economic and monetary union (1989), Report on economic and monetary union in the European Community (Delors Report), April, 17

Committeri M., P. Tommasino (2018), Managing sovereign debt restructurings in the euro zone. A note on old and current debates, Bank of Italy, Questioni di Economia e Finanza (Occasional Papers) No. 451, July

Constâncio V. (2016), Principles of macroprudential policy, Speech at the ECB-IMF Conference on Macroprudential Policy, Frankfurt am Main, 26 April, www .ecb.europa.eu/press/key/date/2016/html/sp160426.en.html

Cooper R. N. (1999), Should capital controls be banished? *Brookings Papers on Economic Activity*, 30(1): 89–125

Coricelli F., A. Cukierman, A. Dalmazzo (2006), Monetary institutions, monopolistic competition, unionized labor markets and economic performance, *Scandinavian Journal of Economics*, 108(1): 36–63

Corsetti G., M. Higgins, P. Pesenti (2016a), Policies and institutions for managing the aggregate macroeconomic stance of the EZ, in R. Baldwin, F. Giavazzi, eds.

Corsetti G., K. Kuester, A. Meier, G. J. Müller (2013), Sovereign risk, fiscal policy, and macroeconomic stability, *The Economic Journal*, 123(566): F99–F132

Corsetti G., K. Kuester, A. Meier, G. J. Müller (2014), Sovereign risk and belief-driven fluctuations in the euroarea, *Journal of Monetary Economics*, 61 (C): 53–73

Corsetti G., L. Feld, P. R. Lane, L. Reichlin, H. Rey, D. Vayanos, B. Weder di Mauro (2015), A new start for the Eurozone: Dealing with debt, monitoring the Eurozone 1, London: CEPR

Corsetti G., L. Feld, R. Koijen, L. Reichlin, R. Reis, H. Rey, B. Weder di Mauro (2016b), Reinforcing the EZ and protecting an open society, VOX, CEPR's Policy Portal, 27 May

Costa A. S., J. R. Figueira, C. R. Vieira, I. V. Vieira (2017), An application of the ELECTRE TRI-C method to characterize government performance in OECD countries, International Transactions in Operational Research, 8 February, htt p://onlinelibrary.wiley.com/doi/10.1111/itor.12394/full

Costantini O. (2015), The cyclically adjusted budget: History and exegesis of a fateful estimate, Institute for New Economic Thinking, W. P. Series 24, October

Cottarelli C., F. Giammusso, C. Porello (2014), Perché la crisi complica la stima del Pil potenziale, www.lavoce.info

Council of the European Union (2015), Broad economic policy guidelines for EU countries, https://eur-lex.europa.eu/legal-content/EN/TXT/HTML/?uri=LEGISSUM:14030202_1&from=ENG

Cova P., G. Ferrero (2015), Il programma di acquisto di attività finanziarie per fini di politica monetaria dell'Eurosistema, Bank of Italy, Questioni di Economia e Finanza (Occasional Papers) 270, April

Cova P., P. Pagano, M. Pisani (2015), Domestic and international macroeconomic effects of the Eurosystem expanded asset purchase programme, Bank of Italy, Temi di discussione 1036, September

Cowen T. (2011), *The Great Stagnation*, New York: Dutton

Cozzi T. (2013), La crisi e i moltiplicatori fiscali, *Moneta e Credito*, 66(262): 129–51

Crafts N. (2013), Long-term growth in Europe: What difference does the crisis make? *National Institute Economic Review*, 224(2): R14-R28

Crafts N. (2014), Secular stagnation: US hypochondria, European disease? in C. Teulings, R. Baldwin, eds.

Cramme O., S. B. Hobolt (2015), Democratizing a macroeconomic union, in O. Cramme, S. B. Hobolt, eds., *Europe in Democratic Politics in a European Union under Stress*, Oxford: Oxford University Press

Creel J., F. Saraceno (2010), European fiscal rules after the crisis, *Journal of Innovation Economics & Management*, 2(6): 95–122

Croci Angelini E., F. Farina, E. Valentini (2016), Contagion across the EZ countries and the core-periphery divide, *Empirica*, 43(1): 197–213

Cugnasca A., Ph. Rother (2015), Fiscal multipliers during consolidation: Evidence from the European Union, ECB W. P. 1863, October

Cukierman A. (1992), *Central Bank Strategy, Credibility, and Independence: Theory and Evidence*, Cambridge: MIT Press

Cukierman A., F. Lippi (1999), Central bank interdependence, centralization of wage bargaining, inflation and unemployment – Theory and evidence, *European Economic Review*, 43(7): 1395–434

Cukierman A., F. Lippi (2001), Labor markets and monetary union: A strategic analysis, *The Economic Journal*, 111(473): 541–61

Curzon Price V. (2011), Institutional competition in the European Union: Causes and consequences of the drive to harmonise, in M. N. Jovanović, ed., pp. 3–20

Dabla-Norris E., K. Kochhar, F. Ricka, N. Suphaphiphat, E. Tsounta (with contributions from P. Sharma and V. Salins) (2015), Causes and consequences of income inequality: A global perspective, IMF Staff D. N., June

da Costa Cabral N., J. R. Gonçalves, N. Cunha Rodrigues (2017), eds., *The Euro and the Crisis*, Heidelberg: Springer

Dalla Pellegrina L., D. Masciandaro, R. V. Pansini (2013), The central banker as prudential supervisor: Does independence matter? *Journal of Financial Stability*, 9(3): 415–27

Dallago B., J. McGowan (1995), eds., *Economic and Political Crises in Europe and the United States: Prospects for Policy Cooperation*, London: Routledge

Dalmazzo A. (2014), Monetary discipline as a substitute for fiscal reforms and market liberalizations, *Economic Notes*, 43(3): 193–210

Damiani M., F. Pompei, A. Ricci (2011), Temporary job protection and productivity growth in EU economies, MPRA_paper_59151.pdf

Danescu E. R. (2012), Economists v. monetarists – agreements and clashes in the drafting of the Werner Report, in A rereading of the Werner Report of 8 October 1970 in the light of the Pierre Werner family archives, Sanem: CVCE, www.cvce.eu

De Boef S. L., L. Keele (2008), Taking time seriously, *American Journal of Political Science*, 52(1): 184–200

De Grauwe P. (1991),Is the European monetary system a DM-Zone? in A. Steinherr, D. Weiserbs, eds., *Evolution of the International and Regional Monetary Systems*, London: Macmillan

De Grauwe P. (2003), *The Stability and Growth Pact in Need of Reform*, University of Leuven, Katholieke Universiteit Leuven, Centrum voor Economische Studiën, International Economics

De Grauwe P. (2006), What have we learnt about monetary integration since the Maastricht Treaty? *Journal of Common Market Studies*, 44(4): 711–30

De Grauwe P. (2009), Keynes' savings paradox, Fisher's debt deflation and the banking crisis, mimeo, www.researchgate.net/publication/252557666_KEYNES%27_SAV INGS_PARADOX_FISHER%27S_DEBT_DEFLATION_AND_ THE_BANKING_CRISIS

De Grauwe P. (2010), The fragility of EZ's institutions, *Open Economies Review*, 21(1): 167–74

De Grauwe P. (2011a), A less punishing, more forgiving approach to the debt crisis in the EZ, Ceps policy brief 230, 18 August

De Grauwe P. (2011b), The European Central Bank as a lender of last resort, VoxEU, 18 August

De Grauwe P. (2014a), Yes, it's the economy, stupid, but is it demand or supply? CEPS Commentary, 24 January

De Grauwe P. (2014b), Macroeconomic policies in the EZ since the sovereign debt crisis, Euroforum KU Leuven, Policy paper 13, September

De Grauwe P. (2015a), Greece is solvent, but illiquid: Policy implications, Vox, CEPR's Policy Portal, July 3, www.voxeu.org/article/greece-solvent-illiquid-policy-implications

De Grauwe P. (2015b), Secular stagnation in the EZ, Vox, CEPR's Policy Portal, 30 January, http://voxeu.org/article/secular-stagnation-EZ

De Grauwe P. (2016), The legacy of the EZ crisis and how to overcome it, *Journal of Empirical Finance*, 39(B): 145–270

De Grauwe P. (2017a), The future of the euro, Lecture given at the University of Perugia, May 15

De Grauwe P. (2017b), Making the EZ sustainable, in A. Bénassy-Quéré, F. Giavazzi, eds.

De Grauwe P., Y. Ji (2013a), Fiscal implications of the ECB's bond-buying programme, Vox, CEPR's Policy Portal, 14 June, http://voxeu.org/article/quantitative-easing-EZ-its-possible-without-fiscal-transfers

De Grauwe P., Y. Ji (2013b), Self-fulfilling crises in the EZ: An empirical test, *Journal of International Money and Finance*, 34(C): 15–36

De Grauwe P., Y. Ji (2013c), Panic-driven austerity and its implication for the EZ, VoxEU CEPR's Portal, 21 February, www.voxeu.org/article/panic-drivenausterity-EZ-and-its-implications

De Grauwe P., Y. Ji (2014a), How much fiscal discipline in a monetary union? *Journal of Macroeconomics*, 39(Issue PB): 348–60

De Grauwe P., Y. Ji (2014b), The fragility of two monetary regimes: The European monetary system and the EZ, *International Journal of Finance & Economics*, 20 (1): 1–15, 10/2014; 20 (1), doi:10.1002/ijfe.1500

De Grauwe P., Y. Ji (2014c), The future of the EZ, *Manchester School*, 82(S1): 15–34

De Grauwe P., Y. Ji (2015a), Quantitative easing in the EZ: It's possible without fiscal transfer, Vox, CEPR Policy Portal, 15 January

De Grauwe P., Y. Ji (2015b), Has the EZ become less fragile? Some empirical tests, *Journal of Policy Modeling*, 37(3): 404–14

De Grauwe P., Y. Ji (2016), How to reboot the EZ and ensure its longterm survival, in R. Baldwin, F. Giavazzi, eds.

De Grauwe P., W. Moesen (2009), Gains for all: A proposal for a common euro bond, *Intereconomics*, 44 (3) doi:10.1007/s10272-009-028

De Grauwe P., W. Vanhaverbeke (1991), Is Europe an Optimum Currency Area? Evidence from regional data, CEPR D. P. 555, May

De Grauwe P., Y. Ji (2012), TARGET2 as a scapegoat for German errors, 2 November, Vox, CEPR's Policy portal, www.voxeu.org

de Haan J., J. Sturm (1992), The case for central bank independence, *BNL Quarterly Review*, 45(182): 305–27 de Haan J., M. Hoeberichts, R. Maas F. Teppa (2016), Inflation in the EZ and why it matters, De Nederlandsche Bank N.V.

de Jong J., N. Gilbert (2018), Fiscal discipline in EMU? Testing the effectiveness of the Excessive Deficit Procedure, DNB W. P. 607, September

Dell'Ariccia G, C. Ferreira, N. Jenkinson, L. Laeven, A. Martin, C. Minoiu, A. Popov (2018), Managing the sovereign-bank nexus, IMF Departmental Paper 18/16

DeLong B., L. H. Summers (2012), Fiscal policy in a depressed economy, mimeo, March 20

Delors Commission (1993), White Paper on Growth, Competitiveness, and Employment – The Challenges and Ways Forward into the 21st Century, COM (93), 700 final 5. 12.1993

del Río P. (2017), Why does the combination of the European Union Emissions Trading Scheme and a renewable energy target make economic sense? *Renewable and Sustainable Energy Reviews*, 74: 824–34

Demertzis M., G. B. Wolf (2016), *The Effectiveness of the European Central Bank's Asset Purchase Programme*, Bruegel Policy Contribution, 2016/10, June

Demertzis M., A. Hughes Hallett, N. Viegi (2004), An independent central bank faced with elected governments, *European Journal of Political Economy*, 20(4): 907–22

Demertzis M., J. Pisani-Ferry, A. Sapir, T. Wieser, G. B. Wolff (2018), One size does not fit all: European integration by differentiation, Policy Briefs 27473, Bruegel, Bruxelles

Denes M., G. Eggertsson, S. Gilbukh (2013) Deficits, public debt dynamics and tax and spending multipliers, *The Economic Journal*, 123(566): F133–F163

Deo S., P. Donovan, L. Hatheway (2011), Euro break up, UBS investment research, 6th September

Depla J., J. von Weiszäcker (2010), The Blue Bond Proposal, Bruegel Policy Brief, 3, May

Dervis K., F. Saraceno (2014), An investment New Deal for Europe, Brookings Blogs – Up 28 Front, September 3, www.brookings.edu/blog/up-front/2014/09/03/an-investment-new-deal-for-europe/

de Wilde P., A. Leupold, H. Schmidtke (2016), Introduction: The differentiated politicisation of European governance, *West European Politics*, 39(1): 3–22

Dhéret C., F. Nicoli, F. Zuleeg (2012), The implications of an EU fiscal union for local and regional authorities, European Policy Centre, European Union, doi:10.2863/64577

Di Bartolomeo G., P. Tirelli, N. Acocella (2015), The comeback of inflation as an optimal public finance tool, *International Journal of Central Banking*, 11(1): 43–70

di Mauro F., A. J. Nagengast, R. Stehrer (2016), On the correction of EZ external imbalances and the pitfalls of bilateral imbalance measures, VOX CEPR's Policy Portal, 29 January, http://voxeu.org/article/pitfalls-EZ-bilateral-trade-imbalance-measures

Di Meglio G., S. Visintin (2014), Efficiency of the services sector: A parametric approach, Universidad Complutense, Madrid, W. P. 1419, July

Dixit A. K. (1996), *The Making of Economic Policy: A Transaction-Cost Politics Approach*, Cambridge: MIT Press

Dixit A., L. Lambertini (2001), Monetary-fiscal policy interactions and commitment versus discretion in a monetary union, *European Economic Review*, 45(4–6): 977–87

Dixit A., L. Lambertini (2003), Symbiosis of monetary and fiscal policies in a monetary union, *Journal of International Economics*, 60(2): 235–47

Dobbs C., M. Spence (2012), Preventing a Eurozone bank and bond run, CEPR's Policy Portal, 15 June

Dolls M. (2018), An unemployment re-insurance scheme for the EZ? Stabilizing and redistributive effects, BertelsmannStiftung, www.bertelsmann-stiftung.de/fileadmin/files/BSt/Publikationen/GrauePublikationen/EZ_Study_Re-Insurance_2018_ENG.pdf

Dolls M., C. Fuest, A. Peichl (2012), Automatic stabilisers and economic crisis: US vs. Europe, *Journal of Public Economics*, 96(3): 279–294

Dolls M., C. Fuest, D. Neumann, A. Peichl (2013), Fiscal integration in the EZ: Economic effects of two key scenarios, ZEW D. P. 13–106

Dolls M., C. Fuest, F. Heinemann, A. Peichl, J. Kock (2015), Reconciling insurance with market discipline: A blueprint for a European Fiscal Union, ZEW D. P. 15–044

Dolls M., C. Fuest, C. Krolage, F. Neumeier, D. Stöhlker (2019), Incentivising structural reforms in Europe? A blueprint for the European Commission's reform support programme, *Intereconomics*, 54(1): 42–6

Dolls M., C. Fuest, J. Kock, A. Peichl, N. Wehrh, C. Wittneben (2014), Automatic stabilizers in the EZ: Analysis of their effectiveness at the member state and Euro Area level and in international comparison, ZEW, November 26

Doluca H., M. Hübner, D. Rumpf, B. Weigert (2012), The European redemption pact: An illustrative guide, German council of economic experts, *Intereconomics*, 47(4): 230–9

Dornbusch R. (1996), Euro fantasies: Common currency as panacea, *Foreign Affairs*, 75(5): 110–24

Dosi G., A. Napoletano, A. Roventini, T. Treibich (2014), The short- and long-run damages of fiscal austerity: Keynes beyond Schumpeter, LEM W. P. 2014/22, November

Dosi G., M. Minenna, A. Roventini, R. Violi (2018), Making the EZ work: A risk-sharing reform of the European Stability Mechanism, LEM Papers Series 2018/20, Laboratory of Economics and Management (LEM), Sant'Anna School of Advanced Studies, Pisa

Downs A. (1957), *An Economic Theory of Democracy*, New York: Harper & Brothers

Draghi M. (2012), Verbatim of the remarks made by Mario Draghi, President of the European Central Bank at the Global Investment Conference in London, 26 July, www.ecb.europa.eu/press/key/date/2012/html/sp120726.en.html

Draghi M. (2014), Unemployment in the Euro Area, Speech by Mario Draghi, President of the ECB, Annual Central Bank Symposium in Jackson Hole, 22 August

Dreger C., J. Wolters (2016), On the empirical relevance of the Lucas critique: The case of Euro Area money demand, *Empirica*, 43(1): 61–82

Dew-Becker I., R. J. Gordon (2008), The role of labor market changes in the slowdown of European productivity growth, NBER W. P. 13840, March

Dreyer J. K., P. A. Schmid (2016), Growth effects of EU and EZ memberships: empirical findings from the first 15 years of the euro, Economic Modelling, 25 October, http://dx.doi.org/10.1016/j.econmod.2016.09.007

Driffill J. (2006), The centralization of wage bargaining revisited: What have we learnt? *Journal of Common Market Studies*, 44(4): 731–56

Dullien S. (2014), The macroeconomic stabilisation impact of a European basic unemployment insurance scheme, *Intereconomics*, 49(4): 189–93

Dullien S., M. Schieritz (2012), German savers should applaud the growing TARGET balances, Vox, CEPR's Policy Portal, 7 May

Dullien S., J. Fernández, M. López, G. Maass, D. del Prado, J. von Weizsäcker (2018), *Fit for Purpose: A German-Spanish Proposal for a Robust European Unemployment Insurance*, Oficina Madrid, Madrid: Friedrich Erbert Stiftung

Dür A., G. Mateo (2014), The Europeanization of interest groups: Group type, resources and policy area, *European Union Politics*, 15(4): 572–94

Dür A., G. Mateo (2016), *Insiders Versus Outsiders: Interest Group Politics in Multilevel Europe*, Oxford: Oxford University Press

Dür A., P. Bernhagen, D. Marshall (2015), Interest group success in the European Union: When (and why) does business lose? *Comparative Political Studies*, 48(8): 951–83

Durand C., S. Villemot (2016), Balance sheets after the EMU: An assessment of the redenomination risk, OFCE W. P. 31

Dustmann C., B. Eichengreen, S. Otten, A. Sapir, G. Tabellini, G. Zoega (2017), *Europe's Trust Deficit: Causes and Remedies*, London: CEPR Press

Duval R., D. Furceri (2016), Time for a supply-side boost? Macroeconomic effects of labor and product market reforms in advanced economies, Chapter 3, IMF World Economic Outlook, April

Dyson K., K. Featherstone (1999), *The Road to Maastricht: Negotiating Economic and Monetary Union*, Oxford: Oxford University Press

ECB (2011), TARGET2 balances of national central banks in the Euroarea, Monthly Bulletin, October, 35–42

ECB (2013), Assessing the retail bank interest rate pass-through in the Euro Area at times of financial fragmentation, Monthly Bulletin, August, 75–91

ECB (2016), Public investment in Europe, ECB Economic Bulletin, Issue 2: 75–88

Ederer S. (2015), Macroeconomic imbalances and institutional reforms in the EMU, WIFO Policy Paper, March 22

EEAG (2011), *The EEAG Report on the European Economy 2011*, Munich: CESifo

EEAG (2013), *The EEAG Report on the European Economy 2013*, Munich: CESifo

EEAG (2014), *The EEAG Report on the European Economy*, Munich: CESifo

EEAG (2015), *The EEAG Report on the European Economy*, Munich: CESifo

EEAS (2017), Permanent Structured Cooperation on defence could be launched by end 2017, 08/ 09/2017, https://eeas.europa.eu/headquarters/headquarters-homepage_en/31832/Permanent%20Structured%20Cooperation%20on%20d efence%20could%20be%20launched%20by%20end%202017

Eggertsson G. B. (2011), What fiscal policy is effective at zero interest rates? in D. Acemoglu and M. Woodford, eds., *NBER Macroeconomics Annual 2010*, 25(2): 59–112

Eggertsson G. B., P. Krugman (2012), Debt, deleveraging, and the liquidity trap: A Fisher-Minsky-Koo approach, *The Quarterly Journal of Economics*, 127(3): 1469–513

Eggertsson G. B., N. R. Mehrotra (2014), A model of secular stagnation, NBER W. P. 20574, October

Eggertsson G. B., A. Ferrero, A. Raffo (2014), Can structural reforms help Europe? *Journal of Monetary Economics*, 61(C): 2–22

Eggertsson G. B., N. R. Mehrotra, L. H. Summers (2016), Secular stagnation in the open economy, *The American Economic Review*, 106(5): 503–7

Eggertsson G. B., R. E. Juelsrud, L. H. Summers, E. Getz Wold (2019), Negative nominal interest rates and the bank lending channel, NBER W. P. 25416, January

Eichenberg R. C., R. J. Dalton (2007), Post-Maastricht blues: The transformation of citizen support for European integration, 1973–2004, *Acta Politica*, 42 (2–3): 128–52

Eichengreen B. (1992), *Should the Maastricht Treaty Be Saved?* Princeton: International Finance Section, Department of Economics, Princeton University, December

Eichengreen B. (1993), European monetary unification, *Journal of Economic Literature*, 31(3): 1321–57

Eichengreen B. (1998a), The European monetary unification: A tour d'horizon, *Oxford Review of Economic Policy*, 14(3): 24–40

Eichengreen B. (1998b), Saving Europe's automatic stabilizers, Macroeconomics, EconWPA, National Institute Economic Review, 1997, 159(1): 92–98, in M. Baimbridge, B. Burkitt, P. Whyman, eds., *The Impact of the Euro: Debating Britain's Future*, London: Macmillan

Eichengreen B. (2010a), The break up of the Euro Area, in A. Alesina, F., Giavazzi, eds., pp. 11–51

Eichengreen B. (2010b), In Europe: Balanced deflation, or more depression, www.bradford-delong.com/2010/12/in-europe-balanced-deflation-or-more-depression.html

Eichengreen B. (2010c), Europe's inevitable haircut, http://prosyn.org/Iej8cAJ

Eichengreen B. (2014), The EZ crisis: The theory of optimum currency areas bites back, Notenstein Academy White Paper Series, November

Eichengreen B. (2015), Secular stagnation: The long view, *The American Economic Review: Papers & Proceedings*, 105(5): 66–70

Eichengreen B. (2017), Can Macron and Merkel agree on how to fix the EZ? The Guardian, 11 September

Eichengreen B., J. Frieden (1994), eds., *The Political Economy of European Monetary Unification*, Boulder: Westview Press

Eichengreen B., J. Von Hagen (1995), Fiscal policy and monetary union: Federalism, fiscal restrictions and no bail-out rule, CEPR D. P. 1247

Eichengreen B., C. Wyplosz (1993), The unstable EMS, Brookings papers on economic activity, economic studies program, *The Brookings Institution*, 24 (1): 51–144

Eisenschmidt J., D. Kedan, M. Schmitz, R. Adalid, P. Papsdorf (2017), The Eurosystem's asset purchase programme and TARGET balances, ECB Occasional Paper Series 196, September

Eleftheriadis P. (2014), Democracy in the EZ, in W. G. Ringe, P. Huber, eds., *Legal Challenges Arising Out of the Global Financial Crisis: Bail-outs, the Euro, and Regulation*, Oxford: Hart Publishing

Emerson M., D. Gros, A. Italianer, J. Pisani-Ferry, H. Reichenbach (1992), *One Market, One Money: An Evaluation of the Potential Benefits and Costs of*

Forming an Economic and Monetary Union, European Economy 44, republished by Oxford University Press: Oxford, 1992

Engelmann D., H.-J. Knopf, K. Roscher, T. Risse (2012), Identity politics in the European Union, in P. Minkinnen, H. Patomäki, eds.

Ercolani V., J. Valle e Azevedo (2018), How can the government spending multiplier be small at the zero lower bound? Bank of Italy Temi di Discussione (W. P.) 1174

Erler A., S. Hohberger (2014), The real costs and profits of TARGET2 balances, Universität Bayreuth, Rechts-und Wirtschaftswissenschaftliche Fakultät, D. P. 02–14, April

Eser F., M. Carmona Amaro, S. Iacobelli, M. Rubens (2012), The use of the Eurosystem's monetary policy instruments and operational framework since 2009, ECB Occasional Paper Series 135

Esposito L. E., G. Gatti, G. Mastromatteo (2019), Sustainable finance, the good, the bad and the ugly: A critical assessment of the EU institutional framework for the green transition, Università Cattolica del Sacro Cuore, Dipartimento di Politica Economica, Quaderno n. 4/febbraio

ESRB (2017), A Review of Macroprudential Policy in the EU in 2016, April

Estevão M. (2005), Product market regulation and the benefits of wage moderation, IMF W. P. 05/191

EuroMemo Group, European Economists for Alternative Economic Policy in Europe (2015), What future for the European Union – Stagnation and polarization or new foundations? Euromemorandum 2015, Transform – European Journal for Alternative Thinking and Political Dialogue, www2 .euromemorandum.eu/uploads/euromemorandum_2015.pdf

European Commission (1990), One market, one money, European Economy, 44, October

European Commission (1991), The economics of EMU. Background studies prepared for European Economy n. 44, "One market, one money," No. 1, Special edition

European Commission (1997), Conclusions of the Ecofin council meeting on 1 December 1997 on a code of conduct for business taxation, in *Official Journal of the European Communities*, 6.1.1998, C 2/1

European Commission (2008), EMU@10: Successes and challenges after 10 years of Economic and Monetary Union, European Economy, 2, June, http://ec.europa .eu/economy_finance/publications/publication_summary12680_en.htm

European Commission (2010), Europe 2020: The European Union strategy for growth and employment

European Commission (2011a), Communication from the Commission to the European Parliament, the Council, the European economic and social committee and the Committee of the regions – A resource-efficient Europe – Flagship initiative under the Europe 2020 Strategy Brussels, COM(2011) 21, 26.1.2011

European Commission (2011b), The costs of not implementing the environmental acquis. Final report, ENV.G.1/FRA/2006/0073, September

European Commission (2011c), Green Paper on the feasibility of introducing Stability Bonds, MEMO/11/820, Brussels, 23 November 2011, http://ec .europa.eu/economy_finance/articles/governance/2011–11–23-green-paper-stability-bonds_en.htm

European Commission (2012), The distributional effects of fiscal consolidation in nine EU countries, Research Note 01/2012

European Commission (2013), Multiannual financial framework 2014–2020 and EU budget 2014, Bruxelles

European Commission (2014a), The Platform's Manifesto and policy recommendations, Bruxelles

European Commission (2014b), Communication from the Commission to the European Parliament, the Council, the European Economic and Social Committee and the Committee of the Regions. 2014 European Semester: Country-specific recommendations, COM(2014) 400 final Brussels, 2.6.2014

European Commission (2014c), Taking stock of the Europe 2020 strategy for smart, sustainable and inclusive growth, COM(2014) 130 final, Brussels

European Commission (2016a), Consultation document review of the EU macro prudential policy framework. Briefing, http://ec.europa.eu/finance/consulta tions/2016/macroprudential-framework/docs/consultation-document_en.pdf

European Commission (2016b), Towards a Positive Fiscal Stance for the Euro Area. November 16, https://ec.europa.eu/info/sites/info/files/2017-european-semester-communication-fiscalstance_en_1.pdf

European Commission (2017a), Rome Declaration of the Leaders of 27 Member States and of the European Council, the European Parliament and the European Commission, http://europa.eu/rapid/press-release_STATEMENT-17–767_en .htm

European Commission (2017b), President Jean-Claude Juncker's State of the Union Address 2017, Brussels, 13 September, http://europa.eu/rapid/press-release_SPEECH-17–3165_en.htm

European Commission (2017c), Communication to the European Parliament, the Council, the European Central Bank, the European Economic and Social Committee and the Committee of the Regions on Completing the Banking Union, Brussels, 11.10.2017, COM(2017) 592 final

European Commission (2017d), Reflection Paper on "Deepening of the Economic and Monetary Union", COM(2017) 291, 31 May

European Commission (2017f), Commission sets out Roadmap for deepening Europe's Economic and Monetary Union – Press release, Brussels, 6 December

European Commission (2017g), Communication from the Commission. The Fiscal Compact: Taking Stock Brussels, 22.2.2017, C(2017) 1200 final

European Commission (2018), Towards a stronger international role of the euro, December

European Communities (1975), Report of the study group "Economic and monetary union 1980", Brussels, March

European Monetary Institute (1998), Convergence Report, April

European Systemic Risk Board (2018), Sovereign bond-backed securities: A feasibility study, Volume I: main findings, High-Level Task Force on Safe Assets, January

Everaert L., W. Schule (2008), Why it pays to synchronize structural reforms in the euro area across markets and countries, *IMF Staff Papers* 55, 356–66

Fantacone S., P. Garalova, C. Milani (2015), Deficit strutturali e politiche di bilancio: I limiti del modello europeo, *Rivista di Politica Economica*, 104(1/3): 127–52

Farhi E., I. Werning (2017), Fiscal unions, *The American Economic Review*, 107(12): 3788–834

Faria A., P. R. Lane, P. Mauro, G. M. Milesi-Ferretti (2007), The shifting composition of external liabilities, *Journal of the European Economic Association*, 5(2–3): 480–90

Farina F., R. Tamborini (2002), Le politiche macroeconomiche di stabilizzazione in Europa nel nuovo regime di unione monetaria, in F. Farina e R. Tamborini, eds., *Da Nazioni a Regioni. Mutamenti Strutturali e Istituzionali dopo l'Ingresso nell'Unione Monetaria Europea*, Bologna: Il Mulino

Farina F., R. Tamborini (2015), *Europe's Great Divide*. A geo-economic-political map, mimeo

Fatás A., I. Mihov (2003a), On constraining fiscal policy discretion in EMU, *Oxford Review of Economic Policy*, 2003 19(1): 112–31

Fatás A., I. Mihov (2003b), The case for restricting fiscal policy discretion, *The Quarterly Journal of Economics*, 11(8): 1419–47

Fatás A., L. H. Summers (2016a), Hysteresis and fiscal policy during the Global Crisis, CEPR Vox 12 October

Fatás A., L. H. Summers (2016b), The permanent effects of fiscal consolidations, NBER W. P. 22374, June, then in *Journal of International Economics*, 112(C): 238–50, 2018

Favero C. A., V. Galasso (2015), Demographics and the secular stagnation hypothesis in Europe, CEPR D. P. 10887, October

Favero C. A., A. Missale (2012), Sovereign spreads in the Eurozone: Which prospects for a Eurobond? *Economic Policy*, 27(70): 231–73

Fazi T., G. Iodice (2016), Why further integration is the wrong answer to the EMU's problems: The case for a decentralised fiscal stimulus, *Journal for a Progressive Economy*, 15 November. www.eunews.it/wp-content/uploads/2016/05/Fazi-Iodice-Progressive-Economy.pdf

Featherstone K. (2004), The political dynamics of external empowerment: The emergence of EMU and the challenge to the European social model, in A. Martin, G. Ross, eds., *Euros and Europeans: Monetary Integration and the European Model of Society*, Cambridge: Cambridge University Press, pp. 226–47

Featherstone K. (2001), The political dynamics of the vincolo esterno: The emergence of EMU and the challenge to the European Social Model, Queen's Papers on Europeanisation, No. 6/2001

Featherstone K. (2014), ed., *Europe in Modern Greek History*, London: Hurst

Featherstone K. (2015), External conditionality and the debt crisis: The "Troika" and public administration reform in Greece, *Journal of European Public Policy*, 22(3): 295–314

Featherstone K. (2016), Conditionality, democracy and institutional weakness: The Euro-crisis trilemma, *Journal of Common Market Studies*, 54 (9): 48–64

Federal Ministry for Economic Cooperation and Development (2017), *Africa and Europe – A New Partnership for Development, Peace and a Better Future. Cornerstone of a Marshall Plan with Africa*, Berlin: BMZ, January

Feld L. P. (2016), Is German (macro-) economic policy different? in G. Bratsiotis. D. Cobham, eds., *German Macro: How It's Different and Why That Matters*, Brussels: European Policy Centre, pp. 42–54

Feld L., C. Schmidt, I. Schnabel, V. Wieland (2016a), Causes of the EZ crisis: A nuanced view, VOX CEPR's Policy Portal, 22 March, http://voxeu.org/, also in R. Baldwin, F. Giavazzi, eds.

Feld L., C. Schmidt, I. Schnabel, V. Wieland (2016b), Completing Maastricht 2.0 to safeguard the future of the EZ, VOX CEPR's Policy Portal, 23 March (http://voxeu.org/), in R. Baldwin, F. Giavazzi, eds.

Feldkirchery M. (2012), The determinants of vulnerability to the global financial crisis 2008 to 2009: Credit growth and other sources of risk, Oesterreichische Nationalbank, October 31

Feldstein M. (1997), The political economy of the European Economic and Monetary Union: Political sources of an economic liability, *The Journal of Economic Perspectives*, 11(4): 23–42

Feldstein M. (2012), An optimistic case for the euro, Project Syndicate, Oct 30

Feldstein M. (2017), Lasciare l'euro? Ora è complicato (Leaving the euro? Now it is complicated), il Sole 24 ore, 27 April

Fernandez-Villaverde J. (2014), Discussion of "Can structural reforms help Europe?" by G. Eggertsson, A. Ferrero, A. Raffo, *Journal of Monetary Economics*, 61(C): 23–31

Fernandez-Villaverde J., L. Garicano, T. Santos (2013), Political credit cycles: The case of the Euro Zone, *The Journal of Economic Perspectives*, 27(3): 145–66

Ferrara M., P. Tirelli (2017), Equitable fiscal consolidations, *Economic Modelling*, 61(C): 207–23

Fidora M., C. Giordano, M. Schmitz (2018), Real exchange rate misalignments in the Euro Area, Bank of Italy, Temi di discussione (W. P.) 1162, January

Figari F., A. Paulus, H. Sutherland (2015), The design of fiscal consolidation measures in the European Union: Distributional effects and implications for macroeconomic recovery, EUROMOD W. P. EM5/15

Fiorentini R, G. Montani (2014), A Keynesian recovery policy for the European Union, *Bulletin of Political Economy*, 8(2): 145–74

Fiori G., G. Nicoletti, S. Scarpetta, F. Schiantarelli (2012), Employment effects of product and labour market reforms: Are there synergies? *The Economic Journal*, 122(558): 79–104

Fisher I. (1933), The debt-deflation theory of the Great Depression, *Econometrica*, 1 (4): 337–57

Fitoussi J.-P. (2007), Le rôle des institutions et des normes sociales dans la détermination des politiques économiques, *Revue de l'OFCE*, 102(3): 109–24

Fitoussi J.-P., J. Creel (2002), How to reform the ECB, Center for European Reform, London, October

Fitoussi J.-P., E. Laurent (2009), Macroeconomic and social policies in the EU 15: the last two decades, Sciences Po Publications 2009–21

Fitoussi J.-P., F. Saraceno (2006), The Brussels-Frankfurt-Washington Consensus: Old and new tradeoffs in economics, in W. Mitchell, J. Muysken, T. van Veen, eds., *Growth and Cohesion in the European Union: The Impact of Macroeconomic Policy*, Cheltenham: Edward Elgar

Fitoussi J.-P., F. Saraceno (2013), European economic governance: The Berlin–Washington consensus, *Cambridge Journal of Economics*, 37(3): 479–96

Flassbeck H., C. Lapavitsas (2015), *Against the Troika: Crisis and Austerity in the EZ*, London and New York: Verso

Fleming J. M. (1962), Domestic financial policies under fixed and under floating exchange rates, *IMF Staff Papers*, 9(3): 369–79

Follesdal A., S. Hix (2006), Why there is a democratic deficit in the EU: A response to Majone and Moravcksic, *Journal of Common Market Studies*, 44(3): 533–62

Forbes K., D. Reinhardt, T. Wieladek (2016a), Banking de-globalisation: A consequence of monetary and regulatory policies? BIS Papers 86, September

Forbes K., M. Fratzscher, T. Kostka, R. Straub (2016b), Bubble thy neighbour: Portfolio effects and externalities from capital controls, *Journal of International Economics*, 99(C): 85–104

Forder J. (1996), On the assessment and implementation of "institutional" remedies, *Oxford Economic Papers*, 48(1): 39–51

Forder J. (2001), The theory of credibility and the reputation-bias of policy, *Review of Political Economy*, 13(1): 15–26

Foresti P. (2013), How do debt constraints affect fiscal and monetary policies interaction in a strategic monetary union? *Journal of Game Theory*, 2(2): 13–17

Foster J. B., R. McChesney (2012), *The Endless Crisis: How Monopoly-Finance Capital Produces Stagnation and Upheaval from the USA to China*, New York: Monthly Review Press

Frangakis M., C. Hermann, J. Huffschmid, K. Lóránt (2010), eds., *A Critique of European Policies and Proposals for Alternatives*, London: Palgrave Macmillan

Frankel J. (1993), Discussion on Buiter et al (1993), pp. 92–97

Frankel J. A., A. K. Rose (1997), Is EMU more justifiable ex post than ex ante? *European Economic Review*, 41(3–5): 753–60

Frankel J. A., A. K. Rose (2002), An estimate of the effect of common currencies on trade and income, *The Quarterly Journal of Economics*, 117(2): 437–466

François A., C. Le Gall, R. Magni Berton (2014), Is the European Union a ruler? A natural experiment on attribution of responsibility, Sciences Po Grenoble W. P. 19, February

Fransen L., G. del Bufalo, E. Reviglio (2017), Boosting investments in social infrastructure in Europe. Report of the High-Level Task Force on Investing in Social Infrastructure in Europe chaired by Romano Prodi and Christian Sautter, 1st December, Bruxelles

Franzini M., M. Raitano (2016), Economic inequality and its impact on intergenerational mobility, in M. Franzini, M. Pianta, J. K. Galbraith, F. Bogliacino, V. Maestri, M. Raitano, G. Bosch, T. Kalina, eds., Forum on Wealth and Income Inequality in Europe, Intereconomics, 51(2): 331–5

Fratianni M. (1994), What went wrong with the EMS and European Monetary Union, in B. Abegaz, P. Dillon, D. H. Feldman, P. F. Whiteley, eds., *The Challenge of European Integration. Internal and External Problems of Trade and Money*, Boulder: Westview Press, pp. 219–36

Fratzscher M. (2017), Germany's low investment rate leaves its infrastructure creaking, *The Economist*, 17 June

Fratzscher M., M. Lo Duca, R. Straub (2013), On the international spillovers of US quantitative easing, ECB W. P. 1557, June

Frenkel R. (2012), What have the crises in emerging markets and the Euro Zone in common and what differentiates them? www.itf.org.ar/pdf/lecturas/lectura67 .pdf

Frenkel J. A., M. Goldstein (1991), Monetary policy in an emerging European economic and monetary union: Key issues, *IMF Staff Papers*, 38(2): 356–73

Friedman M. (1953), The case for flexible exchange rates, in M. Friedman, ed., *Essays in Positive Economics*, Chicago: The University of Chicago Press

Friedman M. (1960), *A Program for Monetary Stability*, New York: Fordham University Press

Friedman M. (1962), Should there be an independent monetary authority? in L. B. Yeager, ed., *In Search of a Monetary Constitution*, Cambridge: Harvard University Press

Friedman M. (1968), The role of monetary policy, *The American Economic Review*, 58(1): 1–17

Friedman M. (1969), The optimum quantity of money, in M. Friedman, ed., *The Optimum Quantity of Money and Other Essays*, Chicago: Aldine

Friedman M. (1996), Un entêtement suicidaire. Unification économique, unification politique et souveraineté. Entretien exclusif avec M. Friedman par Robert Lozada, Géopolitique, No. 53, Monnaie unique, le débat interdit: 58–66

Furceri C., P. Loungani (2015), Capital account liberalization and inequality, IMF W. P. 15/243

Furceri D., A. Zdzienicka (2015), The euro area crisis: Need for a supranational fiscal risk sharing mechanism? *Open Economies Review*, 26(4): 683–710

Gabor D. (2014), Learning from Japan: The European Central Bank and the European sovereign debt crisis, *Review of Political Economy*, 26(2): 190–209

Gabrisch H., K. Staehr (2015), The euro plus pact: Competitiveness and external capital flows in the EU countries, *Journal of Common Market Studies*, 53(3): 558–76

Galati G., R Moessner (2013), Macroprudential policy: A literature review, *Journal of Economic Surveys*, 27(5): 846–78

Galbraith J. K. (1987), *Economics in Perspective. A Critical History*, Boston: Houghton Mifflin Co.

Galbraith J. K. (2016), *Welcome to the Poisoned Chalice: The Destruction of Greece and the Future of Europe*, Yale: Yale University Press

Galì J., T. Monacelli (2008), Optimal monetary and fiscal policy in a currency union, *Journal of International Economics*, 76(1): 116–32

Galor O., O. Moav (2004), From physical to human capital accumulation: Inequality and the process of development, *Review of Economic Studies*, 71 (4): 1001–26

Gambacorta L., B. Hofmann, G. Peersman (2014), The effectiveness of unconventional monetary policy at the zero lower bound: A cross-country analysis, *Journal of Money, Credit and Banking*, 46(4): 615–42

Gambetti L., A. Musso (2017), The macroeconomic impact of the ECB's expanded asset purchase programme (APP), ECB W. P. Series 2075, June

Garin A. (2016), Putting America to work, where? The limits of infrastructure construction as a locally-targeted employment policy, Taubman Center W. P. 2016/01

Garofoli G., S. Holland (2017), Alternative economic policies in Europe: An introduction, *The European Journal of Comparative Economics*, 14(1): 3–12

Gaulier G., V. Vicard (2012), Current account imbalances in the Euro Area: Competitiveness or demand shock? Banque de France, Quarterly Section of Articles, No. 27, Autumn

Gawel E., S. Strunz, P. Lehmann (2014), A public choice view on the climate and energy policy mix in the EU – How do the emissions trading scheme and support for renewable energies interact? *Energy Policy*, 64(S): 175 82

Geithner T. (2014), *Stress Test: Reflections on Financial Crises*, New York: Crown Publ. Group

Genser B. (2003), Coordinating VATs between EU member states, *International Tax and Public Finance*, 10(6): 735–52

Georgiadis G. (2015), Determinants of global spillovers from US monetary policy, ECB W. P. 1854, September

Ghosh A. R., J. I. Kim, E. G. Mendoza, J. D. Ostry, M. S. Qureshi (2013), Fiscal fatigue, fiscal space and debt sustainability in advanced economies, *The Economic Journal*, 123(566): F4–F30

Giannone D., M. Lenza, H. Pill, L. Reichlin (2011), Non-standard monetary policy measures and monetary developments, ECB W. P. 1290, January

Giannone D., M. Lenza, H. Pill, L. Reichlin (2012), The ECB and the interbank market, ECB W. P. 1496, November

Gianviti F., A. O. Krueger, J. Pisani-Ferry, A. Sapir, J. Von Hagen (2010), A European mechanism for sovereign debt crisis resolution: A proposal, Bruegel Blueprint Series, Vol. X, A European mechanism for sovereign debt

Giavazzi F., M. Pagano (1988), The advantage of tying one's hands: EMS discipline and central bank credibility, *European Economic Review*, 32(1): 55–75

Giavazzi F., M. Pagano (1990), Can severe fiscal contractions be expansionary? Tales of two small European countries, in O. J. Blanchard, S. Fischer, eds., *NBER Macroeconomics Annual 1990*, 5: 75–122, Cambridge: MIT Press

Giavazzi F., M. Pagano (1996), Non-Keynesian effects of fiscal policy changes: International evidence and the Swedish experience, *Swedish Economic Policy Review*, 3(1): 67–112

Giavazzi F., L. Spaventa (1990), The "New" EMS, CEPR D. P. No. 369, Centre for Economic Policy Research

Gibson H. D. (2003), Realignment probabilities and reputation effects in the EMS, *Oxford Economic Papers*, 55(2): 314–35

Giordano R., M. Pericoli, P. Tommasino (2013), Pure or wake-up-call contagion? Another look at the EMU sovereign debt crisis, in Bank of Italy, The sovereign debt crisis and the Euro Area, Workshops and Conferences, No. 14, July, pp. 53–82

Girardi A., P. Paesani (2008), Structural reforms and fiscal discipline in Europe, *Transition Studies Review*, 15(2): 389–402

Giraud G., T. Kockerols (2015), Making European Banking Union Macro-Economically Resilient, Cost of Non-Europe Report, European Parliament, June

Glick R., A. K. Rose (2016), Currency unions and trade: A post-EMU reassessment, *European Economic Review*, 87(C): 78–91

Goecke H., M. Hüther (2016), Regional convergence in Europe, *Intereconomics*, 51 (3): 165–71

Goldback R., H. Zimmermann (2015), Germany in the context of the multilevel reform process, in R. Mayntz, ed., *Negotiated Reform. The Multilevel Governance of Financial Regulation*, Frankfurt-on-Main: Campus, pp. 139–61

Gomes S., P. Jacquinot, M. Mohr, M. Pisani (2011), Structural reforms and macroeconomic performance in the Euro Area countries: A model-based assessment, ECB W. P. 1323

Goodhart C. A. E. (1975), *Problems of Monetary Management: The U.K. Experience*, in Papers in Monetary Economics, Vol. I, Sydney: Reserve Bank of Australia

Goodhart C. A. E. (1998), Two concepts of money: Implications for the analysis of optimal currency areas, *European Journal of Political Economy*, 14(3): 402–32

Gopinath G., S. Kalemli-Ozcan, L. Karabarbounis, C. Villegas-Sanchez (2015), Capital allocation and productivity in South Europe, NBER W. P. 21453, March

Gourinchas P.-O., M. Obstfeld (2012), Stories of the twentieth century for the twenty-first, *American the Economic Journal: Macroeconomics*, 4(1): 226–65

Gourinchas P.-O., H. Rey, K. Truempler (2012), The financial crisis and the geography of wealth transfers, *Journal of International Economics*, 88(2): 266–83

Gordon R. J. (1976), Recent developments in the theory of inflation and unemployment, *Journal of Monetary Economics*, 2(2): 185–219

Gordon R. J. (2012), Is US economic growth over? Faltering innovation confronts the six headwinds, NBER W. P. 18315, August

Gordon R. J. (2014), The turtle's progress: Secular stagnation meets the headwinds, in C. Teulings, R. Baldwin, eds.

Graham L., D. J. Snower (2008), Hyperbolic discounting and the Phillips Curve, *Journal of Money, Credit and Banking*, 40(3): 427–48

Greenwald B., J. E. Stiglitz (1988), Imperfect information, finance constraints and business fluctuations, in M. Kohn, S. Tsiang, eds., *Finance Constraints, Expectations and Macroeconomics*, Oxford: Oxford University Press

Greenwald B., J. E. Stiglitz (1990), Macroeconomic models with equity and credit rationing, in R. G. Hubbard, ed., *Asymmetric Information, Corporate Finance and Investment*, Chicago: University of Chicago Press

Greenwald B., J. E. Stiglitz (1993), Financial market imperfections and business cycles, *Quarterly Journal of Economics*, 108(1): 77–114

Gregory M., D. Weiserbs (1998), Changing objectives in national policymaking, in J. Forder, A. Menon, eds., *European Union and National Macroeconomic Policy*, London: Routledge

Griffith-Jones S., G. Cozzi (2016), Investment-led growth: A solution to the European crisis, ch. 7 in M. Mazzucato, M. Jacobs, *Rethinking Capitalism: Economics and Policy for Sustainable and Inclusive Growth*, Chichester: Wiley-Blackwell

Gros D. (2014), A fiscal shock absorber for the EZ? Insurance with deductible, *Intereconomics*, 49(4): 199–203

Gros D (2016), Structural reforms as a panacea? The European productivity and growth puzzle. *Intereconomics*, 51(6): 318–20

Gros D. (2017a), An evolutionary path towards a European Monetary Fund, Scrutiny paper provided in the context of Economic Dialogues with the President of the Eurogroup in the Economic and Monetary Affairs Committee, European Parliament, May

Gros D. (2017b), The EZ's hidden strength, Project Syndicate, June 2

Gros D., A. Belke (2016), *Banking Union as a Shock Absorber. Lessons for the EZ from the US*, CEPS, London: Rowman & Littlefield International

Gros D., T. Mayer (2010), Towards a Euro(pean) Monetary Fund, Policy Brief 202, Centre for European Policy Studies (CEPS), Brussels, February

Gros D., T. Mayer (2011), EFSF 2.0 or the European Monetary Fund, CESifo Group Munich, CESifo DICE Report 3/2011: 31–38, www.cesifo-group.de/DocDL/dic ereport311-forum5.pdf

Gros D., T. Mayer (2012), A German sovereign wealth fund to save the euro, Vox, CEPR's Policy Portal, 28 August

Gros D., N. Thygesen (1992), *European Monetary Integration*, London: Longman

Grunfeld F. (2017), The snow isn't greener on the other side: Scandinavian nations, Hamodia, December 19

Gualtieri R. (2009), L'Europa come vincolo esterno, in P. Craveri, A. Varsori, eds., *L'Italia nella Costruzione Europea. Un Bilancio Storico (1957–2007)*, Milan: Angeli

Guderjan M. (2012), Local government and European integration – beyond Europeanisation? *Political Perspectives*, 6(1): 105–28

Guerrieri V., G. Lorenzoni (2011), Credit crises, precautionary savings, and the liquidity trap, NBER W. P. 17583

Guglielminetti E. (2016), The labor market channel of macroeconomic uncertainty, Bank of Italy W. P. 1068, June

Guibourg G., M. Jonsson, B. Lagerwall, C. Nilsson (2015), Macroprudential policy: Effects on the economy and the interaction with monetary policy, *Sveriges Riksbank Economic Review*, 2: 29–46

Guiso L., P. Sapienza, L. Zingales (2016), Monnet's error? *Economic Policy*, 31(86): 247–97

Guzzo, V., A. Velasco (1999), The case for a populist central banker, *European Economic Review*, 43(7): 1317–44

Haberler G. (1952), The Pigou effect once more, *Journal of Political Economy*, 60(3): 240–6

Habermas J. (2012), *The Crisis of the European Union: A Response*, Cambridge: Polity

Haentjens M., L. Janssen (2015), New national solutions for bank failures: Game-changing in the UK, Germany and the Netherlands? *Journal of Financial Regulation*, 1(2): 294–7

Haidar J. J. (2015), Can the euro survive? *The World Economy*, 38(3): 553–67

Hale T., K. Allen (2017), Hopes for European "safe" bonds lean on pre-crisis techniques, *Financial Times*, August 15, www.ft.com/content/06917b7a-7e a1-11e7-ab01-a13271d1ee9c

Hall P. A. (2014), Varieties of capitalism and the Euro Crisis, *West European Politics*, 37(6): 1223–43

Hall R. E. (2011), The long slump, *American Economic Review*, 101(2): 431–69

Hall R. E. (2014), Quantifying the lasting harm to the US economy from the financial crisis, NBER W. P. 20183, April

Handler H. (2012), The EZ: Piecemeal approach to an Optimum Currency Area, WIFO W. P. 446

Harashima T. (2007), Why should central banks be independent? Munich Personal RePEc Archive Paper 1838, 15 January

Harashima T. (2011), A mechanism of inflation differentials and current account imbalances in the Euro Area, Munich Personal RePEc Archive Paper 28121, 18 January

Hartmann P., F. Smets (2018), The first twenty years of the European Central Bank: Monetary policy, CEPR Discussion Papers 13411

Hayek F. A. (1960), *The Constitution of Liberty*, Chicago: The University of Chicago Press

Hayo B. (1998), Inflation culture, central bank independence and price stability, *European Journal of Political Economy*, 14(2): 241–63

Hayo B., C. Hefeker (2010), The complex relationship between central bank independence and inflation, in P. L. Siklos, M. T. Bohl, and M. E. Wohar (eds.), *Challenges in Central Banking*, Cambridge: Cambridge University Press, pp. 179–217

Hebous S. (2010), The effects of discretionary fiscal policy on macroeconomic aggregates: a reappraisal, Goethe University, Frankfurt, July 2009, Munich personal Repec archive Paper 23300, http://mpra.ub.uni-muenchen.de/23300/

Hefeker C. (1994), German Monetary Union, the Bundesbank and the EMS collapse, *BNL Quarterly Review*, 47(191): 379–98

Hein E. (2012), *Macroeconomics of Finance-Dominated Capitalism – And Its Crisis*, Cheltenham: Elgar

Hein E., T. Niechoj (2005), Guidelines for sustained growth in the EU? The concept and consequences of the Broad Economic Policy Guidelines, IMK W. P. 2/2005, http://nbn-resolving.de/urn:nbn:de:101:1-2008081458

Hein E., A. Truger (2005), European Monetary Union: Nominal convergence, real divergence and slow growth? An investigation into the effects of changing macroeconomic policy institutions associated with monetary union, Macroeconomics 0501011, EconWPA

Hein E., A. Truger (2017), Opportunities and limits of rebalancing the EZ via wage policies: Theoretical considerations and empirical illustrations for the case of Germany, Hans-Böckler-Stiftung, FMM W. P., Nr. 6, July

Heinemann F. (2019), Europe goes to the polls: Ten priorities for reforming the EU and the EZ, ZEW Position Paper

Heinemann F., T. Grigoriadis (2013), Origins of reform resistance and the Southern European regime, WWWforEurope W. P. Series 20

Henning C. R. (1998), Systemic conflict and regional monetary integration: The case of Europe, *International Organization*, 52(3): 537–73

Hermann C., J. Flecker (2012), *Privatization of Public Services: Impacts for Employment, Working Conditions, and Service Quality in Europe*, London: Routledge

Heyes J. (2013), Flexicurity in crisis: European labour market policies in a time of austerity, *European Journal of Industrial Relations*, 19(1): 71–86

Hibbs D. J. (1977), Political parties and macroeconomic policy, *American Political Science Review*, 71(4): 1467–87

Hix S. (2015), Democratizing a macroeconomic union in Europe, in O. Cramme, S. B. Hobolt, eds.

Hobolt S. B., C. Wratil (2015), Public opinion and the crisis: The dynamics of support for the euro, *Journal of European Public Policy*, 22(2): 238–56

Hobson J. (1909), *The Industrial System: An Inquiry into Earned and Unearned Income*, London: Longmans

Hobza A., S. Zeugner (2014), The "imbalanced balance" and its unravelling: Current accounts and bilateral financial flows in the Euro Area, European Union, Economic and Financial Affairs, Economic Papers 520, July, http://ec .europa.eu/economy_finance/publications/

Holland S. (2016), *Beyond Austerity – Democratic Alternatives for Europe*, Nottingham: Spokesman

Hondroyiannis G. (2014), Comment on De Grauwe P., Y. Ji (2014a), How much fiscal discipline in a monetary union? *Journal of Macroeconomics*, 39(B): 361–3

Honkapohja S. (2016), Monetary policies to counter the zero interest rate: An overview of research, *Empirica*, 43(2): 235–56

Hooghe L. (2000), Euro-socialists or Euro-marketeers? EU top officials on capitalism, *Journal of Politics*, 62(2): 430–54

Hooghe L., G. Marks (2010), Types of multi-level governance, in H. Enderlein, S. Wälti, M. Zürn, eds., *Handbook on Multi-level Governance*, Cheltenham: Edward Elgar, ch. 1, pp. 17–31

Horn G. A., A. Watt (2017), Wages and nominal and real unit labour cost differentials in EMU, European Economy D. P. 059, July

Horn G. A., F. Lindner, S. Stephan, R. Zwiener (2017), The role of nominal wages in trade and current account surpluses. An econometric analysis for Germany, IMK Report 125e, June

Hoskyns C. (2018), *Democratizing the European Union. Issues for the Twenty-first Century*, New York: Routledge

Horváth B., W. Wagner (2016), Macroprudential policies and the Lucas critique, in Bank for International Settlements (BIS), Macroprudential policy, BIS papers No. 86, Basel, September, pp. 39–44

Hristov N., O. Hülsewig, T. Wollmershäuser (2018), Capital flows in the Euro Area and TARGET2 balances, CESifo W. P. 6877, January

Hughes Hallett A. J. (2000), Aggregate Phillips curves are not always vertical: Heterogeneity and mismatch in multiregion or multisector economies, *Macroeconomic Dynamics*, 4(4): 534–46

Hughes Hallett A. (2008), Coordination without explicit cooperation: Monetary-fiscal interactions in an era of demographic change, European Economy, Economic Papers 305, February

Hughes Hallett A., Acocella N. (2018), Stabilization and expanded commitment: A theory of forward guidance for economies with rational expectations, *Macroeconomic Dynamics*, 22(1): 122–34

Hughes Hallett A., Acocella N. (2019), Forward guidance reassessed: Stabilizability under endogenous policy rules, *Journal of Macroeconomics*, 59(C): 325–35

Hughes Hallett A., D. N. Weymark (2007), Fiscal leadership and central bank design, *Canadian Journal of Economics*, 40(2): 607–27

Hughes Hallett A., J. Libich, P. Stehlík (2011), Welfare improving coordination of fiscal and monetary policy, *Czech Economic Review*, 5(1): 7–26

Hughes Hallett A., J. Libich, P. Stehlík (2014), Monetary and fiscal policy interaction with various degrees of commitment, *Czech Journal of Economics and Finance*, 64(1): 2–29

Hüttl P., D. Schoenmaker (2016), Should the "outs" join the European banking union? Bruegel Policy Contribution, Issue 2016/03, February

Illes A., M. J. Lombardi (2013), Interest rate pass-through since the financial crisis, BIS Quarterly Review, September, pp. 57–66, http://ssrn.com/abstract=2401570

Illing G., S. Watzka (2013), Fiscal multipliers and their relevance in a currency union – A survey, *German Economic Review*, 15(2): 259–71

ILO (2013), *Global Wage Report*, Geneva: ILO

Ingram J. C. (1959), State and regional payments mechanisms, *The Quarterly Journal of Economics*, 73(4): 619–32

Inman R. P. (1996), Do balanced budget rules work? US experience and possible lessons for the EMU, NBER W. P. 5838, February

Insee (2014), Les niveaux de vie en 2012, Première No. 1513 – September

International Monetary Fund (2010), *World Economic Outlook: Recovery, Risk, and Rebalancing*, World economic and financial surveys, October, Washington: IMF

International Monetary Fund (2012), *World Economic Outlook: Coping with High Debt and Sluggish Growth*, October, Washington: IMF

International Monetary Fund (2013a), *Toward a Fiscal Union for the Euro Area: Technical Background Notes*, Washington: IMF, September

International Monetary Fund (2013b), The functions and impact of fiscal councils, 16 July

International Monetary Fund (2014a), World Economic Outlook, April, Chapter 3

International Monetary Fund (2014b), Euro Area Policies: 2014 Article IV Consultation-Staff Report; Press Release; and Statement by Executive Director, IMF Country Reports, 14/2014

International Monetary Fund (2016), World Economic Outlook, April

in 't Veld J. (2019), Quantifying the economic effects of the Single Market in a structural macromodel, European Economy D. P. 094

in 't Veld J., M. Larch, M. Vandeweyer (2012), Automatic fiscal stabilisers: What they are and what they do, European Economy, Economic Papers 452, April

Iversen T., D. Soskice, D. Hope (2016), The EZ and political economic institutions, *Annual Review of Political Science*, 19(1): 163–85

James H. (2012), *Making the European Monetary Union*, Cambridge: Harvard University Press

Janssen R. (2010), Greece and the IMF: Who exactly is being saved? CEPR, July

Japan Statistics Bureau (n. d.), www.stat.go.jp/english/data/roudou/results/month/index.htm

Jara H. X., H. Sutherland (2014), The effects of an EMU insurance scheme on income in unemployment, *Intereconomics*, 49(4): 193–8

Jarociński M., B. Maćkowiak (2017), Monetary-fiscal interactions and the Euro Area's malaise, ECB W. P. Series 2072, June

Jaumotte F., C. Osorio Buitron (2015), Inequality and labor market institutions, IMF, SDN/15/14, July

Jeffery C. (1997), ed., *The Regional Dimension of the European Union: Towards a Third Level in Europe?* London: Routledge

Jimeno J. F. (2015), Long-lasting consequences of the European crisis, ECB W. P. 1832, July

Jin H., E. K. Choi (2014), Profits and losses from currency intervention, *International Review of Economics and Finance*, 29(C): 47–56

Johnson H. J., A. Swoboda (1973), eds., *The Economics of Common Currencies*, London: George Allen & Unwin

Johnston A., A. Regan (2016), European monetary integration and the incompatibility of national varieties of capitalism, *Journal of Common Market Studies*, 54(2): 318–36

Jones B. (2015), Asset bubbles: Re-thinking policy for the age of asset management, IMF W. P. 15/27, February

Jones E. (2003), Liberalized capital markets, state autonomy, and European monetary union, *European Journal of Political Research* 42(2): 197–222

Jonung L., E. Drea (2009), The euro: It can't happen. It's a bad idea. It won't last. US economists on the EMU, 1989–2002, European Economy Economic Papers, 395, December

Jordan A., A. Lenschow (2010), Environmental policy integration: A state of the art review, *Environmental Policy and Governance*, 20(3): 147–58

Jovanović M. N. (2015), *The Economics of International Integration*, Cheltenham: Edward Elgar

Jovanović M. N. (2011), ed., *International Handbook on the Economics of Integration. Competition, Spatial Location of Economic Activity and Financial Issues*, vol. II, Cheltenham: Edward Elgar

Juncker J. C., D. Tusk, J. Dijsselbloem, M. Draghi, M. Schulz (2015), Completing Europe's Economic and Monetary Union, https://ec.europa.eu/commission/sit es/beta-political/files/5-presidents-report_en.pdf

Kaldor N. (1971), The dynamic effects of the common market, The New Statesman, 12 March, repr. in *Further Essays on Applied Economics – Collected Economic Essays*, vol. 6, London: Duckworth, 1978, Chapter 12, pp. 187–220

Kaminsky G. L., P. Vega-García (2016), Systemic and idiosyncratic sovereign debt crises, *Journal of the European Economic Association*, 14(1): 80–114

Kara G. I. (2016), Systemic risk, international regulation, and the limits of coordination, *Journal of International Economics*, 99(C): 192–222

Keefer P., D. Stasavage (2002), Checks and balances, private information, and the credibility of monetary commitments, *International Organization*, 56(4): 751–74

Kelly N. J., P. K. Enns (2010), Inequality and the dynamics of public opinion: The self-reinforcing link between economic inequality and mass preferences, *American Journal of Political Science*, 54(4): 855–70

Kenen P. B. (1995), ed., *Understanding Interdependence: The Macroeconomics of the Open Economy*, Princeton: Princeton University Press

Keohane R. O., S. Hoffmann (1994), Institutional change in Europe in the 1980s, in R. O. Keohane, S. Hoffmann, eds., *The New European Community Decisionmaking and Institutional Change* (1st ed. 1991), Boulder: Westview Press, pp. 237–55

Keynes J. M. (1936), *The General Theory of Employment, Interest and Money*, London: Macmillan

King M. (1995), Comment on J. B. Taylor's,*The Monetary Policy Implications of Greater Fiscal Discipline, in Budget, Debt, and Deficits: Issues and*

Solutions. Denver, Colorado: Federal Reserve Bank of Kansas City, 1995, pp. 151–70

King M. (2014), Monetary policies and macro-prudential policies, in Banca d'Italia, Conference in Memory of Tommaso Padoa-Schioppa, Rome, 16 December 2011, Proceedings, November 2014

Kirsanova T., C. Machado, A. P. Ribeiro (2018), Sustainable policy equilibria in a monetary union, mimeo, February 20,

Kiyotaki N., J. Moore (1997), Credit cycles, *Journal of Political Economy*, 105(2): 211–48

Kiyotaki N., J. Moore (2002), Balance-sheet contagion, *The American Economic Review*, 92(2): 46–50

Knill C., D. Lehmkuhl (1999), How Europe matters: Different mechanisms of Europeanization, European Integration Online Papers (EIOP), 3(7), https://pdfs .semanticscholar.org/c7af/83f50463c0c33e489bafec75e1a86eeab6bb.pdf

Knill C., D. Liefferink (2013), The establishment of EU environmental policy, in A. Jordan, C. Adelle, eds., *Environmental Policy in the EU: Actors, Institutions and Processes*, 3rd ed., London: Routledge

Knopf B., N. Koch, G. Grosjean, S. Fuss, C. Flachsland, M. Pahle, M. Jakob, O. Edenhofer (2014), The European Emissions Trading System (EU ETS): Ex-post analysis, the market stability reserve and options for a comprehensive reform, FEEM W. P. 79

Kohn D. L. (2010), The Federal Reserve's policy actions during the financial crisis and lessons for the future, Carleton University, Ottawa, 13 May

Kollman K. (1998), *Outside Lobbying: Public Opinion and Interest Group Strategies*, Princeton: Princeton University Press

Kollmann R., M. Ratto, W. Roeger, J. in't Veld, L. Vogel (2015), What drives the German current account? And how does it affect other EU member states? European Commission economic papers, Directorate-general for economic and financial affairs, Unit communication, *Economic Policy*, 30(81): 47–93

Korinek A., A. Simsek (2016), Liquidity trap and excessive leverage, *The American Economic Review*, 106(3): 699–738

Krajewski M. (2014), Human rights and austerity programmes, in T. Cottier, R. M. Lastra, C. Tietje, L. Satragno, eds., *The Rule of Law in Monetary Affairs*, Cambridge: Cambridge University Press

Krugman P. (1987), Economic integration in Europe: Conceptual issues, in T. Padoa Schioppa, ed., *Efficiency, Stability and Equity: A Strategy for the Evolution of the Economic System of the European Community*, Oxford: Oxford University Press, App. A

Krugman P. (1993), Lessons of Massachusetts for EMU, in F. Giavazzi, F. Torres, eds., *The Transition to Economic and Monetary Union in Europe*, Cambridge: Cambridge University Press, pp. 241–61

Krugman P. (1999), O Canada – A neglected nation gets its Nobel, Slate, October 10, URL www.slate.com/articles/business/the_dismal_science/1999/10/o_canada.html

Krugman P. (2009), Financial policy despair, *The New York Times*, 22 March

Krugman P. (2013), *Revenge of the Optimum Currency Area*, in NBER Macroeconomics Annual, 2012, Chicago: University of Chicago Press

Krugman P. (2014), Four observations on secular stagnation, in C. Teulings, R. Baldwin, eds.

Krugman P., M. Obstfeld (2003), Case study: Is Europe an optimum currency area? in P. Krugman, M. Obstfeld, eds., *International Economics: Theory and Policy*, Boston: Addison-Wesley, pp. 625–7

Kydland F. E., E. C. Prescott (1977), Rules rather than discretion: The inconsistency of optimal plans, *Journal of Political Economy*, 85(3): 473–92

Laffan B., S. Mazey (2006), European integration: The European Union – reaching an equilibrium, in J. Richardson, ed., ch. 2., pp. 31–54

Lagarde C. (2010), It takes two to tango. Transcript of interview with Christine Lagarde, *Financial Times*, March 15

Lagarde C. (2015), Lifting the small boats, Address at Grandes Conferences Catholiques, Brussels, June 17, www.imf.org/external/np/speeches/2015/0617 15.htm

Lakatos I. (1970), Falsification and the methodology of scientific research programmes, in I. Lakatos, A. Musgrave, eds., *Criticism and the Growth of Knowledge*, New York: Cambridge University Press, pp. 91–196

Lama R., P. Rabanal (2012), Deciding to enter a monetary union: The role of trade and financial linkages. IMF W. P. 12/240, October

Lamo A. (2017), Did recent reforms facilitate EU labour market adjustment? ECB Research Bulletin No. 38, 14 September

Lane P. R. (2012), The European sovereign debt crisis, *The Journal of Economic Perspectives*, 26(3): 49–67

Lane P. R. (2013), Capital flows in the Euro Area, European Economy, Economic Papers No. 497, April

Lane P. R., P. McQuade (2013), Domestic credit growth and international capital flows, ECB W. P. 1566, July

Lane P. R., G. M. Milesi-Ferretti (2012), External adjustment and the global crisis, *Journal of International Economics*, 88(2): 252–65

Lane P. R., G. M. Milesi-Ferretti (2014), Global imbalances and external adjustment after the crisis, IMF W. P. 14/151, August

Langfield S., M. Pagano (2016), Bank bias in Europe: Effects on systemic risk and growth, *Economic Policy*, 31(85): 51–106

Larch M., A. Turrini (2009), The cyclically-adjusted budget balance in EU fiscal policy making: A love at first sight turned into a mature relationship, Economic Papers 374, March

Lavoie M., E. Stockhammer (2013), eds., *Wage-Led Growth: An Equitable Strategy for Economic Recovery*, London: Palgrave Macmillan

Leander A., S. Guzzini (2012), Economic and Monetary Union and the crisis of the European social contracts, in P. Minkinnen, H. Patomäki, eds.

Le Borgne E., B. Lockwood (2002), Candidate entry, screening, and the political budget cycle, IMF W. P. 02/48

Lee N. A. (2016), Fluid Dynamics: Emergency Liquidity Assistance during the Eurocrisis, M.A. Thesis, European University Institute, Florence, 30 September

Lehndorff S. (2015), ed., *Divisive Integration. The Triumph of Failed Ideas in Europe – Revisited*, Brussels: European Trade Union Institute

Leitemo K. (2004), A game between the fiscal and the monetary authorities under inflation targeting, *European Journal of Political Economy*, 20(3): 709–24

Lelkes O., K. Gasior (2012), Income Poverty and Social Exclusion in the EU. Situation in 2008 and Trends, European Centre for Social Welfare Policy and Research, Vienna, Policy Brief, January

Lenarčič A., K. Korhonen (2018), A case for a European rainy day fund, European Stability Mechanism, D. P. Series No 5, November

Lenza M., J. Slacalek (2018), How does monetary policy affect income and wealth inequality? Evidence from quantitative easing in the euro area, ECB W. P. Series No 2190, October

Leruth B., C. Lord (2015), Differentiated integration in the European Union: A concept, a process, a system or a theory? *Journal of European Public Policy*, 22(6): 754–63

Levich R. M., G. Majnoni, C. M. Reinhart (2002), eds., *Ratings, Rating Agencies and the Global Financial System*, New York: Springer

Lewis V., M. Roth (2017), The financial market effects of the ECB's asset purchase programs, Deutsche Bundesbank D. P. No 23

Liberatore A. (1997), The integration of sustainable development objectives into EU policy-making. Barriers and prospects, in S. Baker, M. Kousis, D. Richardson, eds., *The Politics of Sustainable Development: Theory, Policy and Practice within the European Union*, London: Routledge, Ch. 5, pp. 108–26

Liikanen Report (2012), *High-Level Expert Group on Reforming the Structure of the EU Banking Sector*, Final Report, European Commission, Brussels

Lindbeck A., D. Niepelt (2006), The stability pact: Rationales, problems, alternatives, *Kyklos*, 59(4): 579–600

Liobikien G., M. Butkus (2017), The European Union possibilities to achieve targets of Europe 2020 and Paris agreement climate policy, *Renewable Energy*, 106: 298–309

Lippi F. (2002), Revisiting the case for a populist central banker, *European Economic Review*, 46(3): 601–12

Lippi F. (2003), Strategic monetary policy with non-atomistic wage setters, *Review of Economic Studies*, 70(4),909–19

Lohmann S. (2000), Sollbruchstelle: Deep uncertainty and the design of monetary institutions, *International Finance*, 3(3): 391–411

Lohmann S. (2003), Why do institutions matter? An audience-cost theory of institutional commitment, *Governance*, 16(1): 95–110

Lucas R. E. (1976), Econometric policy evaluation. A critique, *Journal of Monetary Economics, Supplement, Carnegie-Rochester Conference Series on Public Policy*, 1: 19–46

Lucas R. E. (1996), Nobel lecture: Monetary neutrality, *Journal of Political Economy*, 104(4): 661–82

Ludlow P. (1982), *The Making of the European Monetary System. A Case Study of the Politics of the European Community*, London: Butterworth Scientific

Maćkowiak B., F. P. Mongelli, G. Noblet, F. Smets (2009), *The Euro at Ten – Lessons and Challenges*, Frankfurt: ECB

Maestri V., F. Bogliacino, W. Salverda (2014), Wealth inequality and the accumulation of debt, ch. 4 in W. Salverda, B. Nolan, D. Checchi, I. Marx, A. McKnight, I.G. Tóth, H. van de Werfhorst, eds., *Changing Inequalities in Rich Countries: Analytical and Comparative Perspectives*, Oxford: Oxford University Press

Majone G. (1996), *Regulating Europe*, London: Routledge

Majone G. (2014a), The general crisis of the European Union. A genetic approach, in J. E. Fossum, A. J. Menéndez, eds., *The European Union in Crises or the European Union as Crises?* Oslo: ARENA Report 2/14

Majone G. (2014b), *Rethinking the Union of Europe Post-Crisis: Has Integration Gone too Far?* Cambridge: Cambridge University Press

Majone G. (2015), The deeper Euro-Crisis or: The collapse of the EU political culture of total optimism, European University Institute, Dept of Law W. P. 2015/10

Malinen T., P. Nyberg, H. Koskenkylä, E. Berghäll, I. Mellin, S. Miettinen, J. Ala-Peijari, S. Törnqvist (2017), How to leave the EZ: The case of Finland, mimeo

Marani U., C. Altavilla (2001), Is there a deflationary bias in European economic policies? mimeo

Marcussen M. (1997), The role of "ideas" in Dutch, Danish and Swedish economic policy in the 1980s and the beginning of the 1990s, in P. Minkkinen, P. Heikki, eds., *The Politics of Economic and Monetary Union*, Dordrecht: Kluwer

Marelli E., M. Signorelli (2017), *Europe and the Euro Integration. Crisis and Policies*, London: Palgrave Macmillan

Margerit A., M. Magnus, B. Mesnard (2017), The EU macro-prudential policy framework, European Parliament, Economic Governance Support Unit, 17 March www.europarl.europa.eu/RegData/etudes/BRIE/2016/587379/IPOL_BRI(2016)587379_EN.pd

Marimon R. (2018), A new fiscal and monetary framework for the EMU? The EU presidents' roadmap in 2018, in R. Marimon, T. Cooley, eds., *The EMU after the Euro Crisis: Lessons and Possibilities Findings and Proposals from the Horizon 2020 ADEMU Project*, A VoxEU.org eBook, https://voxeu.org/The-emu-after-the-crisis

Marin D., J. Schymik, J. Tscheke (2015), Europe's export superstars – It's the organisation! Bruegel W.P. 5

Marotzke P., R. Anderton, A. Bairrao, C. Berson, P. Tóth (2017), Asymmetric wage adjustment and employment in European firms, ECB W. P. Series 2103, October

Marrazzo P. M., A. Terzi (2017), Structural reform waves and economic growth, ECB W. P. 2111, November

Marzinotto B., A. Sapir, G. Wolff (2011), What kind of fiscal union? Bruegel Policy Brief 2011/6

Masciandaro D., M. Quintyn (2016), The governance of financial supervision: Recent developments, *Journal of Economic Surveys*, 30(5): 982–1006

Masciandaro D., D. Romelli (2018), To be or not to be a euro country? The behavioural political economics of currency unions, Bocconi W. P. 83, July

Matthijs M., M. Blyth (2015), eds., Conclusion. *The Future of the Euro: Possible Futures, Risks, and Uncertainties, The Future of the Euro*, Oxford: Oxford University Press, pp. 249–69

Matthijs M., K. McNamara (2015), The Euro Crisis' theory effect: Northern saints, southern sinners, and the demise of the Eurobond, *Journal of Economic Integration*, 37(2): 229–45

Mayer T. (2009), The case for a European Monetary Fund, Intereconomics, May/June: 136–141

McGuire P., G. von Peter (2009), The US dollar shortage in global banking, BIS Quarterly Review, March, pp. 47–63

McKinnon R. (1996), *Default Risk in Monetary Unions, Background Report for the Swedish Government Commission on EMU*, Stockholm: Swedish Government

McKinnon R. (2002), Optimum currency areas and the European experience, *Economics of Transition* 10(2): 343–64

McKinsey&Company (2017), Basel "IV": What's next for banks? Implications of intermediate results of new regulatory rules for European banks, April

McNamara K. R. (1998), *The Currency of Ideas: Monetary Politics in the European Union*, London: Cornell University Press

McNamara K. R. (2006), Economic governance, ideas and EMU: What currency does policy consensus have today? *Journal of Common Market Studies*, 44(4): 803–21

Meade J. E. (1957), The balance of payments problems of a European free trade area, *The Economic Journal*, 67(267): 379–96

Mediobanca (2017), Italy. Re-denomination risk down as time goes by, 19 January

Meinusch A., P. Tillmann (2014), The macroeconomic impact of unconventional monetary policy shocks, Joint D. P. Series in Economics by the Universities of Aachen, Gießen, Göttingen, Kassel, Marburg, Siegen, No. 26

Melvin M., M. P. Taylor (2009), The global financial crisis: Causes, threats and opportunities. Introduction and overview, *Journal of International Money and Finance*, 28(8): 1243–5

Menna L. (2016), Optimal fiscal and monetary policies under limited asset market participation, *Italian Economic Journal*, 2: 363–83

Merler S. (2015), Squaring the cycle: Financial cycles, capital flows, and macro-prudential policy in the Euro Area, Bruegel W. P. 2015/14, November, http://bruegel.org/2015/11/squaring-the-cycle-capital-flows-financial-cycles-and-ma cro-prudential-policy-in-the-euro-area-2/

Messori M., S. Micossi (2018), Counterproductive proposals on Euro Area reform by French and German economists, CEPR Policy Insight 2018/04, February

Meyer D. (2012), Currency disintegration: Two scenarios of withdrawal, *Applied Economics Quarterly*, 58(3): 171–91

Michie J. (2000), Economic consequences of EMU for Britain, in M. Baimbridge, B. Burkitt, P. Whyman, eds., *The Impact of the Euro*, London: Palgrave Macmillan

Micossi S. (2015), The monetary policy of the European Central Bank (2002–2015), CEPS Special Report 109, CEPS, Brussels, May

Micossi S. (2016), EZ stability still under threat of a 'bad shock', Voxeu.org, 20 August

Micossi S., G. Bruzzone, M. Casella (2014), Bail-in provisions in state aid and resolution procedures: Are they consistent with systemic stability? *CEPS Policy Brief* 318, May 9, pp. 1–9, www.ceps.eu/download/publication/?i d=8497&pdf=PB%20318%20SM%20et%20al%20Bail-in%20Provisions%20i n%20State%20Aid%20and%20Resolution%20Procedures%20final_0.pdf

Michailidou A. (2017), The Germans are back: Euroscepticism and anti-Germanism in crisis-stricken Greece, *Journal of National Identities*, 19 (1): 91–108

Miller M., Sutherland A. (1993), The Walters critique of the EMS: A case of inconsistent expectations, *The Manchester School*, 59(S1): 23–37

Mills D. Q. (2015), Assessment of the EU's management of the EZ crisis, in B. Dallago, J. McGowan, eds., Ch. 5, pp.84–95

Milone L. M. (2015), Structural reforms in the European Union after the global crisis: Problems and prospects, Sapienza University of Rome, Department of Economics and Law, W. P. 171

Milone L. M. (2017), The path of European structural reforms after the crisis: What has changed? Sapienza University of Rome, Department of Economics and Law: mimeo

Minenna M. (2016), *The Incomplete Currency: The Future of the Euro and Solutions for the EZ*, New York: Wiley

Minenna M. (2017), Ora serve un vero Fondo Salva Stati, *Corriere della Sera*, 21 August

Minenna M. (2018), Why a rebooted ESM is much better than an EMF, Social Europe, 1 February, www.socialeurope.eu/forging-esm-2-0-reach-proper-fiscal-union

Minkkinen P., H. Patomäki (2012), eds., *The Politics of Economic and Monetary Union*, Heidelberg: Springer

Minsky H. (1982), *Can "It" Happen Again! Essays on Instability and Finance*, New York: Sharpe M.E.

Mishkin F. S. (2011), Monetary policy strategy: Lessons from the crisis, NBER W. P. 16755, February

Mishkin F. S., K. Schmidt-Hebbel (2007), Monetary policy under inflation targeting: An introduction, in F. S. Miskin, K. Schmidt-Hebbel, eds., *Monetary Policy Under Inflation Targeting*, Santiago: Central Bank of Chile, Ch. 1, pp. 1–22

Misuraca G., C. Kucsera, F. Lipparini, C. Voigt, R. Radescu (2016), ICT-Enabled Social Innovation to support the implementation of the Social Investment

Package – Mapping and Analysis of ICT-enabled Social Innovation initiatives promoting social investment in integrated approaches to the provision of social services: IESI Knowledge Map 2015, European Commission

Modigliani F. (1961), Long-run implications of alternative fiscal policies and the burden of the national debt, *The Economic Journal*, 71(284): 730–55

Modigliani F., R. Brumberg (1954), Utility analysis and the consumption function: An interpretation of cross-section data, in K. Kurihara, ed., *Post-Keynesian Economics*, New Brunswick: Rutgers University Press, pp. 388–436

Mody A. (2015), Living (dangerously) without a fiscal union, Bruegel, Bruxelles W. P. 3

Molloy R., C. L. Smith, A. K. Wozniak (2011), Internal migration in the United States, IZA D. P. 5903, August

Monastiriotis V., S. Zartoloudis (2010), Beyond the crisis: EMU and labour market reform pressures in good and bad times, London School of Economics, European Institute, Europe in Question D. P. 3

Monfort Ph. (2012), The role of international transfers in public investment in CESEE: The European Commission's experience with Structural Funds, The European Commission, W. P. 02/2012

Monnet J. (1976), *Mémoires*, Paris: Fayard

Monti G. (2002), Article 81 EC and public policy, *Common Market Law Review*, 39 (5): 1057–99

Moravcsik A. (2002), In defence of the "Democratic Deficit": Reassessing legitimacy in the European Union, *Journal of Common Market Studies*, 40(4): 603–24

Moro B. (2016), The European crisis and the accumulation of TARGET2 imbalances, Ch. 6, in B. Moro, V. A. Beker, *Modern Financial Crises. Argentina, United States and Europe*, Heidelberg: Springer

Mortensen J. B. (2013), Economic policy coordination in the Economic and Monetary Union: From Maastricht via the SGP to the Fiscal Pact, CEPS Working Document 381, August

Moschovis G., M. C. Servera (2009), External imbalances of the Greek economy: The role of fiscal and structural policies, *ECFIN Country Focus*, VI(6): 1–6

Mosconi F. (2015), *The New EU Industrial Policy*, London: Routledge

Mouabbi S., J.-G. Sahuc (2018), Evaluating the macroeconomic effects of the ECB's unconventional monetary policies, 23 May, http://dx.doi.org/10.2139/ssrn .2909856

Muellbauer J. (2013), Conditional eurobonds and the EZ sovereign debt crisis, *Oxford Review of Economic Policy*, 29(3): 610–45

Mundell R. A. (1961), The theory of optimum currency areas, *The American Economic Review*, 51(4): 657–64

Mundell R. A. (1963), Capital mobility and stabilization policy under fixed and flexible exchange rates, *The Canadian Journal of Economics and Political Science/Revue Canadienne d'Economique et de Science politique*, 29(4): 475–85

Mundell R. A. (1973a), Uncommon arguments for common currencies, in H. Johnson, A. Swoboda, eds., pp. 114–32

Mundell R. A. (1973b), A plan for a European currency, in H. Johnson, A. Swoboda, eds., pp. 143–73

Mundell R. A. (1997), Updating the agenda for Monetary Union, in M. I. Blejer, J. A. Frenkel, L. Leiderman, A. Razin, in co-operation with D. M. Cheney, eds., *Optimum Currency Areas: New Analytical and Policy Developments*, Washington D.C.: International Monetary Fund, pp. 29–48

Musgrave R. A. (1959), *The Theory of Public Finance: A Study in Public Economy*, New York: McGraw Hill

Myrdal G. (1957), *Economic Theory and Underdeveloped Regions*, London: G. Duckworth

Naastepad C. W. M., S. Storm (2007), OECD demand regimes (1960–2000), *Journal of Post Keynesian Economics*, 29(2): 211–46

National Commission on the Causes of the Financial and Economic Crisis in the United States (2011), *The Financial Crisis Inquiry Report: Final Report of the National Commission on the Causes of the Financial and Economic Crisis in the United States*, Washington: US Government PO

Nelson M., S. Roth (2017), *Basel IV. The Next Generation of Risk Weighted Assets*, New York: Eiley

Neri S. (2013), The impact of the sovereign debt crisis on bank lending rates in the Euro Area, Bank of Italy, Questioni di Economia e Finanza Occasional Papers 170, June

Neri S., A. Notarpietro (2014), Inflation, debt and the zero lower bound, Bank of Italy, Questioni di Economia e Finanza Occasional Papers 242, October

Neri S., A. Notarpietro (2015), The macroeconomic effects of low and falling inflation at the Zero Lower Bound, Bank of Italy Temi di Discussione, W. P. 1040, November

Neri S., T. Ropele (2015), The macroeconomic effects of the sovereign debt crisis in the Euro Area, Bank of Italy Temi di discussione, W. P. 1007, March

Neugebauer F. (2018), The effects of ECB's Asset Purchase Announcements on Euro Area government bond yields, mimeo, April 19

Newig J., T. M. Koontz (2014), Multi-level governance, policy implementation and participation: The EU's mandated participatory planning approach to implementing environmental policy, *Journal of European Public Policy*, 21(2): 248–67

Newman M. (2006), After the "permissive consensus": Still searching for democracy, in J. Richardson, ed., ch. 18, pp. 377–98

Nickell S. (2007), Discussion on C. Wyplosz (2006), European Monetary Union: The dark sides of a major success, *Economic Policy*, 21(46): 247–53

Nicolaides P. (2013), Is withdrawal from the European Union a manageable option? A review of economic and legal complexities, Bruges European Economic Policy Briefings 28

Nicoletti G., S. Scarpetta (2005), Product market reforms and employment in the OECD countries, OECD Economics Department W. P. 472

Nicoli F. (2017), Democratic legitimacy in the era of fiscal integration, *Journal of European Integration*, 39(4): 389–404

Nieminen M. (2014), Trade imbalances within the Euro Area and with respect to the Rest of the World, January 16, http://ssrn.com/abstract=2380229 or http://dx.doi.org/10.2139/ssrn.2380229

Nikolov P., P. Pasimeni (2019), Fiscal stabilization in the United States: Lessons for monetary unions, The Levy Economics Institute of Bard College Skidmore College W. P. 926, April

Nocciola L., D. Żochowski (2016), Cross-border spillovers from macroprudential policy in the Euro Area, in Bank for International Settlements (BIS), Macroprudential policy, BIS papers No. 86, Basel, September, pp. 45–48

Nordhaus W. D. (1975), The political business cycle, *Review of Economic Studies*, 42(2): 169–90

Nordvig J. (2014), *The Fall of the Euro: Reinventing the EZ and the Future of Global Investing*, New York: Mc-Graw Hill

Notten G., A. C. Guio (2016), The impact of social transfers on income poverty and material deprivation, ImPRovE W. P. 16/17, Herman Deleeck Centre for Social Policy – University of Antwerp

Nowzohour L., L. Stracca (2017), More than a feeling: Confidence, uncertainty and macroeconomic fluctuations, ECB W. P. 2100, September

Nuti D. M. (2013), Austerity versus development, Paper presented at the "International Conference on Management and Economic Policy for Development", Kozminski University, Warsaw, 10–11 October 2013

Oates W. E. (1972), *Fiscal Federalism*, New York: Harcourt Brace Jovanovich

Oatley T. H. (1998), *Monetary Politics: Exchange Rate Cooperation in the European Union*, Ann Arbor: University of Michigan Press

Obstfeld M. (2012), Does the current account still matter? NBER W. P. 17877

Obstfeld M. (2013), *Finance at Center Stage: Some Lessons of the Euro Crisis*, *European Economy – Economic Papers 493, Directorate General Economic and Financial Affairs (DG ECFIN)*, European Commission, Brussels

Obstfeld M., K. Rogoff (2002), Global implications of self-oriented national monetary rules, *The Quarterly Journal of Economics*, 117(2): 503–35

OECD (2009), *The Political Economy of Reform*, Paris: OECD Publishing

OECD (2015a), *Economic Surveys*. Japan – Overview, April, Paris: OECD Publishing

OECD (2015b), *In It Together: Why Less Inequality Benefits All*, Paris: OECD Publishing

OECD (2016), *Economic Policy Reforms 2016: Going for Growth. Interim Report*, Paris: OECD Publishing

Ollivaud P., D. Turner (2015), The effect of the global financial crisis on OECD potential output, OECD Journal: *Economic Studies*, 2014: 41–60

Olson M. (1965), *The Logic of Collective Action: Public Goods and the Theory of Groups*, Cambridge: Harvard University Press, revised ed. 1971

Olsson A. (2009), Euroscepticism revisited – Regional interest representation in Brussels and the link to citizen attitudes towards European integration, Paper prepared for delivery at the 11th Biennial International Conference of the European Union Studies Association, Los Angeles, California, April 23–25

Onorante L. (2006), Interaction of fiscal policies on the Euro Area: How much pressure on the ECB? European University Institute W. P. 2006/9

Orphanides A. (2017), The fiscal-monetary policy mix in the Euro Area: Challenges at the zero lower bound, CEPR D. P. 12039, 15 May

Orphanides A. (2018), Monetary policy and fiscal discipline: How the ECB planted the seeds of the EZ crisis, in S. Eijffinger, D. Masciandaro, eds., *Hawks and Doves: Deeds and Words. Economics and Politics of Monetary Policymaking*, Ch. 12, London: CEPR Press, February

Ostry J. D., A. Berg, S. Kothari (2018), Growth-equity trade-offs in structural reforms, IMF W. P. No 18/5

Ostry J. D., A. Berg, C. G. Tsangarides (2014), Redistribution, inequality, and growth, IMF D. N. 14/02X, April

Ozkan F. G., D. F. Unsal (2014), On the use of monetary and macroprudential policies for small open economies, IMF W. P. 14/112, June

Ozkan F. G., A. C. Sibert, A. Sutherland (2000), Monetary union, entry conditions and economic reform, EPRU W. P. 2000–03, University of Copenhagen, www.econ.ku.dk/epru/.

Ozkan F. G., A. C. Sibert, A. Sutherland (2004), Monetary union and the Maastricht inflation criterion: The accession countries, *Economics of Transition*, 12(4): 635–52

Padoa Schioppa T. (1982), I mercati europei dei capitali fra liberalizzazione e restrizioni, *Bancaria*, 34(6): 616–25, repr. as European capital markets between liberalization and restrictions, in T. Padoa Schioppa (1985) (ed.), *Money, Economic Policy and Europe*, Brussels: Commission of the European Community

Palma J. G. (2009), The revenge of the market on the rentiers. Why neo-liberal reports of the end of history turned out to be premature, *Cambridge Journal of Economics*, 33(4): 829–69

Palley T. (2009), *America's Exhausted Paradigm: Macroeconomic Causes of the Financial Crisis and the Great Recession, New American Contract Policy Paper*, Washington, DC: New America Foundation

Papadimitriou D. B., M. Nikiforos, G. Zezza (2013), *The Greek Economic Crisis and the Experience of Austerity. A Strategic Analysis*. Annandale-on-Hudson, New York: Levy Economics Institute of Bard College, July

Pagano M., P. Volpin (2010), Credit ratings failures and policy options, *Economic Policy*, 25(62): 401–31

Papaioannou E. (2016), Needed: A European institutional union, in R. Baldwin, F. Giavazzi, eds.

Pâris P., C. Wyplosz (2014), PADRE: Politically Acceptable Debt Restructuring in the EZ, Geneva Special Report on the World Economy 3, ICMB and CEPR

Pasimeni P. (2014), An optimum currency crisis, *The European Journal of Comparative Economics*, 11(2): 173–204, http://eaces.liuc.it

Pasimeni P. (2016), Instability and stagnation in a Monetary Union, Institute for New Economic Thinking, Apr 11

Passamani G., R. Tamborini, M. Tomaselli (2015), Sustainability vs. credibility of fiscal consolidation. A principal-components test for the Euro Zone, *Journal of Risk Finance*, 16(3): 321–43

Perotti R. (1996), Growth, income distribution, and democracy, *Journal of Economic Growth*, 1(2): 149–87

Perotti R. (2013), The "Austerity Myth": Gain without pain? in A. Alesina, F. Giavazzi, eds., *Fiscal Policy after the Financial Crisis*, Chicago: University of Chicago Press

Perotti R. (2017), Investimenti dimezzati. Ecco il grande inganno del Piano Juncker, La Repubblica, 15 May

Phelps E. S. (1967), Phillips curve, expectations of inflation and optimal unemployment over time, *Economica*, 34(135): 254–81

Philippart E., G. Edwards (1999), The provisions on closer co-operation in the Treaty of Amsterdam: The politics of flexibility in the European Union, *Journal of Common Market Studies*, 37(1): 87–108

Piattoni S., L. Polverari (2016), eds., *Handbook on Cohesion Policy in the EU*, Cheltenham: Edward Elgar

Piketty T. (2013), *Le Capital au XXIe Siècle*, Paris: Éditions du Seuil, Engl. Transl.: *Capital in the Twenty-first Century*, Cambridge: Harvard University Press, 2014

Pisani-Ferry J. (2012), The euro crisis and the new impossible trinity, Bruegel Policy Contribution 2012/1, January

Pisani-Ferry J. (2013), The known unknowns and unknown unknowns of European Monetary Union, *Journal of International Money and Finance*, 34(0): 6–14

Pisani-Ferry J. (2014), *The Euro Crisis and Its Aftermath*, Oxford: Oxford University Press

Pisani-Ferry J. (2016), The EZ's Zeno paradox – and how to solve it, in R. Baldwin, F. Giavazzi, eds.

Pisani-Ferry J., A. Sapir, G. B. Wolff (2011), An evaluation of IMF surveillance of the Euro-area, Bruegel Blueprint Series, 14

Pisani-Ferry J., A. Sapir, G. B. Wolff (2013), EU-IMF assistance to Euro Area countries. An early assessment, Bruegel Blueprint Series, XIX

Pissarides C. (1997), The need for labor-market flexibility in a European economic and monetary union, *Swedish Economic Policy Review*, 4(2): 513–45

Pissarides C. (2016), Rebooting Europe: Closer fiscal cooperation needed, in R. Baldwin, F. Giavazzi, eds.

Pitelis C. N., P. Kelmendi (2011), European industrial policy: Perspectives, trends and a sustainability-focused new framework, in M. N. Jovanović, ed., pp. 21–44

Poghosyan T. (2017), Cross-country spillovers of fiscal consolidations in the Euro Area, IMF W. P. 17/140, June

Porter M. (1990), *The Competitive Advantages of Nations*, New York: Free Press (republished with a new introduction, 1998)

Portes R. (1993), EMS and EMU after the fall, *The World Economy*, 16(1): 1–16

Posen A. (1994), *Is Central Bank Independence the Result of Effective Opposition to Inflation? Evidence of Endogenous Monetary Policy Institutions*, Harvard University, Cambridge Mass: mimeo

Posen A. (2015), Rebalancing cooperation and independence by central banks, in P. Catte, A. Gerali, F. Passacantando, eds., *Money and Monetary Institutions*, Rome: Bank of Italy

Praet P. (2013), Forward guidance and the ECB, in W. den Haan, ed., Forward guidance perspectives from central bankers, scholars and market participants,

A VoxEU.org eBook, 6 August, www.ecb.europa.eu/press/key/date/2013/html/sp130806.en.html

Prasad E., R. Rajan, A. Subramanian (2007), Foreign capital and economic growth, *Brookings Papers on Economic Activity*, 38(1): 153–230

Prodi R., A. Quadrio Curzio (2011), EuroUnionBond, here is what must be done, Il Sole 24 Ore 23.08

Quadrio Curzio A. (2011), On the different types of Eurobonds, *Economia Politica*, 28(3): 279–94

Quint D., P. Rabanal (2014), Monetary and macroprudential policy in an estimated DSGE model of the Euro Area, *International Journal of Central Banking*, 10(2): 169–236

Radojičić J., B. Krstić (2017), Structural reforms of the banking sector. Regulatory approaches and implications, *Economics and Organization* 14 (2): 117–26

Ramajo J., M. Marquez, G. Hewings, M. Salinas (2008), Spatial heterogeneity and interregional spillovers in the European Union: Do cohesion policies encourage convergence across regions? *European Economic Review*, 52(3): 551–67

Ravallion M. (2016), *The Economics of Poverty. History, Management and Policy*, New York: Oxford University Press

Rebooting Consensus Authors (2015), Rebooting the EZ: Step 1 – Agreeing a Crisis narrative [12], VoxEU, 20 November

Reichlin L. (2014), Monetary policy and banks in the Euro Area: The tale of two crises, *Journal of Macroeconomics*, 39(PB): 387–400

Reinhardt D., L. A. Ricci, T. Tressel (2010), International capital flows and development: Financial openness matters, IMF, WP/10/235, October

Reinhart C. M., V. Reinhart (2009), Capital flow bonanzas: An encompassing view of the past and present, in J. Frankel, C. Pissarides, eds., *NBER International Seminar on Macroeconomics 2008*, Chicago: University of Chicago Press, pp. 9–62

Reinhart C. M., K. S. Rogoff (2010), Growth in a time of debt, *American Economic Review*, 100(2): 573–78

Reinhart C. M., C. Trebesch (2016), Sovereign debt relief and its aftermath, *Journal of the European Economic Association*, 14(1): 215–51

Rey H. (2012), Comments on J. C. Shambaugh (2012), The euro's three crises, *Brookings Papers on Economic Activity*, 43(1): 219–27

Ribeiro M. P., R. Beetsma (2008), The political economy of structural reforms under a deficit restriction, *Journal of Macroeconomics*, 30(1): 179–98

Richardson J. (2006a), ed., *European Union. Power and Policy-Making*, New York: Routledge

Richardson J. (2006b), Policy-making in the EU: Interests, ideas and garbage cans of primeval soup, in J. Richardson, ed., ch. 1, pp.3–30

Rinaldi D. (2016), A new start for social Europe, Institute Jacques Delors, Studies and Reports, February

Ritzen J., J. Haas (2016), A substainable Euro Area with exit options, IZA Policy Paper 120

Robinson J. A., R. Torvik (2009), A political economy theory of the soft budget constraint, *European Economic Review*, 53(7): 786–79

Rodriguez-Pose A. (2013), Do institutions matter for regional development? *Regional Studies*, 47(7): 1034–47

Rodrik D. (1999), Where did all the growth go? External shocks, social conflict, and growth collapses, *Journal of Economic Growth*, 4(4): 385–412

Rodrik D. (2013), Roepke lecture in economic geography – Who needs the nation-state? *Economic Geography*, 89(1): 1–19

Rodrik D. (2015), The future of European democracy, in L. van Middelaar, P. Van Parijs, eds., *After the Storm. How to Save Democracy in Europe*, Tielt: Lannoo Publ., pp. 55–65

Rodrik D. (2017), Does Europe really need fiscal and political union? Project Syndicate, Dec 11

Roeger W., J. Varga, J. in 't Veld, L. Vogel (2019), A model-based assessment of the distributional impact of structural reforms, European Economy, D. P. 091, February

Rogoff K. (1985), The optimal degree of commitment to an intermediate monetary target, *Quarterly Journal of Economics*, 100(4): 1169–89

Rose A. K. (2007), Checking out: Exits from currency unions, *The Capco Institute Journal of Financial Transactions*, 19: 121–8

Rossi L., E. Beccalli (2018), Economies or diseconomies of scope in the EU banking industry? in D. Díaz, I. Belén, O. Samuel, P. Molyneux, eds., *Corporate Governance in Banking and Investor Protection. From Theory to Practice*, Heidelberg: Springer, pp. 123–47

Rossi S. (2016), The euro must be abandoned to achieve European monetary integration, *International Journal of Political Economy*, 45(1): 72–84

Rossi S. (2017), A structural-reform proposal for a two-speed European Monetary Union, in da Costa Cabral, Gonçalves, Cunha Rodrigues, eds.

Roth A., G. B. Wolff (2018), Understanding (the lack of) German public investment, Bruegel Blog, June 19

Russack S. (2019), *Direct Democracy in the EU: The Myth of a Citizens' Union*, London: Rowman & Littlefield International

Sadeh T., A. Verdun (2009), Explaining Europe's monetary union: A survey of the literature, *International Studies Review*, 11(2): 277–301

Samuelson P. A. (1964), Theoretical notes on trade problems, *Review of Economics and Statistics*, 46(2): 245–154

Sanchez J. L. D., A. Varoudakis (2013), Growth and competitiveness as factors of EZ external imbalances. Evidence and policy implications, The World Bank, Policy Research W. P. 6732, December

Santoni G. J. (1986), The Employment Act of 1946: Some history notes, Federal Reserve Bank of St. Louis Review, November, pp. 5–16

Sapir A. (2016), The EZ needs less heterogeneity, in R. Baldwin, F. Giavazzi, eds.

Sapir J. (2011), S'il faut sortir de l'euro, Document de travail, Cemi-Ethess, 6 Avril

Sapir J. (2017), L'euro, fonte strutturale di squilibrio, Vocidallestero, agosto 1

Sapir A., D. Schoenmaker (2017), We need a European Monetary Fund, but how should it work? Bruegel Policy Brief, May 29

Saraceno F., R. Tamborini (2016), How can it work? On the impact of quantitative easing in the EZ, LUISS School of European Political Economy, W. P. 01/2016

Sargent T. J., N. Wallace (1975), Rational expectations, the optimal monetary instrument, and the optimal money supply rule, *Journal of Political Economy*, 83 (2): 241–54

Sargent T. J., N. Wallace (1981), Some unpleasant monetarist arithmetic, *Federal Reserve Bank of Minneapolis Quarterly Review*, 5(3): 1–17

Savona P. (2015), The future of the euro still lies in its past, *International Atlantic Journal*, 43(2): 407–14

Scharfstein D., J. Stein (1990), Herd behavior and investment, *The American Economic Review*, 80(3): 465–79

Scharpf F. W. (2001), Notes toward a theory of multilevel governing in Europe, *Scandinavian Political Studies*, 24(1): 1–29

Scharpf F. W. (2002), The European social model: Coping with the challenges of diversity, *Journal of Common Market Studies*, 40(4): 645–70

Schäuble W. (2017), Non-paper for paving the way towards a Stability Union, mimeo, reproduced, e.g., in Astrid Rassegna, 23/10/2017– No. 271 (14/ 2017)

Schelkle W. (2006), The theory and practice of economic governance in EMU Revisited: What have we learnt about commitment and credibility? *Journal of Common Market Studies*, 44(4): 669–85

Schelkle W. (2013), Monetary integration in crisis: How well do existing theories explain the predicament of EMU? *Transfer: European Review of Labour and Research*, 19(1): 37–48

Schimmelfennig F., B. Rittberger (2006), Theories of European integration: Assumptions and hypotheses, in J. Richardson, ed., ch. 4, pp. 73–96

Schimmelfennig F., T. Winzen (2014), Instrumental and constitutional differentiation in the European Union, *Journal of Common Market Studies*, 52(2): 354–70

Schmidt V. A. (2009), Re-envisioning the European Union: Identity, democracy, economy, *Journal of Common Market Studies*, 47, Annual Review: 17–42

Schmidt V. A. (2013), Democracy and legitimacy in the European Union revisited: Input, output and "throughput", *Political Studies*, 61(1): 2–22

Schmitt-Grohé S., M. Uribe (2004) Optimal fiscal and monetary policy under sticky prices, *Journal of Economic Theory*, 114(2): 198–230

Schmitz B., J. von Hagen (2011), Current account imbalances and financial integration in the Euro Area, *Journal of International Money and Finance*, 30 (8): 1676–95

Schuck P. (2014), *Why Government Fails So Often: And How It Can Do Better*, Princeton: Princeton University Press

Schularick M., A. M. Taylor (2012), Credit booms gone bust: Monetary policy, leverage cycles, and financial crises, 1870–2008, *The American Economic Review*, 102(2): 1029–61

Semmler W., A. Semmler (2013), The macroeconomics of the fiscal consolidation in the European Union, IMK W. P., www.boeckler.de/pdf/p_wp_imk_122_2013 .pdf

Semmler W., B. Young (2017), Re-booting Europe: What kind of Fiscal Union – What kind of Social Union? The New School for Social Research, Department of Economics, W. P. 13/2017, March

Sen A. K. (2009), *The Idea of Justice*, Cambridge: Harvard University Press

Sensoy A., E. Hacihasanoglu, A. M. Rostom (2015), European Economic and Monetary Union sovereign debt markets, World Bank Policy Research W. P. 7149

SEP Economists (2017), A rebuttal to an editorial on EZ reform proposals, Letter to the editors of *Le Monde* and *Frankfurter Allgemeine Zeitung*, LUISS School of European Political Economy (SEP), 2 October

Serra N., J. E. Stiglitz (2008), *Initiative for Policy Dialogue*, Oxford: Oxford University Press

Shambaugh J. C. (2012), The euro's three crises, *Brookings Papers on Economic Activity*, 43(1): 157–231

Shiller R. J. (2008), *The Subprime Solution: How Today's Global Financial Crisis Happened, and What To Do about It*, Princeton: Princeton University Press

Shiller R. J. (2015), *Irrational Exuberance*, 3rd ed., Princeton: Princeton University Press

Sibert A. (1999), Monetary integration and economic reform, *The Economic Journal*, 109(452): 78–92

Sibert A., A. Sutherland (2000), Monetary union and labour market reform, *Journal of International Economics*, 51(2): 421–35

Siebert H. (1990), The harmonization issue in Europe: Prior agreement or a competitive process? in H. Siebert, ed., *The Completion of the Internal Market*, Tübingen: Mohr, pp. 53–75

Simonazzi A., A. Ginsburg, G. Nocella (2013), Economic relations between Germany and Southern Europe, *Cambridge Journal of Economics*, 37(3): 653–75

Sims C. A. (2008), Inflation expectations, uncertainty, the Phillips curve, and monetary policy, Conference Series [Proceedings], Federal Reserve Bank of Boston, vol. 53

Single European Act (Treaty establishing the European Communities), https://eur opa.eu/european-union/sites/europaeu/files/docs/body/treaties_establish ing_the_european_communities_single_european_act_en.pdf

Sinn H. W. (2003), Ist Deutschland noch zu retten? Munchen: Econ (English transl in H. W. Sinn (2007), *Can Germany Be Saved? The Malaise of the World's First Welfare State*, Cambridge: MIT Press)

Sinn H. W. (2011), The ECB stealth bailout, VoxEu, June 1

Sinn H. W. (2012a), Fed versus ECB: How TARGET debts can be repaid, Vox, CEPR's Policy Portal, 10 March

Sinn H. W. (2012b), TARGET losses in case of a euro breakup, Vox, CEPR's Policy Portal, 22 October

Sinn H. W. (2018), The ECB's fiscal policy, *International Tax Public Finance*, 25(6): 1404–33

Sinn H. W., T. Wollmershäuser (2011), Target loans, current account balances and capital flows: The ECB's rescue facility, NBER W. P. 17626, November

Sinn H. W., T. Wollmershäuser (2012), Target balances and the German financial account in light of the European balance-of-payments crisis, CESifo W. P. 4051

Smeets H. D. (1990), Does Germany dominate the EMS? *Journal of Common Market Studies*, 29(1): 37–52

Smets F. (2014), Financial stability and monetary policy: How closely interlinked? *International Journal of Central Banking*, 10(2): 263–300

Solow R. M. (1956), A contribution to the theory of economic growth, *The Quarterly Journal of Economics*, 70(1): 65–94

Soskice D., T. Iversen (1998), Multiple wage-bargaining systems in the single European currency area, *Oxford Review of Economic Policy*, 14(3): 110–24

Soskice D., T. Iversen (2000), The nonneutrality of monetary policy with large price or wage setters, *Quarterly Journal of Economics*, 115(1): 265–84

Spendzharova A., E. Versluis, E. Radulova, L. Flöthe (2016), Too much, too fast? The sources of banks' opposition to European banking structural reforms, *Journal of Banking Regulation*, 17(1–2): 133–45

Spolaore E. (2013), What is European integration really about? A political guide for economists, *The Journal of Economic Perspectives*, 27(3): 125–44

Spolaore E. (2015), The political economy of European integration, in H. Badinger, V. Nitsc, eds., *Handbook of the Economics of European Integration*, Ch. 26, New York: Routledge, pp. 435–48

Standard&Poors (2017), How S&P Global Ratings would assess European Safe bonds (ESBies), RatingsDirect, 25 April

Steinbach A. (2016), The structural reforms in EU member states: Exploring sanction-based mechanisms, Ademu WP 2016/045, September

Steinberg F., M. Vermeiren (2016), Germany's institutional power and the EMU regime after the crisis: Towards a Germanized Euro Area? *Journal of Common Market Studies*, 54(2): 388–407

Steinherr A. (1994), *30 Years of European Monetary Integration from the Werner Plan to EMU*, New York: Longman

Stiglitz J. E. (2009), Obama's ersatz capitalism, *The New York Times*, March 31

Stiglitz J. E. (2013), A revolution in monetary policy: Lessons in the wake of the global financial crisis, C. D. Deshmukh Lecture, 3 January, Reserve Bank of India, Mumbai

Stiglitz J. E. (2016), *The Euro: How a Common Currency Threatens the Future of Europe*, New York: W.W. Norton

Stiglitz J. E. (2017), The fundamental flaws in the Euro Zone framework, in N. da Costa Cabral, J. R Gonçalves, N. Cunha Rodrigues, eds.

Stockhammer E. (2008), Wage flexibility or wage coordination? Economic policy implications of the wage-led demand regime in the Euro Area, *European Journal of Economics and Economic Policies: Intervention*, 5(1): 54–62

Stockhammer E. (2011), Peripheral Europe's debt and German wages: The role of wage policy in the Euro Area, *International Journal of Public Policy*, 7(1/2/3): 83–96

Stockhammer E. (2015), Rising inequality as a cause of the present crisis, *Cambridge Journal of Economics*, 39(3): 935–58

Stockhammer E., O. Onaran (2012), Rethinking wage policy in the face of the euro crisis. Implications of the wage-led demand regime, *International Review of Applied Economics*, 26(2): 191–203

Stockhammer E., D. P. Sotiropoulos (2014), The costs of internal devaluation, *Review of Political Economy*, 26(2): 210–33

Stockhammer E., O. Onaran, S. Ederer (2009), Functional income distribution and aggregate demand in the Euro Area, *Cambridge Journal of Economics*, 33(1): 139–59

Stöllinger R., N. Foster-McGregor, M. Holzner, M. Landesmann, J. Pöschl, R. Stehrer (2013), A "Manufacturing Imperative" in the EU – Europe's position in global manufacturing and the role of industrial policy, Vienna: Wiener Institut für Internationale Wirtschaftsvergleiche Research Report 391, October

Storm S., C. W. M. Naastepad (2012), Wage-led or profit-led supply: Wages, productivity and investment, ILO, Conditions of Work and Employment Series No. 36

Storm S., C. W. M. Naastepad (2015), Crisis and recovery in the German economy: The real lessons, *Structural Change and Economic Dynamics*, 32(C): 11–24

Storm S., C. W. M. Naastepad (2016), Myths, mix-ups and mishandlings: What caused the EZ crisis? *International Journal of Political Economy*, 45(1): 46–71

Storm S., C. W. M. Naastepad (2017), Bhaduri–Marglin meet Kaldor–Marx: Wages, productivity and investment, *Review of Keynesian Economics*, 5(1): 4–24,

Story J. (1988), The launching of the EMS: An analysis of change in foreign economic policy, *Political Studies*, 36(3): 397–412

Story J., M. De Cecco (1993), The politics and diplomacy of monetary union: 1985–1991, in J. Story, ed., *The New Europe: Politics, Government and Economy since 1945*, Oxford: Blackwell

Stráský J., G. Claveres (2019), A European fiscal capacity can avoid permanent transfers and improve stabilization, VoxEU, 28 January

Strassberger M., L. Sysoyeva (2015), The institutional developments of the European banking supervision, *European Journal of Economics and Management Sciences*, 3: 42–45

Stubb A. C-G. (1996), A categorization of differentiated integration, *Journal of Common Market Studies*, 34(2): 283–95

Summers L. H. (2014a), US economic prospects: Secular stagnation, hysteresis, and the zero lower bound, *Business Economics*, 49(2): 65–73

Summers L. H. (2014b), Reflections on the "New Secular Stagnation Hypothesis," in C. Teulings, R. Baldwin, eds.

Svensson L. E. O. (1997), Optimal inflation targets, "conservative" central banks, and linear inflation contracts, *The American Economic Review*, 87 (1): 98–114

Svensson L. E. O. (2012), Comment on Michael Woodford, "inflation targeting and financial stability," *Sveriges Riksbank Economic Review*,1: 33–9

Svensson L. E. O. (2016), Cost-benefit analysis of leaning against the wind: Are costs larger also with less effective macroprudential policy? IMF W. P., WP/16/3

Tabellini G. (2016), Building common fiscal policy in the EZ, in R. Baldwin, F. Giavazzi, P. C. Paris, eds.

Wyplosz (2014), The PADRE Plan. Politically Acceptable debt restructuring in the EZ, VoxEU, January

Tabellini G. (2017a), Which fiscal union? in A. Bénassy-Quéré, F. Giavazzi (2017a), eds.

Tabellini G. (2017b), Reforming the EZ: Structuring vs restructuring sovereign debts, Voxeu.org, 23 November

Tabellini G., C. Wyplosz (2006), Supply-side policy coordination in the European Union, *Swedish Economic Policy Review*, 13(1): 101–56

Tamborini R. (2015), Heterogeneous market beliefs, fundamentals, and the sovereign debt crisis in the Euro Zone, *Economica*, 82 (s1): 1153–76

Tancioni M. (2015), Non solo Grecia. Riflessioni sulle implicazioni del vincolo valutario europeo, Menabò di Etica ed Economia, No. 26, 16 July, www .eticaeconomia.it

Tavlas G. S. (1993a), The theory of optimum currency areas revisited, *Finance and Development*, 30(1): 32–5

Tavlas G. S. (1993b), The "New" theory of optimum currency areas, *The World Economy*, 16(6): 663–85

Tcherneva P. R. (2011), Fiscal policy effectiveness: Lessons from the Great Recession, Levy Economics Institute of Bard College, W. P. 649, January

Tepper J. (2012), A primer on the euro breakup: Default, exit and devaluation as the optimal solution, Variant Perception, 16 February

Teulings C., R. Baldwin (2014), eds., *Secular Stagnation: Facts, Causes and Cures*, London: A VoxEU.org eBook, CEPR

Thatcher M. (2006), European regulation, in J. Richardson, ed., ch. 15, pp. 311–28

Thimann C. (2015), The microeconomic dimensions of the EZ crisis and why European politics cannot solve them, *The Journal of Economic Perspectives*, 29(3): 141–64

Thwaites G. (2015), Why are real interest rates so low? Secular stagnation and the relative price of investment goods, Bank of England Staff W. P. 564

Thygesen N. (2016), Why did Europe decide to move to a single currency 25 years ago?*Intereconomics*, 51(1): 11–16

Tizzano A. (2000), Quelques observations sur la coopération internationale en matière de concurrence, *Revue du Droit de l'Union Européenne*, 1: 75–100

Tobin J. (1986), The monetary and fiscal policy mix, *Federal Reserve Bank of Atlanta Economic Review*, 71(7): 4–16

Tomlin B., L. Fung (2015), Exchange rate movements and the distribution of productivity, *Review of International Economics*, 23(4): 782–809

Tornell A., A. Velasco (2000), Fixed versus flexible exchange rates: Which provides more fiscal discipline? *Journal of Monetary Economics*, 45(2),399–436

Torój A. (2017), A solution method for DSGE models with regionally biased monetary policymakers: the case of ECB voting reform, May 15, mimeo

Torres F. S. (2013), The EMU's legitimacy and the ECB as a strategic political player in the crisis context, *Journal of European Integration*, 35(3): 287–300

Tørsløv, T. R., L. S. Wier, G. Zucman (2018), The missing profits of nations, NBER W. P. 24701, August

Tranholm-Mikkelsen J. (1991), Neo-functionalism: Obstinate or obsolete? A reappraisal in the light of the new dynamism of the EC, *Millennium*, 20 (1): 1–22

Trichet J.-C. (2010), Reflections on the nature of monetary policy non-standard measures and finance theory, Opening address at the ECB Central Banking Conference, Frankfurt, 18 November

Truger A. (2015), Implementing the Golden Rule for public investment in Europe: Safeguarding public investment and supporting the recovery, Materialien zu Wirtschaft und Gesellschaft W. P. 138 – Reihe der AK-Wien, März

Ubide Á. (2015), Stability bonds for the Euro Area, Peterson Institute for International Economics, Policy Brief 15–19

Unison (n.d.), The future of the public services in Europe, The Center of European Reform

van Aarle B., J. Engwerda, A. Weeren (2018), Effects of debt mutualization in a monetary union with endogenous risk premia: Can Eurobonds contribute to debt stabilization? *Structural Change and Economic Dynamics*, 44(C): 100–14

van Oyen T. S., M. Elmer (2016), Testing for explosive behavior in the NASDAQ and STOXX 600 Europe Technology indices, MSc Finance thesis, Lund University, May

van Parijs Ph. (2017), Building a Europe for the people, Social Europe, 24 May, www.socialeurope.eu/author/philippe-van-parijs

van Rixtel A., G. Gasperini (2013), Financial crises and bank funding: Recent experience in the Euro Area, BIS W. P. 406, March

Verdun A. (2010), Economic and Monetary Union, in M. Cini, N. Pérez-Solórzano Borragán, eds., *European Union Politics*, Oxford: Oxford University Press, pp. 324–39

Villeroy de Galhau F., J. Weidmann (2016), Europa braucht mehr Investitionen (Europe needs more investment), *Sueddeutsche Zeitung*, 8 Februar

Veugelers R. (2014), Public R&I budgets for smart fiscal consolidation, SIMPATIC W.P., presented at the second annual SIMPATIC conference, The Hague, April 2–4,2014, www.simpatic.eu

Visco I. (2015), EZ challenges and risks, London, Wharton, University of Pennsylvania, Second Annual Meeting of the Zell/Lurie Real Estate Center, 6 May

Von Hagen J. (1992), Fiscal arrangements in a monetary union: Some evidence from the US, in D. Fair, C de Boissieux, eds., *Fiscal Policy, Taxes, and The Financial System in an Increasingly Integrated Europe*, Dordrecht: Kluwer Academic Publishers

Von Hagen J., B. Eichengreen (1996), Federalism, fiscal restraints, and European monetary union, *The American Economic Review*, 86(2): 134–8

Walsh C. E. (1995), Optimal contracts for central bankers, *American Economic Review*, 85(1): 150–67

Walsh C. E. (2009), Inflation targeting: What have we learned? *International Finance*, 12(2): 195–233

Walters A. (1990), *Sterling in Danger*, London: Fontana

Watt A. (2010), From End-of-Pipe Solutions towards a golden wage rule to prevent and cure imbalances in the Euro Area, December 2010, www.social-europe.eu /2010/12/from-end-ofpipe-solutions-towards-a- golden-wage-rule-to-prevent-and-cure-imbalances-in-the-euro-area/

Weber A. (1991), EMU and asymmetrical and adjustment problems in the EMS. Some empirical evidence, in Commission of the European Communities (1991)

Werner P. (1970), Report to the Council and the Commission on the realisation by stages of economic and monetary union in the Community, Luxembourg, 8 October

Wessels W. (1997), An ever closer fusion? A dynamic macropolitical view on integration processes, *Journal of Common Market Studies*, 35(3): 267–99

Westermann F. (2012), Two types of capital flight: Will a common deposit insurance help to stabilise the TARGET2 imbalances? Vox, CEPR's Policy Portal, 16 October

Wettestad J. (2014), Rescuing EU emissions trading: Mission impossible? *Global Environmental Politics*, 14(2): 64–81

Whelan K. (2011), Professor Sinn misses the target, VoxEu, June 9, www.voxeu.org /article/there-hidden-EZ-bailout

Whelan K. (2012), TARGET2: Germany has bigger things to worry about, Vox, CEPR's Policy Portal, 29 April

Wildasin D. (1997), Externalities and bailouts: Hard and soft budget constraints in intergovernmental fiscal relations, World Bank Policy Research W. P. 1843

Wilkinson R., K. Pickett (2009), *The Spirit Level: Why More Equal Societies Almost Always Perform Better*, London: Allen Lane

Willett T. D. (1994), Some often neglected aspects of the political economy of European monetary integration, in B. Abegaz, P. Dillon, D. Feldman, P. Whiteley, eds., *The Challenge of European Integration*, Boulder: Westview Press

Willett T. D. (2000), Some political economy aspects of EMU, *Journal of Policy Modeling*, 22(3): 379–89

Williams J. C. (2011), Unconventional monetary policy: Lessons from the past three years, Economic Letter, 2011-31, Federal Reserve of San Francisco, October

Williamson J. (1999), Comment on Cooper (1999), *Brookings Papers on Economic Activity*, 1999(1): 130–5

Wittman D. (1977), Candidates with policy preferences: A dynamic model, *Journal of Economic Theory*, 14(1): 180–9

Wohlgemuth M. (2007), Learning through institutional competition, Freiburger Diskussionspapiere zur Ordnungsökonomik 07/9

Wolff G. (2016), European Parliament testimony on EDIS, 23 May, Bruegel

Wollmann H. (2014), Public services in European countries between public/ municipal and private sector provision – and reverse? in C. Nunes Silva, J. Bucek, eds., *Fiscal Austerity and Innovation in Local Governance in Europe*, Farnham: Ashgate, pp. 49–76

Woodford M. (1996), Control of the public debt: A requirement for price stability, NBER W.P. 5684, July; a shorter version was published in G. A. Calvo and M. King, eds., *The Debt Burden and its Consequences for Monetary Policy*, London: Macmillan, 1997

Woodford M. (2003), *Interest Rate and Prices*. Princeton: Princeton University Press

Woodford M. (2007), The case for forecast targeting as a monetary policy strategy, *The Journal of Economic Perspectives*, 21(4): 3–24

Woodford M. (2008), Forward guidance for monetary policy: Is it still possible? Vox, CEPR's Policy Portal, 17 January

Woodford M. (2009), Comment on Williams, Heeding Daedalus: Optimal inflation and the zero lower bound, *Brookings Papers on Economic Activity*, 40(2): 38–45

World Bank (2007), Social exclusion and the EU's social inclusion agenda, Paper prepared for the EU8 Social Inclusion Study, mimeo

Wyplosz C. (1991), Monetary Union and fiscal policy discipline, CEPR D. P. 488

Wyplosz C. (1997), Why and how it might happen, *The Journal of Economic Perspectives*, 11(4): 3–21

Wyplosz C. (2006), European monetary union: The dark sides of a major success, *Economic Policy*, 21(46): 208–61

Wyplosz C. (2012), The coming revolt against austerity, CEPR's Policy Portal, 2 May, http://voxeu.org

Wyplosz C. (2017a), A European Monetary Fund? Scrutiny paper provided in the context of Economic Dialogues with the President of the Eurogroup in the Economic and Monetary Affairs Committee European Parliament, May

Wyplosz C. (2017b), The euro and ordoliberalism, in T. Beck, H.-H. Kotz, eds., *Ordoliberalism: A German Oddity?* A VoxEU.org eBook, 145–52

Yellen J. L. (2009), A Minsky meltdown: Lessons for central bankers, Presentation to the 18th Annual Hyman P. Minsky Conference on the State of the US and World Economies, "Meeting the Challenges of the Financial Crisis" organized by the Levy Economics Institute of Bard College, New York City, April 168

Zemanek H. (2010), *Asymmetric International Risk Sharing in the Euro Area*, mimeo, ifo Institute www.cesifo-group.de

Zemanek H., A. Belke, G. Schnabl (2010), Current account balances and structural adjustment in the Euro Area, *International Economics and Economic Policy*, 7 (1): 83–127

Zodrow G. R. (2003), Tax competition and tax coordination in the European Union, *International Tax and Public Finance*, 10(6): 651–71

Index

Printed in the United States
By Bookmasters